Gender in the Middle Ages

Volume 15

FEMALE DESIRE IN CHAUCER'S
LEGEND OF GOOD WOMEN
AND MIDDLE ENGLISH ROMANCE

Gender in the Middle Ages

ISSN 1742-870X

Series Editors
Jacqueline Murray
Diane Watt

Editorial Board
Clare Lees
Katherine J. Lewis

This series investigates the representation and construction of masculinity and femininity in the Middle Ages from a variety of disciplinary and interdisciplinary perspectives. It aims in particular to explore the diversity of medieval genders, and such interrelated contexts and issues as sexuality, social class, race and ethnicity, and orthodoxy and heterodoxy.

Proposals or queries should be sent in the first instance to the editors or to the publisher, at the addresses given below; all submissions will receive prompt and informed consideration.

Professor Jacqueline Murray, Department of History, University of Guelph, Guelph, Ontario, N1G 2W1, Canada

Professor Diane Watt, School of Literature and Languages, University of Surrey, Guildford, Surrey GU2 7XH, UK

Boydell & Brewer Limited, PO Box 9, Woodbridge, Suffolk IP12 3DF, UK

Previously published volumes in the series are listed at the end of this book.

FEMALE DESIRE IN CHAUCER'S *LEGEND OF GOOD WOMEN* AND MIDDLE ENGLISH ROMANCE

Lucy M. Allen-Goss

D. S. BREWER

© Lucy M. Allen-Goss 2020

All Rights Reserved. Except as permitted under current legislation no part of this work may be photocopied, stored in a retrieval system, published, performed in public, adapted, broadcast, transmitted, recorded or reproduced in any form or by any means, without the prior permission of the copyright owner

The right of Lucy M. Allen-Goss to be identified as the author of this work has been asserted in accordance with sections 77 and 78 of the Copyright, Designs and Patents Act 1988

First published 2020
Paperback edition 2023

D. S. Brewer, Cambridge

ISBN 978-1-84384-570-6 hardback
ISBN 978-1-84384-679-6 paperback

D. S. Brewer is an imprint of Boydell & Brewer Ltd
PO Box 9, Woodbridge, Suffolk IP12 3DF, UK
and of Boydell & Brewer Inc.
668 Mt Hope Avenue, Rochester, NY 14620–2731, USA
website: www.boydellandbrewer.co.uk

A CIP catalogue record for this book is available
from the British Library

The publisher has no responsibility for the continued existence or accuracy of URLs for external or third-party internet websites referred to in this book, and does not guarantee that any content on such websites is, or will remain, accurate or appropriate

CONTENTS

Acknowledgements	vi
Abbreviations	vii
Author's Note	viii
Introduction: The Origins of Female Desire	1
1. The Silencing of Female Desire in the 'Legend of Philomela'	35
2. The Traumatised Narrative of the Alliterative *Morte Arthure*	61
3. 'As Matter Appetiteth Form': Desire and Reciprocation in the 'Legend of Hipsiphyle and Medea'	83
4. Stony Femininity and the Limits of Desire in *The Sowdone of Babylon*	111
5. Veiled Interpretations and Architectures of Desire in the 'Legend of Thisbe' and the 'Legend of Ariadne'	141
6. Opening Mechanisms, Enclosing Desire: The Erotic Aesthetics of *Undo Your Door*	165
Conclusion: The Ends of Desire	187
Bibliography	197
Index	219

ACKNOWLEDGEMENTS

Writing this book was, at times, an emotional experience, as a book about female desire should be. I feel very warmly towards the many people who contributed perspectives and ideas, but also shared their feelings on the subject in its diversity of medieval and modern manifestations. Daisy Black, Katherine Collins, Laura Kalas, Roberta Magnani, Laura Varnam and Diane Watt all read drafts of chapters and provided vital sounding boards. Sarah Baechle and Carissa Harris shaped my thinking about sexual violence, and about the forms women's resistance to it might take. Justin Bengry and Rachel Moss both, in different ways, challenged me to think about the personal aspects of writing in the field of history of the emotions.

This book began as lectures delivered in the English Faculty at the University of Cambridge, and as classes taught there and at King's and Newnham College. There could not have been a better or more stimulating place to write this book, and I am immeasurably grateful to have had the freedom to explore my ideas with such brilliant, generous students and colleagues. In particular, Hester Lees-Jeffries sparked off many productive ideas about Chapter One, Hannah Piercy made me think more carefully about romance, and Jackie Tasioulas continued to make me feel as at home in medieval literature as she did when she first taught me as an undergraduate. Since 2018, I have been a research associate at the Centre for Medieval Studies at the University of York. I particularly thank Nicola McDonald for enjoyable discussions of *Undo Your Door*, both then and during my time as a doctoral candidate at York from 2009 to 2014. I am also grateful to the participants and organisers of the Gender and Medieval Studies conferences of 2017–19, who responded generously to papers based on several chapters of this book. Jonathan Hsy and Mary Flannery kindly shared work with me; David Raybin and Susanna Fein, anonymous readers at *the Chaucer Review* and at Boydell and Brewer, all gave me painstakingly thoughtful and helpful feedback. Caroline Palmer kept me going through the difficult bits. Above all, Alex da Costa read, supported, encouraged and made me believe this book could be and should be written. I owe her many thanks.

At home, Helen and David Allen provided practical support when it was most needed; Elisabeth Allen-Goss provided impractical – but much appreciated – companionship and comfort, and proof of the generative potential of female desire. This book is for her, and for her mother.

ABBREVIATIONS

BoD	*The Book of the Duchess*, in *The Riverside Chaucer*, gen. ed. Larry D. Benson
CT	*The Canterbury Tales*, in *The Riverside Chaucer*, gen. ed. Larry D. Benson
EETS	Early English Text Society
e.s.	extra series
o.s.	original series
F and G	The two distinct versions that survive of the *Legend* Prologue.
MED	Hans Kurath and Robert E. Lewis, eds, *Middle English Dictionary* (Ann Arbor, MI: University of Michigan Press, 1999)
Mets	Ovid, *Metamorphoses Books*, trans. Frank Justus Miller, 2 vols (London: William Heineman, 1916)
Parl	*The Parliament of Fowles*, in *The Riverside Chaucer*, gen. ed. Larry D. Benson
PMLA	*Publications of the Modern Language Association of America*
T&C	*Troilus and Criseyde* in *The Riverside Chaucer*, gen. ed. Larry D. Benson

AUTHOR'S NOTE

This book is deeply indebted to queer theory, to medievalists who use queer theory and to the communities of self-identified queer scholars who have inspired and influenced my work. I recognise the value that these scholars place upon the term they choose. 'Queer' resists binary categories; it posits a generously inclusive sense of political and affective community. It is polemical in its capacity to enable speakers to withhold and retreat from that exhausting process of constantly making oneself legible within society's categories ('are you straight or gay? A man or a woman?'). Queer theory resists the idea that queerness exists only in the minority, on the margins and in the current moment. In laying claim to such seemingly stable, unchanging concepts as time and space, and such culturally valued structures as language and history, queer theory resists the restriction of the queer subject. By positing that time might be 'queer', or that the interpretation of *lacunae* in language might parallel the erotic fingerings of gaps suggestive of queer desire, scholars take ownership of these concepts.

Yet I have been reluctant to use the term 'queer' in this book. 'Queer', we are told, has been reclaimed. Its pejorative sense belongs to the past. This commonplace statement has strangely disorienting implications. It mobilises the past as a container for those 'ugly feelings' we might wish did not exist, that inward-directed shame or outward-directed disgust at 'queer' desires and bodies.[1] Yet for some people, these do remain a present emotional response to the term 'queer'. In this note, I suggest that the practice of taking ugly emotions out of the picture distorts the relationship between past and present, particularly in the context of medieval conceptions of desire and the body.

As I wrote this note, I thought of the medieval writer whose views on language most strongly shape this book. I imagined Alan of Lille transported from his comfortable room at the University of Paris in the twelfth century, to attend a conference where a queer theorist colleague speaks. He would be quite at home with the idea of sodomy queering language; he would be puzzled by the dissent of a conservative scholar who objects to the way that sexuality is 'brought into everything these days'. He would relate to Sara Ahmed's description of how female same-sex desires 'disorient' our ways of inhabiting the world; he would understand when Elizabeth Freeman writes

---

[1] Sianne Ngai, *Ugly Feelings* (Cambridge, MA: Harvard University Press, 2005).

Author's Note

of a 'queer time', pulled out of joint by the desirous fingers of lesbian readers.[2] Yet these ideas would not convey to Alan a polemical defence of queer subjectivity, a celebratory centring of the queer subject. The emotion that radiates from Alan's writings on sexuality and the desiring body is disgust at its deviancies: horror at same-sex desire and shock at masculinity degenerating into femininity. Alan seeks to stigmatise, to mark out as damaging and deforming, the sexuality that disrupts language. To use the term 'queer' in the context of medieval representations of desire is, I would argue, to perform a displacement of these 'ugly emotions', similar to that displacement I recognise in the assertion that 'queer' is a reclaimed term in the twenty-first century. The term does not stand counter to hegemonic constructions of sexuality and the body in medieval culture and thought: it accords with them. It does not disrupt, disturb or trouble medieval writers' understanding of the relations between embodiment and desire: it only confirms them. For these reasons, I have avoided the term 'queer' in this book. The terms I use in preference are sometimes openly, sometimes implicitly, pejorative (describing desires as 'deviant' or 'dissident'); sometimes they emphasise orientation towards another gendered body ('same-sex desire') or resistance to codes of gendered behaviour ('gender nonconformity'). They overlap, but also act as a reminder that no single comfortable term exists; that the illusion of congruence between medieval and modern perspectives is exactly that – illusory.

---

[2] Sara Ahmed, *Queer Phenomenology: Orientations, Objects, Others* (Durham, NC and London: Duke University Press, 2006), pp. 91–95; Elizabeth Freeman, *Time Binds: Queer Temporalities, Queer Histories* (Durham, NC: Duke University Press, 2010), p. 110.

INTRODUCTION:
THE ORIGINS OF FEMALE DESIRE

> And the Lord God said: It is not good for man to be alone: let us make him a help like unto himself. ... The Lord God cast a deep sleep upon Adam: and when he was fast asleep, he took one of his ribs, and filled up flesh for it. And the Lord God built the rib which he took from Adam into a woman: and brought her to Adam. And Adam said: This now is bone of my bones, and flesh of my flesh; she shall be called woman, because she was taken out of man.[1]
> (Genesis 2: 21–23)

This passage from Genesis encapsulates the fundamental tensions that attend on medieval representations of female desire. At the moment of his creation, man is complete. His body can only be diminished. But the creation of woman leaves an absence, and she has no fixed definition without reference to that diminished masculinity. Woman is so called, *because she was taken out of man*. She is constantly defined in the negative and constantly troubled by absences, missing pieces and incomplete beginnings. Her construction follows a prosthetic logic, both in the literal sense that it involves the substitution of one body part (flesh) for another (the rib), and in the epistemic sense Derrida proposes, where the prosthetic is both 'compensatory and vicarious ... an adjunct, a subaltern instance which takes-(the)-place'.[2] A prosthetic both

---

[1] 'dixit quoque Dominus Deus non est bonum esse hominem solum faciamus ei adiutorium simile sui. ... inmisit ergo Dominus Deus soporem in Adam cumque obdormisset tulit unam de costis eius et replevit carnem pro ea et aedificavit Dominus Deus costam quam tulerat de Adam in mulierem et adduxit eam ad Adam dixitque Adam hoc nunc os ex ossibus meis et caro de carne mea haec vocabitur virago quoniam de viro sumpta est'. All Latin quotations are from the Vulgate unless otherwise stated.

[2] Jacques Derrida, *Of Grammatology*, 2nd edn (Baltimore, MD: Johns Hopkins University Press, 1998), p. 145. Several scholars have made important use of theories of prosthesis in relation to the female body. In particular, Mitchell and Snyder argue that the literary representation of disabled bodies results in a form of narrative prosthesis that seeks to explain and 'close' the gaps manifested in those bodies and Tory Vandeventer Pearman has acknowledged that this theory resonates with medieval constructions of the female body as innately 'disabled'. See David T. Mitchell and Sharon L. Snyder, *Narrative Prosthesis: Disability and the Dependencies of Discourse* (Ann Arbor, MI: University of Michigan Press, 2000) and Tory Vandeventer Pearman, *Women and Disability in Medieval Literature* (New York: Palgrave Macmillan, 2010), pp. 20–23. For discussion of prosthesis in relation to female masculinity, see Judith Halberstam, *Female Masculinity* (Durham, NC: Duke University Press, 1998), pp. 3–5. In this reference, as elsewhere, I refer to Halberstam's work using the name under which it was published, in line with

supplements and announces a pre-existing lack, taking the place of what is missing and simultaneously acting as an ever-visible reminder of that lack, by its difference from the substance it replaces. The problem of incompleteness, of prosthetic desire and absent masculine body parts, haunts the imaginary of female desire from Eve onwards.

In a subversive visual twist on the narrative of Genesis, found in a manuscript copied in France in the early fourteenth century, we find the story of the temptation in Eden reflected forwards. In Paris, Bibliothèque nationale de France, MS Fr. 25526, beneath text from Jean de Meun's portion of the *Roman de la Rose*, there stands a woman clad in a habit and wimple.[3] Beside her, a fruit tree bears a startling crop of pear-like penises that evoke the forbidden apples of the Tree of Knowledge.[4] As the nun reaches for these organs seemingly removed from a male body, her plucking of phallic fruit recalls the moment of Eve's creation from Adam's rib. It also – and predictably – sexualises that moment, glossing the rib as a phallus. The two separate acts of removal are contained in a single image, as if to make Eve responsible for the method of her own making. What does it all mean? In the absence of any explanation from the text it accompanies, the image has fascinated and bewildered viewers. Patently, it depicts an act of female desire, of appetite: a hunger for fruit. Yet since this appetite is carnal (and directed at a sexual member), it is also metaphorical lust. Leading us away from Eve's story, the nun's habit might recall the sex-starved nuns of *fabliaux* and anti-clerical literature, with the disembodied penises as metonyms for longed-for male bodies. Or those peculiar fruit might be interpreted as sexual prosthetics (playing to the well-worn innuendos of the sexual shenanigans of cloistered women).[5] The plucking of the fruit, though it might express a sexual desire, might equally well be a contemptuous castration, a power-hungry grab for what the phallus

---

Halberstam's stated preferences. See http://www.jackhalberstam.com/on-pronouns/. Accessed 8/3/2019.

[3] Paris, Bibliothèque nationale de France, MS Fr. 25526, f. 106v. The image has no direct support in the written text, and its sources and meanings are much debated. See Sylvia Huot, *The Romance of the Rose and its Medieval Readers: Interpretation, Reception, Manuscript Transmission* (Cambridge: Cambridge University Press, 1993), pp. 273–322; and *Rethinking the Romance of the Rose: Text, Image, Reception*, eds Kevin Brownlee and Sylvia Huot (Philadelphia, PA: University of Pennsylvania Press, 1992).

[4] For the pear as a symbol of luxuria, see Joan Baker and Susan Signe Morrison, 'The Luxury of Gender: *Piers Plowman* B. 9 and *The Merchant's Tale*', in *William Langland's Piers Plowman: A Book of Essays*, ed. Kathleen M. Hewett-Smith (New York: Routledge, 2001), pp. 41–68 (p. 56); Kenneth Bleeth, 'The Image of Paradise in the Merchant's Tale', in *The Learned and the Lewed: Studies in Chaucer and Medieval Literature*, eds Larry Benson and David Strains (Cambridge, MA: Harvard University Press, 1974), pp. 45–60.

[5] I will discuss this body of writing in greater detail below, but for a summary, see Ruth Mazo Karras, *Sexuality in Medieval Europe: Doing Unto Others*, 2nd edn (New York: Routledge, 2005), pp. 87–119.

Introduction

signifies, or a yearning for the tools and appurtenances of female masculinity. Female desire splinters off into multiple competing questions, all ending in uncertainty. Equally, however, female desire generates multiple competing narratives, all extending into new possibilities.

This difficulty of knowledge, and this productivity of desire, is fundamental to this book. It is a difficulty and a productivity that is inescapably related to medieval theorisations of the female body. The female body exists in prosthetic relation not only to a causative absence in the male body, but also in relation to the substance with which that absence is supplemented: the flesh. As Karma Lochrie points out, the antonym of the masculine spirit is not the body (that bounded, organic unity), but the flesh, the inchoate raw material that pre-exists organisation.[6] Like the flesh, the female body refuses to observe its boundaries, refuses to be closed and stabilised. Medieval surgical and theological discourses code the flesh as a 'natural prosthesis' of the body, uniquely capable of substituting for other organs and filling gaps.[7] Likewise, the fleshly female body is unique in its capacity to swell in pregnancy and gestate the body of another human being. Yet this same swelling extension is also the corollary of a pre-existing lack. The female body was held to be incapable of shaping its own substance, incapable of giving form to the raw material it contains. In the words of the influential seventh-century etymologist Isidore of Seville, woman (*mulier*) takes her very name from her 'softer' (*mollier*) material composition.[8] Her soft body is as formless as warm sealing wax, awaiting an impregnating stamp. Centuries later, the same idea is reflected in Trevisa's fourteenth-century English definition of the distinctions between men and women: 'in the male [body] beþ vertues formal and of schapinge and werchinge, and in þe femel material, suffringe, and passiue.'[9] Without masculine 'schapinge', the female body lacks structure; it cannot give form to the foetus in the womb, but only the matter, the contribution of the mother (*mater*). Indiscriminate and inchoate, simultaneously excessive and insufficient, the female body is always in need of structuring masculinity to give its teeming possibilities shape and purpose.

My focus in this book is the spectrum of female desires that do not answer to structuring masculine desire and that seek to resist being orientated

---

[6] Karma Lochrie, *Margery Kempe and Translations of the Flesh* (Philadelphia, PA: University of Pennsylvania Press, 1994), p. 3.

[7] Katie L. Walter brings Derrida's characterisation of the supplement to bear on the medieval discourse. See Walter, 'Fragments for a Medieval Theory of Prosthesis', *Textual Practice* 30.7 (2016): 1345–63 (pp. 1346–47).

[8] Isidore of Seville, *The Etymologies of Isidore of Seville*, eds Stephen A. Barney, W. J. Lewis, J. A. Beach and Oliver Berghof (Cambridge: Cambridge University Press, 2006), p. 224.

[9] John Trevisa, *On the Properties of Things: John Trevisa's Translation of Bartholomaeus Anglicus De proprietatibus rerum*, ed. M. C. Seymour, 3 vols (Oxford: Clarendon Press, 1975–88), vol. 1, p. 306.

towards a masculine body. These desires are necessarily difficult to represent. If masculine structuring is needed to make the origins of the female body visible, its boundaries secure and its meanings legible, then female bodies and desires that deviate from orientation towards masculinity deviate also from that which would give them visibility, substance and articulation. Sara Ahmed writes of the way in which social norms shape bodily occupations of space. Repeated orientations towards bodies of the opposite gender create 'lines' of habit and expectation (sexual 'orientations'), from which it becomes hard to deviate.[10] Reciprocally, as bodies perform habitual motions, they set down expectations of the ways in which bodily movement '"toward" objects shapes the surfaces of bodily and social space'.[11] To 'bodily and social space' we might add textual and and rhetorical spaces. Women who diverge from these 'lines' become illegible to onlookers, because they appear to have mislaid or mistaken their direction towards an acceptable object of desire.[12] What can such women be trying to reach? 'A woman cannot speak of her pleasure', Lacan insists; Cixous (sharply deconstructing the statement) observes that female desire puzzles masculinist logic, not only because the female exists outside the articulate realm Lacan depicts as governed by the relationship between phallus and logos, but because the question of what women want is always presumed to be rhetorical. It begs the masculine answers 'nothing' or 'nothing ... without me'.[13] Women without men disturb all sorts of boundaries. This is true in the most literal sense: single women have been claimed as a major source of cultural and social anxiety in later medieval Europe; lesbians frighten society into denial of their existence.[14] It is also true in the much more abstract and intellectual sense Judith Butler articulates when she claims for the material body (the body coded as feminine in medieval discourse) a prosthetic capacity of epistemic redirection. The flesh is hard to pin down. 'The thought of materiality [of the body] invariably moved me into other domains', she writes in the preface to *Bodies that Matter*, concluding: 'I could not *fix* bodies as simple objects of thought ... this movement beyond their own boundaries, a movement of boundary itself, appeared to be quite

---

[10] Sara Ahmed, *Queer Phenomenology*, p. 91.
[11] Ibid., p. 68.
[12] Ahmed describes the 'misreading' of such aberrant desires in *Queer Phenomenology*, pp. 95–96.
[13] Hélène Cixous, 'Castration or Decapitation?', trans. Annette Kuhn, *Signs* 7.1 (1981): 41–55 (p. 45).
[14] As Judith Bennett and Amy Froide observe, in their work on medieval 'singlewomen', the very concept of the unattached secular woman was a disturbing one for late medieval male writers, living in societies where a large proportion of the female population was not (and might never be) married. See Judith M. Bennett and Amy M. Froide, 'A Singular Past', in *Singlewomen in the European Past, 1250–1800*, eds Judith M. Bennett and Amy M. Froide (Philadelphia, PA: University of Pennsylvania Press, 1999), pp. 1–37.

Introduction

central to what bodies "are"'.¹⁵ The material body lacks its own fixity, its own stable orginary definition, but endlessly redirects attention beyond its own boundaries, pushing at the limits of what it means to be flesh.

Moreover, the very category of the feminine itself is not stable, but like the flesh, it is ever ready to be extended to cover defects in the originary masculine. Unruly, stigmatised and otherwise incomplete male bodies are pejoratively located within this category, extending its porous boundaries.¹⁶ These male bodies complicate the gendered organisation of sexual and erotic desire. Placed in intimate, erotic or sexual contact with male bodies precariously coded as feminine or female-performing, women may perform the actions and inhabit the bodily situations associated with same-sex desires. Depending on the perception and performance of femininity, then, sexual and erotic encounters cross and re-cross the boundaries between licit and illicit, crystallising seemingly unremarkable female desires into more startling manifestations of atypical and aberrant sexual desire. As a consequence, much of this book focuses on what we might call surrogate or vicarious embodiments: moments in which the genders of bodies are unstably related to the desires circulating within and between those bodies, and in which a masculine body may act as a surrogate for female experience, or a female body may vicariously claim male same-sex intimacies as its blueprint for affection. In the texts I discuss, male bodies are made to articulate prior female experiences, standing as surrogates for female bodies and subjected to imitations of the same sexual violence, objectification or sexualisation. This strategy makes the emotions arising from those experiences more visible, since, according to medieval definitions of female flesh that rely on perceptions of absence, the female body always threatens to make the desires it discloses incomplete and fragmentary. Yet at the same time, by transferring female experiences and emotions onto male bodies, these texts risk a form of 'epistemic injustice', that systematic devaluing of women's capacity to bear witness to their own experiences.¹⁷ More, the slippage between masculine bodies and feminised affective positions produces what Anna Kłosowska identifies, in another

---

15 Judith Butler, *Bodies that Matter: On the Discursive Limits of 'Sex'*, 2nd edn (New York: Routledge, 2011), p. ix.
16 As Sharon Farmer puts it, to some male Christian writers, the category of the feminine 'included a broad variety of persons possessing male bodies … including racialised groups (Jewish men, for example, who were sometimes thought to menstruate) and men who engaged in receptive same-sex activities'. Sharon Farmer, 'Introduction', in *Gender and Difference in the Middle Ages* (Minneapolis, MN: University of Minnesota Press, 2003), pp. ix–xxvii (p. xi).
17 See Suzanne M. Edwards, *The Afterlives of Rape in Medieval English Literature* (New York: Palgrave Macmillan, 2016); Elizabeth Robertson and Christine M. Rose, *Representing Rape in Medieval and Early Modern Literature* (New York: Palgrave, 2001), p. 2; Miranda Fricker, *Epistemic Injustice: Power and the Ethics of Knowing* (Oxford: Oxford University Press, 2007); Gayatri Chakrvorty Spivak, 'Can the Subaltern Speak?', in *Marxism and*

context of vicarious desire, as '*effects* of same-sex desire and *effects* of gender bending' (italics mine).[18] Redirections of affect, activity and intimacy cause men's interactions with men superficially to resemble same-sex desires or gender nonconformities. The counterpart to the invisibility of female desire and emotion is therefore the excessive visibility – the over-identification – of male 'queer' desires and practices. One aim of this book is therefore to re-examine representations of male same-sex desire or masculine gender nonconformity and to search for hidden narratives of unexpressed female emotion beneath them.

As will be clear, the spectrum of female embodied desires I discuss is, because those desires are defined in the negative as not orientated towards masculinity, both wide and difficult to visualise. Female same-sex desires patently belong within this group, but they are not the limit of the focus of this book. It extends to cover many often-unnamed desires: desires for male femininity; desires to emulate the homosocial intimacies of men; desires to organise the penetrably sexualised female body into something harder and more contained; desires to transform the masculine body into something more penetrably erotic or sexualised; desires to assert the boundaries and aversions of the body. Carolyn Dinshaw describes her focus as desires defined by their outsider status: 'lives, texts, and other cultural phenomena left out of sexual categories back then ... and those left out of current sexual categories now'.[19] I also seek to extend this enquiry into sexualities that exist *in potentia*, in the spaces that we might find by reading 'against the grain' and in the moments where constellations of embodied affects and double meanings let us glimpse a sexuality that might have been. To make these desires visible, I draw on research into masculinities, as well as on femininities and female sexualities; notably, I look to Halberstam's work establishing female masculinity as its own field of study rather than as a mirror image or a subcategory of masculinity in general, and on the work of Clare Lees, Ruth Mazo Karras and Isabel Davis.[20] The desires I discuss often, like the disembodied penis fruits, blur the boundaries between animate and inanimate, human and non-human, natural and artificial. The bodies within and between which these desires circulate are often unstably constructed, having less in common with the

---

the *Interpretation of Culture*, eds Cary Nelson and Lawrence Grossberg (Urbana, IL: University of Illinois Press, 1988), pp. 271–313.

[18] Anna Kłosowska Roberts, *Queer Love in the Middle Ages* (New York: Palgrave Macmillan, 2005). p. 17.

[19] Carolyn Dinshaw, *Getting Medieval: Sexualities and Communities, Pre- and Postmodern* (Durham, NC and London: Duke University Press, 1999), p. 1.

[20] Halberstam, *Female Masculinity*; Clare A. Lees, ed., *Medieval Masculinities: Regarding Men in the Middle Ages* (Minneapolis, MN: University of Minnesota Press, 1994); Ruth Mazo Karras, *From Boys to Men: Formations of Masculinity in Late Medieval Europe* (Philadelphia, PA: University of Pennsylvania Press, 2002); Isabel Davis, *Writing Masculinity in the Later Middle Ages* (Cambridge: Cambridge University Press, 2007).

Introduction

post-medieval (Cartesian) model of embodiment as stable, material and fixed, and more in common with Deleuze and Guattari's concept of the assemblage, or Haraway's idea of the hybrid: a body always in the process of becoming, of extending itself, of containing within itself mobile component parts that may combine and recombine in different ways.[21] Consequently, I rely on studies of liminality and marginality, especially work on the monstrous, the hybrid and the prosthetic, notably the works of Jacques Derrida and David Wills, of Jeffrey Jerome Cohen, Margrit Shildrick and Astrida Neimanis, and of the contributors to the recent special issue of *Textual Practice* devoted to prosthesis.[22] Harnessing this work, I explore the ways in which female desires reorient not only the somatic and the emotional, but also the textual and hermeneutic constructions through which medieval and modern writers express themselves.

I argue that, in the late fourteenth century, Chaucer inaugurates an interrogation of the available modes of representing women's emotions, desires and aversions, carried out primarily through his most radically disruptive poem, the *Legend of Good Women*.[23] This text engages deeply and often antagonistically with the hermeneutic tradition stretching from the Latin of Jerome and Alan of Lille; it is most strongly rooted in the great vernacular response to that tradition, the *Roman de la Rose*.[24] Yet I argue that Chaucer's interrogation does not remain stably contained within the *Legend*, but spreads from it to influence a genre of writing seldom associated with hermeneutic or poetic complexity, the genre of Middle English romance. Despite the ongoing scholarly push to rescue Middle English romance from the low prestige

---

[21] Gilles Deleuze and Félix Guattari, *A Thousand Plateaus: Capitalism and Schizophrenia*, translated by Brian Massumi (Minneapolis, MN: University of Minnesota Press, 1987); Donna Haraway, 'A Cyborg Manifesto: Science, Technology, and Socialist-Feminism in the Late Twentieth Century', in *Simians, Cyborgs and Women: The Reinvention of Nature* (New York: Routledge, 1991), pp. 149–81.

[22] Derrida, *Of Grammatology*, passim; David Wills, *Prosthesis* (Stanford, CA: Stanford University Press, 1995); Margrit Shildrick, 'Reimagining Embodiment: Prostheses, Supplements and Boundaries', *Somatechnics* 3.2 (2013): 270–86 and 'Border Crossings: The Technologies of Disability and Desire', in *Culture-Theory-Disability: Encounters Between Disability Studies and Cultural Studies*, eds Anne Waldschmidt, Hanjo Berressem and Moritz Ingwersen (Bielefeld: Transcript, 2017), pp. 137–69; Jeffrey Jerome Cohen, *Stone: An Ecology of the Inhuman* (Minneapolis, MN and London: University of Minnesota Press, 2015); Jeffrey Jerome Cohen, *Medieval Identity Machines* (Minneapolis, MN: University of Minnesota Press, 2003); Astrida Neimanis, *Bodies of Water: Posthuman Feminist Phenomenology* (London: Bloomsbury, 2016); Chloe Porter, Katie L. Walter and Margaret Healy, eds, *Prosthesis in Medieval and Early Modern Culture* (Special Issue) *Textual Practice* 30.7 (2016).

[23] All quotations from Chaucer's works are from *The Riverside Chaucer*, gen. ed. Larry D. Benson, 3rd edn (Oxford: Oxford University Press, 2008). They are given in parentheses in the text.

[24] See Alastair J. Minnis, *Magister Amoris: The* Roman de la Rose *and Vernacular Hermeneutics* (Oxford: Oxford University Press, 2001).

accorded to it in twentieth-century scholarship, the genre remains cut off from comparisons to Latin and European literary debates. I demonstrate, however, that the romances respond to a Chaucerian pressure to change the ways in which women's bodily agency, and women's violently suppressed desires, may be made visible, thinkable concepts. By seeking out the silences and absences in the hermeneutic record, and by investigating the constellations of innuendos and resonances that might suggest a lesbian-like erotic, we can recentre women within the hermeneutic paradigms. I argue that Chaucer's *Legend* inaugurates an interrogation of the visibility of female desires in just such a context. Female desires are central structuring devices of both the *Legend* and the romances, and they offer a radically new way to think about textual interpretation for Chaucer and his fifteenth-century descendants.

A WOMAN-SHAPED GAP IN MEDIEVAL HERMENEUTICS

The field of scholarship concerned with medieval deviant desires is huge and ever-expanding, but it remains organised – with a few notable exceptions – around a telling absence of attention to the desires and embodied emotions of women. In part this absence is authentic. The medieval hermeneutic tradition is often silent about the role of female desires. Yet although medieval references to deviant female sexual activities do certainly exist and are occasionally categorised conveniently in parallel with their masculine equivalents, scholars have been slow to treat female desire as anything but an unremarked mirror-image of male desire, or an absence.[25] There are several recent landmark studies relating to female same-sex desire. For example, Noreen Giffney, Michelle M. Sauer and Diane Watt edited a set of radically interventionalist essays under the title *The Lesbian Premodern*; Anna Kłosowska and Karma Lochrie both make female desire central to their studies, respectively *Queer Love in the Middle Ages*, and *Heterosyncrasies: Female Sexuality When Normal Wasn't*.[26] Yet the subject remains, in Jacqueline Murray's apt phrase, 'twice marginal and twice invisible'.[27] In particular, I argue, this neglect damages our understanding of medieval hermeneutic, epistemic and poetic practices, all of which are persistently and interrogatively related to sexual and gendered categories by medieval writers. In this section of my introduction, therefore,

---

[25] Thomas of Chobham, *Summa confessorum*, ed. F. Broomfield (Louvain: Nauwelaerts, 1968), p. 400; see also Lochrie, *Heterosyncrasies: Female Sexuality When Normal Wasn't* (Minneapolis, MN: University of Minnesota Press, 2005), p. 33.

[26] *The Lesbian Premodern*, eds Noreen Giffney, Michelle M. Sauer and Diane Watt (New York: Palgrave Macmillan, 2011); Kłosowska, *Queer Love in the Middle Ages*; Lochrie, *Heterosyncrasies*. See also *Same Sex Love and Desire Among Women in the Middle Ages*, eds Francesca Canadé Sautman and Pamela Sheingorn (New York: Palgrave, 2001).

[27] Jacqueline Murray, '"Twice Marginal and Twice Invisible": Lesbians in the Middle Ages', in *The Handbook of Medieval Sexuality*, eds Vern L. Bullough and James A. Brundage (New York: Garland, 1996), pp. 191–222.

Introduction

I seek to redress that imbalance, and to show how we might reinterpret the hermeneutic traditions, by which Chaucer's *Legend* and the late medieval romances are so deeply influenced.

The combined efforts of many scholars have demonstrated the wide gulf between medieval and contemporary constructions of sexuality and gender. In medieval Christian thought, the expectation that relations between men and women will break down and become dysfunctional is axiomatic, following the blueprint of Eve. As Karma Lochrie observes, in twentieth- and twenty-first-century debates, the terms 'normal' and 'natural' are employed polemically, to construct or contest moral boundaries. To condemn something as 'unnatural' is to imply its moral repugnance; to insist something is 'quite normal' is to imply it is deserving of moral acceptance. By contrast, medieval models of desire that look back to the theology of the Fall presume that the 'natural' is necessarily subject to corruption.[28] In this context, though desires exist on a contested spectrum, some better or worse than others, all are part of an expectation of disruptive relations between men and women, a means of expressing the dysfunctions that result from Eve's sin.[29] I coin the term 'heterodeviancy' to describe this ruling expectation. The desires I discuss are 'deviant' (or in Middle English 'deviaunt') because they are rooted in the (carnal) sin of Eve.[30] That female sin's consequence is the structuring of male–female relations such that those relations produce dysfunctions and disruptions, including a wide spectrum of female desires no longer orientated towards their proper origin and target.[31] The term captures the general expectation of human propensity to sin, but also gestures towards the fact that, as Dinshaw puts it, medieval women are 'in some sense always already perverse'.[32]

It is the epistemic, hermeneutic and poetic implications of female desire that interest me in this book, and nowhere is masculine ambivalence concerning those implications more evident than in writings of St Jerome. Epistemic

---

[28] Karma Lochrie, *Covert Operations: The Medieval Uses of Secrecy* (Philadelphia: University of Pennsylvania Press, 1999), p. 225; Lochrie, *Heterosyncrasies*, pp. 1–25.

[29] Although I think that the most convincing consensus view is that medieval sexualities were not understood in terms of binaries, there are opposing arguments, for example those Simon Gaunt makes in relation to medieval French literature. See Gaunt, 'Straight Minds/"Queer" Wishes in Old French Hagiography', in *Premodern Sexualities*, eds Louise Fradenburg and Carla Freccero, with the assistance of Kathy Lavezzo (New York and London: Routledge, 1996), pp. 155–73.

[30] For the meanings of the Middle English adjective and noun, see *MED* 'deviaunte' (n and adj). The *MED* accords the term a possible, but not automatic, application to sexuality, and cites its use in the Middle English translation of the *Roman de la Rose*. See also Michelle M. Sauer, *Gender in Medieval Culture* (London: Bloomsbury, 2015), pp. 67–68; Alastair J. Minnis, *Fallible Authors: Chaucer's Pardoner and the Wife of Bath* (Philadelphia, PA: University of Pennsylvania Press, 2008), p. 2.

[31] Here, again, I draw on Ahmed, *Queer Phenomenologies*, especially pp. 19–20.

[32] Dinshaw, *Getting Medieval*, p. 13. She draws on Lochrie, *Covert Operations*, pp. 177–228.

anxiety about the unbounded female body underpins Jerome's paradigmatic analogy between textual interpretation and sexual subjugation, expressed in terms of a masculine hermeneutic search for knowledge.[33] Jerome compares the Classical or pagan text he reads to the beautiful captive woman described in the book of Deuteronomy. 'Is it surprising', he asks his correspondent,

> that I too, admiring the fairness of her form and the grace of her eloquence, desire to make that secular wisdom which is my captive and my handmaid, a matron of the true Israel? Or that, shaving off and cutting away all in her that is dead, whether this be idolatry, pleasure, error or lust, I take her to myself clean and pure, and begat by her servants for the Lord?[34]

Denuded of both her clothes and her nails, representing her only possible means of resistance and witnessing her unspoken or unrecorded aversion, the woman in the analogy is there to be subjugated and overpowered. The reader desirous of this attractive feminine text is urged to 'make her bald, and cut off her alluring hair, that is to say, the graces of style, and pare away her dead nails, and wash her in niter'.[35] The boundaries of the female body are thus disrupted or set aside through a series of overtly violent actions – stripping, shearing and paring, corrosive washing, and finally sexual penetration. Importing a Pauline emphasis on the 'dead' flesh, Jerome's depiction of the hair and nails as 'dead' parts of a living body brings living and dead flesh into disturbing congruence. His construction of these parts of the body as extraneous, as removable as clothing, troubles our sense of the female body as an entity with clear boundaries. Above all, the image of washing this body with nitre or caustic soap indicates the erosion of the skin, the very surface that marks the margin of the body, and the abrasive shifting of bodily boundaries inwards to the raw flesh. The hair, nails and even the skin are coded as devious prosthetic supplements to feminine flesh: evidence of an innate female capacity to move beyond that which is essential. Following Jerome, writers depict the female body as a blank tablet or unwritten page, bearing witness to the need for structures to keep that body static and contained, as the wax tablet is contained within its

---

[33] Carolyn Dinshaw inaugurates the tradition of interpreting Jerome's gendered hermeneutic in the context of vernacular literature in *Chaucer's Sexual Poetics* (Madison, WI: University of Wisconsin Press, 1989), pp. 22–23. For further discussion of Jerome, and of the development of medieval hermeneutics, see Jill Mann, *Feminizing Chaucer*, 2nd edn (Cambridge: D. S. Brewer, 2002), p. 1; Rita Copeland, *Rhetoric, Hermeneutics, and Translation in the Middle Ages: Academic Traditions and Vernacular Texts* (Cambridge: Cambridge University Press, 1995), pp. 37–62; Catherine M. Chin, *Grammar and Christianity in the Late Roman World* (Philadelphia, PA: University of Pennsylvania Press, 2008), pp. 82–85.

[34] Letter 70, in *Jerome: Letters and Select Works*, trans W. H. Fremantle, in *A Select Library of Nicene and Post-Nicene Fathers of the Christian Church*, ed. Philip Schaff and rev. Henry Wace, 2nd series, vol. 6 (New York: Christian Literature Company, 1893), p. 149.

[35] Letter 66, in *Jerome*, trans. Fremantle, p. 138.

wooden frame, or as the page is cut to size and stitched into the codex. Images of women's bodies as texts that simultaneously require containment and suffer assaults on their integrity and their boundaries are persistent presences in the hermeneutic tradition.

Yet when medieval writers discuss the ways in which dissident sexual or gendered activity might be imagined in terms of reciprocal damage to the structure of language, they focus entirely on masculine deviations. To illustrate this, I turn to the twelfth-century theologian Alan of Lille. His *De planctu Naturae* offers a lively illustration of how textual and sexual interactions should uphold each other. In an extended analogy relating creation to inscription, and the act of writing to penetrative insemination, Alan attacks the perversions caused when Venus takes over the pen, the 'calamum prepotentem' or 'potent tool', that properly belongs to the goddess Nature.[36] The word Alan uses, 'calamum', literally means a reed and is commonly the word for a pen, but it is also a euphemism for the penis. This pen, which should inseminate the page (pagina/vagina) and cause it to bear fruitful words, deviates from 'orthography' into 'falsigraphy' (*De planctu*, p. 845). Instead of recording the decorous marriages between masculine and feminine nouns, it scripts a monstrous and incomprehensible confusion.[37] Nature weeps, to see how

> The sex of active nature shudders shamefully, as it thus declines into the passive form. A man turned woman ... is both predicate and subject, he becomes likewise of two declensions, he pushes the laws of grammar too far. (*De planctu*, lines 8–20).[38]

At the narrative level, Alan explains, the effect of such deviation is akin to the distortion of all the famous stories of true love. Achilles is dissolute; Pyramus no longer desires Thisbe. Abandoning Helen, 'Paris with Paris devises monstrous, unspeakable acts'.[39] Much ink has been spilled by scholars

---

[36] Alan of Lille, *De planctu Naturae*, ed. Nikolaus M. Häring, *Studi Medievali* 19 (1978), p. 845. Subsequent quotations are from this edition are given in the text, with line references for the verse and page references for the prose. Translations are adapted from *The Plaint of Nature*, trans. James J. Sheridan (Toronto: Pontifical Institute of Mediaeval Studies, 1980).

[37] See Jan Ziolkowski, *Alan of Lille's Grammar of Sex: The Meaning of Grammar to a Twelfth-Century Intellectual* (Cambridge: Medieval Academy, 1985); Susan Schibanoff, 'Sodomy's Mark: Alan of Lille, Jean de Meun, and the Medieval Theory of Authorship', in *Queering the Middle Ages*, eds Glenn Burger and Steven F. Kruger (Minneapolis, MN: University of Minnesota Press, 2001), pp. 28–56 (pp. 34–35).

[38] Actiui generis sexus se turpitur horret
Sic in passiuum degenerare genus.
Femina uir factus ...
predicat et subiect, fit duplex terminus idem.
Grammatice leges ampliat ille nimis.

[39] Non modo Tyndaridem Phrygius venatur adulter,
Sed Paris in Paridem monstra nefanda parit.

eagerly probing the knotty question of precisely *what* sexual deviancies are intended by each salacious innuendo or suggestive simile that punctuates Alan's polemic.[40] This confusion of gender results in the human equivalent of a grammatical fault: 'the human race ... adopts a highly irregular metaplasm when it inverts the rules of Venus, introducing barbarisms in its arrangement of genders'.[41] In grammatical terms, the reason metaplasm offends Alan is that it is a change in the orthography of a word, an expansion or elision that changes the metrical value without changing the sense, and may thus be regarded as a sterile or unproductive change, bringing no new meaning but only the distortion of form. Alan does not mention this further detail, but amongst the types of metaplasm listed in Donatus' Latin grammar (that ubiquitous school text) is *prosthesis*, the addition of syllables at the beginning of a word. Men who deviate from their proper sexual role might thus be seen to be engaging in a feminising degradation of language, much as men overwhelmed by Venus were thought to engage in a feminising abandonment of *ratio* to *libido*.[42]

The same emphasis on human sexual deviancy (or, specifically, masculine sexual deviancy) as cause and consequence of uncommunicative and sterile textual practice is translated from Alan's work into many subsequent contexts. Most influential and provocative amongst them is, of course, the great fourteenth-century French poem, the *Roman de la Rose*, which was to underpin much of Chaucer's poetic endeavour. Begun around 1230 by Guillaume de Lorris, the *Roman* is a vast poem, owing most of its length

---

Non modo per rimas rimatur basia Thysbes
Pyramus, huic Veneris rimula nulla placet.

('No longer does the Trojan adulterer pursue the daughter of Tyndareus, but Paris with Paris engages in monstrous, unspeakable things. No longer does Pyramus seek Thisbe's kisses through the cracks [in the wall], but the little chink of Venus no longer pleases him.' De planctu, lines 51–54.)

[40] See, for example, William Burgwinkle, *Sodomy, Masculinity and Law in Medieval Literature: France and England, 1050–1230* (Cambridge: Cambridge University Press, 2004), pp. 170–99. In recent years, the tendency to conflate references to 'unnatural' sexual activity with sodomy and sodomy with 'homosexuality' has been rigorously interrogated. Scholars such as James A. Schultz, Karma Lochrie and Robert Mills demonstrate that the contemporary binaries of heterosexuality and homosexuality do not obtain, and that the medieval category of *sodomia* was both more diverse, and much less liable to use the gender of participants as an organising principle, than post-medieval models of sexual dissidence. See James A. Schultz, 'Heterosexuality as a Threat to Medieval Studies', *Journal of the History of Sexuality* 15.1 (2006): 14–29; Lochrie, *Heterosyncrasies*, pp. 1–25; Robert Mills, *Seeing Sodomy in the Middle Ages* (Chicago, IL and London: University of Chicago Press, 2014).

[41] 'Humanum namque genus ... in constructione generum barbarizans, Venereas regulas inuertendo nimis irregulari utitur metaplasmo'.

[42] See Marilynn Desmond, *Reading Dido: Gender, Textuality and the Medieval Aeneid* (Minneapolis, MN and London: University of Minnesota Press, 1994), pp. 74–98.

to its second author, Jean de Meun, who added a long continuation several decades later. The *Roman* reiterates the conflation of the penis with the pen or 'stylus', and condemns the sterile insubordination of those men who refuse their proper sexual activities:

> those who do not write with their styluses ... on the beautiful precious tablets that Nature did not prepare for them to leave idle ... may they, in addition to the excommunication that sends them all to damnation, suffer, before their death, the loss of their purse and testicles, the signs that they are male![43]
> (pp. 323-34)

As punishment for the hermeneutic failure to understand Nature's decree to reproduce, these men suffer the reciprocal consequence, to lose their penis and testicles, and in this way, men who refuse to write – or to procreate – contribute to the ever-expanding category of not-quite-men, men who threaten to slip through into the porous category of the feminine, men who do not signify as men.

In this long tradition of hermeneutic writing, the focus on masculine deviancy is accompanied by a curious absence of speculation regarding possible deviancies of women, anxiously though Jerome and his ilk seek to persuade their readers of the need to police women's ever-ready propensity to transgress. Innuendos and monitory examples bypass what women might or might not do while men deviate from their affections. We do not know what emotions animate the undesired, unkissed women who function as blank canvases or 'precious tablets', nor what 'unspeakable' activities Helen might devise with Helen. Nonetheless, one particular form of female sexual activity *is* visible within the medieval discourses I have discussed here, and it can serve as a litmus test for the threats and possibilities of aberrant, autonomous or resistant female desire in general. This form of desire is, unsurprisingly, one that involves bodily prosthesis. Scholars of the *De planctu Naturae*, notably Alexandre Leupin, David Rollo and Susan Schibanoff, have drawn attention to the many paradoxes and self-contradictions of Alan's work, including the reliance on metaphorical language to

---

[43] cil qui des greffes n'escrivent ...
es beles tables precieuses
que Nature por estre oiseuses
ne leur avoit por ce prestees
...
o tout l'esconmeniemant
qui touz les mete a dampnemant
puis que la se veulent aherdre,
ainz qu'il muirent, puissant il perdre
et l'aumosniere et les estalles,
don il ont signe d'estre malles!
(19599-637)

condemn metaphor, the seductive delight in desires or figures proclaimed to be deviant, and, above all, the construction of an unnatural Nature, a female goddess wielding a phallic pen.[44] In the historical context, too, the image of a woman with a phallic prosthesis carries explosive implications. Carolyn Dinshaw argues persuasively that, for medieval participants, it is this object, rather than any specific sexual act, that is synonymous with female same-sex activity. A 'long unbroken habit of thought ... linked female same-sex relations with dildos'.[45] Descriptions in penitential codices make salacious suggestions about this, as for example:

> They do not put flesh to flesh as in the fleshly genital member of one into the body of the other, since nature precludes this, but they do transform the use of that part of their body into an unnatural one: it is said they use instruments of diabolical operations to excite desire.[46]

These 'instruments' evidently attracted more censure than other sexual activities between women. A penitential attributed to Bede distinguishes between sex acts between women that are carried out 'by means of a device' (*per machinam*) and sex acts between women that are not: the former category attracts a much longer penance. Sex acts between women that do not involve some kind of phallic substitute are depicted as mere enjoyable absurdities, as in the gleefully eloquent euphemisms of the twelfth-century poet Étienne de Fougères concerning women who 'joust shield to shield' and have 'no pestle in their mortar'. By contrast, the idea of prosthetic sexual activity earns censorious comment, such as Caxton's gloss on Ovid's tale of Iphis and Ianthe, or the verdict of capital punishment returned to the German Katharina Hetzeldofer.[47]

---

[44] Alexandre Leupin, *Barbarolexis: Medieval Writing and Sexuality*, trans. Kate M. Cooper (Cambridge, MA and London: Harvard University Press, 1989), pp. 59-78; David Rollo, *Kiss My Relics: Hermaphroditic Fictions of the Middle Ages* (Chicago, IL and London: University of Chicago Press, 2011), pp. 77-144; Susan Schibanoff, *Chaucer's Queer Poetics: Rereading the Dream Trio* (Toronto, Buffalo, NY and London: University of Toronto Press, 2006), pp. 199-257; Mark D. Jordan, *The Invention of Sodomy in Christian Theology* (Chicago, IL: University of Chicago Press, 1997), p. 71.

[45] Dinshaw, *Getting Medieval*, pp. 89-90. See also Robert L. A. Clark, 'Jousting without a Lance: The Condemnation of Female Homoeroticism in the *Livre Des Manières*', in *Same Sex Love and Desire Among Women*, eds Sautman and Sheingorn, pp. 143-77; Robert Mills, 'Homosexuality: Specters of Sodom', in *A Cultural History of Sexuality in the Middle Ages*, ed. Ruth Evans (Oxford: Blackwell, 2011), pp. 57-80 (pp. 62-63).

[46] Quoted by Edith Benkov, 'The Erased Lesbian: Sodomy and the Legal Tradition in Medieval Europe', in *Same Sex Love and Desire among Women*, eds Sautman and Sheingorn, pp. 101-22 (p. 104).

[47] This text, the story of Iphis and Ianthe, is discussed by Mills in *Seeing Sodomy*, p. 243. See also Helmut Puff, 'Female Sodomy: The Trial of Katherina Hetzeldofer (1477)', *Journal of Medieval and Early Modern Studies* 30.1 (2000): 41-61; William Caxton,

Introduction

This method offers potential for rediscovering hidden narratives of female desire by widening the spectrum of possible contexts in which they may be situated. Judith Bennett's influential work on historical women's same-sex relations provides a model.[48] She puts forward the ingenious approach of using representational strategies, rather than proof of sexual activities, as her evidence of same-sex intimacy. Bennett examines the memorial brass dedicated to two never-married women, demonstrating that the brass appropriates the established iconography used to memorialise married couples, and thus codes the women's intimacy as quasi-marital. She coins the term 'lesbian-like' to describe this, and it is a useful means of making visible same-sex intimacies between women in the (almost ubiquitous) context of a paucity of evidence about sexual practices. As Bennett herself acknowledges, the approach also carries the risk of perpetuating stereotypes of 'lesbian' intimacy as non-sexual (and lesbian sex as 'not sex', a stereotype that persists). In response, I make a complementary intervention, suggesting we might think of a 'lesbian-like erotic' that widens the spectrum of practices we might recognise as relating to same-sex sexual and erotic contact between women. There are many moments in the texts I discuss in this book where women are associated with practices, the activities and (especially) the prosthetic objects that are part of the established vocabulary for referring to female same-sex sexual activity. These women, in inverse relation to Bennett's couple, might be seen as expressing or performing a 'lesbian-like erotic', a constellation of behaviours that suggest the workings of lesbian sex without corresponding evidence of female–female intimacy or emotional attachment.

I propose a spectrum of embodiments, literary tropes and emotional relations that merit reinvestigation as possible locations of occluded, erased or simply overlooked female desire. We may look to the silences of the hermeneutic tradition, where women's desires are conspicuous only for the absence of men to respond to them. We may look to the moments where masculine sexual and textual violence overwrites a female desire or subjugates a female body, where aversion offers a negative image of a desire *not* to be so treated, a desire not to be so touched, penetrated, structured or inscribed. We may look to moments where women seek to appropriate or embody forms of 'masculine' agency, equipping themselves with literal or metaphorical prostheses. We may identify a 'lesbian-like erotic', to uncover further moments of what resembles female sexual desire, hidden within women's narratives or women's relations that do not, on the surface, appear anything but conventionally orientated towards masculine desire. We may re-examine innuendos of male same-sex intimacy and sexual activity, to recentre the desires of women missing from

---

The Booke of Ovyde Named Methamorphose, ed. Richard J. Moll (Toronto and Oxford: Pontifical Institute of Mediaeval Studies/Bodleian Library, 2013), IX, lines 919–1078.

[48] Judith Bennett, 'Remembering Elizabeth Etchingham and Agnes Oxenbridge', in *The Lesbian Premodern,* eds Giffney, Sauer and Watt, pp. 131–43.

such accounts. All of these overlapping and complementary strategies must be pulled together to create a composite picture of the female desires that are so often inarticulate in medieval and modern discussions of desire.

This search amongst negatives and absences, amongst the unspoken, the conjectural and the subtextual, amongst prosthetic gaps and absences, aligns my work with recent theorisations of a medieval female same-sex erotic, which seek to transform the unknown, absent or imperfect from a source of failure to a marker of possibility. Anna Kłosowska and Lara Farina identify a female erotic organised around the *lacunae*, the gaps and seams and interstices, that permeate medieval representations of female desire.[49] This anticipates the process described by Horne and Lewis, whereby 'lesbians and gays have … to form identities out of appropriations and adaptations of existing codes', or the 'lesbian' mode of reading that proceeds through patchworking together of materials, through *lacunae* and omissions.[50] Reframing these features as sites of potential pleasure rather than imperfection, they raise the possibility of a distinctively female erotic that enjoys its own discontinuous materiality. Elizabeth Freeman argues that, in the asynchronous narratives of 'lesbian erotohistoriography', one may find 'a kind of visceral encounter between past and present figured as a tactile meeting, as a finger that in stitching, both touches and is touched, and that in reading, pokes and caresses the holes in the archival text even as it sutures them'.[51] This eroticism of fingers and holes, of incomplete or penetrable surfaces, enables a mode of 'lesbian' reading that is not bound by rigid temporal or narrative structures, and which resists orientation towards expected trajectories of desire and embodiment.[52] In contemporary contexts, lesbian-identified readers gravitate towards certain types of narrative, which provide ambivalent portrayals of heterosexual romances, or sufficiently suggestive silences and gaps surrounding female–female interaction, to accommodate lesbian or lesbian-like readings. Examples include stories set in all-female or female-dominated communities. A similar fascination with gaps and silences, with spaces closed to male participation, with apertures giving secret access, permeates medieval depictions and constructions of female same-sex desire and activity. This provides a means of thinking through *lacunae* to a distinctively female-coded form of desiring, which can serve as a litmus test for the wide spectrum of non-male-orientated

---

[49] Lara Farina, 'Lesbian History and Erotic Reading', in *The Lesbian Premodern*, eds Giffney, Sauer and Watt, pp. 49–60; Kłosowska, *Queer Love in the Middle Ages*, pp. 69–116.

[50] Peter Horne and Reina Lewis, 'Introduction, Reframed – Inscribing Lesbian, Gay and Queer Presences in Visual Culture', in *Outlooks: Lesbian and Gay Sexualities and Visual Culture*, eds Peter Horne and Reina Lewis (London: Routledge, 1996), pp. 1–12 (p. 4).

[51] Elizabeth Freeman, *Time Binds: Queer Temporalities, Queer Histories* (Durham, NC: Duke University Press, 2010), p. 110.

[52] See Ahmed, *Queer Phenomenology*, pp. 91–95.

Introduction

female desires that are the focus of this book. Consequently, the inarticulacies of female desire – both in medieval expression and modern scholarship – offer not only limitations, but also possibilities. The prosthetic origins of that desire, within a female body always organised around an absence in a male body, give it both nebulous openness, and also the means to think beyond established structures: the supplementary and lacking character of the prosthetic itself.

PENETRATING THE HERMENEUTIC BODY: CHAUCER'S *LEGEND OF GOOD WOMEN*

The primary site through which I explore medieval representations of female desire is a somewhat unlikely candidate: Chaucer's much-denigrated and often overlooked *Legend of Good Women*.[53] The *Legend*'s lukewarm critical reception has often been linked to the heavy-handed hints of boredom with which the narrator treats his material: a threadbare collection of just nine legends drawn from Classical literature, which ends abruptly just before the conclusion of the final narrative.[54] Scholarship has long been dominated by the assumption that, whatever its successes or failures, its sincerities or cynicisms, the *Legend* is socio-emotional project, a work whose primary focus is the emotions and the wrongs of women. Carolyn Dinshaw sees the

---

[53] In 1972, Robert Worth Frank challenged the prevailing dismissive assessment of the *Legend*, but even so it remains under-studied in comparison to the earlier dream visions, let alone *Troilus and Criseyde* or the *Canterbury Tales*. See Frank's 'The Legend of the *Legend of Good Women*', *Chaucer Review* 1.1 (1966): 110–33 and *Chaucer and the 'Legend of Good Women'* (Cambridge, MA: Harvard University Press, 1972), pp. 189–210. Twelve manuscript witnesses to the *Legend* survive, plus a first print edition by Thynne in 1532, which for a Chaucer's work represents a fairly modest circulation in manuscript and a late entry into print culture. The picture of the *Legend*'s popularity and influence is rather muted in comparison to the *Canterbury Tales*, *Troilus and Criseyde* or even *The Parliament of Fowls* (fifteen manuscripts and a 1478 edition by Caxton). The critical edition of the *Legend* discusses its manuscripts. See Janet Cowen and George Kane, eds, *Geoffrey Chaucer: The Legend of Good Women* (East Lansing, MI: Colleagues Press, 1995).

[54] For details of the individual legends and their sources, see Amanda Holton, *The Sources of Chaucer's Poetics* (Aldershot: Ashgate, 2008). Chaucer invites the comparison to the *Heroides* in his 'Man of Law's Prologue' (*CT* II, lines 53–76). See also Lisa J. Kiser, *Telling Classical Tales: Chaucer and the Legend of Good Women* (Ithaca, NY: Cornell University Press, 1993); Copeland, *Rhetoric, Hermeneutics, and Translation*, pp. 186–97; Suzanne Hagedorn, *Abandoned Women: Rewriting the Classics in Dante, Boccaccio, and Chaucer* (Ann Arbor, MI: University of Michigan Press, 2004), pp. 21–46, 130–58; Marilynn Desmond, 'The *Translatio* of Memory and Desire in *The Legend of Good Women*: Chaucer's Vernacular *Heroides*', *Studies in the Age of Chaucer* 35 (2013): 179–207. For Chaucer's use of Boccaccio, see David Wallace, *Chaucer and the Early Writings of Boccaccio* (Cambridge: D. S. Brewer, 1985); Carolyn Collette, *Rethinking Chaucer's Legend of Good Women* (York: York Medieval Press, 2014), pp. 35–49.

text as a satire on 'passive' women.⁵⁵ Sheila Delany interprets it as a corrective to the representations of women in 'courtly love' and 'clerical misogyny'.⁵⁶ Nicola McDonald and Joyce Coleman view the entire project as a 'ludic' form of flirtation between the sexes in the royal court.⁵⁷ Several scholars, including Hansen, Hume and most recently Burger, see the *Legend*'s target as the limited, effeminising or restrictive rhetoric and rules of courtly love.⁵⁸ Collette argues for the *Legend* as a humanist theorising of love as a 'moral force', made possible by recognition of the 'alterity' of the Classical source material, and enabling an interrogation of the tensions between women's emotional satisfaction and their social constraint.⁵⁹ Finally, a recent special issue of *the Chaucer Review* sets out to 'read the *Legend* as a central work in Chaucer's exploration of women's emotional lives'.⁶⁰ This consensus, and the accompanying scholarly tendency to gloss over the legends in favour of the lengthy prologue that precedes them, have done a disservice to the *Legend*.⁶¹ I argue that the text's primary focus is hermeneutic, not social or emotional.

The hermeneutic focus of the *Legend* is evident from its orientation of itself in relation to Jerome (as an exemplar) and to Jean de Meun (as monitory example). A stern God of Love rebukes the narrator for the 'heresye' (F, line 330) of translating the *Roman* 'in pleyn text, withouten nede of glose' (F, line 328), and

---

⁵⁵ Dinshaw, *Chaucer's Sexual Poetics*, p. 75.
⁵⁶ Sheila Delany, *The Naked Text: Chaucer's Legend of Good Women* (Berkeley, CA, Los Angeles, CA and Oxford: University of California Press, 1994), p. 139.
⁵⁷ Nicola McDonald, 'Chaucer's *Legend of Good Women*, Ladies at Court and the Female Reader', *Chaucer Review* 35.1 (2000): 22–42; Joyce Coleman, 'The Flower, the Leaf, and Philippa of Lancaster', in *The* Legend of Good Women: *Context and Reception*, ed. Carolyn P. Collette (Cambridge: Cambridge University Press, 2006), pp. 33–58.
⁵⁸ Elaine Tuttle Hansen, 'The Feminization of Men in Chaucer's *Legend of Good Women*', in *Seeking the Woman in Late Medieval and Renaissance Writings: Essays in Feminist Contextual Criticism*, eds Janet Halley and Sheila Fisher (Knoxville, TN: University of Tennessee Press, 1989), pp. 51–70; see also Elaine Tuttle Hansen, *Chaucer and the Fictions of Gender* (Berkeley, CA, Los Angeles, CA, and Oxford: University of California Press, 1992), pp. 1–12; Cathy Hume, *Chaucer and the Cultures of Love and Marriage* (Cambridge: D. S. Brewer, 2012), pp. 175–207; Glenn Burger, '"Pite renneth soone in gentil herte": Ugly Feelings and Gendered Conduct in Chaucer's *Legend of Good Women*', *Chaucer Review* 52.1 (2017): 66–84.
⁵⁹ Collette, *Rethinking Chaucer's* Legend, pp. 1–5.
⁶⁰ It is revealing of the *Legend*'s precarious popularity that, even here, it is still necessary for the editors of the special issue to reiterate Worth's argument of 1972 and to 'reject the idea that the *Legend* is an unsuccessful experiment'. Susanna Fein and David Raybin, 'About this Issue', *Chaucer Review* 52.1 (2017): 1–2 (p. 1).
⁶¹ Frank's sharp observation that they are 'all of the *Legend* that the mid-twentieth century is willing to take to its bosom' still holds uncomfortably true, but one suspects some of this enthusiasm for the prologues is born of familiarity, or of enjoyment of the academic parlour game of trope-spotting. See Frank, *Chaucer and the* Legend, p. 11. The prologue exists in two versions, F and G. For details, see Cowen and Kane eds, *The Legend*, pp.124–26.

Introduction

castigates his slanderous treatment of Criseyde and other women. As penance, the narrator undertakes to construct a 'gloryous legende' that will expose the perfidy of men and shed light on 'goode women' (F, lines 473–74): a gendered inversion of previous poetic practice. However, this ostensibly kindly focus on feminine emotion works in much the same way as Chaucer's depiction of the Pardoner would work in the *Canterbury Tales*, affording an opportunity to play with ideas about linguistic supplementation, bodily disintegration and *auctoritas*, deeply influenced by Jean de Meun. The *Legend* constructs a poetics of desire marked with *lacunae* and excisions, permeated by the struggle to extend, to supplement, to take up vicarious positions and to move beyond itself. We might call it a prosthetic poetics of desire, a poetics that anticipates the 'eunuch hermeneutics' Dinshaw associates with the Pardoner's signal genital lack and rhetorical supplement.[62] Yet the *Legend* differs both from the earlier formulations of the *Roman* and from the later *Canterbury Tales* in that it considers how women's always already prosthetic bodies and desires might offer new and distinct rhetorical possibilities, transforming commonplace hermeneutic tropes into inverted fragments of themselves and breaking away from the great governing image of the naked female body as the surface on which to write. Responding to tropes of poetic inspiration that echo through the hermeneutic tradition from Jerome and Alan of Lille to the *Roman de la Rose*, Chaucer constructs his own inverted images. He maps the poetic structures through which textual and sexual reproduction are typically analogised onto bodies of the opposite gender. To understand the implications of this, we must look firstly to the *Roman*, and then to the Pardoner of the *Canterbury Tales*, whose take on the imagery of the *Roman* sheds light on Chaucer's *modus operandi* in the *Legend*.

The *Roman* opens with Guillaume de Lorris' conventional take on the trope of Nature as a creative inspiration. Inheriting a version of Jerome's image of the veiled pagan text that may be traced through Alan of Lille, Macrobius and William of Conches, Guillaume describes Nature ('la terre' or 'the earth') clothing herself in the colours of a hundred pairs of flowers.[63] These colours

---

[62] Carolyn Dinshaw, 'Eunuch Hermeneutics', *English Literary History* 55.1 (1988): 27–51.
[63] 'A new dress ... so ornate ...
that there are a hundred pairs of colours in it
of the grass and the flowers, blue, white
And many other colours.'
(pp. 31–32)

novele robe ... si cointe ...
Que de colors i a c peire
l'erbe et le flors blanches et perses
Et de maintes colors diverses.'
(lines 60–64)

All quotations from the Rose refer by line number to *Le Roman de la Rose*, ed. Felix Lécoy, 3 vols (Paris: Fermin-Didot, Champion, 1914–24). Modern English translations

or integuments of rhetoric adorn the body of Nature, inspiring the desiring activities of all natural things, including the poet's own writing.[64] After this, Jean de Meun's image of poetic inspiration is rather a shock. The God of Love foretells the coming of one Jean de Meun, the only poet worthy to complete the poem left unfinished at the death of its first author. 'Here Guillaume shall rest', the God of Love declares; 'May his tomb be full of balm, of incense, of myrrh, and aloes!' (p. 187). [65] Seemingly eulogistic, these lines neatly dispose of Guillaume. As he is memorialised, he is depicted as a dead body, rotting its fertile matter into the text of the *Rose* and providing the raw material for the continuation. Transformed into matter, his body is feminised, leaving centre stage clear for Jean de Meun as sole and virile *auctor*. Yet the play of necrotic generativity does not end here. Earlier in the *Roman*, Jean de Meun's goddess Reason had asserted that it is mere accident that the word for 'relics' is not 'testicles'.[66] The enshrinement of Guillaume in a tomb filled with incense and spices codes the dead author as a kind of textual relic and, equivalently, a textual *coille*. He is thus both feminine matter and masculine inseminating property, a hermaphroditic and doubled image of poetic inspiration that radically complicates the earlier and simpler image of 'natural' poetic inspiration drawn from a desirable (and lively) female body.[67]

We know, of course, that Chaucer was familiar with this passage from the *Roman*, and his later use of it in the *Canterbury Tales* clarifies the overlooked

---

refer by page number to *The Romance of the Rose*, trans. Charles Dahlberg, 3rd edn (Princeton, NJ: Princeton University Press, 1995).

[64] Bloch observes that 'the breaking of the poet's silence and the awakening of sexual desire are explicitly bound to the cloaking of Nature's body'. Howard R. Bloch, *The Scandal of the Fabliaux* (Chicago, IL: University of Chicago Press, 1986), p. 33.

[65] Cy se reposera Guillaume
Dont le tombel soit plain de bausme
D'encens, de mirre, d'aloez ...
(lines 11135–37).

[66] If I, when I gave names to things
had called testicles 'relics'
and named relics 'testicles',
you ... would reply to me, saying that 'relics'
was a base word, and ugly.
(p. 135)

se je, quant mis les nons aus choses
...
coilles reliques apelasse
et reliques coilles clamasse
tu ... me redeïsses de reliques
que ce fust lez moz et vilans.
(lines 7078–85).

[67] I am indebted to Marco Nievergelt, who discussed the imagery of doubling in the *Rose* in the context of this passage in a seminar given at the University of York, 12 February 2019.

Introduction

hermeneutic innovations of the *Legend*.[68] As Carolyn Dinshaw has argued, Chaucer's Pardoner displays the workings of an 'eunuch hermeneutics' rooted in this provocative exchangeability of *coilles* and *reliques*. Although he is cheerfully frank about the fact that the 'relikes' (*CT*, I, line 701 he carries are no more than 'pigges bones', (*CT* I, line 700) the Pardoner audaciously suggests, 'I have relikes and pardoun in my male ... Com forth, sire Hoost, and offre firste anon / And thou shalt kisse the relikes everychon' (*CT* VI, lines 920-44). The Host's response signals both his familiarity with the *Roman* and his penetration of the Pardoner's genital meaning, as he reverts to French to retort: 'I wolde I hadde thy coillons in myn hond / In stide of relikes' (*CT*, VI, lines 952-53). Yet in his anger he betrays his complicity in the very fiction he attacks, attributing to the Pardoner those very 'coillons' we have been given to understand he does not possess. The exchange between the two characters thus testifies to the persuasive power of the Pardoner's rhetoric, which, like a prosthesis, simultaneously advertises and augments his lack. For the Pardoner as for Jean de Meun's Reason, the image of the 'relique' that is also a 'coille' is part of a hermeneutics based on presumptively masculine genital lack. The Pardoner's 'eunuch hermeneutic' follows a Lacanian logic, whereby articulation proceeds from the perception of phallic lack. However, as we have seen, the phallic lack in relation to which the female body is organised is of a different order, and the female body has somatic, as well as a rhetorical, means of self-extension. The *Legend* considers a prosthetic economy centred upon female bodies and their prosthetic desires. The effect is of a shift in the way language is produced, the way meaning is produced, within the sexual logic of Chaucerian (indeed, of medieval) poetics.

This shift in the way language is produced lies behind Chaucer's adaptation of the two images of poetic inspiration borrowed from the *Legend*. First, Chaucer transforms Guillaume's trope of Nature as a female body. Launching into an ostensibly tedious and stereotyped take on the dream-vision tradition, he races through the clichés of the *locus amoenus* with its flowers and birds, the dream of the beautiful lady and the bumbling poet narrator who bemoans his own shortcomings. The setting is wearily familiar; the textually masturbatory pleasures of self-citation are as present here as anywhere else in Chaucer.[69] It is no surprise to find the poet inspired by springtime growth and beauty, gazing at

---

[68] The volume of scholarship on the Pardoner is vast. In addition to Dinshaw's 'Eunuch Hermeneutics', see Rollo, *Kiss My Relics*, pp. 226-28; Marijane Osborn, 'Transgressive Word and Image in Chaucer's Enshrined "Coillons" Passage', *Chaucer Review* 37 (2003): 365-84; Minnis, *Fallible Authors*; Glenn Burger, 'Kissing the Pardoner', *PMLA* 107 (1992): 1143-56; Vern L. Bullough with Gwen Whitehead Brewer, 'Medieval Masculinities and Modern Interpretations: The Problem of the Pardoner', in *Conflicted Identities and Multiple Masculinities: Men in the Medieval West*, ed. Jacqueline Murray (New York and London: Garland, 1999), pp. 93-110.

[69] The God of Love lists *Troilus and Criseyde* as a crime to stand alongside the 'heresye' of

> the smale, softe, swote gras,
> That was with floures swote enbrouded al.
> ...
> Forgeten hadde the erthe his pore estat
> Of wynter, that hym naked made and mat,
> And with his swerd of cold so sore greved;
> Now hath th' atempre sonne all that releved,
> That naked was, and clad him new agayn.[70]
> (F, lines 118–29)

There can be no doubt this is a version of Jerome's naked feminine text with its rhetorical *integument*: here is the imagery of violent sexual penetration, of a naked body 'sore greved' by a phallic 'swerd of cold'. In the G prologue, the passage is even preceded by an explicit reference to Englishing of a 'naked text' (G, line 86). Here too are the details drawn from Guillaume de Lorris, equating the naked body with the earth that is covered in 'enbrouded', stitch-like, floral garments. Yet, there is a twist. This body newly clad is not 'la terre'; it is not the female goddess Nature or the feminine-gendered earth, which we found in the *Roman* and will find again in the *Canterbury Tales*' General Prologue.[71] The *Legend*'s earth takes consistently masculine pronouns. Interrupting what has seemed boringly familiar imagery, this unexpected masculine nakedness carries all the shock value of indecent exposure. This substitution of a male body for a feminine nakedness affronts presumptions of gendered desire. Instead of erotic unveiling, it is a hermeneutic invitation to penetrate a naked masculine body.

The *Legend* makes a display of attempting to conceal the sodomitical implications of this image. Hastily, the narrator takes refuge in the relief of a pun that covers the naked body, 'relev[ing]' (re-leafing) it in clothing once again. This same verdant covering of leaves and flowers is itself personified. Identified with the daisy flower, beloved of the narrator, it takes form as a woman dressed in green and crowned with a diadem of white flowers. She is revealed to be 'quene Alceste / That turned was into a dayeseye' (F, lines 512–13). Alceste is the flower that sprinkles the meadows, the 'enbrouded' grasses that cover the body of the personified earth. In her prosthetic derivation from that earthy body, the Adamic body that 'God ... mad of erthe' (F, line 286 and G, line 189), Alceste is figure of Eve. In her position relative to the 'naked erthe', she is the rhetorical *integument*, the veil of language over

---

Chaucer's translation of the *Roman*; the narrator's muse counters a veritable catalogue of early Chauceriana, from the *House of Fame* to 'Origenes upon the Maudeleyne' (F, line 428).

[70] For discussion of this passage, see Delany, *The Naked Text*, pp. 71–74.
[71] Dinshaw has argued that the General Prologue, by contrast, operates according to an insistently binary logic, with the feminine earth/nature inseminated by the masculine rain that penetrates it. See *Getting Medieval*, pp. 117–20.

the truth of the text. Alceste is the figure through which Chaucer justifies a new hermeneutic project and creates something fresh from the discarded fragments of a sterile dream-vision tradition.

Through her, the *Legend* thus proposes a need for feminine rhetoric to cover undesirable masculine truths, for a feminine *integument* to veil that exposed and sodomitically inviting masculine body. This exciting possibility is tempered with typically Chaucerian equivocation, as Chaucer grafts onto this hermeneutic structure the imagery of poetic inspiration drawn from Jean de Meun's section of the *Roman*, looking to his more complex and disturbing image of poetic inspiration, the image of the textual relic. In the *Roman* it is the God of Love who describes Guillaume's body in its tomb. In the *Legend* he returns, to name Alceste, the narrator's muse who famously 'chees to dye' for her husband (F, line 513), as 'my relyke' (F, line 321). The identification confirms the rhetorically supplementary capacity of Alceste, already established through her position as the daisy that covers the 'naked erthe', coding her as a textual *coille*. The indication of the God of Love's possessive pronoun is that the body Alceste supplements is his; she is his 'relyke'. Yet it is the narrator who is portrayed as impotent in connection with her, 'thereto nothing able'. Angrily, the God of Love rebukes his attempt to come close to the daisy, insisting:

> 'Yt were better worthy, trewely,
> A worm to neghen ner my flour than thow ...
> For thow', quod he, 'art therto nothing able.
> Yt is my relyke, digne and delytable,
>   And thow my foo.'
> (F, lines 317–22)

The imagery of worms, with their age-old associations with death and the dead body, suggests a bodily corruptibility, a property definitively unshared by true relics. Like the Pardoner's paraphernalia of deception, Alceste is coded as a false relic almost before the epithet is attached to her. Not only this, but the same language aligns the narrator with the agents of putrefaction and destruction, with 'worm[s]' that eat into the flesh of the flower, coding his desire as an inappropriate and necrotic form of carnal lust.[72] Like heresy, the narrator's desire is misaligned, a hunger that fastens too literally on the flesh. The idea is ubiquitous in Wycliffite rhetoric concerning misdirected devotion towards relics, and that rhetoric is permeated with language

---

[72] Grace M. Jantzen has argued that such 'necrophilic' imagery underpins a masculinist theology, as contrasted with a feminist theology of flourishing. See Jantzen, *Becoming Divine: Towards a Feminist Philosophy of Religion* (Bloomington, IN: University of Indiana Press, 1999), passim.

relating deviant sexual desires to deviant religious desires.[73] The narrator's desire for the relic, for rhetorical supplementation, is evidence of his hermeneutic failure, his preference for the dead flesh over the vivifying spirit.

Unlike the Pardoner, Alceste does not and seemingly cannot author her own narrative, and her poetics is a poetics of surrogacy, translated onto a masculine body. In the *Legend* prologues, Chaucer's narrator describes how he, puppet-like, is made to speak and write by ventriloquising the voice of his muse and patron:

> My word, my werk ys knyt so in youre bond
> That, as an harpe obeieth to the hond
> And maketh it soune after his fyngerynge,
> Ryght so mowe ye oute of myn herte bringe
> Swich vois, ryght as yow lyst, to laughe or pleyne.
> (F lines 89–93)

The image of poetic creation is also an image of bodily violation. Controlling fingers force a 'vois' out of the heart itself, invading the chest cavity to pull at the strings of the 'hert in-with my sorwfull brest' (F, line 86) as if plucking the strings of a harp. This resulting expression, the 'word' and 'werk', is 'knyt so in [the] bond' of the inspiring muse that it is not only obedient to her command, but also cleaves to that bond as to flesh, just as the penetrated body might cleave to a material object binding it. Insofar as the probing fingers of the narrator's beloved recall Freeman's 'lesbian erotohistoriography', with its imagery of female fingers penetrating feminine bodily spaces, this passage is suggestive of a Chaucerian narratorial discomfort with taking in the position of feminised, penetrated lover.[74] Chaucer never escapes this squeamishness about the prosthetic desires he describes; he finds no way to allow his female characters to express desire without their prostheses making them monstrous, aggressive and inadequate, supplemented and yet surgically reduced.

This sense of the failure of a feminine-bodied hermeneutic project circumscribes the *Legend*'s very structure. The image of the relic extends out into the body of the poem, standing not for the supplementary *coille* but for that which is broken, fragmented and incomplete in female bodies. The *Legend* is a hagiographic form, a 'Seintes Legende', as the Man of Law would have it (*CT* II, line 61), and in the body of the text are nine stories of women repeatedly mutilated and fragmented through the effects of desire. These stories are notoriously truncated with Chaucerian *occupatio*, rendering them incomplete textual as well as physical *corpora*. The female protagonists are secular saints and their bodies potential relics, but like the 'pigges bones' (*CT* I line 700) the *Canterbury Tales*' Pardoner will produce from his purse, they are false

---

[73] See Dinshaw, *Getting Medieval*, pp. 88–90.
[74] Freeman, *Time Binds*, pp. 103–10.

Introduction

saints, their stories all taken ultimately from pre-Christian sources. It remains profoundly uncertain whether or not these feminine fragments have the capacity to engage in the rhetorical supplementation and the provocation of desire for fiction that we see in the Pardoner.[75] Thus the *Legend* equivocates. It makes the case for a poetics that relies on the imagining of female desires. It makes the case for turning the old paradigms of hermeneutics and *auctoritas* on their heads, for visualising transgressively authoritative female desires that seek to script their own aversions and refusals as well as their own intimacies and erotic relations. Yet it also casts doubt upon the results of such an experiment. Like a reliquary filled with false relics, the contents of the *Legend* are so many absences and *lacunae*, endlessly seeking something beyond themselves to give them definition. The prosthetic economy of desire operates across the *Legend*, and extends from it into late medieval English romance.

SURROGACIES OF DESIRE IN ROMANCE

From its twelfth-century origins as a genre, romance has concerned itself with the question of how much can be known about a woman's embodied desires. Chaucer's own 'Wife of Bath's Tale' provides a nastily polished take on the topic, framing a violent rape as the epistemic necessity that precipitates a knightly quest to discover 'what thyng is it that wommen moost desiren' (*CT* III, line 905). The narrative rests on the premise that female desire is opaque, even resistant to discovery. The triumphant conclusion, 'wommen desiren to have sovereynetee' (*CT* III, line 1038), is circumscribed by the frame narrative, in which the Wife of Bath offers her own *sententia* on gendered interpretation: 'Who peyntede the leon, tel me who?' (*CT* III, line 692). Together, these quotations exert a centrifugal paradox upon the text, pulling apart the central principle of the narrative. Women desire to have control, yet the narrative – written by a man – can only give a man's perspective. Yet, despite this, Middle English romance is rarely treated as a genre implicated in wider hermeneutic debates in which Chaucer participates, especially those I have discussed in this introduction. Indeed, the history of medieval and post-medieval objections to romance as a genre read very much like the history of medieval and

---

[75] Several surviving manuscripts give physical form to this similarity, treating the individual legends as entries in a *Legenda*. See Laura J. Getty, '"Other Smale Ymaad Before": Chaucer as Historiographer in the "Legend of Good Women"', *Chaucer Review* 42.1 (2007): 48–75 (p. 58). Steven F. Kruger refers to Cleopatra's grave as a 'shrine-pit'; V. A. Kolve's study of the iconography of the *Legend* includes a detailed comparison of Cleopatra's entombment, naked in a pit full of snakes, to the emerging imagery of the *memento mori* tradition. See Kruger, 'Passion and Order in Chaucer's *Legend of Good Women*', *Chaucer Review* 23.3 (1989): 219–235 (p. 235, n. 14); Kolve, 'From Cleopatra to Alceste: An Iconographic Study of *The Legend of Good Women*', in *Signs and Symbols in Chaucer's Poetry*, eds John P. Hermann and John J. Burke (Tuscaloosa, AL: University of Alabama Press, 1981), pp. 130–78 (pp. 145–51).

post-medieval objections to the disorderly, desirous and desirable female body. Romances seduce and distract; they entertain and tempt; they lead good men and women away from godly pursuits. The thirteenth-century cleric William of Nassington condemns the 'vanitee' of these 'fantoums' or fictions; three centuries later the humanist distaste of Roger Ascham is focused on their 'baudrye'.[76] Even fictions comment on fictions, as Dante's Francesca cites the romance of Lancelot and Guinevere as the 'galeotto' or go-between that seduced herself and her lover Paolo into the adulterous kiss that was to be their downfall.

The genre often positions itself in opposition to the tropes of literary *paternitas*, and especially to those that begin to coalesce around the figure of Chaucer, *auctor*, in the fifteenth century.[77] Already generically poised to seek alternatives to the idea that seminal paternal authority is required for correct textual production, the fifteenth-century romances I discuss have vested interests in exploring the generative possibilities of women. Despite the example of the 'Wife of Bath's Tale' cited above, Chaucer and Middle English romance are often seen to pull in opposite directions. Studies relating the genre of romance to his work tend to focus on earlier romances, *fabliaux* or *chanson* that provided models for individual tales in the *Canterbury Tales*, or to discuss Chaucer himself as a 'romance' writer.[78] Chaucer is often claimed as post-medieval before the fact, a poet whose work looks forward to, and generates, the poetry of later ages. His prestige is intimately related to his place in post-Chaucerian and post-medieval literary genealogies, as 'father Chaucer', and 'the father of English literature'. The recent 'romance turn' of early twenty-first-century medieval scholarship responds to a widespread perception of romance as anchored in the past, as old-fashioned and clunky as Chaucer's parody of it in *The Tale of Sir Thopas*. Thus, Putter and Gilbert argue that twentieth-century scholarship of popular romance reflects a kind of 'embarrassment' at the genre and at its supposed vested interests in maintaining the retrogressive power structures of the 'medieval' period. McDonald and Little comment that romance is *the* quintessential popular marker of 'the Middle

---

[76] William of Nassyngton, 'Speculum Vitae', lines 36 and 48; quoted and discussed by Melissa Furrow, *Expectations of Romance: The Reception of a Genre in Medieval England* (Cambridge: D. S. Brewer, 2009), pp. 1–42; For Ascham, see James Simpson, 'Derek Brewer's Romance', in *Traditions and Innovations in the Study of Medieval English Literature: The Influence of Derek Brewer*, eds Charlotte Brewer and Barry Windeatt (Cambridge: D. S. Brewer, 2013), pp. 154–172 (p. 160).

[77] See Samantha Katz Seal, *Father Chaucer: Generating Authority in* The Canterbury Tales (Oxford: Oxford University Press, 2019); Roberta Magnani, 'Constructing the Father: Fifteenth Century Manuscripts of Chaucer's Works', unpublished PhD thesis, Cardiff University, 2010, pp. 1–52.

[78] Carol F. Heffernan, *The Orient in Chaucer and Romance* (Cambridge: D. S. Brewer, 2003); Corinne Saunders, 'Affective Reading: Chaucer, Women and Romance', *Chaucer Review* 51.1 (2016): 11–30.

Introduction

Ages itself, a Middle Ages that is by turns magical, barbarous, childish, absurd, but above all archaic, a thing of the past'.[79] Rooted in an idealised and fictionalised past, romance's stock material of battles and bloodshed, rapacious knights and lovers' adventures resonates with popular reconstructions of medieval worlds from *Monty Python* to *Game of Thrones*. The genre's origins in twelfth-century French make it easy to read English romances of the fourteenth and fifteenth centuries as doubly dated, and romance studies has been slow to break away from the studies of sources and analogues that weld these more recent romances to their antecedents. As a literary tradition, they seem nostalgic for an earlier Europe and thus, paradoxically, firmly insular, cut off from the contemporary world beyond England.

The new and ongoing intertextual conversations and discourses that are common to studies of much late medieval English writing, notably that of Chaucer, rarely feature in studies of romances. Geographies and locations speak loudly. Where Chaucer is 'cosmopolitan' or 'London-based', romance still reads as 'provincial' or 'rural' and thus belonging to the 'before' (ignoring the considerable overlap between Chaucer and romance in fifteenth-century manuscripts).[80] Where Chaucer is 'courtly', romance is imbricated in the world of the 'gentry' (again, ignoring the considerable gap between the audiences Chaucer interpellates in texts such as the *Legend*, and the actual milieux in which manuscripts of that text circulated). These polarising characterisations of Chaucer and Middle English romance go some way to explaining why, even in very recent years, romance seems a stranger to the wider European conversations otherwise so readily drawn into the ambit of late medieval English literature. We might expect, for example, to find *some* scholarship relating Middle English romance to the *Roman de la Rose*, as one of the most influential and prolifically copied vernacular works circulating in the later medieval period, but we look in vain for references to that text in recent introductions to romance, including those that make the case for a reassessment of romance's reach and influence.[81]

---

[79] Katherine C. Little and Nicola McDonald, 'Introduction', in *Thinking Medieval Romance*, eds Katharine C. Little and Nicola McDonald (Oxford: Oxford University Press, 2018), pp. 1–14 (p. 1).

[80] Halberstam cites the rural as a space that is 'before' the urban spaces contingent to it in his analysis of queer asynchronicity. See Jack Halberstam, *In A Queer Time and Place: Transgender Bodies, Subcultural Lives* (New York: New York University Press, 2005), and M. W. Bychowski, Howard Chiang, Jack Halberstam, Jacob Lau, Kathleen P. Long, Marcia Ochoa and C. Riley Snorton, '"Trans Historicities": A Roundtable Discussion', *Transgender Studies Quarterly* 5.4 (2018): 658–85 (p. 662). For discussion of manuscript overlaps, see Chapter 3, pp. 107–8 and Chapter 5, pp. 156–8.

[81] Several edited collections have been published in the past couple of decades, purporting to introduce Middle English romance as a genre, or to assess the state of romance scholarship. In McDonald's *Pulp Fictions* the *Roman* is mentioned once, and then only as a point of contrast between Chaucer's use of imagery (drawn from the *Roman*) and

This presents us with an enormous puzzle. Romance is, after all, the genre that was to underpin so much of sixteenth- and seventeenth-century literature, that was to represent, in fact, the future of English fiction. The romances I discuss in this book reflect the topicality and serious appeal of the genre, spreading across the period from *c*. 1400 to *c*. 1500. My first chapter on romance focuses on the graphic, tragic Arthurian poem known as the alliterative *Morte Arthure* (written *c*. 1400), and its afterlife in Malory's *Morte Darthur*. Through Malory, this poem travels into early print, and was to become part of the best-known English version of the Arthurian narrative in post-medieval England. My second romance chapter considers the early fifteenth-century *Sowdone of Babylon*, one of a large family of narratives concerned with Saracen–Christian conflict and conversion, and with the imbrication of desire for religious relics with lust for a female body. It belongs to a huge, spreading set of stories about race and desire, which may be traced into the popular fictions of the twentieth- and twenty-first-century mass market. The theorisations of femininity and fluidity with which it engages endure, submerged, in some of the most cutting-edge philosophies of gender and the body circulating today. Thirdly, I look at the romance known variously as *The Squire of Low Degree* or *Undo Your Door*, probably composed *c*. 1500, and its provocative and parodic narrative of a princess who displays decidedly deviant sexual desires. It spread like wildfire through early modern poetry and drama, was used by Shakespeare as a ubiquitous signifier of ambitious and crude striving for social status, and was woven into Spenser's *Faerie Queene*. Mobile, these romances move beyond their medieval origins to take positions in later culture and literature. Yet none has ever achieved the 'canonicity' of a romance such as *Sir Gawain and the Green Knight*. The volume of scholarship dedicated to each is small compared to the attention Chaucer's work garners, and often that work is dedicated to placing these texts in the context of their earlier sources, dragging them backwards in time, as I have argued is typical of much romance scholarship. An aim of this book is to relocate these romances within the mainstream of later medieval hermeneutic and rhetorical discourse, to reveal their dialogic engagements with Chaucer and, through him, with continental and cosmopolitan literary traditions.

This book sets out to rethink romance as a mode of writing about female desire and female bodily agency that is innovative and contemporary, rather

---

that found in *Sir Degrevant*. See Arlyn Diamond, '*Sir Degrevant*: What Lovers Want', in *Pulp Fictions of Medieval England*, ed. Nicola McDonald (Manchester: Manchester University Press, 2004), pp. 82–101 (p. 95). In Putter and Gilbert's *Spirit of Medieval Popular Romance* it merits a single mention in a footnote. See Jane Gilbert, 'Gender, Oaths and Ambiguity in *Sir Tristrem* and Béroul's *Roman de Tristan*', in *The Spirit of Medieval Popular Romance: A Historical Introduction*, eds Ad Putter and Jane Gilbert (Harlow: Pearson Education, 2000), pp. 237–57 (p. 255). It is entirely absent from McDonald and Little's recent *Thinking Medieval Romance*.

than isolated and retrograde. I look beyond the plots – often studied almost in isolation from the poetics of romances – to the unspoken spaces of innuendo and subtext, where we find hints of deviant desires seldom expressed openly. To read like this presumes for romance an audience it has often been denied: an audience of subtle readers, willing to unpick intertextual resonances and to recognise tropes from a wide range of other types of writing, from hagiography to medicine to dream visions to religious invective. Some of this writing is in English, but much is in French, or even Latin. Yet, despite the 'manuscript turn' of the last couple of decades of medieval studies, it still often forgotten that many romances circulate in precisely such a company of textual material.[82] In Household Books (or miscellanies, or whatever we choose to call them), romances circulate alongside Latin treatises of spiritual medicine or English remedies and prayers, alongside saints' lives and devotional poems and the wealth of late medieval material concerned with the practice of orthodox and heterodox religion. Some manuscripts are truly plurilingual, code-switching back and forth between English, Latin and French; others, less linguistically rich, replicate in English materials drawn from continental debates such as the *Querelle des Femmes*, or draw into the ambit of their romances the works of Chaucer, Gower, Lydgate and Hoccleve. This seems to me evidence enough that it is worthwhile imaging readers who might subject romances to deep, thoughtful attention, who might catch an allusion to the myth of Philomela, a reference to the *Roman de la Rose* or a resonant similarity to the *Twelve Conclusions of the Lollards*.

Why might such readers seek out romance? I argue that the hermeneutic importance and the desirability of romance are fundamentally the same. Both as a seductive fiction and as a perpetual source of new iterations of narrative and new theorisations of gender and sexuality, romance conveys an endlessly generative interest in extending beyond what has been done before, in proliferating and supplementing older narratives, in transgressing new boundaries. These qualities of romance are, of course, what gives the genre its racy sensationalism, and what allows it at times to be crude, violent or gruesome, yet they are also qualities germane to the prosthetic feminine hermeneutic Chaucer proposes and then so jealously circumscribes. This attraction to novelty is a strong feature of recent studies of romance. Nicola McDonald, for example, claims that romance's fascination with the marvellous, with strange objects and inventions, spreads its influence forward to the most futuristic of contemporary genres, 'science fiction and fantasy', while Patricia Ingham places the genre

---

[82] We could date the 'manuscript turn' to the publication of Ralph Hanna's *Pursuing History: Middle English Manuscripts and their Texts* (Stanford, CA: Stanford University Press, 1996). See also *Book Production and Publishing in Britain, 1375–1475*, eds Jeremy Griffiths and Derek Pearsall (Cambridge: Cambridge University Press, 2007); *The Production of Books in England 1350–1500*, eds Daniel Wakelin and Alexandra Gillespie (Cambridge: Cambridge University Press, 2011).

at the centre of her wide-ranging study of the ways in which medieval literatures and cultures related to 'now-ness', novelty, technological and intellectual innovation.[83] Yet I argue that romances do not seek novelty purely for its own sake, but because it is a form of prosthetic extension of that which is established. That is to say, romances embrace new technologies rather than new objects. Romances engage with technologies of surrogate representation, technologies of surrogate desire that enable the female body to extend its emotional experience outside expected bodily constraints, to construct new somatic possibilities for expressing emotion or aversion.[84] In this, romances are perfectly positioned to take up from Chaucerian and continental traditions of poetry the question of how female desires may be made visible. The romances I discuss share a fascination with the processes of reworking and reusing old material, which gives them a patchwork, piecemeal and yet 'lesbian-like' erotic quality. Making pointed (and pointedly disintegrative) reference to Chaucer's works, to the emerging myth of Chaucerian literary *paternitas* and to the cherished paradigms of Classical literature on which Chaucer draws, these texts position themselves as subversive respondents to the canon. They revisit the problem of representation with which Chaucer grapples in the *Legend*: the question of how representing women's unspoken, hidden or marginalised desires might stimulate or reconfigure poetic practice.

NAVIGATING DESIRE

The structure of this book falls into three sections, each opening with a chapter on a legend or legends from Chaucer and a paired romance. I begin with Chaucer's 'Legend of Philomela', the thematic centre of the *Legend*. Chaucer's text radically reshapes the ancient tale of rape and mutilation that leaves Philomela tongueless and forces her to communicate her plight through an alternative *textus* woven on her loom. Instead of concentrating on the revenge (which he omits), Chaucer explores the significance of the loom as a prosthetic device. In rendering Philomela both a rape survivor and a lesbian-like figure, simultaneously, Chaucer overlays a queasy sense of active desire on the depiction of a woman whose volition is overwhelmed (a device he explores again in the 'Legend of Lucrece'). Through her, he poses the question whether a

---

[83] Nicola McDonald, 'The Wonder of Middle English Romance', in *Thinking Medieval Romance*, eds McDonald and Little, pp. 13–36 (p. 14). Chapters Three and Four of Patricia Ingham's book concentrate on romance: see Patricia Clare Ingham, *The Medieval New: Ambivalence in the Age of Innovation* (Philadelphia, PA: University of Pennsylvania Press, 2015), pp. 75–140.

[84] I am indebted to Cohen's work on 'identity machines', which in turn draws on Deleuze and Guattari's work on the 'desiring machine' of the body. See Cohen, *Medieval Identity Machines*, pp. xi–xxx; and Deleuze and Guattari, *Anti-Oedipus: Capitalism and Schizophrenia*, trans. Robert Hurley, Mark Seem and Helen R. Lane (London and New York: Continuum, 2004), pp. 1–8, 38–44.

Introduction

woman can articulate her experience of sexual violence and aversion in any way except by taking on tools and strategies that construct her as sexually deviant, thus attributing to her a sexual desire at the very moment at which her volition is violently overruled.

The same problem – the articulation of a woman's experience of rape – surfaces within the alliterative *Morte*. The text features a female martyr, whose remains are memorialised in a church built on the site of her death. Grotesquely violated in death, she is a Philomela figure, her silenced pain and grief ventriloquised and, I will argue, used to structure the remainder of the text. In this narrative, rape occupies a relatively small textual space, occurring within the early stages of the long poem, and swiftly forgotten by many scholars of the text. However, it lingers in the subtext in a manner that both disrupts and, paradoxically, lends a coherence to the remainder of the narrative. The text is punctuated by disconcerting elements of masculine gender nonconformity, from intimate and intense homosocial grieving that tips over into 'womanly' behaviour, to bizarre and crude acts of violence described by means of puns suggestive of anal penetration. The rape – submerged early on within the text – is replayed over and over on the bodies of male characters, producing the appearance of male same-sex activity, in a classic trauma-induced omission. As the text insistently returns to details omitted from the account of the rape, it reinserts the omitted detail into the text, like a flashback interrupting a trauma victim's experience. Consequently, the text takes us inside the structure of the traumatised mind, replaying the rape over and over, insisting upon its continued visibility. As with the 'Legend of Philomela', rape produces the semblance of same-sex activity, but where in the Philomela narrative the ambiguities are concentrated on the rape survivor's own, ambiguously interpreted body, here they are explored through the bodies of men, raising the question of whether women's experiences of sexual violence may be emotionally realised without translation into a masculine gendered context.

My third chapter focuses on Chaucer's legends of Dido, Hipsiphyle and Medea. These women's deviant desires are closely related to the construction of their bodies as aberrant, flawed by sterility, self-harm or quasi-emasculatory violence. In recounting Dido's story, Chaucer draws on an already well-established subtext of hints as to Dido's virago-like desire for an emasculated or womanish man, and this narrative prepares for a more radical reinterpretation. The story of Hipsiphyle and Medea is the *Legend*'s only paired narrative, a tale of two women successively abandoned by Jason during his pursuit of the golden fleece. Hipsiphyle, Jason's first lover, exhibits a desire for male femininity, while her successor Medea's desire is rooted in a desire for sameness and for the homosocial intimacies modelled by Jason and his companion Hercules. Medea's desire is written in a manner that capitalises on the absences and disparate fragments of the earlier narrative of Jason, Hercules and Hipsiphyle, in a way that resembles the 'lesbian-like' desire for silences, gaps and *lacunae*, as theorised by Kłosowska. Her emotions thus slip between categories of same-sex desire, resembling both male homoerotic relations and lesbian-like attraction. Chaucer establishes a poetic structure that resembles the bodies of the women it contains: excessive, yet lacking; desirous of male femininity yet unable to take on a fully masculine, phallic *auctoritas*. In its endless, cyclic repetition, his story of Jason suggests that, when female desire is placed at the centre of the *relicta* narrative, the narrative itself becomes sterile, its point or *telos* lost in a manner akin to castration.

In my fourth chapter, I explore the early fifteenth-century *Sowdone of Babylon*. A unique translation, it is a version of the highly popular French *chanson de Fierabras*, set during the wars between Charlemagne and the Saracen Sultan of Babylon. The narrative concerns the recovery of the relics of Christ's crucifixion, stolen by Fierabras from Rome and guarded by his beautiful sister Floripas, who falls in love with a French knight and (like her brother), ultimately converts, returning the relics to the French court. Drawing on work by Robyn Malo and Seeta Chaganti on relic discourse, and by Dinshaw and Lochrie on the imbrications of the heretical and the queer, this chapter explores the ways in which the pleasures of the forbidden overlap in the discourses of heterodox religion and of 'deviant' desires.[85] In seeking to construct herself as somatically impenetrable, Floripas rejects the imagery of female excess and fluidity that surround her in the sources and analogues of her text. The narrative exhibits an unease about both relics and idols, which I locate in the context of fifteenth-century religious writings that treat both relics and women's sexuality (especially women's same-sex desire) as objects of suspicion.

In my fifth chapter, I argue that the legends of Thisbe and Ariadne reconstruct, in parodic form, Jerome's image of the veiled captive woman who is analogous to the desirable naked body or 'matter' of a text. Yet as each narrative enacts a self-consuming process, they also expose the cynical limitations Chaucer places upon such parodic modes of interrogation. Utilising familiar tropes and images of female same-sex desire, the two narratives simultaneously defer authority from female protagonists to male narrators. Ultimately, although they find (limited) space for female sexual desire to display authority and autonomy, both narratives – and that of Ariadne, the later, more than that of Thisbe, the earlier – circumscribe this authority within male-dominated structures of representation.

In my final chapter, I focus on the late fifteenth-century romance *Undo Your Door* (or *The Squire of Low Degree*). *Undo Your Door* is a parodic reworking of Chaucerian tropes and of earlier Middle English romances, a

---

[85] Robyn Malo, *Relics and Writing in Late Medieval England* (Toronto: University of Toronto Press, 2013); Seeta Chaganti, *The Medieval Poetics of the Reliquary: Enshrinement, Inscription, Performance* (New York: Palgrave Macmillan, 2008); Dinshaw, *Getting Medieval*, p. 6; Lochrie, *Heterosyncrasies*, pp. 47–70.

Introduction

tale whose heroine manoeuvres behind the walls of her chamber to secure her beloved, even in the face of dastardly challenges from a malcontent steward. The romance borrows from a wide range of visual and verbal discourses to evoke the various mechanisms used to manipulate boundaries between inside and outside, from the hinge of a window to the panels of a triptych to the pages of a manuscript, exploring the ways in which these mechanisms construct the viewer, reader or doer as mistress of her own sexuality. In a text consumed by inaction, the moving parts of inanimate mechanisms constitute a substitute focus for human activity, underlying a wider eroticised aesthetic of fragmentation and reassembly, which resonates with much contemporary work on lesbian erotics of the narrative and the text.

A crucial claim I make in these chapters is that Chaucer and the writers of romance inherit a hermeneutic that has no space, no place, for female sexuality that is autonomous and orientated away from masculinity. That sexuality is felt as an act of displacement, rather than a presence in itself. Insinuations of deviancy append themselves to the women of the *Legend* like foreign objects stuck into a body; innuendos of sodomy and necrophilia and images of bodily fragmentation, stone-like inanimacy and death disrupt the romances. The difficulty of expression that attends this female desire is felt in the *lacunae* and ambiguities that permeate the *Legend*, and the disjunctive and disorientating transfers of emotion and experience from body to body that animate the romances. Again and again, these texts puzzle and disturb scholars, who draw attention to their inarticulate, incoherent, inappropriate content, their awkward puns and odd innuendos and strange, unexpected double meanings. Readily, these elements are interpreted as signs of poetic failure or (in the case of romance) generic insufficiency. Yet I argue that these gaps and tensions, these moments of terseness and these insistent, displaced subtexts might not be aesthetic failures or moments of inattention, but strategies for representing the female emotion and desire occluded by that tradition. This book therefore places one of Chaucer's most under-valued poems, the *Legend of Good Women*, at the heart of a medieval hermeneutic debate about the representation of female desire, and at the start of a process of interrogation of that debate, which was to spread from Chaucer to the English romances of the late fourteenth and fifteenth centuries. I argue that Chaucer treats the sufferings of women at the hands of men as a linguistic problem, a series of experiences that threaten the fabric of his text, resulting in a notoriously truncated, abbreviated and awkward poem. Disruptions to relations between men and women cause damage to the figurative levels of language, and the individual legends explore how different figures of speech buckle under the strain of communicating the emotional states of Chaucer's women. This destabilisation of language enables interrogation of the grammatical moralising tradition of Jerome, Alan of Lille and Jean de Meun. A structure full of holes, from hypometric lines to unfinished stories, the *Legend* constantly invites readers to take up unfinished threads or probe empty spaces, to collect the 'debris' of sources to which Chaucer repeatedly gestures. This mode of response recreates the experiences scholars persistently associate with female same-sex desire, gesturing towards a lesbian hermeneutic. Yet while Chaucer seeks always to contain the potential of his developing hermeneutic with authorial circumscription, the romances interrogate *auctoritas* – sometimes, explicitly, this Chaucerian *auctoritas* – and locate it as part of the matter interrogated, reworked and reconfigured, through the transformative force of female desire. As the romances develop the hermeneutic project I see originating in the *Legend*, they construct representations of female desire that rapidly become not only palpable, but enticing, tantalising, and audacious.

1

THE SILENCING OF FEMALE DESIRE IN THE 'LEGEND OF PHILOMELA'

This chapter confronts the fundamental problem of representing female desire, according to the hermeneutic theories I discuss in the introduction to this book. How can we speak of that which has no definition without reference to an originating masculine desire, unless we speak of it in relation *to* that masculine desire? At its most brutal, the paradigm we are looking at is Jerome's analogy of rape to textual interpretation, which proposes female desire as an irrelevance to the masculine making of meaning. It is this act of rape, and the silencing that results from it, that lie at the centre of Chaucer's 'Legend of Philomela', a text that seeks to explore how female desire might be given space to speak within a context in which it is almost automatically silenced. Raped and mutilated, Philomela weaves her story in tapestry, after her rapist cuts out her tongue.[1] Taking up her narrative from a host of Classical and medieval sources, Chaucer enacts a parallel mutilation. Slashing through the familiar plot, he replicates the damage done to Philomela's body by cutting out the traditional conclusion to her story,

---

[1] Chaucer's primary Latin source for the legend is the version of the tale found in Ovid's *Metamorphoses*; he also clearly draws quite extensively on the Old French tale found in the early fourteenth-century *Ovide Moralisé*, an enormous compilation of retold works of Ovid, which incorporates a version of the *lai de Philomela* attributed to Chretien de Troyes. Latin quotations are from Ovid, *Metamorphoses, Books I–VIII*, trans. Frank Justus Miller (London: William Heineman, 1916); hereafter *Mets*. Subsequent references will be given in parentheses in the text by book and line number, with translations from the same volume. Old French quotations are from Cornelius de Boer, ed., *Ovide Moralisé: Poème du commencement du quatorzième siècle*, 4 vols (Amsterdam: Johannes Müller, 1915–38). Chaucer's use of the *Metamorphoses* and the *Ovide Moralisé* have been much discussed. The question of whether Chaucer tended to work primarily from Ovid in the original or from paraphrases such as the *Moralisé* has been debated in the context of his corpus as a whole. See A. J. Minnis, 'A Note on Chaucer and the *Ovide Moralisé*', *Medium Ævum* 48 (1979): 254–57 or, for an opposing view, John M. Fyler, *Chaucer and Ovid* (New Haven, CT and London: Yale University Press, 1979), p. 17. However, Chaucer's use of the *Moralisé* for this particular legend has long been acknowledged. See J. L. Lowes, 'Chaucer and the *Ovide Moralisé*', *PMLA* 33 (1918): 302–25.

leaving only an inarticulate 'remenaunt' (line 2383) to which he refuses to give voice. This much-remarked disruption is one of many disjunctive moments within the expected sequence of the narrative, and it serves to conflate two mutilated bodies: the textual corpus of the Philomela myth, and the tongueless, violated woman.[2] As such, the 'Legend of Philomela' pointedly recalls Jerome's hermeneutic, and invites readers to reflect upon that traditional conflation of female body with feminised text, to try to understand what is missing, or inarticulate, within the traditional hermeneutic paradigm with which we are presented. Yet as the 'Legend' interrogates Jerome's paradigm, it illustrates the remarkable power of that hermeneutic denial of female desire, repeatedly representing attempts to articulate female desire as splintering off into images of deviancy and sexual dissidence. For Philomela, there is no way to articulate a female emotional experience, except by taking on the tools and linguistic strategies gendered masculine, a process that causes her to resemble other women whose appropriation of masculine tools indicates their sexual deviancy.[3] As women seek to voice their emotions, they are forced to take on the *habitus*, the stance, the rhetorical or somatic devices associated with female deviant desires. Yet, while this might seem to represent the final cruelty of Chaucer's hermeneutic exploration – the demonstration that when women speak of emotion, they code themselves as deviant – it also carries hope for a new rhetoric of female desire. The disruption of the traditional structures of meaning (poetic and narrative, spatial and temporal) makes space for the voicing of female emotions and results in a text centred around *lacunae* and incompleteness, around the recombination of materials and the reassembly of fragments. These *lacunae* reveal a new axis of meaning, a feminine hermeneutic orientated away from the masculine paradigm. In her theory of a lesbian erotohistoriography, Freeman posits a distinctively lesbian ethos of touch, emotion and recuperation, realised in texts and textiles made up of *lacunae* and reworked material, of textile construction and of female hands moving through material spaces that represent the female body.[4] I argue that the 'Legend of Philomela' evokes this same ethos, raising the possibility that a feminine hermeneutic might find, if not a voice, then a recuperative *habitus* allowing the violated body to process the narrative of its violation.

---

[2] For a range of perspectives on the ending of Chaucer's *Legend*, see Delany, *The Naked Text*, pp. 220–21; Hagedorn, *Abandoned Women*, p. 161; Collette, *Rethinking Chaucer's Legend*, p. 111.

[3] See my discussion of the 'lesbian' goddess Nature, and of sexual prostheses, in the introduction.

[4] See Freeman, *Time Binds*, pp. 95–135.

The Silencing of Female Desire

DISORIENTED BODIES AND DISPLACED TEXT

The excision of the ending of Philomela's story in the *Legend* is often read as proof of the poem's crude aesthetic and cynical outlook.[5] In the traditional narrative, which circulated widely in medieval Europe in both Latin and vernacular versions, the recently married Athenian princess Procne begs her Thracian husband Tereus to bring her young sister to visit her.[6] On meeting Philomela in Athens, Tereus is overtaken by a burning lust. Instead of transporting the young woman to his court in Thrace, he takes her to a remote wilderness where he rapes her, then cuts out her tongue to prevent her reporting the crime. In her lonely prison, Philomela takes to her loom, weaving a tapestry that carries the story of her rape. This tapestry reaches Procne, and reveals the violence Philomela has suffered. Reunited, the two sisters carry out a horrific revenge, murdering Procne's son Itys and feeding the child's stewed flesh to his unsuspecting father. When Tereus finds out he rushes to murder the women and the gods intervene, transforming all three figures into birds. The truncation of this narrative in the 'Legend of Philomela' is carried out just before the sisters plot their revenge; as a result, it omits the gory scenes of infanticide and cannibalism, and the avian metamorphosis. Critics of the *Legend* have claimed that the omission of this material deprives Philomela of agency, as if to imply that the vindication of a 'goode' woman (the text's purported project) is compatible only with the demonstration of her suffering.[7] However, the 'Legend of Philomela'

---

[5] For discussion of the *Legend*'s reputation as a poetic failure or insincere project see, for example, Frank, *Chaucer and* The Legend, p. 138, and Delany, *The Naked Text*, p. 213; Betsy McCormick, Leah Schwebel and Lynne Shutters, in their introduction to the 2017 special issue of *the Chaucer Review* dedicated to the *Legend of Good Women*. See 'Introduction: Looking Forward, Looking Back on the *Legend of Good Women*', *Chaucer Review* 52 (2017): 3–11. For a range of perspectives on the ending of the text, see Collette, *Rethinking Chaucer's* Legend, p. 111; Delany, *The Naked Text*, pp. 220–21; Hagedorn, *Abandoned Women*, p. 161 and Holton, *The Sources of Chaucer's Poetics*, p. 50. For Jerome, see Letter 70, in *Jerome*, trans. Fremantle, p. 149, and Dinshaw, *Chaucer's Sexual Poetics*, pp. 22–23; Mann, *Feminizing Chaucer*, p. 1.

[6] For discussions of medieval versions of the Philomela narrative, see two essays in in *Representing Rape*, ed. Robertson and Rose: E. Jane Burns, 'Raping Men: What's Motherhood Got to Do With It?', pp. 127–60, and Nancy A. Jones, 'The Daughter's Text and the Thread of Lineage in the Old French Philomena', pp. 161–88. For discussion of rape in the *Legend*, including that of Philomela, see Corinne J. Saunders, 'Classical Paradigms of Rape in the Middle Ages: Lucretia and Philomela', in *Rape in Antiquity*, ed. Susan Deacy and Karen F. Pierce (London: Classical Press of Wales, 1997), pp. 243–66; Richard Ireland, 'Lucrece, Philomela (and Cecily): Chaucer and the Law of Rape', in *Crime and Punishment in the Middle Ages*, ed. T. S. Haskett (Victoria, BC: University of Victoria, 1998), pp. 37–61; Corinne J. Saunders, *Rape and Ravishment in the Literature of Medieval England* (Cambridge: D. S. Brewer, 2001), pp. 265–311; Miranda Griffin, *Transforming Tales: Rewriting Metamorphosis in Medieval French Literature* (Oxford: Oxford University Press, 2015), pp. 55–60.

[7] Dinshaw, *Chaucer's Sexual Poetics*, p. 75.

offers far more than a cynical equation of feminine virtue with passivity and pain. The poem calls attention to its own disruptions and its own discontinuous materiality, telescoping time, space and narrative structure, dwelling upon its own *lacunae*, and marking its broken ending with conspicuous *occupatio*. The text is permeated with images of structural deformation, beginning with the deformation of the source material of Philomela's story. Yet, through this disorder and disorientation, it offers the debris from which a feminine hermeneutic may be (re)constructed, to allow for the voicing of female emotions and desires.

In its opening lines, the 'Legend of Philomela' purports to be concerned with divinely mandated form and structure. Apostrophising God as 'giver of the formes', the narrator castigates Tereus for his crimes, which cause distortions to that divine structure, and which he labels 'foule' (line 2240). As a pun, hinting at the bird transformation readers might expect to come at the end of the story, the word 'foule' would seem to confirm the divine ordering of language itself: a deep structure of the universe, through which truths to come are revealed in words. Yet, this illusion rapidly crumbles. Chiming with this pun, avian transformations and bird-voices spill forwards into the 'Legend of Philomela', and their function is not only to generate (false) expectations concerning the shape of the plot that is to unfold, but also to expose the duplicity and the gendered ambiguities of language. Images of the traditional metamorphosis of Philomela haunt the prologues to the *Legend*, as Chaucer alludes to his *Parliament of Fowls* with its Tereus-like 'false lapwynge, ful of trecherye' (*Parl*, line 347) and his *Troilus and Criseyde* with its image of 'the swalowe Proigne' whose song recalls 'whi she forshapen was ... [and] how Tereus gan forth hire suster take' (*T&C* II, lines 64–69).[8] The garden of the prologues, over whose 'enbrouded' carpet of flowers the narrator walks, is home to birds who sing their defiance of another figure of 'trecherye': the Tereus-like fowler who 'had hem betrayed with his sophistrye' (F, line 137). Language here is the birdsong that makes an inarticulate twittering of female pain, that 'jangling' associated, as Karma Lochrie reminds us, with the gossip of women, and coded as a form of 'abjected' speech.[9] And it is also the patriarchal discourse of violence and power, the 'sophistrye' that entraps women as a net entraps a bird. In the 'Legend of Philomela' itself, language begins to unravel, as the narrator characterises Tereus as a 'slaunder of man': a man whose very name causes mimetic distortions within the linguistic 'formes' of the universe and the eyes of the reader.[10] As the narrator says:

---

[8] In the *Parliament* Chaucer anticipates, or shares a source with, Gower in his portrayal of Tereus transformed into a 'lappewincke ... the brid falseste of alle' (*CA* V, lines 6046–47).

[9] Lochrie, *Covert Operations*, pp. 68–69.

[10] D. Vance Smith, 'Destroyer of Forms: Chaucer's Philomela', in *Readings in Medieval*

> Whan that I his foule storye rede,
> Myne eyen wexe foule and sore also
> Yit last the venym of so longe ago,
> That it enfecteth hym that wol beholde
> The storye of Tereus.
> (lines 2239–43)

Although the lines' surface message is one of condemnation of men, its imagery is borrowed from the antifeminist tradition. The mention of a 'venym' that affects the eyes recalls medical tradition, wherein women's menstrual blood was understood as a poisonous substance that could circulate through the body. Sauer notes that men were warned to avoid menstruating women, 'so as to evade their venym'.[11] Perhaps reflecting this association of ideas, one manuscript of the *Legend* reads 'wemyn' rather than 'venym', attributing the root cause of linguistic deformation to women rather than men, women rather than their rapists.[12] The scribal error neatly proves the point it mistakenly makes, that linguistic deformations are irrevocably associated with 'wemyn'. At the same time, the phrase 'slaunder of man' (line 2231), applied to Tereus, casts Tereus' own sex as the target of his corrosive energies, giving the phrase unmistakably sodomitic implications that recall Alan of Lille's description of the corruption of language through deviant masculine desire. Language, which briefly seemed to figure forth divine creation in formal order, becomes a fluid and slippery medium, insinuatingly aligning its negative implications with female bodies and with corrupt masculinity. Amid this chaotic disorder of language, Tereus' act of rape appears as a perverted echo of Jerome's hermeneutic paradigm, for like Jerome, Tereus penetrates a woman's body that is simultaneously a Classical *fabula*. Yet whereas Jerome claims this quasi-sexual despoiling as a means of separating the truth of language from its veil of rhetorical ornament, for Tereus the rape of Philomela is sign and symbol of the linguistic deformation spreading corrosively from text to reader.

This provocative deformation of Jerome's hermeneutic paradigm is part of a larger concern with rape, rhetoric and the voicing or silencing of female emotions, which pervades the *Legend*.[13] In the earlier 'Legend of Lucrece', which functions as a thematic introduction to some of the themes of the 'Legend of Philomela', Chaucer exposes the power imbalance that lies at the heart of hermeneutic practice when reading texts about women, showing how rhetoric works to entrap the unfortunate Lucrece in a position of both literal

---

Textuality: Essays in Honour of A. C. Spearing, eds Christina Maria Cervone and D. Vance Smith (Cambridge: D. S. Brewer, 2016), pp. 135–56 (pp. 148–49).

11 Sauer, *Gender in Medieval Culture*, p. 69.
12 London, British Library MS Additional 12524.
13 For discussion of the canonical status of rape in Western literature, see Elizabeth Robertson and Christine M. Rose, 'Introduction', in *Representing Rape*, ed. Robertson and Rose, pp. 1–20 (p. 3).

and hermeneutic (or epistemic) vulnerability. The narrative draws on a wider tradition of thinking about sexual violence towards women, which Chaucer acknowledges as he alludes to the writings of St Augustine. 'Austyn hath gret compassioun/ Of this Lucresse' (lines 1690–91), he observes, rather disingenuously recalling St Augustine's famous discussion of Lucrece's innocence or guilt concerning her rape.[14] Augustine offers an image of the impenetrable soul of a chaste woman, which has a long history as an architectural trope, rooted in the scriptural depiction of the Virgin Mary as *porta clausa*, a locked gate.[15] A truly chaste woman never consents in her soul and thus remains spiritually intact. However, the same conflation of the female body with its architectural surrounds enables a correspondingly insinuating discourse of female guilt. As Sheila Delany has demonstrated, accumulated hints of complicity or sexual willingness undermine the portrayal of Lucrece as a chaste and virtuous wife, subtly and disturbingly suggesting that, as her body is conflated with its architectural surroundings, therefore any architectural rupture, breach or unguarded entrance connotes a corresponding openness of her body to sexual contact.[16] While Lucrece's rapist Tarquinius is engaged in a drawn-out siege in war, a battering at resistant walls, Lucrece innocently expresses the hope, 'God wolde the wallis weryn fallen adoun!' (line 1726), unpleasantly forshadowing the coming assault on her own bodily integrity. Returning home, Collatine and Tarquinus find the entrances to Lucrece's home suggestively open: no porter blocks the gate through which they enter 'prively' (line 1716); they go in through the 'estris' (line 1715), an enclosed space or courtyard garden and also an innuendo for female genitalia.[17] Later, Tarquinius makes his solitary way into the house unimpeded, via a 'prive halke' (line 1780) – a secret nook, but also a cavity in the body, implicitly genital in connection with 'prive' – as if already penetrating Lucrece's body as he prepares to penetrate her domestic space. Indeed, the point of entry to the house itself is suggestively ambiguous. The narrator expresses uncertainty about whether Tarquinius enters 'by wyndow or by other gyn' (line 1784), and the word 'gyn' means not only a device or structure but also a trick or stratagem; it is frequently used in collocation with the punning genital term 'queynte'.[18] The violence of the trope lies in the asymmetry of understanding and intention concerning its operation. As the architectural metaphors of the text redefine interior and exterior bodily space, they reveal that Lucrece's body has always been vulnerably open to sexual violence, for this openness is exterior to the body she herself knows. In turn, this is a form of epistemic violence. Female bodily space is stretched thin, as the

---

[14] See Saunders, *Rape and Ravishment*, p. 268.
[15] See Edwards, *The Afterlives of Rape*, pp. 7–9.
[16] See Delany, *The Naked Text*, pp. 146–47.
[17] See Florence Percival, *Chaucer's Legendary Good Women* (Cambridge: Cambridge University Press, 1998), p. 274, and Delany, *The Naked Text*, p. 146.
[18] See *Middle English Dictionary* headword gin(ne) (n.), and Chapter Six of this book.

boundaries of Lucrece's body are metaphorically displaced outwards, in order that larger and larger epistemic and ethical structures (responsibility for rape; responsibility to guard against sexual entry) are located within her female body. Unaware of any conflation between her body and the ruptures she welcomes or the entrances she leaves open, Lucrece is placed in a position of vulnerable innocence. Entrants to her house and to her story (including readers, implicated by the narrator's innuendo) are in a position of greater knowledge about those boundaries and the bodily vulnerabilities they disclose.

The 'Legend of Philomela' likewise represents established rhetorical tropes as the systems through which violated women are alienated from their own bodies and implicated within discourses of alien emotion and desire. The text retains from the earlier 'Legend of Lucrece' the imagery that conflates the female body with the architecture that surrounds it; in particular, it draws upon the language used to depict the cells and enclosures of religious women, professionally chaste and protected from masculine sexual violence. In literature written for anchorites and women religious, and increasingly disseminated to lay audiences across the fourteenth century, the chaste female body is pictured as a cell within a cell, and the walls of the anchorhold are pictured as the outermost limits of her body.[19] As Suzanne Edwards has argued, literature written for and to anchorites seeks to construct the anchorhold as the definitive space of protection for women, and is therefore laden with monitory images of the sexual violence they might encounter outside its walls.[20] The narrative of Philomela concentrates its architectural allusions on the moment immediately following Philomela's mutilation, placing Philomela in an unpleasantly twisted version of the containment envisaged in anchoritic literature. Preparing to rape his victim, Tereus drags her to a 'derke cave', (line 2312) and after the violation:

> ... with his swerd hire tonge of kerveth he,
> And in a castel made hire for to be
> Ful pryvely in prisoun everemore.
> (lines 2234–36)

The 'castel' appears as if from nothing, in the middle of what we have been given to understand is a remote wilderness. In these lines, the specific space of Philomela's violated mouth and body is eclipsed by the much larger shifting of architecture around her, as the vaginal 'derke cave' in which the rape was located only moments before is transformed into an enclosing 'castel'. The lines suggest a distorted form of the anchoritic ceremony. Texts recording the rituals through

---

[19] *Ancrene Wisse* describes the body as 'the house of my soul'. Elsewhere in the same text, the author reminds his audience that the womb, in which Christ was a recluse, is a narrow dwelling ('for wombe is nearow wununge, þer ure Lauerd wes recluse'): *Ancrene Wisse*, ed. Robert Hasenfratz (Kalamazoo, MI: Medieval Institute Publications, 2000), p. 142.

[20] Ibid., p. 72.

which anchorites were committed to their cells focus particular attention on the tongue, depicting it as a gateway to sexual sin and representing control and silence of the tongue as the means by which women were somatically enclosed.[21] Unpleasantly literalising this idea, the 'Legend of Philomela' represents the violent control and silencing of the tongue as the prequel to sudden enclosure. These disconcerting and distorting implications are reinforced by the grammar of the poetry. The anaphoric paralleling of the lines implies a causal relation, as if the act of excision of the tongue effected the translocation of Philomela from a cave to an imprisoning castle in a single stroke: 'with his swerd hire tonge of kerveth he, / And in a castel made hire for to be'. The depiction slices into our sense of narrative chronology, as time is protracted or doubled, for the action of the phallic sword on the tongue drags a memory of the rape back into the text from the earlier lines, setting in parallel Philomela's violated genitalia and her violated mouth. Time is also telescoped; the intermission between the sword falling and the bolt of the prison slamming into place is cut out, as if sword and prison bolt are one and the same.

Whereas in the anchoritic literature Edwards discusses, imagined sexual violence is a constant possibility (or threat) lying *outside* the anchorhold and in the future, in Chaucer's version sexual violence is *prior to* quasi-anchoritic enclosure. Enclosure does not protect Philomela from sexual violence, it protects her violator from discovery. Worse, it implicates her in a discourse of censorious anxiety concerning female chastity, for literature written for and about enclosed women persistently worries about their ongoing propensity to transgress. In particular, the imagery of the tongue's control prior to architectural enclosure amid the threat of masculine sexual violence is part of the familiar constellation of ideas that recur in anchoritic literature concerned with enclosed women's vulnerability to same-sex desires.[22] The *Ancrene Wisse*, for example, warns its audience that some enclosed women 'of hire ahne suster haveth ... i-beon i-temptet' ('have been tempted by their own sisters'), while Aelred's *De institutione inclusarum* cautions female recluses against the belief that men are the only threat to chastity.[23] Accordingly, as Chaucer

---

[21] See E. Jane Burns, *Bodytalk: When Women Speak in Old French Literature* (Philadelphia, PA: University of Pennsylvania Press, 1993), p. 204; E. A. Jones, 'Ceremonies of Enclosure: Rite, Rhetoric and Reality', in *Rhetoric of the Anchorhold: Space, Place and Body within the Discourses of Enclosure*, ed. Liz Herbert McAvoy (Cardiff: University of Wales Press, 2008), pp. 34–49 (p. 42–43).

[22] Watt, Sauer and Lochrie all explore the same-sex implications of anchoritic space and literature. See Diane Watt, 'Why Men Still Aren't Enough', *GLQ: A Journal of Lesbian and Gay Studies* 16.3 (2010): 451–64; Michelle M. Sauer, 'Representing the Negative: Positing the Lesbian Void in Medieval English Anchoritism', *Thirdspace* 3.2 (2004): 70–88 (p. 70), consulted online on 20 February 2016 at http://www.thirdspace.ca/articles/3_2_sauer.htm; Lochrie, Heterosyncrasies, pp. 26–46.

[23] *Ancrene Wisse*, ed. Hasenfratz, II, lines 180–81; *Aelred of Rievaulx's De institutione inclusarum: Two English Versions*, eds John Ayto and Alexandra Barratt, EETS o.s.

The Silencing of Female Desire

reverses a narrative of anchoritic enclosure to entrap Philomela within the quasi-protective walls that are no longer of any use to her violated body, he also locates her within a discourse of suspicion of female sexual desires. Insofar as this imagery insinuates the presence of sexual desire where it might seem absent (that is, in the emotions of a raped woman), the strategy is not dissimilar to that Chaucer used in the 'Legend of Lucrece', with its imagery of architectural/sexual openness. The hinted same-sex desires that cling to the trope of the enclosed woman are likewise pejorative in their application to Philomela, disturbing in that they replace her overt aversion with the suspicion of deviant emotion.

This combination of disoriented, truncated narrative structure, deformed textual embodiment and the insinuation of same-sex desire prepares us for the profoundly odd and jarring ending to Chaucer's 'Legend of Philomela'. The text ends abruptly after Philomela is freed from her prison, depriving her of the revenge on Tereus she typically orchestrates, and (in the views of many readers of the text) reducing her vengeful agency to bland suffering. The sequence of events is simple. After Procne unfolds the tapestry her sister wove and sees its message of rape and mutilation, she hurries to the castle where her sister is imprisoned, finding her weeping and alone. The two women pull each other into a wordless embrace, lamenting together. In this strange in-between moment, before the looming threat of female vengeance, filicide and cannibalism that typically follows, the voice of the narrator intervenes:

> And thus I late hem in here sorwe dwelle.
> The remenaunt is no charge for to telle,
> For this is al and som.
> (lines 2382–84)

Frozen in her sorrow, held in her sister's embrace, Philomela's story is suspended. The abrupt ending leaves her in a state of arrested narrative development. Yet this sudden ending is not only poetic brutality: it is also (and uncomfortably) the means whereby Chaucer makes space for a feminine hermeneutic. Eschewing the standard metamorphosis of the central characters, Chaucer avoids the transformation that is so ambiguously caught between 'refuge from and reminder of ... trauma', between escape and imprisonment in a bird's body.[24] Ending his story at the moment of Philomela's rescue from prison, Chaucer pointedly withholds resolution. The disorientations to plot and narrative, time and space, vividly realise the difficulty of

---

2 (London: Oxford University Press, 1984), p. 287. For a summary of this tradition of writing, see Karma Lochrie, 'Between Women', in *The Cambridge Companion to Medieval Women's Writing*, eds Carolyn Dinshaw and David Wallace (Cambridge: Cambridge University Press, 2003), pp. 70–90 (pp. 77–81).

[24] Mary Flannery, 'Gower's Blushing Bird, Philomela's Transforming Face', *Postmedieval* 8.1 (2017): 35–50 (p. 40).

giving voice to women's emotions of desire and aversion within the structures of medieval rhetoric and poetics. In Chaucer's hands, the poem seems actively to resist the articulation of Philomela's story, disarticulating its own chronological and spatial structures in the process. The insinuating language through which Philomela's body is alienated from itself and incorporated into a foreign discourse of quasi-anchoritic enclosure makes her legible from a medieval perspective as a figure of potentially deviant desire. This resonates with the poetic and narrative disorientations of the text, which may also be understood in terms of disorienting or deviant desire. Freeman and Ahmed both, as I observed in my introduction, theorise temporal and spatial asynchrony and disorientation in terms of 'queer' sexual desire, specifically of *women*'s 'queer' sexual desires. Caught in an arrested narrative trajectory, displaced from the foreshadowed progress of her story, Philomela is located in what they might call a 'queer time and space': a narrative space that pulls away from expectations. The damage Chaucer does to the textual body of the Philomela myth may, therefore, be seen not only as mimetic cruelty towards its heroine, but also as the cause and consequence of twisting Jerome's hermeneutic paradigm, and attempting to give voice to female emotion. With profoundly misogynistic logic, the 'Legend of Philomela' represents rhetoric as a system that can only represent female emotion that is not orientated responsively towards masculine desire as deviancy or inarticulacy.

A BODY WITH MISSING BITS: PHILOMELA'S PROSTHETIC VOICE

The source of this deviant voice that floats up through the subtext of the 'Legend of Philomela' is, of course, the female body: that body coded as incomplete and excessive, inherently prosthetic and limited, which I discuss in the introduction. With her tongueless mouth and violated body, Philomela cannot speak of her emotions or desires, yet her body's physical presence is eloquent testimony to the essential condition of women within an economy of desire that excludes female speech and agency. The representation of Philomela's body is therefore of crucial importance, standing (as it does) as a metonym for women's suffering bodies and women's silenced narratives more generally. Yet in Chaucer's version of the narrative, Philomela's body is the site of yet more strange *lacunae*, more seemingly inexplicable departures from sources, and more insinuatingly excessive subtextual innuendos that jostle awkwardly to fill the gaps left in the *Legend*'s text. The result is, I argue, the construction of Philomela's body as deviant, and indicative of sexual deviancy.

At the crucial moment immediately following her rape, Philomela's body – already so disoriented in time and space – is virtually written out of the narrative. The swiftly mobilised architectural imagery takes the place of any description of Philomela's mutilation, and the sense of speed almost, but not quite, distracts us from the omission. However, it is striking in the context of

Chaucer's departures from his Latin and French sources. Chaucer is unique in leaving out any details of the mutilation of Philomela that would testify to her pain and her injury. In Chaucer's Latin source, Ovid's *Metamorphoses*, the rapes (plural) are described with euphemistic verbs, 'superat' ('forced', *Mets* VI, line 525) and 'fertur' ('assailed', *Mets* VI, line 561), and the account culminates, gruesomely, with the excised tongue itself. As Philomela struggles to call out

> He seized her tongue with pincers, and cut it off with his cruel sword. Her tongue's root was left quivering, while the rest of it lay on the dark soil, vibrating and trembling, and moving like the tail of a mutilated snake, it writhed, as if, in dying, it were searching for some sign of her.[25]

The image of the writhing tongue is curiously alienating, despite the horror that should stir our sympathy. It attributes movement and volition – or at least, the appearance of volition – to the severed object, locating these properties that contribute to the definition of an autonomous self outside the body of the violated woman. Yet this externalising of Philomela's agency into her separated tongue also externalises, and therefore publicises, her internal pain and suffering. This externalisation and display continue in the account of Philomela's tapestry, for Ovid specifies the purple colour of the designs Philomela weaves: 'purpureas ... notas' or 'purple marks' (*Mets* VI, line 577), as if her blood continues to flow though the tapestry that replaces the speech of her butchered tongue. Blood is a consistent emphasis of the Philomela tradition, and would continue after Chaucer, as Gower describes how the flood of gore across Philomela's face made her almost unrecognisable and Shakespeare compares the bleeding limbs of his Lavinia (an analogue of Philomela) to spurting fountains.[26] By contrast, blood is pointedly absent from Chaucer's text. Chaucer rewrites the episode, restraining the gory somatic content, and replacing it with the description of architectural space that links Philomela to a wider discourse of sexual violence. Chaucer describes Philomela's rape with a bluntness very different from Ovid's euphemistic

---

[25] ... conprensam forcipe linguam
abstulit ense fero. radix micat ultima linguae,
ipsa iacet terraeque tremens inmurmurat atrae,
utque salire solet mutilatae cauda colubrae,
palpitat et moriens dominae vestigia quaerit
(*Mets* VI, lines 556–60).

[26] Gower claims that 'what with blod and what with teres ... He made hire faire face uncouth': *Confessio Amantis*, ed. Russell A. Peck with Latin translations by Andrew Galloway, 3 vols (Kalamazoo, MI: Medieval Institute Publications, 2004), V, lines 5692–94. Subsequent quotations from the *Confessio* are taken from this edition and given by book and line numbers in the text. Shakespeare's Marcus refers to Lavinia's 'crimson river of warm blood, / Like to a bubbling fountain stirr'd with wind' (*Titus Andronicus*, Act II, sc. 4, 1086–87).

verbs. 'By force ... he hath reft hire of hire maydenhede' (lines 2324–25), the narrator states, unambiguously. Delany comments positively on the 'integrity and power' of Chaucer's version of the tale, and Blud argues that, in contrast to Gower's more gory and graphic version, it 'evokes conventional sympathy'.[27] It is certainly tempting to see this rewriting as an attempt to steer clear of Ovid's sensationalising impulses and their grotesque externalisation of Philomela's volition and movement to her severed tongue. In Chaucer, no surgical pincers (nor Gower's nastily ironic sewing shears) hold the struggling tongue; once Tereus' sword has swung down, there is no further description of wound or wounded body, either as external evidence of pain or as voyeuristic image of writhing limbs, but only the architectural imagery of the 'castel' (line 2335) and 'prisoun' (line 2336).

This rewriting accommodates a less sympathetic set of connotations, which extend the imagery of same-sex desire already identified. The lack of blood and gore assimilates Philomela into two radically opposed discourses of unbleeding female bodies, female bodies that contain rather than displaying the visible, somatic witnesses to their internal feelings. Firstly, of course, Philomela's lack of visible wounding, pain or blood might be read as a transcendence of the violence she suffers, a move away from Ovid's sensationalising imagery. Blood, or rather its absence, marks a particular kind of spiritual and sexual identity in women. Bettina Bildhauer succinctly examines this mode of demarcation, noting that as blood affirms the integrity of the body, those bodies that naturally bleed are 'exclud[ed] from such integrity', their bleeding 'marking gender'.[28] To bleed is to be feminine and fragmented; to be bloodless is to transcend messy femininity, to adopt a kind of saintly and contained female masculinity. The Virgin's body, and in particular her womb, were characterised as expanses of whiteness and shining incorruptibility, very different from the bloody flesh of a normal woman's body.[29] Constructing Philomela's body as bloodless and enclosed, Chaucer returns her to a quasi-virginal, quasi-saintly state, as if to locate her protectively outside the timeline in which the rape has occurred. In this line of thought, the bloodless body in its enclosure is like the body of the anchorite, contained in a somatic and architectural resistance to sexual violence. However, the same lack of bleeding could, alternatively, be read in the light of medical theories of the natural and healthy functions of female bleeding. The female body, being regularly cleansed of blood in the form of menses, was held to be naturally colder and less given to emissions of humours than the male body. Avicenna – whom Chaucer cites in his catalogue of medical authorities in the

---

[27] Delany, *The Naked Text*, p. 149; Victoria Blud, *The Unspeakable, Gender and Sexuality in Medieval Literature 1000–1400* (Cambridge: D. S. Brewer, 2017), p. 158.

[28] Bettina Bildhauer, *Medieval Blood* (Cardiff: University of Wales Press, 2006), p. 1.

[29] Jacqueline Tasioulas, '"Heaven and Earth in Little Space": The Foetal Existence of Christ in Medieval Literature and Thought', *Medium Ævum* 76 (2007): 24–48.

General Prologue (line 432) – writes that the natures and bodies of women whose menstrual cycles were interrupted became 'similar to the natures of men ... and [they experience] expulsion of superfluities in the way that men expel them'.[30] Women whose bodies retained blood in this unnatural way were thought to develop sexual desires that were 'masculine' in their assertiveness.[31] If bleeding marks the female body, then the lack of natural blood in a female body is symptomatic of sexual deviancy.[32] The mutilation, and Chaucer's unique treatment of it, positions Philomela uncomfortably between two opposing traditions of viewing female bodies, the first aligning Philomela with saintly women transcending their bloody bodily natures to retain their virginity, and the second aligning her with women exhibiting 'deviant' sexual desires. Neither discourse fits comfortably with her status as a rape survivor.

The bloodlessness of Philomela's body in Chaucer's legend results from the rejection of Ovid's sensational depiction of the writhing, bleeding severed tongue, yet this lump of flesh does not lose its symbolic potential in the Middle English text. It remains saturated with connotations. The metonymic relationship between tongue and female genitalia is commonplace. The Old French word *langue* can mean both tongue and clitoris, and *fabliaux* frequently exploit the pun with references to women's 'two tongues'.[33] To speak of violence towards the tongue of a woman, and violence with a sexual component, is to suggest symbolic violence to her clitoris as well. Some medical writers held that the anatomical cause of female same-sex desire was an excessively sized clitoris, and therefore that a cure was the excision or partial excision of this member, the analogue for the lingual mutilation Philomela undergoes.[34] Philomela's mutilation thus functions as a 'thematic site' or Lacanian *point de capiton* (quilting point) drawing together disparate discourses of female sexuality and sexual violence.[35] Like the knot that anchors threads running through separate layers of fabric, to which Lacan refers, Philomela's missing tongue links ideas of the female tongue/clitoris to ideas of the unnaturally unbleeding female body, and to the recommendation of cliterodectomy to treat women whose symptoms include desire for other women, allowing us to arrive at a reading of Philomela's mutilation as a form of denial of female

---

[30] The quotation is from Avicenna's *Liber canonis* and is quoted, translated and discussed by Lochrie, *Heterosyncrasies*, p. 88.
[31] Ibid.
[32] I extrapolate from Bildauer, *Medieval Blood*, p. 1.
[33] Burns, *Bodytalk*, pp. 48–51.
[34] Guy de Chauliac prescribes the cutting of the clitoris, but states that this should be an incomplete excision (as, notably, Gower makes the glossectomy in his version of the tale), 'for drede of bledynge'. See Lochrie, *Heterosyncrasies*, p. 87.
[35] Jacques Lacan, *The Psychoses (The Seminar of Jacques Lacan, Book III: 1955-1956)*, ed. Jacques Alain-Miller, trans. R. Grigg (New York: Norton, 1993), pp. 258–70.

sexuality or even 'lesbian' castration.[36] Chaucer's *lacuna*, his omission of the lurid imagery of Philomela's mutilated flesh and bloody tongue, makes visible the tensions within the discourses available for representation of violated female sexuality, showing how easily female aversion to male sexual violence can be made to look like transgressive female desire punished.

These troubling implications are intensified by the process, and especially the object, whereby Philomela finds a substitute means of communicating. She weaves her story on a loom, and its wooden frame and shuttle take the place of her severed tongue. The loom functions as a prosthesis, an object that takes the place of the absent tongue but also draws attention to its ongoing absence. Prostheses are 'ontologically unstable ... claimed neither by the body nor by the world ... they thereby violate the coherence and integrity of the body-image'.[37] Philomela's body is metaphorically invaded by a thing belonging in her violated mouth, yet also horrifically foreign to that space. Indeed, the loom is also suggestive of further oral violation, its wooden shuttle displacing Philomela's tongue. This image of the prosthetic taking the place of what was in the mutilated mouth is capitalised on in Shakespeare's extension of the Philomela narrative, as he depicts the raped woman struggling to guide a disconcertingly phallic staff to trace words with her tongueless mouth.[38] This loom disturbs our sense of Philomela's bodily integrity, her selfhood, in much the same way that the quivering, self-propelling remnant of tongue in Ovid disturbed that sense. But where Ovid's severed tongue prompts a purely abject reaction of horror, the loom is more complicated because it is also productive of the voice whose lack it replaces.

For Chaucer, the prosthesis does not reveal Philomela's subjectivity, but implicates her in a very different discourse relating to transgressive female sexuality. In Ovid's account, the contraption on which Philomela weaves is specifically named: it is a *tela*: the word means loom, warp thread and also web (and is grammatically feminine). In the Old French of the *Ovide Moralisé*, we are told Philomela does not lack any 'ostille' (*Moralisé* VI, line 3310) – any tool, any loom – for her work. Chaucer, however, omits to name the structure on which the adult Philomela weaves. The prosthetic loom thus draws attention to a lingual absence and a linguistic absence, to the lack of a tongue and to the lack of a word to name the structure that stands in for that tongue. In Middle English, the word 'loom' is a euphemism for penis: the *Middle English Dictionary* gives this as the first meaning, alongside the meaning of 'a frame

---

[36] Diane Watt identifies Philomela's glossectomy in Gower's *Confessio Amantis* as a form of 'symbolic castration' in *Amoral Gower: Language, Sex, and Politics* (Minneapolis, MN: University of Minnesota Press, 2003), p. 94.

[37] Allon White, 'Prosthetic Gods in Atrocious Places: Gilles Deleuze/Francis Bacon', in *Carnival, Hysteria, and Writing: Collected Essays and Autobiography* (Oxford: Oxford University Press, 1993), pp. 160–77 (p. 173).

[38] *Titus Andronicus*, Act IV, sc. i, stage direction after line 76.

for weaving'.[39] The innuendo has an entirely straightforward origin in the fact that the Anglo-Saxon root *geloma* means simply 'tool' and thus gives rise to both later meanings, and the phallic shape of the shuttle provides obvious justification for it. Genital prosthetics are far from unknown in the *Legend* as a whole: they reappear in the 'Legend of Thisbe', and Delany identifies them in the 'Legend of Ariadne'.[40] Philomela's loom is thus not only a substitute for her tongue but also an object which, like the staff Shakespeare would use in his later version of the tale, suggests a continuing sexual violation of Philomela's already violated oral space.

Before providing Philomela with the object that metaphorically 'gives' her a penis and a means of communication, Chaucer indulges in a unique digression, which intensifies the underlying violence of implication in the use of the loom. We are told that Philomela has the capacity to 'rede and wel ynow endite / But with a penne coude she nat wryte' (lines 2356–57). As Dinshaw reminds us, evoking the commonplace association of the *gloss* (tongue or paratext) with *auctoritas*, this inability makes Philomela 'a prime example of a woman denied the 'proper' means of making meaning'.[41] The association encourages us to relate the inability to wield a pen to the embodied lack of another implement typically understood as necessary to the act of writing: the penis, evocatively conflated with the pen in the hermeneutic tradition. Philomela's loom is, then, triply a substitute: for her tongue, for her pen and for the penis that would give her the authority to control her own sexual and textual narrative. Chaucer's narrative reminds us that what Philomela 'speaks' with after her mutilation is neither a literal nor a metaphoric voice, but a prosthetic, attempting to replace her tongue and, symbolically, attempting to obtain for her the voice in male-dominated discourse which she lacks. It is prosthetic in that it replaces a body part that is missing; it is also prosthetic in Derrida's sense. A 'supplement' within the system of signs, it draws attention to the absence that necessitates its existence, and it exposes as a construct that which has seemed entirely natural: the system of writing itself.[42] As Derrida observes, the written language purports to substitute for speech, as the loom purports to substitute for the tongue, but inevitably, as a prosthetic operation, it draws attention to the incompleteness of speech, and to the emptiness that necessitates its presence. In the context of the 'Legend of Philomela', this prosthetic loom bears witness to the artificiality and limitation of masculinised rhetoric and hermeneutic practice, systems that demand a woman make use of a supplement in order to participate.

These insinuations entrap Philomela yet further in the linguistic treachery that we saw at work in Chaucer's treatment of Lucrece in the 'Legend of

---

[39] See *MED* headword lome (n.)
[40] Delany, *The Naked Text*, pp. 148–49.
[41] Dinshaw, *Chaucer's Sexual Poetics*, p. 81.
[42] Derrida, *Of Grammatology*, p. 145.

Lucrece' and for Philomela in the moments of her imprisonment. Yet they also implicate her within yet another innuendo relating to female same-sex desire. Medieval depictions of female same-sex desire provide a context for interpreting the prosthetic use of the loom as a substitute for that nexus of bodily parts including the tongue, the clitoris and the penis. As I discuss in my introduction, writers including Bennett, Dinshaw and Mills demonstrate that medieval writers interpreted the use of a prosthetic substituting for male genitalia – a dildo – as a defining feature of female same-sex activity.[43] Historical cases of prosecutions for female same-sex desire focus on use of a phallic substitute; writers refer censoriously to women engaging in erotic or intimate relations using such devices.[44] As Philomela seeks a prosthetic substitute for the pen she cannot use, her action renders her legible as a certain kind of woman in medieval understandings of sexual behaviours. Grotesquely, a narrative of sexual violence – of aversion from unwanted desire – produces the spectre of active, 'deviant' female same-sex desire. Philomela's loom arouses an unsettling nexus of puns around the tongue and the genitals, suggestive of female sexual deviancies. Moreover, the verse form itself works to locate Philomela, once again, within the 'queer' textual spaces Freeman discusses. The line that expresses Philomela's essential lack, the lack that necessitates her reliance upon a multiply genitally coded prosthetic, is hypometric. 'But with a penne coude she nat wryte', the narrator says. The verse form underscores the association between Philomela's lack of means to make meaning, and her formal or bodily lack. It calls to mind Freeman's argument that disruptions in metre or tempo reflect and constitute the temporalities in which alternative desires express themselves.[45] The gap in the metre makes a space in which Philomela's desire emerges as deviant, a space in which Philomela's need to supplement her body with a penile prosthetic becomes apparent. In his depiction of Philomela, then, Chaucer represents a female body that is profoundly unnatural, unbleeding and grotesquely prosthetically extended, persistently struggling to fit the established structures of verse form and narrative structure. This somatic, narrative and poetic disorientation and asynchronicity resonates with those forms of writing Freeman and Ahmed associate with the 'queer'. The 'Legend of Philomela' embodies, and bodies forth, a dissonant poetics that struggles to contain itself within expected structures of thought and language, a poetics that codes its female protagonist as sexually and somatically dissident whenever and however she seeks to overcome her silence.

[43] See Murray, 'Twice Marginal and Twice Invisible', pp. 191–222; Robert L. A. Clark, 'Jousting without a Lance', pp. 143–77; Mills, 'Homosexuality: Specters of Sodom', pp. 62–3; Dinshaw, *Getting Medieval*, pp. 89–90.
[44] Puff, 'Female Sodomy', pp. 41–61; Mills, *Seeing Sodomy*, p. 126.
[45] Freeman, *Time Binds*, p. 21

The Silencing of Female Desire

A TEXTILE POETICS FOR THE *LEGEND OF GOOD WOMEN*

In interpreting Chaucer's Philomela as an unwittingly or unwillingly deviant figure, I read the text as a hermeneutic exploration, of which the emotions of a violated woman are collateral damage. As female emotions arising from rape, which are silenced and erased within the traditional hermeneutic paradigm, attempt to break into the poem, they fracture and damage its poetic and narrative structures, in a manner not dissimilar to the linguistic damage Alan of Lille attributes to sodomy. Female deviant desire is not the mirror image of masculine deviant desire, however, for whereas men's active desire only causes semantic damage when it transgresses from its proper object, female desire appears deviant when it simply seeks to speak. However, although the loom implicates Philomela within a discourse of deviant desire painfully unlike her own sexual experience of rape, that is not its only function. In this final part of this chapter, I examine the startlingly innovative way in which Chaucer depicts Philomela's weaving, in a radical departure from the source tradition that has gone entirely unremarked by scholars. Chaucer rejects the traditional association of the tapestry with images of completeness and aesthetic or economic value, instead showing us a rough and crude item, depicted in jagged, hypometric verse, which never succeeds in serving the purpose of catalysing Philomela's revenge or her final transformation into a bird. However, this degraded object has another, very different purpose. As Philomela adopts the *habitus* of weaving, her body is drawn into rhythms of movement and thought that function as therapy for her traumatised mind. Weaving imposes a material discipline entirely different from writing or speech. The process renders narrative structure discontinuous and asynchronous, as the message is built up across slowly accumulating threads; the *lacunae* that strike readers of a poem as jarring or aesthetically displeasing are translated into the necessary apertures and open spaces without which weaving cannot be completed. The process allows Philomela to communicate her violation without reliving her trauma in one painful flood of narrative. In turn, the weaving process (as Chaucer reimagines it) brings a new coherency to the *Legend*, too, offering an explanation for the sudden ending to Philomela's story. Demonstrating that there is no way for Philomela to reclaim that voice from within the communicative traditions of the patriarchy without implicating herself in discourses of deviant desire, the *Legend* offers, instead, an entirely alternative communicative structure.

Long-standing tradition holds that the tapestry Philomela makes is a superlative work of art, an aesthetic triumph that is at best a symbol of *écriture féminine* at its most articulate, and at worst, a horrific justification of masculine violence as an instigator of that feminine pain that produces beauty.[46] Once finished, the tapestry is a valuable object, playing its role in the rhythms of artistic and commercial display and exchange.[47] It is a product, carrying a specific purpose. In the *Metamorphoses*, Philomela weaves on white cloth in purple: the purple is rich in material and symbolic value. It looks back to the narrative with which this book (VI) of the *Metamorphoses* opens, the story of the weaving contest between goddess Athene and mortal Arachne, which likewise features thread of 'Tyrian purple' (Tyrium ... purpura', *Mets* VI, line 61) and its colour is, as we have seen, eloquent of the blood shed during the mutilation, as if the silenced body still speaks its blood loss. In combination with the white cloth, it suggests the colour combinations of Greek ceramic art. The textile is an aesthetically beautiful object, symbolically linked to work of surpassing artistry, and Ovid calls it 'callida': skilful (*Mets* VI, line 576). The Old French only augments this description. There, Philomela is provided with a backstory. Her youthful training, we are told, equipped her with knowledge of an outstanding repertoire of aurally evocative textile designs (*Moralisé* VI, lines 2404-9). The tapestry itself – a 'cortine' (*Moralisé* VI, line 3311) for a bed – is made of differently coloured threads, and it is the collaborative creation of the ad hoc weaving workshop of women who assemble around Philomela in the hope of learning her skills. These women provide Philomela not only with support, but also with the material goods, the multi-coloured threads of 'blue and red, yellow and green', needed for her work (*Moralisé* VI, lines 3330-31).[48] The resulting cloth eloquently evokes the 'colours' of rhetoric. This *cortine* is easily read as a kind of *écriture feminine* or 'bodytalk', 'speaking' through its skilled design and communicating wordlessly between women in networks of support.[49] The eloquence extends to the level of the narrative, as a strand of wordplay elevates the depiction of Philomela's weaving to highly skilled manipulation of French puns that play on her name's similarity to the phase *fil a mené* (weave the thread).[50]

In sharp contrast, Chaucer depicts Philomela's weaving in uneven verse, halting in terms both of versification and of language. He describes how, after a year of work in her prison:

---

[46] See Geoffrey Hartman, 'The Voice of the Shuttle: Language from the Point of View of Literature', *Review of Metaphysics* 23 (1969): 240–58, and in response to him Patricia Klindienst Joplin, 'The Voice of the Shuttle is Ours', in *Rape and Representation*, eds Lynn A. Higgins and Brenda R. Silver (New York: Columbia University Press, 1991, pp. 35–64.

[47] This returning to the rhythms of commerce evokes Freeman's work on rhythm and pattern as structures of chromonormativity, aligned with heterosexuality as a disciplining process for bodies. See Freeman, *Time Binds*, pp. 171–73.

[48] '... fil inde et fil vermoile
Et jaune et vert.'

[49] The term 'bodytalk' is from Burns, *Bodytalk*, p. 7; see also Klindienst, 'The Voice of the Shuttle is Ours', pp. 35–64.

[50] Nancy Jones, 'The Daughter's Text', pp. 170–81.

> She hadde ywoven in a stamyn large
> How she was brought from Athenes in a barge,
> And in a cave how that she was brought;
> And al the thyng that Tereus hath wrought.
> (lines 2360–63)

The first line presents a metrical issue: while three manuscripts feature the three-syllable form 'ywoven', the remaining six offer bisyllabic alternatives, 'wouen' or 'woued', rendering the line hypometric. The third line is likewise hypometric.[51] The lack of syllables draws attention to the oddness, and insufficiency, of the content. The first two lines conclude with a clumsy rhyme that throws what seem semantically and grammatically subordinate details ('large' and 'in a barge') into jarring prominence. The detail of the 'barge' is minor in the context of Philomela's immediate narrative, but it is significant within the larger literary structure of the *Legend* itself. Throughout the text, ships are persistently associated with themes of treachery and ill omen, and the narrator even compares the *Legend* itself to an overloaded 'ship or barge' (line 621), which may be lost if too full of words, requiring the narrator to ignore the 'remnaunt' (line 623) of his material. It is a nasty irony in the context of Philomela's inability to speak.[52] Similarly unpleasant in connotation is the final line, which subsumes under a brief euphemism the rape, the mutilation and the imprisonment, as 'al the thyng that Tereus hath wrought'. The word is repeated only a few lines later, as Procne, receiving the tapestry, 'hath this thing beholde' (line 2373). As a euphemism, it suggests a linguistic squeamishness or reticence that makes emotional sense of Philomela's state of mind, but it is a disingenuous euphemism, for while it hints that the rape and mutilation are too terrible to be mentioned, it is simultaneously commonplace slang for genitalia. Despite this crudeness, the lines lack, along with several syllables, any specific mention of rape or mutilation, while the 'stamyn' – in a line a syllable short – offers the ghost of the word 'stameringe', like a stammering word cut short. The wordplay has precedent of a kind: in Ovid, Philomela's loom is described as 'barbarica' (*Mets* VI, line 576): foreign or 'barbarian', denoting the wilderness of Thrace. The term is onomatopoetic: 'barbarians' are those whose speech resembles a garbled 'bar bar' sound rather than civilised Latin speech; thus, the loom Philomela uses is both a foreign loom and a stammering loom, a loom that render's Philomela's voice foreign to her

---

[51] The line 'And in a cave how that she was brought' is hypometric unless 'brought' is provided with a final e; however, if it is provided with a final e, it disrupts the rhyme with the following line (which would, by contrast, be hypermetric if provided with a final e).

[52] Consider, for example, Cleopatra's unfortunate sea-battle, Dido's bitter equation of the propulsion of Aeneas' fleet to withdrawal of his faith and Ariadne's horror at the sight of Theseus' ships departing without her.

as it stammers out her message. In the Latin, the eloquently blood-coloured tapestry she produces represents a triumph of achievement over equipment; the wordplay is ironic rather than mimetic. In the Middle English, however, it is the tapestry itself – the finished product, and not the means of making it – that is punningly inarticulate.

This inarticulacy emphasises the degraded and degrading nature of Philomela's textile work, exploiting a network of well-known connotations of the textile trade in general. Trafficked women were exploited in hybrid sex-and-textile trade across Europe, while the technology of embroidery was associated with textile work used as a front for the selling of sex or even the trafficking of young women.[53] These seamier implications lurk under descriptions of luxury products in the *Ovide Moralisé* version of Philomela's story, as E. Jane Burns has noted.[54] When Chaucer describes Philomela's experience of textile work during her girlhood in Athens, he borrows this subtext, noting archly that Philomela 'werken and enbroude couthe'. The verb 'wurken' is a common euphemism for sex, while the verb 'enbrouden' means 'to embellish' in the sense of fabricating or fictionalising a verbal account. Although (as we will see) this line depicts a younger Philomela, in a sense its unpleasant implication is magnified by that fact, as it insinuates that, even during her early years, Philomela's innocent girlhood textile work was tinged with anticipatory sexual implication. In the description of Philomela's imprisonment, the association between cloth and sexual violence redoubles. We are told that, after the rape, Tereus kept Philomela imprisoned 'to his usage and his store' (line 2337): the phrase suggests both sexual 'usage' and stockpiling of goods, while the word 'store' puns on the term for a coarse, rough cloth.[55]

It is this roughness that differentiates Chaucer's version of the Philomela narrative from every other version circulating at the time. Initially, Chaucer seems to be following the conventional line, as he pictures Philomela's childhood acquisition of textile skills.

> This woful lady lerned hadde in youthe
> So that she werken and enbroude couthe,
> And weven in hire stol the radevore
> As it of wemen hath be woned yore.

---

[53] For links between the embroidery trade and the sex trade, see Jeremy Goldberg, *Women, Work and Life Cycle in a Medieval Economy: Women in York and Yorkshire, c. 1300–1520* (Oxford: Clarendon Press, 1992), p. 152, and Ruth Mazo Karras, *Common Women: Prostitution and Sexuality in Medieval England* (New York: Oxford University Press, 1996), p. 54. For discussion of associations between fiction and the sex trade, see Jeremy Goldberg, 'John Rykener, Richard II, and the Governance of London', *Leeds Studies in English* NS 44 (2014): 49–70 (p. 51).

[54] E. Jane Burns, *Sea of Silk: A Textile Geography of Women's Work in Medieval French Literature* (Philadelphia, PA: University of Pennsylvania Press, 2009), p. 62.

[55] See *MED*, headword stōre (n.(3)).

The Silencing of Female Desire

(lines 2350–53)

The terminology is specific, as we might expect for a man working in one of the most important textile centres in Europe and responsible for the customs on one of the most lucrative raw materials of the textile trade. A 'stol' is a frame used either for embroidery or for frame-weaving, typically of silk. In proximity to the word 'enbroude', it suggests textile work such as the *opus anglicanum* embroidery on woven silk, made in England and famous throughout Europe.[56] The implication is that, whether weaving or embroidering (or, indeed, embroidering onto silk woven by her own hands), Philomela has been accustomed to expensive equipment and materials. Like her Latin analogue, who forms letters in elegant purple and white, or her French counterpart who weaves intricate patterns in multi-coloured silk, she has the capacity for fine work. Indeed, Chaucer's account is substantially derived from the French narrative's account of Philomela's youth, with which that text begins. Borrowing that depiction of childhood learning, Chaucer displaces it chronologically, incorporating it in a form of flashback, immediately after he describes Philomela's rape. Just after this, he explains that Philomela decided to weave the story of her rape because she had this early training: 'letters can she weve to and fro' (line 2358). The two accounts of textile practice are easily conflated, and many scholars fail to recognise that the first refers to a time chronologically quite distinct from the time of Philomela's imprisonment.[57]

We are told that, during her imprisonment, Philomela weaves 'a stamyn large' (line 2360). The choice of noun is probably influenced by Ovid's Latin term, *stamina* (*Mets* VI, line 576) or thread, but the Middle English cognate has quite different implications. The term has gone unremarked by scholars, but it is odd. The *Middle English Dictionary* glosses 'stamin' as referring to cloth, usually made of wool, or the undergarments made from that cloth, and the quotations it lists are illuminating.[58] Most relate the cloth to clothing for the body or to soft furnishings, and in the former category are several references to the wearing of stamin (or stamin underclothing) by minoresses, anchorites and other enclosed women, or by the religious as a substitute for a hair shirt. It is in this last sense that Chaucer's Parson will use the term, when he refers to the mortification of 'werynge of heyres or of stamyn or of haubergeons on hire naked flessh' (line 1054). Plainly, then, although the term 'stamyn' may evoke the Latin *stamina*, the fabric envisaged here is not Ovid's luxurious purple thread, nor the multi-coloured thread we find in the *Ovide*

---

[56] The *MED* gives 'stol-werk' as embroidery; one of the quotations given refers to orpheys for vestments, which would be embroidered, and another glosses a 'lyncet' or 'werking stole' as an 'instrument for sylke women'. See headword 'stol' (n.).

[57] Blud, for example, truncates the passage as if to indicate Chaucer refers to a single event or time period, in *The Unspeakable, Gender, and Sexuality*, p. 156.

[58] See *MED*, headword 'stamin' (n.), and *CT* X, line 1052.

Moralisé, but something altogether rougher. This 'stamyn large' does not only suggest something very different from the fine 'stol' work of Philomela's youth; it also suggests raw materials not typically used for tapestry at all, poor substitutes more often found in coarse clothing. If the literary source of this fabric is obscure, its physical source within the economics of the tale is not. Philomela is provided with 'hire fille / Of mete and drynk and clothyng at hire wille' (lines 2354–55). The word 'fille', as Nancy Jones observes in regard to the *Ovide Moralisé*, puns on the French for 'thread', and here the mention of clothing raises the possibility of Philomela unravelling garments to acquire the raw material for her weaving.[59] Many scholars, conflating the depiction of Philomela's youthful weaving with her later making of the 'stamyn', misread the implications of Chaucer's representation, and conclude that Philomela, like her earlier analogues, is constructing an object of artistic beauty.[60] But the tapestry is crude in terms of material and content, realised in verse mimetic of its rough, uneven texture, and it is implicated in a wider textile economy marked with reminders of the duplicities of the sex trade. The rough cloth would seem to deepen and emphasise the degrading implications of the loss of voice.

The widespread misreading of Philomela's crude weaving seems to me a significant scholarly omission that carries wide implications for our understanding of Chaucer's work across the *Legend*. Ironically, the *lacunae* of the tapestry Chaucer's Philomela makes seem invisible to the eyes of scholars commenting on the text. These scholars tend to be 'historicist' in their treatment of narrative and source, focusing on the endpoint rather than the 'structures of belonging and duration ... invisible to the historicist eye'.[61] Yet, paradoxically, they are insufficiently open to an entirely historical particularity (if one that is associated with a denigrated form of material record): the material facts of weaving, as practised in the late fourteenth century. It is presumed that what matters is the transmitted shape of a Classical plot, and not the quotidian workings of the weaver's loom. In considering the textile work, and conflating the elegance of silk embroidery with the coarseness of a woven 'stamyn', scholars display a surprisingly scant interest in the materials and production of the medieval textile industry.[62] It seems unlike Chaucer, with his history of employment in close proximity to the textile trade (both in his location in London at the hub of the weaving trade, and in his work as controller of wool customs), to be unaware of these distinctions; indeed, his

---

[59] Jones, 'The Daughter's Text', p. 171.
[60] Collette refers repeatedly to the textile as 'art'. See Collette, *Rethinking Chaucer's* Legend, pp. 111, 134.
[61] Freeman, *Time Binds*, p. xi.
[62] An honourable exception here is E. Jane Burns, who discusses the process of weaving fine silk in some detail in her work on the French text found in the *Ovide Moralisé*. See Burns, *Bodytalk*, pp. 121–25.

vocabulary proves as much. Since the 'manuscript turn' of the past couple of decades, there has been an explosion of scholarship dedicated to exploring the relationship between texts and their material forms or production circumstances, and it is commonplace to acknowledge that we need specialist knowledge of these things in order to understand a text as fully as possible. In particular, close attention to the production of medieval manuscripts raises generative possibilities for reading that which might seem fragmented, damaged, aesthetically inferior or makeshift: all qualities attributed to the *Legend* as a poetic endeavour. For example, Arthur Bahr reads manuscripts from the *Legend*'s fourteenth-century London context as meaningful 'assemblages' rather than the disordered 'miscellanies' they are often considered to be, arguing for the 'integral connection between the forms of matter and the matter of forms'.[63] Kłosowska, as we have seen, analyses nuns' cut-and-pasted books as reflective of an aesthetic, even same-sex erotic, preference for the patchwork, and I have made similar arguments for the texts (including a portion of the *Legend* itself) that circulate in the Findern manuscript (Cambridge, University Library, MS Ff. 1. 6).[64] The making of textiles, likewise, involves materials, methods and tools that shape both the finished product and the movements of bodies and senses, through which that finished product is approached and encountered. In the case of Chaucer's Philomela, such considerations take on particular importance, both because the account is so precise and so detailed in its textile terminology, and because Chaucer's omission of the traditional imagery of a beautiful finished product redirects attention to the specifics of the weaving process itself.

In late medieval England, weaving a tapestry such as Philomela's involves the translating of narrative into cloth. As the weaver works, she deals with a story always viewed in fragments, and in reverse, for the 'wrong' side of the tapestry faces upwards (or outwards) on the loom.[65] The weaver's memory must constantly hold in mind the section to be produced, and her gaze never takes on the whole narrative at once, but is confined to a narrow strip of bare warp threads, which take on density and solidity from the weft as it is woven over them. In order to weave in more than one colour – as one must to weave 'letteres' or images – the weaver must work with discontinuous wefts, that is, with threads of different colours which are woven along the warps to create patches of distinct colour. These threads are then discontinued, to give way to another weft thread in another colour. Where one weft thread ends, it is

---

[63] Arthur Bahr, *Fragments and Assemblages: Forming Compilations in Medieval London* (Chicago, IL: University of Chicago Press, 2013), p. 1.
[64] Kłosowska, *Queer Love in the Middle Ages*, pp. 69–116; Lucy Allen-Goss, 'Queerly Productive: Women and Collaboration in Cambridge, University Library, MS Ff. 1. 6', *Postmedieval* 9.3 (2018): 334–48.
[65] See Thomas P. Campbell, *Tapestry in the Renaissance: Art and Magnificence* (New Haven, CT and London: Yale University Press, 2002).

usually knotted into place, and the space between one weft thread and another can be variously managed. The simplest and fastest approach is to leave a slit in the tapestry, which is then sewn up, juxtaposing the two areas of colour directly.[66] The process of weaving tapestry therefore has its own distinctive scopic implications, organising the perception of time, space and narrative. Philomela's temporality as she weaves is therefore radically different from the 'normal' time of a narrative that progresses from beginning to end; it is both an uneven, disorienting time (like Chaucer's hypometrical, stumbling text) and also regulated, governed by the demands of the material and the organised tension of threads on threads. For a woman in the aftermath of rape, this combination of discontinuous narrative processing and regulated use of time and material has therapeutic potential. The weaving process breaks down the story of violence and trauma into manageable sections, reducing its relentless narrative teleology to something that can be encountered piece by piece. Thus the violent assault on the boundaries of the female body, which we have seen is depicted as an epistemic as well as a somatic and sexual experience, is answered with a creative activity centred upon the drawing together of gaps and *lacunae* and the making of seams and boundaries.

We might say that weaving instils its own *habitus* for dealing with narrative: as one weaves, it becomes customary to segment a narrative into discontinuous sections, to move asynchronously through what will become a coherent message, to change perspectives as the tapestry lengthens and is rolled on the loom. This *habitus* may be understood in terms of what Ahmed says about orientation as a habitual movement along established paths of desire and action, towards what is proximate and familiar. The *habitus* of weaving is quite different from that of poetic text: the narrative lines and paths that desired and desiring bodies follow through poems are teleological, and in the case of the traditional Philomela myth, are set in motion by masculine lust, whose target is a feminine body. Yet weaving offers a maker of narratives a different set of lines, both in terms of what the weaver's body does with her materials and in terms of what the weaver's creative faculties do with her plot and her message. As if taking on a new sexual orientation, Philomela takes on a new set of narrative and bodily habits as she weaves, learning to tell her tale by moving her threads across her loom and within the empty space of the 'shed' between threads. The process vividly anticipates Freeman's reading of the textile and the skin as somehow exchangeable, or overlapping, symbols of feminine erotic pleasure, which contrast with heteronormative experiences of time and touch. As I noted in the introduction, she describes a 'lesbian erotohistoriography' wherein past and present come together 'as a tactile meeting,

---

[66] See Sarah W. Mallory, 'Designing and Defining Tapestries: The Three Stages of Tapestry Production', in *Grand Design: Pieter Coecke van Aelst and Renaissance Tapestry*, ed. Elizabeth Cleland (New York: Metropolitan Museum of Art and Yale University Press, 2014), pp. 110–21.

as a finger that in stitching, both touches and is touched, and that in reading, pokes and caresses the holes in the archival text even as it sutures them'.[67] Freeman's tactile imagery, though it refers to written text in her case, might prompt us to think of how Philomela's weaving differs not only symbolically but also materially from the process of inscription as imagined by the hermeneutic tradition with which Chaucer sceptically engages. In that tradition, the pen is a sharp point; it does not glide over the surface of parchment or paper, but penetrates it, allowing ink to seep into what was once skin. By contrast, Philomela's weaving hands move in spaces left ready for them, and while the strands of her weaving may cling together – may even become felted – the threads do not 'impregnate' each other in a liquid sense, but rub together, touch and entwine. In concentrating attention on weaving as a process rather than on the textile as a finished product, Chaucer raises the possibility of a rhetorical practice that stands as an alternative to the poetic tradition that denies a space for women to articulate desire and emotion. This alternative rhetorical practice is, in keeping with the wider tendency of the 'Legend of Philomela', evocative of practices elsewhere associated with female same-sex desire. As with so much of this text, it is ambivalent. It is further evidence that the articulation of female emotion produces the effects of deviancy no matter how inappropriate to the speaker's situation; it is further hope that female desire may find its own distinct hermeneutic praxis.

CONCLUSION

Truncated in its relation to the source tradition, spatially and temporally unstable in its juxtapositions, journeys and shifting geographies, the 'Legend of Philomela' persistently gestures towards a future – and a transformative reversal of fortunes – that never comes. Weaving with poor, reclaimed thread, in verse of halting and uneven metre, Philomela constructs a textile message that does not secure the revenge she traditionally acquires. Yet this seeming 'failure' of a poetic text is also a complex meditation upon the possibility of a feminine hermeneutic to stand against Jerome's paradigm of masculine inscription. Chaucer's sources render the tapestry Philomela weaves as an object of aesthetic and economic value, an idea that is disconcerting in its stark contrast with the mutilated state of her body. This tapestry is, as we have seen, increasingly closely integrated into the socio-economic networks through which women's work might be exploited. The parallel to the male-authored text that exploits a narrative of female suffering and constructs an object of literary value from that suffering is clear. Chaucer resists this network of connotations, though he does so in a way that is fraught with tensions. In representing Philomela's weaving as a crude process, resulting in a poor-quality piece of

---

[67] Freeman, *Time Binds*, p. 110.

fabric, he retains the visual imagery of degradation instead of replacing it with an object of beauty. In using the aesthetic of that weaving – an aesthetic of content shot through with slits or *lacunae*, of an image viewed in incomplete sections and out of order – he makes the entire *Legend of Good Women* reflect Philomela's voice, the only voice she can have in a textual tradition that represents female textual agency as a form of transgressive disruption. Through Philomela, Chaucer sets up the idea of a feminine hermeneutic that disrupts the rhythm of traditional narrative and poetics, which seeks to find its own modes of expression but which is constantly hampered by its stumbling, stammering asynchronicity, the manifestation of which is the clumsy appendage with which Philomela is equipped, the prosthetic phallus/pen/loom. This ambiguously genital object propels Philomela into multiple competing discourses of deviant female sexuality, which disturbingly replace her aversion and pain with implications of desire. The desire to be a closed, self-authoring female body is, Chaucer demonstrates, impossible to reconcile with the imagery of feminine desirousness, which equips the desiring subject with the (lesbian) phallus that insists upon the desire she denies. This ambivalent treatment of female emotion pervades the *Legend*, and will be an abiding theme of this book. As I explore Chaucer's innovative, provocative engagement with hermeneutic tradition, I encounter, again and again, his painful willingness to insert unwelcome or inappropriate images of female desire into the intimate spaces of narratives of 'goode women'.

2

THE TRAUMATISED NARRATIVE OF THE ALLITERATIVE *MORTE ARTHURE*

The violent silencing of female desire that lies at the heart of Chaucer's 'Legend of Philomela' also pervades the romance that is the subject of this chapter: the alliterative *Morte Arthure*.[1] I argue that, like the *Legend*, this romance presents two almost equally unappealing possibilities: the first, that female desire is simply irrelevant to a poetics founded on rape; the second, that any attempt to articulate or depict female desire must result in sodomitic disruptions to the poetic, narrative and linguistic structures of the text. Written around 1400, the alliterative *Morte* concentrates upon that most enduringly popular subject of romance: the Matter of Britain and the exploits of King Arthur.[2] Rooted in the chronicles of Geoffrey of Monmouth, Layamon and Wace, the poem is permeated by military and political concerns, European campaigns and set-piece jousts, treachery and usurpation and civil war.[3] Women rarely feature, and scenes of love or desire between men and women are entirely absent. Yet I argue that a brutal rape,

---

[1] All quotations are from *The Alliterative Morte Arthure* in *King Arthur's Death: The Middle English Stanzaic Morte Arthur and Alliterative Morte Arthure*, ed. Larry D. Benson and rev. Edward E. Forster (Kalamazoo, MI: Medieval Institute Publications, 1994).

[2] The definition and categorisation of romance as a genre has been endlessly (and not always productively) rehashed; like most romances, the *Morte* has come in for its fair share of debate. In the first, and so far only, monograph dedicated to the text, William Matthews defines it as a tragedy of fortune; it has been placed in the genres of epic and history as well as romance. See Matthews, *The Tragedy of Arthur: A Study of the Alliterative 'Morte Arthure'* (Berkeley, CA and Los Angeles, CA: University of California Press, 1960); Maureen Fries, 'The Poem in the Tradition of Arthurian Literature', in *The Alliterative Morte Arthure: A Reassessment of the Poem*, ed. Karl Heinz Göller (Cambridge: D. S. Brewer 1981), pp. 30–43; Mary Hamel, 'Adventure as Structure in the Alliterative "Morte Arthure"', *Arthurian Intentions* 3.1 (1988): 37–48; K. S. Whetter, 'Genre as Context in the Alliterative *Morte Arthure*', *Arthuriana* 22.2 (2010): 45–65; Dorsey Armstrong, 'The Alliterative *Morte Arthure* and Arthur's Sword of Peace', *Parergon* 25.1 (2008): 81–101.

[3] See Richard J. Moll, *Before Malory: Reading Arthur in Later Medieval England* (Toronto, Buffalo, NY and London: University of Toronto Press, 1996) and Fiona Tolhurst,

early in the text, holds the key to the poem's strangely repetitive structure and odd outbreaks of mingled innuendo and emotion. Drawing on work in trauma theory, I read the *Morte* as a 'traumatised narrative', a narrative whose structure responds to the 'forgotten wound' of the rape, which is repeatedly re-performed through scenes of jarring, comedic or parodic episodes of violence and intimacy between men.[4] As with the 'Legend of Philomela', this displaced representation of silenced female suffering brings coherence to seemingly dissonant, fragmented, repetitive and structurally disarticulated aspects of the poem.[5] The *Morte* thus exemplifies the dynamic we will find in other late medieval English romances. It makes space for the expression of female emotions within and through masculine bodies, yet in so doing, it constructs a hermeneutic wherein female emotion is legible only as it takes on the visible contours of sodomitic masculine desire.

EVERYWHERE AND NOWHERE: FORGETTING RAPE IN THE ALLITERATIVE MORTE ARTHURE

The alliterative *Morte Arthure* is one of several Middle English treatments of the narrative of the death of King Arthur, following the many Latin and French texts that told and retold the famous story. Written some time shortly

---

Geoffrey of Monmouth and the Feminist Origins of the Arthurian Legend (New York: Palgrave Macmillan, 2012).

[4] Cathy Caruth, *Unclaimed Experience: Trauma, Narrative and History* (Baltimore, MD: Johns Hopkins University Press, 1996), p. 5. Rape trauma has been a field of study for several decades. The term was coined by Ann Wolbert Burgess and Lynda Lytle Holmström in their foundational article. See Burgess and Holmström, 'Rape Trauma Syndrome', *American Journal of Psychiatry* 131.9 (1974): 981–86. Several scholars have applied trauma theory to accounts and narratives of medieval rape survival. See, for example, Carissa Harris, '"For Rage": Rape Survival, Women's Anger, and Sisterhood in Chaucer's *Legend of Philomela*', *Chaucer Review* 54.3 (2019): 253–69; Belle S. Tuten, 'Power and Trauma in the "Maid of Arras", *Cantigas de Santa María*', in *Trauma in Medieval Society*, eds Wendy J. Turner and Christina Lee (Leiden and Boston: Brill, 2018), pp. 105–21; and Wendy J. Turner, 'The Leper and the Prostitute: Forensic Examination of Rape in Medieval England', in *Trauma in Medieval Society*, eds Turner and Lee, pp. 122–50.

[5] In trauma theory the association between trauma and repetition or inarticulacy has long been formulated with reference to medieval literary examples, beginning (as Donna Trembinksi notes) with Freud's reading of Tasso's *Gerusalemme Liberata*. See Sigmund Freud, *Beyond the Pleasure Principle*, trans. James Strachey (London and New York: Norton, 1961), pp. 16–17; Jacques Lacan, *The Ego in Freud's Theory and in the Technique of Psychoanalysis* (*The Seminar of Jacques Lacan, Book II: 1954-1955*), ed. Jacques-Alain Miller, trans. Sylvana Tomaselli (New York: Norton, 1991); Caruth, *Unclaimed Experience*, pp. 1–10; Lauren Berlant, 'Trauma and Ineloquence', *Cultural Values* 5 (2001): 41–58; Blud, *The Unspeakable, Gender and Sexuality*, pp. 1–20; Donna Trembinski, 'Trauma as a Category of Analysis', in *Trauma in Medieval Society*, eds Turner and Lee, pp. 19–20.

before 1400, the text survives in an unique manuscript, copied in around 1440 and owned by the Yorkshire landowner Robert Thornton.[6] A few decades later, Malory adapted the alliterative verse almost wholesale into his prose *Morte*, ensuring its continued presence in English literary history.[7] Extending across more than four thousand lines, the poem translates a centuries-old legend of Arthurian nation-building into a deeply contemporary meditation on warfare at home and abroad. Steeped in images of realistic and bloody combat, it reflects the ongoing realities of the Wars of the Roses and the Hundred Years War, which provide important contexts for the unflinchingly gruesome images of women as collateral damage in warfare. The narrative is fast-paced, and resonant of realities contemporary with the poem's late medieval context, with its diplomatic exchanges and hostile encounters, and the strategic preparations of an army. Responding to insulting demands from the haughty Emperor of Rome, Arthur raises an army and crosses the Channel, preparing to wage war. Ultimately, the poem sees Arthur engaged in conflicts across Europe, defeating many enemies, before his own throne is usurped by his nephew and he dies in battle. One interlude, however, distracts from this plot. A giant rapes Arthur's kinswoman, the duchess of Brittany. Arthur defeats this fantastic foe in bloody single combat, stripping him of several macabre symbols of power before he returns to his sober military plans. The rape is never again explicitly mentioned; scholars rarely discuss the event in detail.[8] Salient details of the rape itself remain unarticulated, caught

---

[6] The poem has been dated to the late years of the fourteenth century, possibly as late as the turn of the century. See John Finlayson, 'Two Minor Sources for the Alliterative *Morte Arthure*', *Notes & Queries* 9.4 (1962): 132–33; Finlayson, '*Morte Arthure*: The Date and a Source for the Contemporary References', *Speculum* 42.4 (1967): 624–38; Larry D. Benson, 'The Date of the *Alliterative Morte Arthure*', in *Medieval Studies in Honor of Lillian Herlands Hornstein*, eds Jess B. Bessinger, Jr and Robert R. Raymo (New York: New York University Press, 1976), pp. 19–40; Mary Hamel, ed., *Morte Arthure: A Critical Edition* (New York and London: Garland, 1984), pp. 53–58; and P. J. C. Field, '*Morte Arthure*, the Montagus and Milan', *Medium Ævum* 78.1 (2009): 98–117. For its manuscript context, see the essays in *Robert Thornton and His Books: Essays on the Lincoln and London Thornton Manuscripts*, eds Susanna Fein and Michael Johnston (York: York Medieval Press, 2014), especially Ralph Hanna and Thorlac Turville-Petre, 'The Text of the Alliterative *Morte Arthure*: A Prolegomenon for a Future Edition', pp. 131–56, and John Finlayson, 'Reading Romances in their Manuscript: Lincoln Cathedral Manuscript 91 ("Thornton")', *Anglia* 123.4 (2006): 632–66.

[7] See Edward D. Kennedy, 'Malory and his English Sources', in *Aspects of Malory*, eds Toshiyuki Takamiya and Derek Brewer (Cambridge: D. S. Brewer, 1981), pp. 27–56; Terence McCarthy, 'Malory and His Sources', in *A Companion to Malory*, eds Elizabeth Archibald and A. S. G. Edwards (Cambridge: D. S. Brewer, 1996), pp. 75–95; Ralph Norris, *Malory's Library: The Sources of the* Morte Darthur (Cambridge: D. S. Brewer, 2008), pp. 53–69; Catherine Batt, *Malory's* Morte D'Arthur: *Remaking Arthurian Tradition* (New York and Basingstoke: Palgrave, 2002), pp. 72–78.

[8] There are exceptions: Fiona Tolhurst discusses the rape and its sources in her study of the poem and its source tradition; Geraldine Heng and Jeffrey Jerome Cohen both

within a wider pattern of silences and omissions that characterises the *Morte*'s treatment of its marginalised female characters. Yet I argue that these silences and omissions linger within the subtext of the *Morte*, prompting questions about the way in which the poem denies overt space to the expression of female desires and emotions.

The *Morte* introduces the rape as a temporal, poetic and narrative disruption, which breaks unexpectedly into the main structure of the text. An unexpected messenger arrives at Arthur's camp, bringing news that a giant is terrorising the nearby lands. The giant kills and eats children (lines 849–50); later we find that he also keeps enslaved women who prepare his meals and endure horrific sexual violation (lines 1029–32). He has captured the duchess of Brittany, and plans to rape her, too. This news interrupts the brisk military realism with a dream-like sequence of adventure into an 'improbable' legendary past of giants and myth.[9] The action of the text slows dramatically, suspending Arthur in time as he rides off after the giant. Sunk in images of pastoral stasis, Arthur rides along a tree-lined riverside, with 'frithes … flourisht with flowres full many' (line 925) and 'swowing of water and singing of birds' (line 932). As Anne Clark Bartlett observes, the passage is reminiscent of the courtly love tradition's *locus amoenus*, and might be read as a homoerotic element, a romantic passage coding Arthur's subsequent battle with the giant as quasi-sexual.[10] We might also see this lyric voice as evocative of the *pastourelle* genre, with its stock figures of ravished maidens.[11] These dissonantly desirous and ominously violent resonances culminate with the sound Arthur hears: 'of the nightingale notes the noises was sweet' (line 930). The songbird evokes the metamorphosis of Philomela, for whom the nightingale is almost a byword; as we have seen, Chaucer himself names a bird in order to conjure up the whole narrative of Procne, Tereus and Philomela in his *Troilus and Criseyde*.[12] With unpleasant irony, the nightingale allusion and *pastourelle* imagery evoke the

---

    discuss the representation of the giant as racially coded rapist. See Tolhurst, *Feminist Origins of Arthurian Legend*, p. 112; Heng, *Empire of Magic: Medieval Romance and the Politics of Cultural Fantasy* (New York: Columbia University Press, 2003), pp. 115–80; Cohen, *Of Giants: Sex, Monsters and the Middle Ages* (Minneapolis, MN: University of Minnesota Press, 1999), pp. 152–57.

[9] Marco Nievergelt, 'Conquest, Crusade and Pilgrimage: The Alliterative *Morte Arthure* in its Late Ricardian Crusading Context', *Arthuriana* 20.2 (2010): 89–116 (pp. 93–94).

[10] Anne Clark Bartlett, 'Cracking the Penile Code: Reading Gender and Conquest in the Alliterative "Morte Arthure"', *Arthuriana* 8.2 (1998): 56–76.

[11] See Carissa Harris, 'Rape Narratives, Courtly Critique, and the Pedagogy of Sexual Negotiation in the Middle English Pastourelle', *Journal of Medieval and Early Modern Studies* 46.2 (2016): 263–87.

[12] Chaucer evokes the tale with the lines quoted in the previous chapter: 'The swalowe Proigne, with a sorowful lay, / Whan morwen com, gan make hire waymentynge / Whi she forshapen was' (*T&C* II, lines 64–66). See L. O. Aranye Fradenburg, *Sacrifice Your Love: Psychoanalysis, Historicism, Chaucer* (Minneapolis, MN: University of Minnesota Press, 2002), pp. 218–28.

rape, which must be happening in the same chronological space as Arthur's journey to prevent it, transferring it into the present moment even as it occurs outside the present location. It is only in this allusive and dislocated form that the rape ever features within the chronological present of the *Morte*, for Arthur is doomed to arrive too late. The duchess dies without ever entering the narrative; her aged foster mother is left to recount the horrors of her suffering over her newly dug grave. The narrative trajectory bends away from her, as it does from the raped women slaves who attend the giant, leaving their final fate unmentioned. The interlude works to deny the raped women not only their rescue (which comes too late), but also their place within the narrative present. Violence is overlaid with imagery of romantic desire; the reality of the rape is segregated from the main trajectory of the narrative as if to relegate it to an unreal space of legend and the past.

The rape subplot is not, however, an unusual element within the *Morte* tradition, although the *Morte* poet does make radical innovations on his sources, transforming the way in which the rape is represented.[13] In the accounts of Geoffrey of Monmouth and Wace, Arthur arrives at the scene of the rape to find his kinswoman dead, and an old woman – her foster mother – grieving over her grave. Both accounts express a kind of narrative reluctance concerning the rape, which is reported second-hand by the old woman. In Geoffrey's version, the old woman explains that the giant intended to rape the duchess, but when he touched her, she died. The giant therefore raped the old woman in place of her charge. In Wace's version, too, the old woman is raped, but there is some ambiguity as to whether the younger has been raped, or abducted and not raped.[14] With squeamish delicacy, the poet implies that her death results from the imposition of the giant's body: 'He was too huge, too large, too ugly, too gross and too heavy. He made her soul leave her body.'[15] This description blends weighty physical detail with euphemism: the fact that it is the young woman's intangible soul that is juxtaposed with the giant's body suggests reluctance to name the act as rape. The verse ventriloquises the woman's emotion, suggesting a sympathetic linguistic reluctance to place

---

[13] This episode is discussed by John Finlayson, 'Arthur and the Giant of St Michael's Mount', *Medium Ævum* 33 (1964): 112–20, and Tolhurst, *Feminist Origins of Arthurian Legend*, p. 112.

[14] For this ambiguity, see Tolhurst, *Feminist Origins of the Arthurian Legend*, pp. 76–77. She notes that only the verb 'ravir' (to rape or to abduct) is used of the girl, while the old woman describes her own experience with the more explicit terms 'purgesir' (to have intercourse with) and 'desforcier' ('to have forced intercourse with').

[15] Trop fu ahueges, trop fu granz,
Trop laiz, trop gros e trop pesanz
L'aume li fist del cors partir.

I. D. O. Arnold and M. M. Pelan, La Partie arthurienne du Roman de Brut (Paris: Klincksiek, 1962), lines 11409–11. Translation by Tolhurst, Feminist Origins of the Arthurian Legend, p. 76.

her physical body against that of the giant. The ambiguities and omissions in the earlier versions of the narrative seek to distance the woman's body from (narrative) violation. As Heng puts it with reference to Geoffrey, the author 'chivalrously allows the aristocratic maiden to perish without sexual despoiling'.[16] A reluctance to imagine the rape of a young woman is thus a well-established facet of the narrative tradition. It is not (seemingly) one shared by the poet of the *Morte*, who provides a far more graphic, gruesome and explicit account. Again, the event is reported by the duchess's grieving foster mother, who explains

> 'Here the duchess dere – today was sho taken –
> Deep dolven and dede, diked in moldes.
> He had murthered this mild by mid-day were rungen,
> Withouten mercy on molde, I not what it ment;
> He has forced her and filed and sho is fey leved;
> He slew her unsely and slit her to the navel.
> And here have I baumed her and buried thereafter.'
> (lines 975–81)

The act of rape is in no way hidden or euphemised. The old woman says that the giant 'has forced ... and filed' (line 979) the duchess, and Arthur accuses the giant of the same act later ('this fair lady ... thou has fey leved/ And thus forced on folde', 1070–71). The explicitness is worth noting, for as Ruth Karras and Corinne Saunders note, romance is often squeamish about rape, either normalising it as a 'courtly' inevitability, depicting it as a threat rarely realised or hedging it about with 'mitigating' factors that obscure the boundaries of female consent.[17] The account of the *Morte* is startlingly explicit, startlingly unambiguous in its depiction of rape.

The graphic imagery of rape expands into the surrounding text. The giant forces his way into the narrative before time, as Arthur (prior to the event) dreams of a bloody single combat between two monsters, which foreshadows his own combat with the giant (lines 759–804). After the giant's death, he is reanimated in the memory by the repetition of the stock phrase referring to giants 'engendered with fendes' (line 2111) later in the poem. Both excessive detail and excessive vagueness attend the descriptions of his body, which involve a strange mixture of euphemism and innuendo. As Heng notes, the anatomical detail of his genitals is the subject of obtrusive ambiguity, with the tellingly euphemistic phrase, 'breekless him seemed' making the giant's naked lower body paradoxically obscure, and emphasised.[18] The suggestion of rape clings to his actions, even when not explicitly part of that act: his cannibalistic meals of men and animals, 'broched' (line 1050) or skewered together, gesture

---

[16] Heng, *Empire of Magic*, p. 44.
[17] Karras, *Sexuality in Medieval Europe*, p. 164; Saunders, *Rape and Ravishment*, p. 187.
[18] Heng, *Empire of Magic*, p. 123.

towards the sexual consumption of the duchess's similarly penetrated body, and the reference to this food as 'rewful bredes' (line 1049) puns on one of the *Morte* dialect's words for women, 'birdes' (line 1052), as if to underline the similarity. Indeed, the old woman makes the association clear, warning Arthur that the giant keeps

> Three balefull birdes his broches they turn,
> That bides his bedgatt, his bidding to work;
> Such four sholde be fey within four houres
> Ere his filth were filled that his flesh yernes.
> (lines 1029–32)

Turning spits ('broches') on which human flesh sizzles, these women are evidently to be forced to satisfy carnal lusts, and the knowledge of the duchess's fate colours the reference to the giant's 'bedgatt' (going to bed) with hints of sexual activity. Compounding the horror of the description of the duchess's rape, these lines likewise suggest that the excess of the giant's body ('his flesh') cannot be satisfied ('filled'), but consumes the female bodies it penetrates. In this microcosmic repetition of the duchess's rape, the author of the *Morte* insistently places the gruesome imagery before our eyes.

This pervasive imagery of rape may be understood as a repeated, fragmentary attempt to evoke the paradigmatic rape narrative of Philomela, to which the *Morte* first alludes through its reference to the nightingale song Arthur hears as he rides towards Mont St Michel. The female figures of the narrative combine to produce a ghostly reflection of Philomela, colouring the subplot of rape with a vivid reminder of the poetic significance of the silencing of women's emotions. The raped and mutilated duchess is, like Philomela, deprived of a voice with which to speak of her trauma; her story is ventriloquised, not through cloth but through the speech of her grieving foster mother. A textile imagery of violence augments this depiction of silenced and vicarious speech, evoking Philomela's weaving. Early in the poem, Arthur's allies determine to avenge the historic rapes perpetrated by Roman invaders, recalling how '[w]hen the Romans regned they … ravished our wives' (lines 293–94), and they seek to respond in symbolic kind, with quasi-sexual violence visited on the heraldic banner of Emperor Lucius: 'I shall aunter me ones his egle to touch / That borne is in his banner … and rive it in sonder' (lines 360–62). The verb 'touchen' has underlying sexual implications, while 'rive' carries connotations of violence and sexual conflict, and puns on the verb 'reven', meaning to rape or abduct women.[19] The textile motif, the eagle on the banner, stands as surrogate both for Lucius' own body, and for the bodies of raped women, for whom retributive justice is sought. This imbrication of rape and textile-making

---

[19] See *MED*, s.v, 'tŏuchen' (v. (6)); *MED*, s.v. 'rīven' (v.(2) (6)) and *MED*, s.v. 'rēven' (v. (2) (e)).

with heraldry recurs later, as the knight Cleges alludes to the story behind the symbol woven onto his heraldic banner, which may be traced back through Chrétien de Troyes and the *Roman d'Eneas* to Ovid's story of the weaving contest between Athena and Arachne, in which Arachne memorialised the rapes of mortal women by the gods.[20] Rape, whether remembered or avenged, becomes part of the heraldic machinery through which Arthur's men express their martial identities, and nowhere is this more true than in Arthur's own case. Defeating the giant of Mont St Michel, Arthur takes as a trophy of victory the giant's cloak, which we are told was

> spunnen in Spain with special birdes
> And sithen garnisht in Greece full graithely togeders ...
> And borderd with the berdes of burlich kings.
> (lines 999–1002)

This object is the textile work by women. The 'birdes' exploited in this work bear witness to the extension of the giant's rapacious consumption of human flesh through sexual and cannibalistic means to a scale of pan-European exploitation, calling to mind the long-standing association between sexual exploitation and the textile trade, which we saw in the previous chapter.[21] Like the women of the French Philomela narrative that we find in the *Ovide Moralisé*, who form a transnational workshop around the titular character and help her to produce a textile of value, the women who make the giant's cloak are anonymous, faceless presences whose story is obscure. The beard-cloak ties the anonymous duchess together with the legendary Philomela, and together with the generations of women, real and fictional, for whom textile-making is intimately linked with sexual violence. This refraction of the Philomela *topos* into three sets of female bodies is a virtual dissection of that single figure into multiple bodies, an act of textualised violence that recalls Chaucer's unpleasantly mimetic 'cutting' of his text in the 'Legend of Philomela'. Yet at the same

---

[20] Cleges (Cligès) enters the Arthurian court via Chrétien's poem of the same title; the poem also alludes to Chrétien's retelling of the Philomela myth from Book VI of the *Metamorphoses*, from which comes the tale of the weaving contest between Athena and Arachne. This Ovidian myth also features in the *Roman d'Eneas*, which describes the heraldic banner that Aeneas, Cleges' ancestor, hung from his lance in 'Brut time / At the citee of Troy' (lines 1695–96). See Chrétien de Troyes, *Cligès*, in *The Romances of Chrétien de Troyes*, ed. Joseph J. Duggan (New Haven, CT and London: Yale University Press, 2001); *Eneas: Roman du XIIe siècle*, ed. J. J. Salverda de Grave, 2 vols (Paris: Champion, 1964), lines 4527–35; and *Eneas: A Twelfth-Century French Romance*, ed. and trans. John A. Yunck (New York: Columbia University Press, 1974); *Mets* VI, lines 70–100. For discussion, see Christopher Baswell, *Virgil in Medieval England: Figuring the Aeneid from the Twelfth Century to Chaucer* (Cambridge: Cambridge University Press, 1995), pp. 181–83.

[21] For parallels to this imagery of enslaved women textile workers in Arthurian literature, see Burns, *Sea of Silk*, p. 61.

time, this process of absorbing images and reflections of rape narratives into the heraldic symbolism of the *Morte* enables – or requires – the men of the poem to wear and carry the rapes of the women who remain silent. As we will see, it is part of a wider imagery of men taking on the stories of raped women.

Despite this omnipresent imagery and language of rape, the *Morte* description manages to elide a considerable amount of detail and to contain a remarkable degree of incoherence in its actual description of the rape at Mont St Michel. In the old woman's speech, the vivid deictics ('here … here') locate the rape precisely in the present space, inescapably close. Yet the precipitous replacement of the recently living woman with a bare mound of earth performs the opposite temporal function, suggesting a deceptively large gap of time since the rape, a suggestion augmented by the mention of embalming, which implies preservation in time. The actual moment of death jumps about in the narrative, emerging in three different lines of a putatively chronological account, first 'dede', then 'murthured' and finally slain ('he slew her'). In the description of the unnamed, unstably numbered women whom the giant keeps captive, there is plenty of penetrative imagery of spitted meat and lustful flesh, but at the last minute the text takes refuge in ambiguity, allowing the possibility of reading the giant's consumption of the women as cannibalistic rather than sexual. In this confusion, it is easy almost to overlook a crucial point: the old woman's speech refuses to specify the weapon the giant used to kill his victim (rare in a poem that constantly mentions and names the swords, lances and spears its aggressors use). 'He slew her unslely and slit her to the navel', she says, and the image manages to be both graphic and vague. Was this an act of genital penetration, with death the consequence of the rape? Or was the duchess raped and, separately, stabbed up to the navel with an unspecified weapon? The passage does not spare readers' imagination with euphemism, yet the detail remains obscure.

The rape subplot of the *Morte* offers a puzzling anomaly of poetic structure, a confusing mixture of romantic imagery and gruesome horror, of graphic violence and strangely reluctant silence. The marked temporal dilation that introduces the episode sets the rape aside from the main narrative, as if to distance it from the rest of the poem; the old woman's puzzlingly ambiguous omission of crucial detail elides a key question about the dead duchess's experience. The poem seeks to forget the duchess, to bury her as quickly as possible, far away from the main action of the poem. Yet at the same time, the persistent allusions to the giant's rapacious appetite and his genital region, to the archetypal rape survivor Philomela and to the anonymous slave-women who await the same fate as the duchess, keep the idea of rape present within the narrative both before and after her death. Rape is thus both everywhere and nowhere, both omnipresent and unarticulated. Both the structure of this episode, with its temporal distortion, compression and distance from the main narrative, and the key omission at its centre, may be understood in terms of the operations of traumatised memory.²² In their work on trauma and memory, Martin Conway, Katrin Hohl and C. W. Pleydell Pearce have established that the reports of trauma survivors tend to be 'temporally compressed' and fragmented, with painful material suppressed.²³ Similarly, the omitted detail in the foster mother's account of the rape corresponds with what Linda Alcoff and Laura Grey observe in their work with contemporary rape survivors, that omissions and suppressions of memory 'may be functional for the survivor', enabling them to censor that which is too painful from their explicit narratives.²⁴ Nor are these uniquely post-medieval understandings of the effects of what we might call trauma on memory. As Donna Trembinksi notes, medieval medical texts discuss how such emotions might disrupt 'an individual's ability to create memory, [and] also ... to recall already formed memories'.²⁵ She describes how the manuscripts of the *Prose Salernitan Questions* locate this loss of memory within the semantic region: that is, the type of omission is likely to relate not to large-scale personal memories but to letters or words, such as the omitted detail of the penis in the foster mother's account.²⁶ As we will see, the idea of sexual violence remains permanently trapped beneath the subtext of the poem, persistently seeping out into the surrounding structures of the narrative. The rape of the duchess of Brittany will emerge not as an inconsequential interruption to the main plot of the *Morte*, nor as a jarringly dissonant deviation into the realms of myth and fantasy, but as a poetic attempt to replicate through narrative structure the traumatised memories of a survivor of rape.

---

22 The application of trauma theory to medieval culture is discussed by Wendy J. Turner and Christina Lee, 'Conceptualising Trauma for the Middle Ages', in *Trauma in Medieval Society*, eds Turner and Lee, pp. 3–12, and Trembinski, 'Trauma as a Category of Analysis', pp. 13–24. Trembinski, in particular, stresses the need to interpret apparent 'symptoms' of the post-medieval condition within their original medieval contexts (pp. 20–21).

23 Katrin Hohl and Martin A. Conway, 'Memory as Evidence: How Normal Features of Victim Memory Lead to the Attrition of Rape Complaints', *Criminology and Criminal Justice* 17.3 (2016): 248–65. For the term 'time-compressed' the authors cite Martin A. Conway and C. W. Pleydell Pearce, 'The Construction of Autobiographical Memories in the Self Memory System', *Psychological Review* 107 (2000): 261–88.

24 Linda Alcoff and Laura Grey, 'Survivor Discourse: Transgression or Recuperation?', *Signs* 18.2 (1993): 260–90 (p. 274).

25 Donna Trembinski, 'Comparing Premodern Melancholy/Mania and Modern Trauma: An Argument in Favour of Historical Experiences of Trauma', *History of Psychology* 14.1 (2011): 80–99 (p. 90). Mary Carruthers indicates that medieval authors were well aware of the association between strong emotion and memory, putting this to use in memory-training exercises. See Carruthers, *The Book of Memory: A Study of Memory in Medieval Culture*, 2nd edn (Cambridge: Cambridge University Press, 2008), pp. 168–71.

26 Trembinksi, 'Comparing Premodern Melancholy/Mania and Modern Trauma'.

SURROGATE BODIES, BORROWED EMOTIONS

To date, the rape of the duchess of Mont St Michel has not loomed large in scholarship of the poem, which is preoccupied with the inconsistencies of the poem's treatment of its masculine heroes. A recent editor of a journal issue dedicated to the *Morte* refers to the text as 'divided against itself' and 'fundamentally fragmented'; it displays a 'weird and macabre sense of humour' that sometimes becomes 'ridiculous'.[27] This fragmentation has, since Matthews first identified the poem as a tragedy, often been interpreted as part of a wider emphasis on the disintegration of chivalric masculinity that results in Arthur's downfall.[28] In 1981, Karl Heniz Göller extended the argument with the influential suggestion that this disintegration may be related to 'effeminate' displays of emotion between men, including outbursts of grief and affection during scenes of loss and death.[29] Unfortunately, as we will see, this tempting interpretative strategy raises some difficulties. The weeping, swooning and kissing that struck Göller in the 1980s as 'effeminate' might, more recent scholars demonstrate, be read as conventionally masculine in a medieval chivalric context; the interpretation of Arthur and his knights as degenerate failures is, as Fiona Tolhurst and K. S. Whetter argue, rooted in an anti-war stance that may be attributed more to the twentieth-century politics of its early scholars than to the late fourteenth century.[30] I argue that there *is* a coherency to the poem's repetitious scenes of grieving intimacy, but conclude that the poem is not anti-war but anti-rape. By recognising the structural significance of the rape episode for the later stages of the text, we can identify the representative strategy that underlies its seeming silence about women, as well as its seemingly incoherent content.

---

[27] Marco Nievergelt, 'Introduction: The Alliterative *Morte Arthure* in Context', *Arthuriana* 20.2 (2010): 3-4 (p. 3) and Nievergelt, 'Conquest, Crusade and Pilgrimage', p. 91; Karl Heinz Göller, 'Reality versus Romance: A Reassessment of the Alliterative *Morte Arthure*', in *The Alliterative* Morte Arthure: *A Reassessment of the Poem*, ed. Karl Heinz Göller (Cambridge: D. S. Brewer, 1981), pp. 15-29 (p. 25).

[28] See Matthews, *The Tragedy of Arthur*; Gillian Adler, '"ȝit þat traytour alls tite teris lete he fall": Arthur, Mordred, and Tragedy in the Alliterative *Morte Arthure*', *Arthuriana* 25.3 (2015): 3-21; Dana M. Oswald, *Monsters, Gender and Sexuality in Medieval English Literature* (Cambridge: D. S. Brewer, 2010), pp. 159-98; Heng, *Empire of Magic*, pp. 115-79; Cohen, *Of Giants: Sex, Monsters and the Middle Ages*, p. 157.

[29] Göller, 'Reality versus Romance', pp. 15-29.

[30] Fiona Tolhurst and K.S. Whetter, 'Memories of War: Retracting the Interpretative Tradition of the Alliterative *Morte Arthure*', *Arthuriana* 29.1 (2019): 88-108. They draw attention to the legal defence of Arthur's actions discussed by Elizabeth Porter, 'Chaucer's Knight, the Alliterative Morte Arthure, and Medieval Laws of War: A Reconsideration', *Nottingham Medieval Studies* 27 (1983): 56-78 and Juliet Vale, 'Law and Diplomacy in the Alliterative *Morte Arthure*', *Nottingham Medieval Studies* 23 (1979): 31-46.

If we accept Tolhurst and Whetter's argument that the *Morte* is not an anti-war poem, its anti-rape stance stands out more strongly. Such a stance would fit with mores contemporary with the date of its composition, in a way that simple denunciation of martial violence arguably does not. It has long been acknowledged that the *Morte* is deeply indebted to contemporary imagery of military organisation and statecraft. The text is loaded with descriptions of the day-to-day operations of a nation at war, mentions of safe conducts for diplomats, ransoms for captured men, discussions of the niceties of siege warfare and so on. The real-life conflict against which the *Morte* was written is that of the Hundred Years War, during which measures were taken to restrict the practice of rape as a weapon of warfare, from Richard II's military code of 1385 (perhaps a decade or two before the *Morte* was composed) to Henry V's code of 1419, both of which specifically prohibited rape.[31] By the 1440s, when Thornton's manuscript was being copied, these laws had brought about the convictions of rapists, and chronicles of the war record instances of rape in both England and France. This increasingly condemnatory attitude towards rape as a weapon of war perhaps reflects the peculiar intimacy of the Hundred Years War, during which hostilities were punctuated by long periods of English occupation and by marriages between English soldiers and French women.[32] In such a context, in which both sides lived in proximity to their own civilian casualties and the lingering effects of trauma might persist through decades of intermittent violence, it seems likely that combatants might have witnessed the effects of rape on women they knew and loved. Reports of Mordred's treachery and his men's lawlessness include descriptions of the rape of nuns (line 3539), while Arthur explicitly limits the violence of siege warfare by forbidding his knights to rape women (lines 3080–83). Rape is thus separated from other acts of violence within the poem, condemned in a way they are not.

This condemnation of rape is, of course, most evident in Arthur's treatment of the giant of Mont St Michel; this brutal battle is, also, the only portion of the rape subplot with which scholars discussing Arthur's supposedly degenerate masculinity regularly engage. It is undeniable that Arthur's first response on hearing that a giant intends to rape his kinswoman is to abandon his military plans and ride to her aid. The episode ends with a bloody battle, during which Arthur slashes off the giant's genitals and kills him. Celebrating with his knights after killing the giant, Arthur declares his desire for the giant's

---

[31] For discussion of rape as a weapon of war, see Tuba Inal, *Looting and Rape in Wartime: Law and Change in International Relations* (Philadelphia, PA: University of Pennsylvania Press, 2013), pp. 20–21; Nicola Henry, *War and Rape: Law, Memory and Justice* (London and New York: Routledge, 2011); Theodor Meron, *War Crimes Law Comes of Age: Essays* (Oxford: Oxford University Press, 1998), pp. 1–10.

[32] David Green, *The Hundred Years War: A People's History* (New Haven, CT: Yale University Press, 2014), pp. 202–3.

emblems of violence as his own spoils of victory: 'Have I the kirtle and the club, I covet nought elles' (line 1191). This gruesome conclusion and triumphant appropriation has grabbed much attention. Jeffrey Jerome Cohen argues that when Arthur takes the giant's phallic weapon, his club, he introduces an ethically uncomfortable parallel between conqueror and conquered, as 'regnal and monstrous bodies coincide ... [and] Arthur is implicated in the crimes the giant commits'.[33] Looking ahead in the text, Gillian Adler argues that the castration of the giant foreshadows Arthur's own more metaphorical emasculation, when he loses his wife and his kingdom to his nephew Mordred. Adler concludes that the 'hyper-masculinity' of violent warfare, which Arthur sees as 'fostering solidarity' between men, ends in sterility.[34] Yet Arthur's response to the giant is one sanctioned in English law contemporary with the poem. His attacks on the giant are explicitly focused on the genital region, concluding with a blow that 'Even into the in-mete the giaunt he hittes / Just to the genitals and jagged them in sonder!' (lines 1122–23). Castration is the punishment set out in Bracton's treatise for those who rape virgins.[35] More significantly, the fatal wound Arthur delivers mirrors that inflicted by the giant on his victim. Where she was split to the navel, the giant is reciprocally slashed from the 'in-mete', or intestines, to the genitals. As this reciprocal violence is visited upon the giant, his genitals – omitted from the foster mother's account of the rape – are suddenly brought into explicit focus, but also, his male body becomes a surrogate for her precipitously buried corpse. It is this surrogacy of experience that resonates through the *Morte* as a whole.

This encounter between Arthur and the giant provides an unrecognised organising paradigm for the subsequent interactions between men, which repeat so strangely through the poem and which scholars have found so disconcerting in their emotional intensity. The poem establishes a strong somatic vocabulary of masculine affection, whose intensity is visibly expressed. So, meeting an ally, Arthur 'caught him in armes ... and kissed him full soon' (lines 3515–16); as joy turns to grief, men come to each other 'weepand' (line 2679) over each other's wounds. Arthur 'writhes and weeped with his eyen' (line 1920) at the loss of named knights; Gawain 'gretes' (line 2962) as his comrade falls 'swoonand ... on the swarth' (line 2960). Even in death, affection is expressed in highly physical terms, as Sir Cador, seeing his

---

[33] Cohen, *Of Giants: Sex, Monsters and the Middle Ages*, p. 154; see also Thomas H. Crofts, 'Perverse and Contrary Deeds: The Giant of Mont Saint Michel and the Alliterative *Morte Arthure*', in *The Erotic in the Literature of Medieval Britain*, eds Andrea Hopkins and Cory Rushton (Cambridge: D. S. Brewer, 2007), pp. 116–31 (pp. 120–28).

[34] Adler, 'Arthur, Mordred, and Tragedy', p. 7.

[35] *Bracton de legibus et consuetudinibus Angliae: Bracton on the Laws and Customs of England*, ed. George E. Woodbine, trans. Samuel E. Thorne, 4 vols (Cambridge, MA: The Belknap Press of Harvard University, 1968–77), vol. 2, pp. 414–15. See Saunders, *Rape and Ravishment*, pp. 53–54.

kinsman Sir Berille dead, '[u]mbeclappes the corse, and kisses him oft' (line 1779). This physical intimacy culminates in a display that forms the crux of most scholars' discussions of the supposed 'effeminacy' of the Arthurian court: the mourning of Arthur over the body of Gawain. The king engages in an extended performance of intimacy and grief, as he

> Kneeles down to the corse and caught it in armes,
> Castes up his umbrere and kisses him soon,
> Lookes on his eye-liddes that locked were fair,
> His lippes like to the lede and his lire fallowed.
> (lines 3951–54)

He refers to Gawain in intimate terms: 'My counsel, my comfort, that keeped mine herte!' (line 3960). The narrator continues: 'Then sweltes the sweet king and in swoon falles, / Swafres up swiftly and sweetly him kisses' (lines 3969–70). Ultimately, Arthur's knights seek to bring an end to the performance, stressing its futility: '[i]t is no worship, iwis, to wring thine handes; / To weep als a woman it is no wit holden!' (lines 3977–78). Much emphasis has been placed upon this final simile, as several scholars conclude that acting 'als a woman' is the strongest form of censure that might be directed at a king, and a clear sign of Arthur's degeneracy. Bartlett and Jeff Westover interpret these gestures and displays of emotion as transgressively 'feminine'. For Westover, Arthur's submissive posture of mourning 'violates the normative economy of gender of his culture', while for Bartlett, it provides the ultimate example of the way in which the *Morte* 'links the feminine with defeat and submission'.[36] Heng argues directly that the intimacies between men can be read in a homoerotic light, basing her interpretation on the fact that '[t]ears shed by men, in this romance, are shed over other men; kisses bestowed by men are bestowed on the bodies of their dead comrades'.[37] Yet it is difficult to support these claims about male-on-male kisses, tears and fainting in the context of medieval romance and culture more widely. Scholars of the *Morte* tend to place extremely strong emphasis on the condemnatory potential of the phrase 'als a woman', applied to Arthur's grief, but it is unclear that the single line can carry such definitive weight.[38] Judith Weiss demonstrates that fainting or swooning are actions that achieved their hyper-feminised connotations

---

[36] Jeff Westover, 'Arthur's End: The King's Emasculation in the Alliterative "Morte Arthure"', *Chaucer Review* 32.3 (1998): 310–24 (p. 318); Bartlett, 'Cracking the Penile Code', p. 74.

[37] Heng, *Empire of Magic*, p 174.

[38] There is one exception: in her discussion of the *Morte*, Anne Baden-Daintree somewhat reluctantly acknowledges that Arthur's actions here are not necessarily to be read as feminine. See Anne Baden-Daintree, 'Kingship and the Intimacy of Grief in the Alliterative *Morte Arthure*', in *Emotions in Medieval Arthurian Literature: Body, Mind, Voice*, eds Frank Brandsma, Carolyne Larrington and Corinne J. Saunders (Cambridge: D. S. Brewer, 2015), pp. 87–104 (p. 94).

well after the medieval period: plenty of chivalric knights faint in medieval romances.[39] The point is taken up by Stephanie Trigg, who points out that both tears and fainting have a diverse range of signification in medieval literature and culture, citing the *Chanson de Roland*, where knights weep and faint in their thousands.[40] Finally, a manuscript made at the same time as the *Morte*'s composition immortalises an infamously suspicious image of a kiss between kings Edward III and Philippe VI, which serves to demonstrate the gesture's currency as a diplomatic gesture akin to a handshake.[41] The somatic and gestural vocabulary of Arthur and his knights is therefore suggestive, not of flagrant sodomitical desire or even mild homoeroticism, but of normative chivalric grief.

However, there remains something awkward about this scene. In its repetitiousness, and its repetitive similarity to other acts of grief, love and mourning, the display of emotion takes on a ritualistic aspect, draining it of spontaneity. Following on from other descriptions of men falling, 'swooning' to the ground, of other dead knights kissed and embraced, Arthur's grief seems programmatic, and we see that as men fall in battle, their dead bodies fall into identical affective postures: supine, kissed, embraced. Mary Michelle Poellinger contextualises this with comparison to the religious language of the piercing and penetration of the body of Christ, which is simultaneously an act of violence and a central focus of affective, even eroticised, meditation.[42] Christine Chism identifies a historical parallel: an incident at the Ricardian court, a reinterment ceremony for Richard's dear friend, during which the king gazed at and affectionately touched the three-years-dead corpse.[43] Though none of the corpses of the *Morte* is in a state of advanced decay, that historical event (and Richard's reputation for inappropriate attachments to

[39] Judith Weiss, 'Modern and Medieval Views on Swooning: The Literary and Medical Contexts of Fainting in Romance', in *Medieval Romance, Medieval Contexts*, eds Rhiannon Purdie and Michael Cichon (Cambridge: D. S. Brewer, 2011), pp. 121–34.

[40] See Stephanie Trigg, 'Weeping Like a Beaten Child: Figurative Language and the Emotions in Chaucer and Malory', in *Medieval Affect, Feeling and Emotion*, eds Glenn D. Burger and Holly A. Crocker (Cambridge: Cambridge University Press, 2019), pp. 25–46 (p. 35). Trigg cites the *Morte* as an example of the condemnation of tears as feminine, but – frustratingly – does not justify the comment except by reference to the single episode of Arthur's weeping (p. 40).

[41] The image is found in London, British Library MS Royal 20 C VII, f. 72v, a manuscript of the *Chroniques de France* dated to the last quarter of the fourteenth century. For discussion of it, see Ardis Butterfield, *The Familiar Enemy: Chaucer, Language and Nation in the Hundred Years War* (Oxford: Oxford University Press, 2009), p. xix; see also Carolyn Dinshaw, 'A Kiss is Just a Kiss: Heterosexuality and its Consolations in *Sir Gawain and the Green Knight*', *Diacritics* 24 (1994): 205–26 (p. 210).

[42] Mary Michele Poellinger, '"The rosselde spere to his herte rynnes": Religious Violence in the Alliterative *Morte Arthure* and the Lincoln Thornton Manuscript', in *Robert Thornton and His Books*, eds Fein and Johnston, pp. 157–76.

[43] Chism, 'Friendly Fire', pp. 68–69.

his male companions) might contextualise the ritualistic overtones of the *Morte*'s scenes of mourning.[44] In both the Ricardian ritual and the text, there is a disturbing tension between the intimacy of the embodied activity and the unresponding limbs and lips it involves, which codes the emotion as transgressive and misplaced. The sense of transgressiveness identified by the proponents of the Göller tradition of scholarship may be located not in the 'effeminacy' of kissing, weeping and swooning as individual acts, but in this layered effect of temporal disruption, as emotions are visited and revisited on bodies no longer able to respond.

In its temporally disruptive role, Arthur's grief recalls that other act of temporally disruptive weeping 'als a woman'. As we saw, when the duchess's foster mother weeps over her dead charge, she does not weep over a body but a grave. The text represents the burial as having taken place with precipitous and unnatural haste, such that the body has been 'baumed ... and buried' (line 981) in the matter of hours it seems to have taken Arthur to arrive on scene. Contrasting with this unnatural haste is the dilation of Arthur's mourning, which has the opposite effect of temporal disruption on the text. Anne Baden-Daintree argues that the king's mourning 'places court life in stasis': its immoderate duration and intensity freezes the narrative.[45] We might, then, see the knights' rebuke to Arthur to cease weeping 'als a woman' as relating to the virtue of moderation, often held to be key to masculinity and essential to the distinction of 'the ... man from the woman'.[46] In bringing the action to a halt, Arthur offends against social codes not through the specifics of his gestures or the intimacy of his bodily contact with another male body, but through the temporal inappropriateness of his mourning. Elizabeth Freeman has argued that the regulation of time is what 'binds ... naked flesh ... into socially meaningful embodiment': it is what 'organise[s] individual human bodies toward maximum productivity'.[47] As she points out, this regulation of time is closely related to the social structures that code certain bodily actions and interaction as 'natural' and others as 'unnatural', including of course those actions and interactions relating to gender and sexuality.[48] The protracted mourning of Arthur over Gawain flies in the face of this 'productive' use of time to affirm social bonds, placing it outside the sphere of normative gendered relations that express themselves through the regulation of time or – in medieval terms – through the moderation proper to masculinity. Like Richard II's unnaturally protracted mourning over a body long since dead, Arthur's grief flouts convention. It is 'womanish' not because swoons or

---

[44] See Sylvia Federico, 'Queer Times: Richard II in the Poems and Chronicles of Late Fourteenth-Century England', *Medium Ævum* 79.1 (2010): 25–46.
[45] Baden-Daintree, 'Kingship and the Intimacy of Grief', p. 99.
[46] Karras, *From Boys to Men*, p. 108.
[47] Freeman, *Time Binds*, p. 3.
[48] Ibid.

embraces are homoerotic gestures, but because the immoderate indulgence is associated with a feminine lack of control; it is 'unnatural' not because kisses carry sodomitic implication, but because its extended duration sets Arthur's grief outside the temporal regulations of which reproductive sexuality is a crucial constituent part. Finally, it is an act of mourning that harks back to the past, and thus – like Richard II's macabre disinterment of his lost friend – it inverts the 'natural' progress from life to death to the rituals of burial and to interment. As the poem re-performs its surrogate scene of mourning for the duchess, it drags the memory of her embalmed body from its grave again and again. The initial temporal distortion that sees the duchess precipitously enclosed in her grave and in the generic pastness of myth weighs on the later narrative, making itself felt in interruptions of ever more protracted displays of emotion, until the forward progress of Arthur's army falters, overwhelmed by grief. Female emotions thus haunt the structure and imagery of the *Morte*, radiating outwards from the episode of rape.

PENILE PUNS AND PERSONIFIED PHALLUSES: THE RE-MEMBERING OF RAPE

In its insistent, disruptive repetitions, the *Morte* represents the violent negation of female agency as having an equally violent, damaging effect on language and poetic structure. Yet paradoxically this trauma also gives the text a coherence, imbuing its fractured, macabre and repetitious content with significance. The initial trauma-induced *lacuna* in the account of the rape returns to give coherence to subsequent patterns of disruptively jarring innuendo. In a poem dedicated to charting the tragic story of the death of a famous hero, an emphasis on male genitalia constitutes a tantalisingly provocative seam of punning, and scholars have been quick to draw attention to it. Göller coyly refers to a 'little idiosyncrasy of the poet's, a preoccupation with the penetrative effects of weapons thrust "below the belt"'.[49] In his 1981 article, he identifies several penile innuendos, which, he implies, only confirm this impression of masculine degeneracy. Since then, scholars have gleefully expanded on this interpretation, finding ever-increasing examples of penile innuendo and identifying more and more episodes of hyper- or hypo-masculinity within the Arthurian court.[50] Putting things more bluntly, Bartlett argues that there is a 'penile code' governing the 'sexual logic' of emasculating combat between armies, while Westover coins the term 'genital ethos' to characterise the innuendo permeating the poem.[51] All three scholars

---

[49] Göller, 'Reality versus Romance', pp. 23–24.
[50] For puns, see Bartlett, 'Cracking the Penile Code', pp. 56–76; Westover, 'Arthur's End', p. 318; John William Sutton, 'Mordred's End: A Reevaluation of Mordred's Death Scene in the Alliterative *Morte Arthure*', *Chaucer Review* 37.3 (2003): 280–85.
[51] Bartlett, 'Cracking the Penile Code', p. 56; 'Westover', 'Arthur's End', p. 310.

delve into the poet's language with gusto, uncovering a host of genitally related puns. These puns have, from Göller's work onwards, been understood as part of that atmosphere of 'effeminacy' that has been read into the narrative of the *Morte*. However, taken as they stand, they carry a rather different subtextual force, and their undeniably sodomitic implications may be understood in a different light.

The effect of the penile imagery in the *Morte* derives not only from its content, but also from its accumulation, from simple puns into a rich network of innuendo. Westover describes how, when Lancelot attacks the Roman Emperor Lucius, he stabs him in the belly such that his pennon sticks into the flesh in a manner evocative of phallic penetration: 'Through paunce and plates he perced the mailes / That the proud pensel in his paunch lenges!' (lines 2075–76). The Welsh king kills his adversary:

> With a cruel launce coupes full even
> Aboven the spayre a span, among the short ribbes,
> That the splent and the spleen on the spere lenges!
> (lines 2059–61)

Westover notes that 'spayre' is glossed by Hamel in her edition as 'breeches opening', and is a striking and unusual place from which to measure, suggestive, he argues, of genital preoccupations.[52] Kay's death, too, follows this pattern:

> ... the traitour him hit
> In through the felettes and in the flank after
> That the bustous launce the bewelles entamed,
> That braste at the brawling and broke in the middes.
> (lines 2173–76)

The lance penetrates first his 'felettes' – loins – and then his belly. Similar examples proliferate. Bartlett points out that Gawain's blow to his enemy Priamus' side exposes the liver, 'the origin of sexual passion according to much medieval lore'; Sutton suggests – somewhat controversially – that the 'fente' through which Arthur stabs Mordred is to be understood as the cover protecting his backside, such that the king kills his nephew by driving his sword into his anus.[53]

More examples can be found. The preoccupation with male genitals and penetration permeates the puns and the errors of the text, which spread from the *Morte* itself to Malory's later reworking. Firstly, the word 'pensell', used to

---

[52] Westover, 'Arthur's End', p. 311.
[53] Bartlett, 'Cracking the Penile Code', p. 69; Sutton, 'Mordred's End', p. 280. Tolhurst and Whetter dispute Sutton's interpretation of 'fente' as the cover of the backside (and thus, its sodomitic implication here), in 'Memories of War', p. 99.

describe the pennon Lancelot rams into his enemy's guts, is a pun on 'pentel', or penis.[54] In some scribal hands and dialects (though not those of the scribe who copied the *Morte*), the two words would be orthographically identical, with 'pentel' ('penis') confused with 'pencel' (pennon).[55] Even more overt is the pun found at line 2112, where the *Morte* refers to one 'Sir Ienitall'. This is presumably an error for 'Jonathal', the name which appears in the earlier source texts.[56] However, its phallic sense is intensified by the verb used to describe eponymous knight's action: meeting with a giant, they 'joinen', which carries a sense not only of battle meeting, but also of sexual consummation.[57] There is a revealingly strange echo of this in the Winchester manuscript of Malory's *Morte Darthur*, which is based on the alliterative *Morte*. In Malory's description of Arthur's battle and of the castrating stroke he deals to the giant, the word 'genytrottys' ('genitals') is rubricated.[58] In being rubricated, the word has been treated in the same way as all proper names of the Winchester manuscript, and thus 'genytrottys' is transmuted from ordinary male anatomy to personification. In this section, Malory works quite directly from the earlier alliterative *Morte*, yet this is no ordinary replication of a copying error. It is conceptually, not mechanically, identical to that slip which saw 'Jonathal' replaced with 'Ienitall'. Thus, it replicates the pattern of submerged genital innuendo threatening to break through into the main text and take on a disproportionately human role and agency. Like the grotesquely corporeal giant, these startling innuendos force their way into the text before and after time, threatening to disrupt the structure of the poem, jarring against the elegiac episodes of grief and loss they penetrate.

Remarkably, and rather disconcertingly, the actual rape of the duchess of Mont St Michel (as opposed to the battle fought after her death) features very little in these analyses of genital imagery. None of the authors writing on the penile imagery of the *Morte* make the link between the rape narrative's euphemistic refusal to name the giant rapist's penis and the disconcerting profusion of rape-like penetrations throughout the remainder of the narrative. Westover's entire article on the 'genital ethos' of the poem makes no mention whatsoever of the event, although it mentions the subsequent fight with the giant, and the woman who tells Arthur about the raped woman. Bartlett's omission is less complete, but she spends barely a paragraph on what she refers to as

---

[54] See headwords pintel, n. and pencel, n. in *MED*.

[55] In Thornton's hand, 't' and 'c' are not easily confused. In the Winchester Malory, which uses the *Morte* as a source, the word is typically spelt with a medial 's', the standard secretary long s, which is not identical with secretary 't', having a marked curved ascender and no cross-bar. However, it is not impossible that lost versions of the text would have supported visual confusion.

[56] Benson and Forster, eds, *Morte*, note to line 2112.

[57] *MED*, s.v. joinen. (6).

[58] London, British Library, MS Additional 59678, f. 77v, line 27.

'attempted rape'.⁵⁹ This misreading may have arisen from Matthews' earlier (and more egregious) misreading of the episode, during which he concludes that the duchess was freed, rather than raped and killed.⁶⁰ This lack of interest in the female target of the rape may be seen as part of a wider scholarly preference to imagine scenes devoid of female characters. Bartlett, Westover and Sutton expand on Göller's identification of the *Morte*'s penile puns to envisage a subtext of sexual deviancy, even of sodomy, whose sterile implications ensure the tragic downfall of Arthur's court. In this context, the rape and its giant perpetrator are overshadowed, subsumed into a wider image of emasculation, and we might see the raped duchess as merely collateral damage in a larger conflict over masculine deviant desires and practices. Yet there is an alternative possibility. As Heng has noted, innuendos relating to sodomy are used in other romances (her example is *Richard Coeur de Lion*) in order that the overt 'medium of the joke' may allow for the 'selective, disguised remembering' of larger, unspeakable anxieties and taboos.⁶¹ A similar dynamic of concealment and submerged revelation lies behind Schibanoff's theory of the 'queer decoy', a trope she finds in Chaucer's works, wherein the overtly deviant presentation of one figure draws attention away from other aberrant goings-on.⁶² These arguments illuminate the use of penile imagery of the *Morte*, which might be understood both as a form of 'disguised remembering' of the hidden trauma of sexual violence and as a decoy, directing attention away from that painful episode and towards the comedically violent parodies of it. As the rape is repeatedly played out in surrogate and parodic ways on the bodies of men, the omitted detail of the giant's penis, which the old woman could not bring herself to mention, seems to plunge over and over into the wrong violated bodies.

These repetitions operate not in terms of surface meaning, but at the submerged, subtextual level, the level most easily associated with that which is unconscious, repressed and half-hidden. We may identify them with the 'forgotten wound' Caruth analyses in her influential work on trauma, which 'stubbornly persist[s] in bearing witness' to what has been left unspoken.⁶³ The *Morte* bears witness to the centrality of this wounding and witnessing, even in its own making. The verb typically used of speech, including the writing of the text itself, is 'werpan', which also means 'woven', in the commonplace metaphor from *textere*: a text is a woven object, like cloth on a loom.⁶⁴ The

---

⁵⁹ Bartlett, 'Cracking the Penile Code', pp. 65–66.
⁶⁰ See Matthews, *The Tragedy of Arthur*, p. 185. George Keiser discusses the misreading in 'Edward III and the Alliterative *Morte Arthure*', *Speculum* 48.1 (1973): 37–51 (pp. 42–43).
⁶¹ Heng, *Empire of Magic*, p. 96.
⁶² Schibanoff, *Chaucer's Queer Poetics*, p. 28.
⁶³ Caruth, *Unclaimed Experience*, p. 5.
⁶⁴ *MED*, s.v. 'werpen', v. (6, a), (9, b).

same word used to describe speech – 'warp' – is used of the warp threads of cloth that structure a piece of weaving. The narrator begins with a prayer to God to 'wisse me to warp out some word at this time' (line 9); Arthur uses the same verb: 'To warp wordes in waste no worship it were' at line 150. But the word is, of course, also a contranym, meaning also to distort, or warp.[65] The wounds of the duchess thus make themselves felt in the very fabric of the poem. As Caruth observes, trauma instigates a process of repetition and recurrence, as trauma survivors return to the emotions and experiences they have been unable to process, recognise or articulate.[66] Or, as Trembinksi puts it, the mind of the survivor 'revisits the traumatic event over and over again, in dreams, flashbacks and hallucinations, but that traumatic moment, though often relived, cannot be adequately expressed in language'.[67] Like flashbacks, memories of rape fragment the structure of the text, arising uncontrollably and unpredictably to interrupt seemingly unrelated events, dragging the memory of rape endlessly back into the narrative present. The disruptive force of that episode and its trauma-induced *lacunae* act on the wider structure of the *Morte*, seeping into language and imagery to take up far more space than the literal account itself. Moments of heightened emotion, grief and mourning are experienced not singly, but over and over again; the omitted detail of penile penetration repeatedly interrupts the poem. As the *Morte* brings the omitted detail of the rape back into the subtext over and over, repetition dulls horrific violence into grotesque comedy, and a particular female experience of rape into a generalised impression of violence between men. Rape is robbed of its specificity, constructed as an experience always understood by analogy to other rapes, requiring a communal voice and a multiplicity of evidence, with no single centre.[68] Scholarly responses to the *Morte* betray the fact that most readers would much rather spend time with risqué penile innuendos than with the rape subplot. As Alcoff and Grey point out, even as rape survivors find powerful ways to express their emotions and give voice to their traumas, these same means of expression can 'unwittingly [enable] the recuperation of dominant discourses'.[69] In this case, the surrogate structure of the text both offers representative potential, repeatedly making trauma visible, and also circumscribes that potential, implying that such trauma is *only* properly visible when enacted on male (not female) bodies. Male bodies thus retain their status as the bodies that matter, the bodies that have a place within the dominant discourse. The *Morte* thus expresses a dilemma: can female emotion (let alone female desire) be recuperated from a hermeneutic centred on rape and silencing of women in order for men to speak? Are the men of

---

[65] Ibid., (10, a).
[66] See Caruth, *Unclaimed Experience*, pp. 5–12.
[67] Trembinski, 'Comparing Premodern Melancholy/Mania and Modern Trauma', p. 83.
[68] Edwards, *The Afterlives of Rape*, pp. 2–3.
[69] Alcoff and Grey, 'Survivor Discourse', p. 263.

the *Morte* surrogate voices for the silenced duchess, or do they appropriate her emotion? Is her body fragmented by its ghostly reduplication across other bodies, desecrated by its repeated reanimation, or might we see the poem as a prosthetic structure that 'uncannily extend[s] the boundaries of her embodiment' to render her pain legible after her death?[70]

CONCLUSION

The notoriously fragmented, uneven poetic texture of the *Morte* may be understood not as a reflection of chivalric masculinity disintegrating into homoerotic or sodomitic decay, but as a reflection of the paradigmatically disruptive episode of the rape at Mont St Michel. But to whose benefit is this imposition of coherence on a fragmented structure? In his 'Legend of Philomela', Chaucer envisions a living rape survivor whose mode of response to her experience offers at least some recuperative potential. The author of the *Morte* excludes the possibility. The duchess is always already, and only, a memory within the text. She has no autonomous existence; her story can only be expressed vicariously, and thus the violence of her experience is performed on surrogate bodies and lends itself perilously easily to a slippage from horror to humour as it becomes caught up in the relentless slapstick humour of the penile puns. All that is left to bear witness to female emotion is this sense of *lacunae* and omission, of obscure affective weight dragging backwards on the poem, of something unexpressed. From its opening lines, the poem is both woven and warped, both structured and distorted. This mode of expression – a mode of expression defined by *lacunae* and disjunction – is, as Freeman and Ahmed, Farina and Kłosowska have argued – intrinsic to those female desires that seek to orientate themselves away from masculinity, and which become illegible and inarticulate within the expected structures of language.[71] Yet the poem *is* marked by these things, by the sense of something aslant, out of joint, even 'queer'. Though scholars may seek to reduce the discomfort of the poem to an imagery of degenerate masculinity or sodomitic comedy, it stubbornly resists this simplification of its content. In its insistent reference to the 'wound' that negated female emotion causes within language, the *Morte* sets the stage for a hermeneutic intervention that would find a way to express autonomous female desires.

---

[70] Shildrick, 'Border Crossings', p. 141.
[71] Freeman, *Time Binds*, pp. 103–10; Ahmed, *Queer Phenomenology*, pp. 19–20; Farina, 'Lesbian History and Erotic Reading', pp. 49–60; Kłosowska, *Queer Love in the Middle Ages*, pp. 69–116.

3

'AS MATTER APPETITETH FORM':
DESIRE AND RECIPROCATION IN THE
'LEGEND OF HIPSIPHYLE AND MEDEA'

The 'Legend of Hipsiphyle and Medea' continues Chaucer's exploration of the deformations of language that arise from the attempt to articulate female desire. The tale forms part of a sequence of stories about *relictae*, women abandoned in love, whose paradigmatic example is the Carthaginian queen Dido, subject of Chaucer's third legend. Interpreted as an *exemplum* of hermeneutic practice, her story posits an intimate relationship between reading and desire, which informs the 'Legend of Hipsiphyle and Medea'. Defined by her retrograde position in the text, the *relicta* exerts a pull away from the narrative, geographic and hermeneutic trajectories followed by men. She opens up a space for fluctuating desire, for the back-and-forth of translation, for the seductive pull of texts against teleological history. Many writers, from Virgil onwards, toy with the idea of representing their heroes as deviating briefly from heroic masculinity, or even displaying qualities of what we might call male femininity.[1] Chaucer, however, raises questions about the women's desires, and the ways in which those desires mobilise or unfix, reflect or reveal, the gendered orientation of their bodies. He presents the antagonist of the 'Legend of Hipsiphyle and Medea', the faithless Jason, as a 'queering device', whose studied performance of male femininity exposes the latent deviancies of the women he encounters.[2] Drawing together work by Dinshaw, Freeman and Hsy, I argue that the 'Legend of Hipsiphyle and Medea' shows how the reciprocality of emotion the women seek is fractured into asynchronous,

---

[1] The fact that the term 'male femininity' has not become common currency, unlike its equivalent 'female masculinity', points to an interesting area of omission within the scholarship.
[2] I use this term in relation to Ahmed's coinage of 'straightening devices', which refers to those conceptual and material structures that obscure all of that which does not conform to the 'straight' orientation. A 'queering device' must then reverse the process, drawing into prominence that which has propensity to deviate. See Ahmed, *Queer Phenomenology*, pp. 72, 91–92.

displaced and unsuccessful attempts to script a new language of desire.³ As Jason cynically constructs himself as a desirably feminine copy of Aeneas, Hipsiphyle and Medea fail to perceive the duplicitous mobility of his gendered performances. Their desires are thus imbricated with misreadings and failures of citation; their linguistic lack (of Latin) is analogised to the phallic absence that renders female masculinity impotent and inconclusive.

THE *RELICTA* PARADIGM IN THE *LEGEND*

The *relicta* trope in Classical legend is embedded in tales of men flung from shore to shore, propelled by tides, shipwrecked and washed up, driven here and there by storms. Surrounded by and even submerged in the watery element that medieval philosophers and medics associate with the humoral composition of the female body, at the mercy of lunar tides, these men are temporarily unmoored from masculinity. Sea journeys figure the transitional state between immaturity and virile masculinity. Within these journeys, desire threatens to distract the hero from his ordained destination and the historic progress it represents.⁴ Like the undertow of a wave, constantly dragging a swimmer backwards even as he struggles to push onwards, the *relicta* represents the feminising force that draws men away from duty, reason and fate.⁵ The women who figure the temptations of desire are located on distant shores, 'beyond Troye, estward in the se' (line 1426): women from Colchos and Carthage, Crete and Lemnos and Egypt.⁶ In medieval Christian commentary, Aeneas journeys from Troy to Cathage and onwards to Rome in a trajectory that represents nothing less than the *translatio imperii et studii* that gave the Christian Church its foundation in the West and, in English tradition, led Brutus to found Britain.⁷ This trajectory is only briefly interrupted by Dido and Carthage, yet she remains stubbornly present in the literary imagination

---

3   Dinshaw's discussion of asynchronicity underpins Freeman's concept of 'temporal drag'; I relate this to Hsy's description of the 'back and forth' of translation and its affective disruptions. See Freeman, *Time Binds*, pp. 62–86, 114; Dinshaw, *Getting Medieval*, p. 21, and *How Soon is Now? Medieval Texts, Amateur Readers, and the Queerness of Time* (Durham, NC: Duke University Press, 2012), p. 32; Jonathan Hsy, *Trading Tongues: Merchants, Multilingualism, and Medieval Literature* (Columbus, OH: Columbus University Press, 2013), pp. 72–73.
4   See Desmond, *Reading Dido*, pp. 74–98.
5   See Freeman, *Time Binds*, pp. 59–93. I discuss Freeman's image of the wave in more detail shortly.
6   The association between the East and undisciplined desire underpins pejorative constructions of race in medieval Western Europe, as I discuss in more detail in the next chapter. See Suzanne Conklin Akbari, *Idols in the East: European Representations of Islam and the Orient, 1100–1450* (Ithaca, NY: Cornell University Press, 2009), pp. 155–99.
7   For Chaucer's use of Troy as an anchoring point throughout the Legend, see Collette, *Rethinking the* Legend, p. 121.

of generations of Classical and medieval writers.⁸ Immortalised by Virgil, Dido became famous in medieval Latin and vernacular narrative, despite the fact her encounter with Aeneas is over and done less than halfway through the *Aeneid*. In Ovid's *Heroides*, where the abandoned women of Classical legend burst out into eloquent and emotional voices of their own, Dido speaks bitterly of her betrayal and resolve to kill herself. Her voice echoes down myriad texts, persistently replaying the process of temptation that leads men to wander from their courses and linger with women.

The Carthaginian queen is memorialised as the seducer not only of Aeneas, but also of the (male) reader. She is the emotional centre to which the text turns back even as its narrative moves on, the dangerous figure who threatens to unman the hero with her feminine wiles, emasculating him into abandoning his destiny.⁹ In his famous account of reading Virgil, Augustine pictures himself dissolving into watery emotion on encountering Dido's story: 'I was compelled … to weep for the death of Dido, who killed herself for love, while I bore with dry eyes my most wretched self dying to you, O Lord'.¹⁰ The emotion is a betrayal of the (masculine) self, the saint explains: for instead of weeping for his own immortal soul, he weeps for the memory of a pagan woman, seduced by her sad story into neglecting his own fate. This influential account conflates the reader of the Classical text with its own voyaging protagonist: like Aeneas, Augustine falls for Dido; like the Trojan hero, he inhabits a world of fluid emotion, wherein he loses sight of the fixed endpoint of his personal narrative, tempted into a temporary and false harbour by a beguiling woman. The seas over which Augustine voyages are lines of text; it is the *Aeneid* across which he makes his spiritual journey, and not a real geographic space. We know from his account that he was reading the text as a schoolboy learning grammar; like him, countless generations of medieval schoolboys read of Aeneas and Achilles, Dido, Medea and Cleopatra in lessons on grammar, which were thought to inculcate not only linguistic competency but also that quality Alan of Lille sees as being so intimately linked to grammar: moral rectitude.¹¹ Thus, when Augustine describes his fascination with, and subsequent rejection of, Dido, he is also describing the

---

8   Hagedorn, *Abandoned Women*, pp. 1-3; Desmond, *Reading Dido*; Baswell, *Virgil in Medieval England*, pp. 249-69.
9   Desmond notes that the practice of reading Dido as the central character was a strong, even dominant, tendency in medieval vernacular versions of the narrative, a practice that 'disrupts the patrilineal focus of the *Aeneid*'. See Desmond, *Reading Dido*, p. 2.
10 'cogebar … plorare Didonem mortuam, quia se occident ab amore, cum interea me impsum in his a te morientem, deus, uita mea, siccis occulis ferrem misserimus'. Augustine, *Confessions*, ed. and trans. Carolyn J. B. Hammond, 2 vols (Cambridge, MA: Harvard University Press, 2014-15), I.13.20.
11 See Marjorie Curry Woods, 'Performing Dido', in *Public Declamations: Essays on Medieval Rhetoric, Education, and Letters in Honour of Martin Camargo*, eds Georgiana Donavin and Denise Stodols (Turnhout: Brepols, 2015), pp. 253-65, and *Weeping for*

experience of learning to read rationally, to identify a narrative whose *telos* is the rejection of temporal, fleshly femininity in favour of masculine reason. Like Jerome's *exemplum* of the captive woman of Deuteronomy, Dido's story becomes a hermeneutic analogy, a text about encounters with text. In her desirability, Dido exemplifies the powerful magnetism of lingering over language, the undeniable attraction of getting lost in the Latin text.

In its Classical and early medieval forms, then, the story of Dido explores the situation of men caught in the 'dangerous middle' stages of *translatio*: seeking to cross from shore to shore, from Classical learning to Christian knowledge, from *libido* to *ratio*.[12] As Marilynn Desmond points out, this is an implicitly masculine journey, in which the male hero achieves his mature and virile status not only by rejecting lust and pleasure in favour of duty and fate, but also by rejecting the feminine qualities within himself, which are coded as forms of weakness or degeneracy. Yet as Dido draws attention back to herself, stalling the geographic progress of Aeneas and the chronological progress of the narrative, she works against this teleological masculine progress. Freeman identifies such temporally disruptive activity as a form of 'queer time' in which 'the patriarchal, linear time of "monumental" history' may be 'evacuated' into an 'asynchronous' space in which different times (and unexpected bodies) may touch up against one another in moments of deviant affection.[13] The transmission of the story of Dido from Virgil to Augustine exemplifies this process. Augustine's illicit desire for Dido's story inhabits the same conceptual space as Aeneas' illicit desire for Dido *within* the story. As Dido is dragged out of her narrative chronology to become the embodiment of the text Augustine reads as well as the character in that text, she inhabits a doubled or folded time, evocative of Freeman's concept of 'temporal drag'.[14] This citation of pastness carries with it implications of temporal disorientation, a movement back and forth, exemplified for Freeman by the image of the wave, whose undertow drags backwards even as it moves forwards. 'Temporal drag' aptly describes Augustine's performance of desire for Dido, which looks backward to the original desirous performance of Aeneas, 'citing' that performance out of time, and bearing witness to 'the pull of the past on the present'.[15] Even as Augustine resolves to abandon the pleasures Dido represents, he reanimates

---

Dido: The Classics in the Medieval Classroom (Princeton, NJ: Princeton University Press, 2019).

[12] I adapt the term from Jeffrey Jerome Cohen, *Hybridity, Identity and Monstrosity in Medieval Britain: On Difficult Middles* (New York: Palgrave, 2007), pp. 1–10. For discussion of *libido* and *ratio* see Desmond, *Reading Dido*, p. 77.

[13] See Freeman, *Time Binds*, pp. 57, 59–93. I draw on Dinshaw's theorising of queer touch as a form of time-transgressing affect. See Dinshaw, 'Chaucer's Queer Touches/A Queer Touches Chaucer', *Exemplaria* 7.1 (1995): 75–92.

[14] Freeman, *Time Binds*, p. 62.

[15] Ibid.

the emotion she generates in Aeneas. Like a linguistic citation, this performance of desire is translative, in the sense Jonathan Hsy advances when he identifies a 'fluid' movement 'back and forth' between languages as integral to Chaucer's poetry.[16] Virgil's Dido becomes part of Augustine's text, but Augustine's yearning also floods backwards into Virgil, heightening post-Augustinian readers' sense of Dido's paradigmatic desirability. Hsy associates this undular 'back and forth' with the process of engaging in *translatio* (whether textual or geographic), resulting in the unfixing of a subject's sense of 'affective belonging' in relation to language, country or place.[17] Like Aeneas, journeying from Troy to Rome, Augustine is suspended between his place of origin (the grammar-school class in North Africa where he first encountered Dido) and his destination (the holy city), pulled off course by his affective engagement with Carthaginian pleasure.[18] The *relicta* narrative thus becomes saturated with connections to the 'eddying' of desire, the asynchronous, disorientating and fluid exchanges of language and emotion that frustrate masculine forward progress.[19]

The coding of this desire as illicit is part of a wider emphasis on the dangerousness of degenerate masculinity for men within the *relicta* tradition. Long before he meets Dido, Aeneas' Trojan origins place his masculinity under suspicion; as Delany observes, Troy 'was often represented as the site of debilitating sensuality and, more particularly, of effeminacy'.[20] In the *Aeneid*, Dido's Carthaginian suitor Iarbus refers to the companions of Paris as 'half-male', a slander which, Delany reminds us, remained active even in medieval glosses on Classical texts, citing a twelfth-century example in which Ovid's reference to Paris as a 'Phrygian man' is glossed by a commentator as relating to weakness or effeminacy.[21] The selfish desire of Paris for Helen, which caused

---

16 Hsy, *Trading Tongues*, p. 72.
17 Ibid., p. 23.
18 I use the term 'suspended' with reference to Hsy's claim that distinctive types of language 'take shape in transit, when one's social identifications are temporarily suspended between destinations or diffused across locations'. See Hsy, *Trading Tongues*, p. 23.
19 Eve Kosofsky Sedgwick offers the influential definition, which underlies Freeman's argument, that 'Queer is a continuing moment, movement, motive – recurrent, eddying, *troublant*'. See Sedgwick, *Tendencies* (Durham, NC: Duke University Press, 1993), p. xii.
20 Sheila Delany, 'Geographies of Desire: Orientalism in Chaucer's *Legend of Good Women*', in *Chaucer's Cultural Geography*, ed. Kathryn L. Lynch (New York and London: Routledge, 2002), pp. 225–47 (p. 237).
21 The Latin is 'semiviro' (*Aeneid* IV, line 215). This and subsequent quotations are from Virgil, *Eclogues, Georgics, Aeneid, Minor Poems*, trans. H. Rushton Fairclough, rev. by G. P. Goold, 2 vols (Cambridge, MA: Harvard University Press, 1999). The reference to a 'Phrygio ... viro' is from the *Ars Amatoria* 1, in *Ovid: The Art of Love and Other Poems*, ed. G. P. Goold and trans. H. J. Mozley, 2nd edn (Cambridge, MA: Harvard University Press, 1985), line 54. The gloss is from Ralph Hexter, *Ovid and Medieval Schooling*:

the Trojan war, features in Alan of Lille's catalogue of disorderly desires, the 'gateway drug' leading to the even greater transgression: the 'monstrous acts' that 'Paris with Paris devises'. Schoolboys reading the story of Dido might read of another famous hero led astray by feminising desire: the Greek Achilles, whom Alan castigates in the same passage for 'counterfeit[ing] the bearing of a maiden' in order to attract women's attention (*De planctu*, lines 50–54).[22] Statius' *Achilleid*, a common partner text for grammar teaching to Virgil's *Aeneid*, describes how Achilles fell in love with the princess of Skyros, Deidamia, while disguised in women's clothing.[23] Achilles expresses his fears that the disguise will 'soften' or emasculate him using the verb, *mollire*, which Isidore of Seville famously cited as etymological evidence of the innate link between the woman (*mulier*) and the quality of greater softness (*mollior*; 'softer'), and he abandons Deidamia to fight in the Trojan war.[24] The same vocabulary of condemnation applies to Aeneas himself. The Latin Turnus calls his rival a 'semiviris Phrygis', or 'half-male Trojan' (*Aeneid* XII, line 99), while in the twelfth-century French *Roman d'Eneas*, the Roman Lavinia's mother even describes Aeneas as a sodomite and elaborates on his sexual proclivities at length.[25] Like Achilles, dressed in women's clothing, Aeneas comes to Dido

---

Studies in the Medieval School Commentaries on Ovid's Ars Amatoria, Epistulae Ex Ponto, *and* Epistulae Heroidum (Munich: Arbeo-Gesellschaft, 1986), p. 75 n. 197. See Delany, *The Naked Text*, p. 180.

[22] Paris in Paridem monstra nefanda parit
... Pelides mentitur virginis actus,
Ut sic virgineum se probet esse virum..

[23] For the medieval reception of Statius' works, see Dominique Battles, *The Medieval Tradition of Thebes: History and Narrative in the OF Roman de Thèbes, Boccaccio, Chaucer and Lydgate* (New York and London: Routledge, 2004), pp. 1–18, and Robert R. Edwards, 'Medieval Statius: Belatedness and Authority', in *Brill's Companion to Statius*, eds W. J. Dominik, C. E. Newlands and K. Gervais (Leiden and Boston: Brill, 2015), pp. 497–511.

[24] I discuss this in the introduction, pp. 00–00. See *The Etymologies*, eds Barney, Lewis, Beach, and Berghof, p. 224.

[25] Unques feme n'ot bien de lui
n'en avras tu, si com ge cui,
d'un traitor, d'un sodomite.
(Eneas, ed. Salverda de Grave, lines 8581–83)

'Never did any woman have any good from him, nor do I think you will have, from a traitor and a sodomite.'
(Eneas, trans. Yunck), p. 226.

For discussion of this episode, see Judith Haas, 'Trojan Sodomy and the Politics of Marriage in the Roman d'Eneas', *Exemplaria* 20.1 (2008): 48–71; Noah Guynn, *Allegory and Sexual Ethics in the High Middle Ages* (New York: Palgrave Macmillan, 2007), pp. 51–52; Vincent A. Lankewish, 'Assault from Behind: Sodomy, Foreign Invasion, and Masculine Identity in the Roman d'Eneas', *Text and Territory: Geographical Imagination in the European Middle Ages*, eds Sylvia Tomasch and Sealy Gilles (Philadelphia, PA: University of Pennsylvania Press, 1998), pp. 207–46; Raymond Cormier, 'Taming the

in an always already feminised state; thus there is always the worry that he, like Paris, will give in to further perversions. The spectre of a deviant or 'effeminate' hero generates anxiety and fear of an instability that might spread through the whole text to change the course of history. In abandoning Dido, Aeneas demonstrates his virility because he stabilises his narrative trajectory towards Rome.

In contrast, Dido's own emotions are frozen in a state almost of stasis, heavily anchored by narrative certainty. Virgil depicts her falling reluctantly in love with Aeneas, giving in to her passion and, almost immediately, discovering she has been abandoned and killing herself. Yet it is this last stage of passionate emotion that becomes embedded in the subsequent tradition, as we have seen; Dido's emotion becomes synonymous with the grief and resentment of the *relicta*, the emotion that ends in the self-lacerating violence of suicide. It is this emotion that Ovid expands upon in the *Heroides*, depicting Dido looking back on her love affair as a thing already ended, her desire an emotion of the past, whose futility is always already known. English medieval retellings of Aeneas' story, Christopher Baswell demonstrates, 'dilate' upon Dido and her emotions *because* they represent the slow postponement of desire, while also draining these emotions of their individuality.[26] By persistently treating Dido as an echo of Creusa (Aeneas' wife, lost in Troy) and a shadow of Lavinia (whom he is to marry in Rome), these texts loosen her purchase on the chronological arc of the narrative, transforming her from an individual into a trope of ubiquitous and generic feminine emotion.[27] We could say that, for many medieval readers of the Ovidian tradition, as for Augustine and Ovid, Dido's desire only 'exists' in retrospect, at the point at which its tragic outcome is already known. Whereas generations of (male) poets revisit Aeneas' dangerously fluid yearning, rekindling the same possibilities of deviance translated into new contexts, when these poets come to speak of Dido, they contain her emotion within the narrative space concerned with the retrospect of what has already ended. This relegation of Dido's desire to the end of her text renders that desire null or sterile, containing its affective potential. Thus, while desire *for* Dido is a narratively generative force, giving rise to ever more extensions of the story, the desire Dido herself feels is dislocated from the forward motion of her story, trapped like a fly in amber in the laments that memorialise it.

It is this memorialised desire that Chaucer brings into the vivid present

---

Warrior: Responding to the Charge of Sexual Deviance in Twelfth-Century Vernacular Romance', in *Literary Aspects of Courtly Culture: Selected Papers from the Seventh Triennial Congress of the International Courtly Literature Society*, eds Donald Maddox and Sara Sturm-Maddox (Cambridge: D. S. Brewer, 1994), pp. 153–60; Simon Gaunt, 'From Epic to Romance: Gender and Sexuality in the Roman d'Eneas', *Romanic Review* 83.1 (1992): 1–27.

[26] Baswell, *Virgil in Medieval England*, p. 173.
[27] Ibid., p. 186.

tense in his version of the narrative in the 'Legend of Dido'. The text is Chaucer's second substantial retelling of her story; it is also by far the longest of the legends, and the most insistent to display its status as a translation from Classical material.[28] In it, Chaucer repeatedly directs attention back to other, prior versions of the Carthaginian queen written in Latin and medieval vernaculars, such that these sources exert a constant pull on its Middle English narrative. While these allusions to the 'bok' or 'autour' of Chaucer's sources, to 'Virgil Mantoan' and to 'Naso' or 'Ovyde', suggest an intimacy with these textual predecessors, Chaucer's insistent distinction of his own 'matere' from their content indicates the desire to move beyond them. Participating in the familiar performance of retrospective desire for Dido and subsequent abandonment, Chaucer truncates the story with characteristic *occupatio*. He thus folds into the already convoluted temporality of the *relicta* paradigm another layer of metatextual identification, between the translating poet and the voyaging hero. Like Augustine and Aeneas, Chaucer represents himself as a poet inhabiting an affectively mobile transitional identity, between the Latin of his source material and the English of his writing. Subtly shifting small details of Virgil's Latin, he reconfigures the characterisation of desire and emotion found in his source materials, allowing images of femininity to suffuse the portrait of Aeneas. This shifted emphasis, from a pejorative language of degenerate masculinity imputed to Aeneas by speakers other than Dido to an imagery of desirable femininity perceived in Aeneas *by* Dido, provides the catalyst for Chaucer's representation of Dido's own experience of desire.

The changes Chaucer makes are concentrated in passages otherwise very close to Virgil's Latin, during which Dido first sees Aeneas. In the Latin, the hero has been hidden from sight; suddenly, his mother the goddess Venus raises the cloud of mist that conceals him. At this moment, she 'adflarat' (*Aeneid* I, line 591; imparted) good looks upon her son, making him look 'os umerosque deo similis' (*Aeneid* I, line 589; like a god about the shoulders and the face). Dido, the narrator tells us briefly, 'obstupuit … aspectu' (*Aeneid* I, line 613; was stunned by his looks), but most of what passes between the pair is conversation. Chaucer hugely expands the visual aspect of this scene, and also the sense of interior access to Dido's emotions as she sees Aeneas. More than a dozen lines are spent in establishing Dido's impression of what she sees, much of which focuses on Aeneas' physical features (lines 1057–71). Only then does the narrator explain 'after Venus hadde he swich fayrnesse / That no man myghte be half so fayr, I gesse', (lines 1072–73). This translation preserves the sense of Virgil's Latin, but adds quite a different subtext. The word 'after' may be glossed as 'in imitation of' or 'resembling', suggesting a maternal inheritance

---

[28] Chaucer offers a Dido-centric paraphrase of the beginning part of the *Aeneid* in *The House of Fame*, lines 143–382. See Hansen, *Chaucer and the Fictions of Gender*, pp. 87–107. The 'Legend of Dido' is 444 lines long; the average length is 238 lines.

or similarity, rather than a divine gift.[29] Aeneas is attractive because he looks like his goddess mother, rather than because she has made him look like a god. In this context, the following phrase, 'no man myghte be half so fayr', takes on a certain arch implication: it is no *man* who might so resemble the goddess of feminine beauty. Yet Chaucer does not only suggest that Aeneas' attractive qualities are more feminine than masculine: he also suggests that this interpretation of Aeneas' looks comes from Dido's careful examination. Her searching eye finds these qualities in Aeneas' appearance, pointing to the recognition of Venus' looks in Aeneas' body. Accordingly, we might see Dido's gaze as a queering gaze, a gaze that recognises (and, thus, makes visible to readers who see the scene through Dido's eyes) the qualities of male femininity latent in the ostensibly masculine hero. As this gaze codes Aeneas' desirability as feminine, and his femininity as desirable, it offers an alternative to the narrative sequence in which dissident masculinity is the stuff of pejorative, anti-Trojan accusation.

This subtle shift prepares for a more substantial reconfiguration of the *Aeneid*'s Latin, through which Chaucer stresses that the femininity Dido detects in Aeneas' appearance is reflected in his emotional conduct. One of the most emotive and moving passages of the first book of the *Aeneid* describes how Aeneas, standing in Dido's temple, sees upon the wall a carving that memorialises the recently concluded Trojan war, freezing in time the story of his own people's last defeat. In Virgil, Aeneas responds with a tearful, passionate pride. Telling his companion Achates to banish all fear, he celebrates the lasting fame the tablet represents.[30] In the *Legend*, Aeneas' response is very different:

> 'Allas! ... Thourghout the world oure shame is kid so wyde,
> Now it is peynted upon every syde.
> We, that weren in prosperite,
> Been now desclandred, and in swich degre,
> No lenger for to lyven I ne kepe.'
> And with that word he brast out for to wepe.
> (lines 1027–33)

This lament is full of the language of shame (the very word Aeneas uses)

---

[29] *MED* headword 'after', prep. (10).
[30] 'Weeping, he said: "Now what place, Achates,
What region of the world is not full of our labours?
See, Priam! Here, indeed, virtue has its own reward;
There are tears for things, and mortal things touch the soul.
Lose your fear; this fame will bring you some comfort."'

('... lacrimans, "Quis iam locus" inquit "Achate,
quae regio in terris nostri non plena laboris?
En Priamus! Sunt hic etiam sua praemia laudi;
sunt lacrimae rerum et mentem mortalia tangunt.
Solve metus; feret haec aliquam tibi fama salutem."'
(Aeneid I, lines 459–62)

and this shame is of a very particular sort. A host of references – to fear of slander and desire to die, to worries about further retellings of his story – conflate Aeneas' shame with the sexual shame felt by women. Similar images hang heavy over the 'Legend of Lucrece', where Chaucer links 'shame' with 'fer of sclaunder' (lines 1813–14) as his heroine responds with 'wepynge' (line 1834) and desire for death; further abroad, in *Troilus and Criseyde* it is the fear of being 'rolled ... on many a tongue (*T&C* V.1061) that preoccupies Criseyde. Mary Flannery has argued that shame is 'central to Chaucer's narratives of honourable women', and persistently associated with feminine readiness to die.[31] It thus functions as 'an important dividing line between medieval concepts of masculinity and femininity'.[32] Aeneas' fluid weeping, his shame and desire for death, locate him firmly within the emotional and somatic ambit of femininity. Translating Aeneas, Chaucer takes advantage of the fluidity of language and affect that result during translation, shifting Aeneas' Latin performance of virile pride and fearlessness into a shamefast horror of notoriety that reads as distinctly feminine in Middle English.

Chaucer represents Dido's desire for Aeneas as the direct result of this display of feminine emotion and feminine appearance. Seeing Aeneas weep in shame, Dido feels 'pite' for him, and 'with that pite love com in also' (line 1079). Jill Mann and Glenn Burger have both drawn attention to this juxtaposition of desire and pity, with Mann arguing that Dido's desire cannot involve 'sexual attraction' because its roots lie in pity.[33] Burger, meanwhile, claims that this 'feminine *pite*' takes the place *fin'amor* accords to masculine unrequited love, and this displacement of feminine emotion to a masculine position (that of the desiring lover rather than the yearned-for beloved) results in a 'destructive morass of ugly feelings' that reflects the 'troubling affective gaps and illegibilities' of the *Legend*'s representation of female desire.[34] These readings are salient, because both are (in different ways) denials of a female desire for femininity, or rather, readings that find such a desire (as Burger puts it) 'illegible'. Mann's flat denial of Dido's sexual desire makes little sense of the queen's courtship of Aeneas, a display that is articulated through firmly gendered literary tropes. Like a hunter, Dido pursues Aeneas; the consummation of their love takes place during a literal hunt in which she takes the lead role.[35] As Delany notes, the passage describing this hunt (which ends in the consummation of Dido and Aeneas' lust) is filled with sexual punning, centred on imagery of 'pricking' and a play on the 'brydal' that curbs Aeneas'

---

[31] Mary Flannery, 'A Bloody Shame: Chaucer's Honourable Women', *Review of English Studies* NS 62.255 (2011): 337–57 (pp. 337–38).
[32] Ibid., p. 341.
[33] Mann, *Feminizing Chaucer*, p. 32.
[34] Burger, 'Ugly Feelings and Gendered Conduct', p. 67.
[35] See Hume, *Chaucer and the Cultures of Love and Marriage*, pp. 185–200.

horse and hints at his subordinate role in a marital union.[36] We may read Dido here as a virago, in that she takes the sexually active, desirous role. But this is, of course, to place her within a recognisable context of gender difference in relation to Aeneas' male femininity; it might be understood as what Ahmed calls a 'straightening device'.[37] Burger's identification of Dido's emotion as 'illegibl[e]' within the context of *fin'amor* paves the way for a more interesting reading. Burger convincingly demonstrates that 'affective gaps and illegibilities' permeate the 'Legend of Dido' and the *Legend* more widely.[38] This much-quoted phrase evokes the *lacunae* which, as we have seen, inhere in depictions of female same-sex desire, those bodily orientations and desirous touches that deviate from the linear structures that would make them legible, occupying an affective space that lies 'aslant'.[39] He identifies, in particular, the 'hybrid' positions adopted by Dido, neither active nor passive, as a source of 'troubling gaps and illegibilities'.[40] However, if we interpret Dido's desire as responsive to Aeneas' male femininity, we may see her adoption of the posture of the virago as a reciprocal act rather than an inopportune display of unfeminine aggression: a display of female masculinity that affirms and is affirmed by Aeneas' male femininity. I argue, then, that Dido's desire for Aeneas *is* an active sexual desire, a desire that responds to his male femininity, and which participates not only in the conventional model of the virago, but also in the more fluid and reciprocal model of a female desire that slips out of the structures that would seek to define desire in terms of opposite-gender attraction.

The form of this desire underpins the final section of Chaucer's 'Legend of Dido', in which he almost allows Dido to rewrite her own ending and take on authorial, as well as sexual, agency. After Dido finds out that Aeneas plans to abandon her, she breaks out into a torrent of furious pleading. In Virgil's account, Dido pitifully wishes she had at least conceived a child to comfort her in her abandonment (*Aeneid* IV, lines 327–30); in Ovid's narrative, this possibility is transformed into a reality, and the queen declares that her suicide will bring an end not only to her own life, but also to the life of her unborn child (*Heroides* VII, lines 137–40).[41] The weapon with which Dido stabs herself is,

---

[36] Delany, *The Naked Text*, p. 144.
[37] Ahmed, *Queer Phenomenology*, pp. 71–72. See also Michelle M. Sauer, '"Where are the Lesbians in Chaucer?": Lack, Opportunity and Female Homoeroticism in Medieval Studies Today', *Journal of Lesbian Studies* 11.3/4 (2007): 331–45 (p. 334).
[38] The phrase originates with Ngai's book *Ugly Feelings*, pp. 2–3, from which Burger draws his methodology. See Burger, 'Ugly Feelings and Gendered Conduct', pp. 68–69.
[39] I discuss this in my introduction. See Freeman, *Time Binds*, p. 100; Ahmed, *Queer Phenomenology*, pp. 91–95; Horne and Lewis, 'Introduction, Reframed', pp. 1–12; Farina, 'Lesbian History and Erotic Reading', pp. 49–60; Kłosowska, *Queer Love in the Middle Ages*, pp. 69–116.
[40] Burger, 'Ugly Feelings and Gendered Conduct', pp. 76–77.
[41] Ovid, *Heroides, Amores*, trans. Grant Showerman, rev. G. P. Goold (Cambridge, MA: Harvard University Press, 1914).

from Virgil onwards, represented as Aeneas' sword, left behind, so Virgil indicates, along with his clothing (*Aeneid* IV, lines 346–48). Ovid expands upon the detail, picturing Dido sitting with the sword suggestively positioned in her fertile lap as her tears fall into its blade, soon to be joined by 'tears of blood' ('lacrimis sanguine', *Heroides* VII, line 188). This suggestive juxtaposition of the phallic sword in the fertile lap suggests both Dido's appropriation of Aeneas' masculinity and its imminent destruction. Baswell aptly labels the suicide a 'sterile transgression', a sin against nature that destroys both life and the possibility of new life.[42] In terms of the narrative teleology, it is the ultimate proof that *libido* is unproductive, a human and textual dead end.[43] As Baswell notes, Chaucer intensifies the implications of Ovid's imagery, describing how Aeneas 'lafte ... his swerd *stondynge*' (line 1332) – that is, erect – in pregnant Dido's bed. However, when Chaucer comes to integrate Virgil's account, he makes an important change. Where Virgil has Aeneas leave his 'Trojan clothing' ('Iliacas vestis', *Aeneid* IV, line 648) along with his sword, Chaucer reports that 'A cloth he lafte ... / Which cloth, whan sely Dido gan awake, / She hath it kyst ful ofte for his sake' (lines 1332–37). As the physical affection Dido lavishes on this object implies, the fabric is plainly a poignantly inanimate substitute for Aeneas' body. Yet in transforming Virgil's 'clothing' into 'cloth', Chaucer stresses that this is also raw material, akin to the unformed 'matter' women were thought to contribute to the process of conception, while men contributed the 'form' or vivifying spark. Thus, though Dido's use of Aeneas' sword may be seen as both emasculating and sterilising, her emotional attention to his cloth might be seen as reaffirming what her queering gaze initially saw in his feminine-looking face. Speaking to this cloth, Dido personifies it – she animates the material Aeneas left behind – in order to record her own version of a narrative conclusion. Addressing the cloth with pathetic apostrophe ('O swete cloth', line 1338), she declares 'I have fulfild of fortune al the cours' (line 1340). Patchworking together details from Virgil and Ovid, Chaucer's Dido constructs a generative image of completeness that flies in the face of known history of her suicide, redefining the truncation of suicide as the fulfilment of destiny. She claims an ending that is not premature but preordained: an ending of the type Aeneas achieves in Rome. Yet, as ever, it is Chaucer's narrator – in the micronarrative, another self-identified successor to Aeneas, revisiting Dido in order to abandon her – who has the last word, imposing yet again the stigma of unfinished material on Dido's story and returning the queen to her retrograde position: 'who wol al this letter have in mynde, / Rede Ovyde, and in hym he shal it fynde' (lines 1366–67).

---

[42] Baswell, *Virgil in Medieval England*, pp. 267–68.
[43] This analysis of teleological pressure and its coding of history in terms of 'reproductive futurity' draws upon Lee Edelman's work. See Edelman, *No Future: Queer Theory and the Death Drive* (Durham, NC: Duke University Press, 2004), pp. 1–31.

In his reconfiguration of the paradigmatic *relicta* narrative in the 'Legend of Dido', Chaucer confirms the overarching themes that will run through the less well-known, more provocative 'Legend of Hipsiphyle and Medea', which forms the midpoint of the *Legend* as a whole. The sight of Aeneas performing emotional femininity is what ignites Dido's desire; his performance of femininity constructs her identity in relation to it, and she becomes visible as a lesbian-like lover. The reciprocality of this desire-formation is suggestive of the dynamics of same-sex desire; suggestive, too, of a lesbian-like erotic wherein two feminised bodies take turns to form and to be formed by each other, as if each were that malleable desirous matter coded as quintessentially feminine in medieval medicine and theology. This reciprocality of desire is another kind of back-and-forth, another wave-like structure. In looking back to Virgil and to Ovid, Chaucer's Dido collects the affective materials that articulate her female desire for femininity, constructing it the interstices of those sources. Chaucer allows her to linger for a moment as a protagonist defining the ending of her own text, before cutting her short.

'COY AS IS A MAYDE': MALE FEMININITY IN ACTION

The expansive, lingering structure of the 'Legend of Dido' acts as a disproportionate prelude to the short, crowded and abbreviated 'Legend of Hipsiphyle and Medea', whose narrative structure follows the aimless wanderings of the faithless Jason. There is no implication that Jason will, like Virgil's Aeneas, transcend fleshly desires; rather, the final lines of the narrative suggest a third repetition of the same pattern, as Jason finds 'a thridde wif … the doughter of the kyng Creon' (lines 1660–61). The treacherous antagonist dominates the narrative, securing a far greater number of lines than Chaucer dedicates to either woman. It has been suggested that the narrative structure of the 'Legend of Hipsiphyle and Medea' confirms Chaucer's cynicism concerning the importance of women, for the two female protagonists never meet and are seemingly brought together only by their shared humiliation at Jason's hands, as if proving the necessity of masculinity to give coherence to their feminine presence in the text.[44] The text would thus embody the excess and surplus (with two protagonists crammed into a narrative with space for one) held to define the ungoverned feminine body. However, I argue that the sense of feminine excess in the 'Legend of Hipsiphyle and Medea' is even more organically related to Jason's presence in the text. In his iterative seagoing journeys, Jason resembles nothing so much as the feminine body, as it is described in medieval medical manuals: a body that responds to the cyclic lunar rhythms that govern tides and menstruation; a body that, like a wandering womb, constantly surges about in search of the orgasmic fulfilment

---

[44] Frank, *Chaucer and The Legend*, pp. 82–85.

that might promise to anchor it in place.⁴⁵ His Mediterranean voyaging sees him periodically cast about upon the waves, constantly pursing sexual contact with the lustful restlessness which, we are reminded, was often thought more characteristic of women than men in medieval understanding.⁴⁶ The 'Legend of Hipsiphyle and Medea' thus contains not two but three seemingly 'feminine' characters – though, as we will see, some of Jason's performance of femininity is strategically calculated – and constitutes a productive site for Chaucer's exploration of entanglements of deviant and misdirected female desire.

The opening lines of the 'Legend of Hipsiphyle and Medea' set the tone for the remainder of the text, concentrating firmly upon Jason and his faithless character. The narrator addresses his antagonist with a torrent of vituperation:

> Thow rote of false lovers, Duc Jasoun,
> Thow sly devourere and confusioun
> Of gentil wemen, tendre creatures,
> Thow madest thy recleymyng and thy lures
> To ladyes of thy statly aparaunce,
> And of thy wordes farced with plesaunce,
> And of thy feyned trouthe and thy manere,
> With thyn obesaunce and humble cheere,
> (lines 1368–76)

The language through which Jason is figured forth on the page may be read as a feminising rhetoric, which bears witness to the deformation of its subject's masculinity. The brief opening reference to Jason's seminal *paternitas* as 'rote of false loveres' is immediately undermined, as the generative meaning of the word 'root' is undercut by its own homophonic echo, the 'rote' that means putrefaction, the opposite process to generation. As Nicola McDonald points out, this opening passage is laden with other telling inversions. She cites the proverbial phrase *mulier est hominis confusio*, which the narrator reverses as he introduces Jason as the 'confusioun / Of gentil wemen' (lines 1369–70). McDonald concludes, persuasively, that '[t]he constituent parts of the proverbially deceptive, inconstant, destructive, and sexually insatiable woman are

---

⁴⁵ See Joan Cadden, *Nothing Natural is Shameful: Sodomy and Science in Late Medieval Europe* (Philadelphia, PA: University of Pennsylvania Press, 2013), pp. 133–34. Sarah Harlan-Haughy has identified the moon as a key image of sterile repetition in the 'Legend of Ariadne'. See Harlan-Haughy, 'The Circle, the Maze and the Echo: Sublunary Recurrence and Performance in Chaucer's Legend of Ariadne', *Chaucer Review* 52.3 (2017): 341–60. I am grateful to the delegates of the Gender and Medieval Studies Conference of 2020 for discussion of wandering wombs, fluid imagery and embodied gender, in particular Diane Heath for her paper 'Recreating the "Natural World": The Medieval Oyster as Wandering Womb and her Pearl as Microcosm', presented at Swansea University, 6 January.

⁴⁶ Karras, *Sexuality in Medieval Europe*, p. 5; Cadden, *Nothing Natural is Shameful*, pp. 131–32.

neatly isolated, inverted, and then restitched into a narrative of male villainy'.[47] The argument is tantalising, particularly because, insofar as the passage inverts misogynistic rhetoric to construct its Jason, it is a process that already carries connotations of the construction of femininity. Just as women were understood to be created from Adam's rib (from an interior masculine body part inverted to form the exterior), so too their sexual organs were often represented as inverted versions of male sexual organs.[48] As Jason is constructed from inversions of antifeminist commonplaces, he is constructed in the manner of a woman, constructed from inversions of pre-existing material.

This feminine linguistic construction unspools rapidly into more deeply disordered uses of language, as the narrator struggles to express the relationships between Jason and his lovers without dissolving into hopeless confusions. Jason is first apostrophised as 'devourere', a term suggestive of carnal appetite and thus continuous with the spectrum of desires that includes sexual lust. In embodying this appetite, Jason therefore exhibits a reflection of that quality of *libido* associated with the feminine. In setting out 'lures' made of 'wordes' he enacts a verbal seduction which, likewise, calls to mind the rich tradition of medieval thought in which persuasive words and sexual temptation are particularly associated with women. However, the prey Jason seeks are 'gentil wemen, tendre creatures'. These female targets are then associated with falcons, whose owner controls them by means of his 'reclayming and lures', those gobbets of raw meat used to entice birds of prey back to the wrist, conjuring up the unappetising image of Jason 'devour[ing]' his own falcons. As a literary figure, falcons draw into the connotative frame Chaucer's earlier dream poem, recalling the cross-species female–female relations in the *Parliament of Fowls*. This allusion to female homosociality or homoeroticism will reappear, as Sara Gutman has argued, in the 'Squire's Tale', whose provocative image of 'false fowls' echoes the *Legend*'s false men. That text involves its human and avian female protagonists in an intimate bond, in which masculine lovers are redundant just as male falcons were often surplus to requirements by medieval falconers.[49] Yet the 'tendre' flesh of the women Jason devours suggests not the predator but the prey, while the metaphoric glossing of Jason's 'lures' as 'wordes farced with plesaunce' (stuffed with delicacies, like a prepared dish) troubles the distinction between raw and cooked meat: that intended for the falcon and that stuffed and garnished for the table.[50] Accordingly, distinctions between human and animal are disturbed along the lines both of appetite and of sexuality, and the taboo against eating certain animals (predators) or certain

---

[47] McDonald, 'Chaucer's *Legend*, Ladies at Court', p. 32.
[48] See Sauer, *Gender in Medieval Culture*, p. 26.
[49] Sara Gutmann, 'Chaucer's Chicks: Feminism and Falconry in the "Knights' Tale", "The Squire's Tale", and *The Parliament of Fowls*', in *Rethinking Chaucerian Beasts*, ed. Carolynn Van Dyke (New York: Palgrave, 2012), pp. 69–83 (p. 71).
[50] *MED*, v. farsen (1).

foods (uncooked meats) is invoked. The passage resists a linear reading process, directing attention insistently back to previous terms that retrospectively modify the confused semantic fields of appetite and sexual desire, predators and prey, women and men. As Geraldine Heng points out, 'deliberate linguistic disordering' gives expression to the twin 'disorders of appetite and of bodily desire'; thus, 'unnatural eating is uncannily like unnatural sex'.[51] As he emerges as both the source of appetite or carnal *libido* ('devourere') and its seductive means of satisfaction (the one who sets out 'farced ... lures'), Jason embodies the confusing sameness, the lack of distinction, that is pejoratively associated both with female same-sex relations and with the operations of metaphor. As Alan of Lille observes, in his discussion of the polysemous deviancies of language and gender that transform 'he's' into 'she's', metaphor is one of the most slippery and dangerous figures of speech, confusing categories of active and passive, masculine and feminine. Jason's duplicity is thus represented as cause and consequence of his gender fluidity, and both duplicity and gender fluidity are expressed through a promiscuously signifying, polysemous language.

The performance of gender that follows provides a stark contrast. A most unexpected restraint and silence characterises Jason's wooing of Hipsiphyle. Instead of the promised torrent of words 'farced with plesaunce', Jason stands tongue-tied before the queen of Lemnos. When she speaks to him, we are told he 'answer[es] mekely and stylle' (line 1491) and 'nought he sayde' (1549). Like Aeneas, whose weeping shame evokes quintessentially feminine emotion, Jason is (according to his companion) 'to speke shamfast' (1535); he is 'coy as is a mayde' (line 1548). The simile reminds us that modesty and reluctance to speak are widely associated with feminine virtue: Jason does not simply perform femininity, he performs *virtuous* femininity. He acts like a 'goode woman'. His 'falseness' lies in the dynamic Hansen describes, the 'betrayal of the category of masculinity', with which she charges all of the men of the *Legend*.[52] To Hipsiphyle, however, this performance of feminine virtue is both attractive and desirable. In his depiction of the queen, Chaucer departs pointedly from his sources, moulding his female character into an echo of the character Jason pretends to be. Chaucer's Hipsiphyle is a whitewashed Amazon, a virago transformed into acceptable femininity.[53] Like

---

[51] Heng, *Empire of Magic*, p. 98.
[52] Hansen, *Chaucer and the Fictions of Gender*, p. 3. For discussions of masculinity, see Sauer, *Gender in Medieval Culture*, p. 115; Vern L. Bullough, 'On Being a Male in the Middle Ages', in *Medieval Masculinities*, ed. Lees, pp. 31–45 (p. 32).
[53] I use the term 'whitewashed' with Hipsiphyle's Lemnian identity in mind. As noted above, the *relicta* tradition participates in the pejorative racial ideology in which Eastern origins are associated with deviant femininity or excess. In mentioning Hipsiphyle's Lemnian identity, Chaucer locates her within the ambit of deviant femininity even as he claims to censor this element of his source material.

Jason, Hipsiphyle appears innocent and girlish; remarkably unencumbered for a queen, she first encounters Jason's she 'in hire pleying ... romynge on the clyves by the se' (lines 1469–70). In this description, Chaucer cuts out a substantial chunk of the source material available to him. As Nancy Bradley Warren points out, Chaucer omits the account of Hipsiphyle's women engaging in battle with Jason's troops, throwing spears at them from the walls of the city. She argues that 'the Lemnian women's mass murder of men and armed resistance to male invasion are, in a word, Amazonian', and Statius' Hipsiphyle makes the allusion directly.[54] Indeed, the reputation of the Lemnian women is testified to by none other than Thetis, mother of Achilles. In Statius' *Thebaid*, Thetis rejects the island of Lemnos as a suitable place for her son to engage in the cross-dressed concealment amongst the women that so energises Alan of Lille, on the grounds that Lemnian women are unfavourable to men (*non aequa viris*).[55] By transforming Hipsiphyle from an antagonistic virago into a gentle 'innocent' (line 1546), Chaucer edits out the backstory of her legendary gender nonconformity. Just as Jason's deviantly feminised construction is hidden under a performance of decorous feminine virtue, so too her history as a virago is concealed. This seeming reciprocality or similitude in the construction of Hipsiphyle and Jason as desiring agents casts the lovers as another Dido and Aeneas, and again represents male femininity as a desirable quality to a woman.

However, Chaucer rapidly exposes the layers of deception that complicate this courtship. Teasingly, he flags up his omitted sources throughout the narrative, crowding the text with citations of sources from the 'Argonautycon' (line 1467), 'Guido' and 'Ovyde' (lines 1464–65), and excusing his truncated description of Jason and Hipsiphyle's relationship with instructions to 'rede / Th'orignal, that telleth al the cas' (lines 1557–58). In the original Lemnian context, the duplicitously feminine behaviour Chaucer's Jason displays might (despite Thetis' worries) function like a distorted mirror of Achilles' famous disguise, allowing him to pass under enemy lines and make his conquest, and giving his strategic adoption of a feminine modesty a logical cause. However, Chaucer implies that what draws Jason away from Hipsiphyle is not the *telos* of destiny that draws Aeneas and Achilles to abandon the women they love, but rather (and more cynically) his prior attachment to someone else entirely. Chaucer gives Hercules, Jason's friend, a convincingly intimate knowledge

---

[54] Nancy Bradley Warren, '"Olde Stories" and Amazons: The *Legend of Good Women*, the Knight's Tale, and Fourteenth-Century Political Culture', in *Re-thinking Chaucer's Legend*, ed. Collette, pp. 83–104 (pp. 92–93). Statius writes that 'Amazonio Scythiam fervere tumultu' (Scythia was afire with Amazonian tumult) in book V, line 144 of *The Thebaid, Books 1–7*, ed. and trans. D. R. Shackleton Bailey, 2 vols (Cambridge, MA: Harvard University Press, 2003).

[55] Statius' *Achilleid*, line 206. See Dániel Kozák, 'Traces of the Argo: Statius' *Achilleid* 1 and Valarius' *Argonutica* 1–2', in *Flavian Epic Interactions*, eds Gesine Manuwald and Astrid Voigt (Berlin and Boston, MA: De Gruyter, 2013), pp. 247–66 (pp. 262–64).

of Jason's sexual desirability, hinting at the nature of this relationship. Ostensibly seeking to persuade Hipsiphyle of Jason's worthiness for love, Hercules declares

> wolde God that I hadde yive
> My blod and flesh, so that I myghte live,
> With the nones that he hadde owher a wif.
> (lines 1538–40)

The exclamation may be understood as a conventional phrase, suggesting the self-sacrificing love of a friend. Yet as it conflates two entities of 'flesh and blod' within an affective relationship to Jason, Hercules' speech also betrays a homoerotic desire to give of himself, as Jason's 'wif'. As this suggestive phrase indicates, the intimacy at the centre of this vicarious courtship of Hipsiphyle is not that which might exist between the queen and the hero who has arrived on her shores, but that which already exists between Jason and Hercules. We are soon told that Jason's display of womanly charms is a pre-arranged deception: 'al this was compassed on the nyght / Bytwixe hym Jason and this Ercules' (lines 1443–44). Together, the two men have hatched a cynical plan to 'bedote' (line 1547) the queen. Jason's male femininity may thus be read as a calculated performance, indicating a shrewd awareness of Hipsiphyle's elided Amazonian past and her antagonism towards men, and a recognition that femininity is what this woman is likely to find attractive.[56] For a certain class of readers, Chaucer's omitted source material provides tacit explanation for Jason's performance of femininity, aligning those who recognise the strategic cleverness in a readerly complicity with the two men.

However, Chaucer's narrator rapidly returns to the rhetoric of gender with which he began the 'Legend of Hipsiphyle and Medea', indicating that beneath Jason's studied performance of virtuous maidenly silence is a deviantly feminine quality. Jason abandons Hipsiphyle precipitously, continuing his journey onwards to Colchis, for:

> As mater apetiteth forme alwey
> And from forme into forme it passen may,
> Or as a welle that were botomles,
> Ryght so can false Jason have no pes.
> (lines 1583–86)

Jason is like 'matter' that desires a 'form', like water constantly flowing from a well. In medieval tradition, 'matter' is typically feminine and form masculine, and the relationship between the two illustrates creative acts from God's

---

[56] Hansen has argued that the women of the *Legend* are frequently 'attracted not by otherness and virility, but by the male's temporary or apparent *sameness*, his passivity, coyness, vulnerability, and dependence (and even, in the case of Jason, his looks)'. See Hansen, *Fictions of Gender*, p. 7.

fatherly creation of the world from formless *matter*, to human fathering through the impregnation of maternal *matter* with the semen that gives human life its shape, to the masculinised act of 'writing' one's textual progeny onto the blank and formless 'tabula' of the page.[57] Delany reads Chaucer's inversion of this traditional association of 'matter' with femininity as a rather weak suggestion 'that gender does not matter in sexual ethics'. She finds the lines 'inept'.[58] However, there is strategy behind the choice of words. Jason's protean nature, easily moulded into the shape and demeanour necessary for the task in hand, resembles 'matter' in its plasticity. Meanwhile, the word 'form' means not only a figure or archetype, but also physical appearance, and even beauty. As the authors of the *MED* note, the word suggests its Latin homophone *forma* (the feminine noun meaning 'beauty') and appears to have been used in that sense by the translators of the Wycliffite Bible.[59] When Jason passes from 'forme to forme', he passes from female figure to female figure, from beautiful woman to beautiful woman. Thus, though 'matter' and 'form' are conventionally mapped onto the gender binary, the word 'form' in its associations with the Latin noun and the female body pushes back against that binary, causing an interpretative confusion for readers. Consequently, the image accommodates a formless, protean Jason, but also two feminised properties promiscuously colliding in a single rhetorical figure, two *formae* signally failing to impress any stamp on the matter in question, two women failing to secure any stability from Jason. Like the women of Étienne de Fougères' famous and parodic poem about lesbian sex, these feminised properties collide unproductively, coming to no conclusion or climax.[60]

FEMALE MASCULINITY AND THE SEARCH FOR A LINGUISTIC PROSTHESIS

In yoking together Hipsiphyle and Medea, Chaucer notoriously links two women whose only shared experience is that of abandonment by Jason. The princess of Colchis is Chaucer's most unlikely heroine. Unlike Philomela or Lucrece, or indeed Ariadne or Phyllis, the Medea of Classical and medieval tradition is no piteous innocent, but a scheming, even supernaturally powerful virago.[61] After Jason abandoned her, she murdered their children in revenge; this detail is pointedly omitted in the *Legend*, but was well known to be the

---

[57] I discuss this tradition in the introduction; see also Sauer, *Gender in Medieval Culture*, pp. 15–46; Cadden, *Nothing Natural is Shameful*, pp. 106–38.
[58] Delany, *The Naked Text*, p. 201.
[59] *MED* headword 'forme' (n.).
[60] See Clark, 'Jousting without a Lance', pp. 143–77.
[61] The definitive study of Medea is Ruth Morse's *The Medieval Medea* (Cambridge: D. S. Brewer, 1996).

final, gory act of Medea's relationship with Jason.[62] The removal of Medea's traditional narrative 'end' looks back to Chaucer's treatment of the story of Philomela, but also takes on new significance in the context of Medea's desire for a linguistic prosthesis or 'poynt'. This desire becomes evident as Medea seeks to take on a quasi-masculine role in her courtship of Jason. With the narrative memory of Hipsiphyle's seduction by Jason and Hercules fresh in mind, Medea attempts to replicate the homosocial intimacies of Jason's earlier relationship with Hercules, to succeed where Hipsiphyle failed, and to seduce a Jason who has hitherto seemed feminine. In that she inserts herself into the previous narrative, Medea performs the same substitution as Augustine does, audaciously echoing the saint, and also echoing Chaucer, who has likewise modelled himself on Aeneas as he retells and revisits the legends of *relictae*. In this attempt, Medea makes use of her formidable prowess in rhetoric. Her famous powers of enchantment, which in Chaucer's sources give rise to dramatic scenes of animal magic and concoctions of potions, are represented in the *Legend* as an entirely verbal form of 'sleyghte of ... enchauntement' (line 1650). Yet for all her rhetorical skill and cool logic, she is easily matched by a Jason who demonstrates an unexpected skill in speaking and a duplicitous aptitude for doubled meanings and veiled references, whose meaning the unfortunate Medea fails to penetrate. In attempting to take on a masculine role, Medea succeeds only in presenting herself as a 'capoun': a masculine body *manqué*, a castrated figure, all of whose skilful linguistic strategies are ultimately subscribed by an impenetrably masculine Latinate *auctoritas*.

Medea's early performances of gender and desire are impressively convincing imitations of Herculean masculinity. As she orientates herself in relation to Jason, she imitates Hercules' orientation, and thus locates herself within a would-be homosocial structure of affection. Approaching Jason, Medea represents herself as a quasi-masculine companion rather than a feminine lover, and proposing not affection and intimacy, but practical help in the matter of finding the golden fleece. She avoids the language of romance and adopts a direct and pragmatic tone that echoes the practicality (even the self-serving duplicity) of Jason and Hercules' interactions, as she teaches him how to acquire her father's precious Golden Fleece:

> Tho gan this Medea to hym declare
> The peril of this cas from poynt to poynt,

---

[62] Chaucer plainly knew of this gruesome conclusion to the traditional narrative. Medea appears in his *Book of the Duchess* as 'Medea ... That slough hir children for Jasoun' (lines 726–27), and in the Man of Law's somewhat misleading description of the *Legend* itself, she is condemned for her 'crueltee' for 'thy litel children hanging by the hals / For thy Jason, that was of love so fals' (*CT* II, lines 72–74). In addition, Medea is one of two women (the other is Philomela) who merit a mention in the legends but not in the ballade in the prologues. See F, lines 249–69 and G, lines 203–23, and Delany, *The Naked Text*, p. 200.

> And of his batayle, and in what disjoynt
> He mote stoned.
> (lines 1629–32)

The diction is legalistic: the verb 'declaren' has a connotation relating to legal pronouncements, which is reinforced by the word 'cas', meaning not only a general situation but also a legal case, such as could be argued through a series of 'poynt[s]'.[63] This sets the scene for a marriage agreement that is conducted entirely as a legal arrangement. The consummation of this marriage is entirely elided. Oaths – twice repeated in the climactic position of the narrative, once in the preceding agreement and once in the actual description of its achievement – take the place of sexual intercourse. We are also told that, after making his oath, Jason:

> … goth with hire to bedde;
> And on the morwe upward he hym spedde,
> For she hath taught hym how he shal nat fayle
> The fles to wynne and stynten his batayle;
> And saved hym his lyf and his honour;
> And gat hym a name ryght as a conquerour,
> Ryght thourgh the sleyghte of hire enchauntement.
> (lines 1654–60)

This account of Medea's strategic instruction of Jason, like the oaths he makes to her, occupies the space within the narrative (and within the bedchamber) that we might expect to be taken up with sexual activity. Medea takes the active role as instructor in the martial, rather than marital, arts, teaching Jason how to win his 'batayle'. The insistent repetition of that term represents the contest with the dragon as one of strength and aggression – stereotypically masculine qualities – rather than one of cunning and deception, right up to the final line. Medea's language is a figurative battleground, filled with 'poynts' akin to sword thrusts, through which she manoeuvres Jason into a position of anticipatory victory over the 'dragoun' and into her bed. Her rhetoric functions as a strategy or even a technology, equipping her with the rhetorical 'poynts' that stand in for her non-existent phallus.

Following common patristic logic, female masculinity is praiseworthy, so one way for Chaucer to accommodate Medea, the byword for a vicious woman, into his valorisation of women is to turn her into a masculine figure.[64] Indeed, this sanctioned gender inversion is something he later plays with in the character of the Second Nun, a self-identified 'sone of Eve'

---

[63] See *MED* entries under headwords declaren (v.) 3, cas (n.) 8, pointe (n. 1), 7 and 8.
[64] See Shawn M. Krahmer, 'The Virile Bride of Bernard of Clairvaux', *Church History* 69.2 (2000): 304–27; Bullough, 'On Being a Male', p. 32.

redeemed to masculinity by her virginity.[65] Like Jerome's idealised woman, Medea eschews the stereotypically carnal feminine role in the bedchamber and replaces it with quintessentially masculine activity, forgoing sexual intercourse for the transmission of battle strategies. Like a virginal or masculinised woman, too, her maternal role is erased. Uniquely, Chaucer omits not only Medea's murder of her children, but also her generation of them in the first place. Departing from Medea, we are told Jason 'with hire lafte *his* yonge children two' (lines 1656–57; emphasis mine). Two children of his, certainly, but not explicitly hers. The story lacks not one, but two generative episodes. In Ovid's version, Jason sows the soil of Colchis with dragon's teeth from which fully armed warriors spring up. The episode in the *Metamorphoses* is unmistakably imagined as a form of telluric and supernatural pregnancy (*Mets* VII, lines 121–38). Although it is the soil that is 'teeming', ('gravidae telluris,' *Mets* VII, line 128), the teeth are dragon's teeth 'soaked in strong poison', ('valido praetincta veneno,' *Mets* VII, line 123) and thus they are patently part of Medea's quasi-maternal magic. In Chaucer's version, no such maternal or quasi-maternal activities take place, significantly lessening the negative associations of Medea with infanticide and with the supernatural. Yet if this is a valorisation of a notorious aggressive and murderous character, it is a cynical and superficial one, for the compensatory association of Medea with masculinity is swiftly undercut with hints of gendered aberration and emasculation. In his opening apostrophe to 'false ... Jasoun' (line 1368), the narrator compares this treacherous lover to a 'fox' and his prey to 'capouns' (line 1389). We are told that:

> But certes, it is both routhe and wo
> That love with false loveres werketh so
> ...
> For evere as tendre a capoun et the fox
> Thow he be fals and hath the foul betrayed,
> As shal the good-man that therefore hath payed,
> Al have he to the capoun skille and ryght,
> The false fox wol have his part at nyght.
> (lines 1384–93)

Scholars have struggled with this image. Delany considers it, like other aspects of the text, 'inept'.[66] Rowe suggests that the syntax here might be misleading, intended instead to equate the capon with Jason, and not his female 'prey'.[67]

---

[65] For the reading of this contested line of the 'Second Nun's Prologue', see Catherine S. Cox, *Gender and Language in Chaucer* (Gainesville, FL: University Press of Florida, 1997), pp. 64–65.
[66] Delany, *The Naked Text*, p. 200.
[67] Donald W. Rowe, *Through Nature to Eternity* (Lincoln, NE: University of Nebraska Press, 1988), p. 60.

Isabel Davis sees it as an instance of 'low tone', borrowed from the world of *fabliaux*, and perhaps an indication of doubt whether 'this provincial narrator ... really is the man to handle epic material'.[68] Yet, in a hermeneutic context, the simile makes perfect sense. Its syntax (*pace* Rowe) conflates women, the prey, with bodies that are caponised, castrated. This codes these bodies as not-quite-male (castrated or emasculated) rather than more-than-female. In a Lacanian sense, castration is implicated in the structuring of human language; Dinshaw's influential reading of the Pardoner's endlessly self-supplementing 'eunuch hermeneutic' applies the concept to the *Canterbury Tales*.[69] The Pardoner's incessantly eloquent verbiage is, like his paraphernalia of relics and documents, a form of prosthetic coverage of his somatic lack, a displacement activity that inevitably draws attention back to the perception of that lack. It recalls Halberstam's theorisations of the role of the prosthetic in the construction of masculinity without maleness, discussed in the introduction to this book.[70] Therefore, in her use of linguistic drag, Medea anticipates the prosthetically supplementing rhetoric of the Pardoner. Her language of 'poynt[s]' is both evocative of penetrative force and a reminder of her bodily lack of a 'poynt' with which to drive home her sexual advances on Jason's body. With unpleasantly mimetic effect, Chaucer incorporates this rhetoric into a narrative that is obtrusively doubled and circular, roaming, like Jason, endlessly from woman to woman. Like a castrated body, the damaged *relicta* narrative of the 'Legend of Hipsiphyle and Medea' is circular and iterative rather than teleological, losing its point in a manner that suggests a narrative castration. Her caponised body is by definition both excessive, and surgically reduced. Caponised bodies are bodies that have had a part removed in order to make them fit for human (and vulpine) consumption; they are carnally objectified. We might then see the image of the 'capoun[s]' and the fox as an illustration of the ways in which women's excessive bodies may, like narratives cut short by *occupatio*, be cut down to size in a manner that suggests the quasi-surgical 'containment' of gender nonconforming or sexually deviant female bodies, prescribed in manuals of medieval medicine.

Insinuated into this rhetorical construction of Medea as a Pardoner-like 'eunuch' is a strand of imagery that complicates the desirous activity of the heroine still further. In her erotic encounters with Jason, Medea occupies a peculiarly vicarious position within the narrative. Like a classic lesbian reader, Medea interpolates herself into a love story between a man and a woman, identifying not with the female beloved, but with the masculine pursuer. She identifies not with Jason, that feminised figure, but Jason's companion Hercules, who plays the role of masculine seducer. Inserting

---

[68] Isabel Davis, 'Introduction', in *Chaucer and Fame: Reputation and Reception*, eds Isabel Davis and Catherine Nall (Cambridge: D. S. Brewer, 2015), pp. 1–20 (p. 13).
[69] Dinshaw, 'Eunuch Hermeneutics', pp. 27–51.
[70] Halberstam, *Female Masculinity*, pp. 3–5.

herself into this already homoerotic triangle, Medea casts herself as masculine lover, not feminine or feminised beloved. Immediately after the description of Medea's instructions as to how to battle the dragon, we are told: 'Now hath Jason the fles, and hom is went / With Medea, and tresor ful gret won' (lines 1651–52). This pointed temporal marker ('now') indicates that the statement refers to the preceding pseudo-sexual instruction: the fleece is a sexual euphemism, that which is won in the battle in the bed. As a euphemism, it draws on those common innuendos relating genitalia to animals used for their fur or their pelts, and is strengthened by the secondary connotation of 'tresor' as relating to (female) virginity. In Chaucer's sources, the implications are clear: the treasure is Medea herself. The *Metamorphoses* identify Medea as 'spolia altera' ('another spoil', *Mets* VII, line 157) alongside the fleece. The *Moralisé* likewise conflates 'la toison … et la bele' ('the fleece … and the beauty', *Moralisé* VII, line 645), and claims that no man could 'ravir' ('ravish', *Moralisé* VII, line 696) Medea of her fleece. Yet in the *Legend*, the genitally suggestive fleece is aligned, not with Medea (or Medea's genitals), but with Jason, as the betrayed Medea laments her attraction to Jason's 'yelwe heer' (line 1672). Like Hipsiphyle before her, Medea desires a feminised property in her lover, and attempts the performance of masculinity that would legitimise this desire.

However, no sooner has Chaucer staged this performance of female masculinity and desire for a feminised body than he disrupts it. Jason, until now 'coy as is a mayde', suddenly shrugs off his feminine silence and displays a hidden aptitude for masculine rhetoric. Appearing to Medea as a man 'goodly of his speche', (line1606), who 'coude of love al craft and art pleyner / Withoute bok' (lines 1607–8), he constructs an exclusionary space of obscurely Latinate allusions, which Medea fails to penetrate. On the surface, the reference to the 'craft and art' of love suggests an attractive degree of courtly erudition. The reference to a 'bok' suggests the mannered forms of courtly love, and the phrase 'without bok' therefore indicates an educated eloquence, an ability to produce a memorised or extemporised speech that satisfies the requirements of rhetorically sophisticated courtship. However, the lines also carry an in-joke for readers equally well acquainted with the textual tradition of writings on love, for the English phrase 'al craft and art of love' neatly translates the Latin title of Ovid's famous work, the *Ars Amatoria* or *Art of Love*. Chaucer's Jason derives much of his character from Ovid's works, likely including the *Ars Amatoria*, whose third book warns women of a list of faithless men, headed by 'fallax Iason': false Jason.[71] Thus, the idea of a Jason whose speech falls 'withoute' (outside) the 'bok' of the 'craft and art of love' is a Jason who separates himself from the Ovidian textual tradition in which he is

---

[71] Ovid, *Ars Amatoria*, in *Ovid: The Art of Love and Other Poems*, eds G. P. Goold and trans. H. J. Mozley, 2nd edn (Cambridge, MA: Harvard University Press, 1985), III, line 33.

listed as false, a Jason who situates himself 'withoute' the space in which such warnings occur. Such an implication, reliant as it is on familiarity with Latin language and literature (albeit in the form of one of the most canonical school texts) would tend to exclude readers along axes of gender and education. Male readers might, however, have been accustomed to exploit the gendered connotations of Latin literacy to construct ties of intimacy, as well as the inevitable exclusionary circles beyond those ties. Rachel Moss provides an example drawn from the correspondence of two young men in the Paston circle. Writing to John Paston II, Thomas Daverse quips that, though he will send his friend a promised copy of Ovid's *De Arte Amandi*,

> me thenketh Ouide *de Remedio* were more mete for yow, but yef [unless] ye purposid to falle hastely in my lady Anne P. lappe, as white as whales bon, &c. Ye be the best cheser of a gentellwoman that I know, &c.[72]

As Moss points out, Daverse' intimate tone and confidence his friend would pick up his literary allusions indicate that both men were familiar with romance both as a practice and as a genre. She also identifies a misogynistic undertone to the communication, noting that the casual abbreviations suggest a certain 'dismissive' attitude towards the woman proposed as the overt target of these attentions. The inventory of John Paston III mentions the *Legend* amongst the family's books; it could well be that the poem was read by father as well as by son, and if so, then Thomas Daverse's allusion to Ovid's *Art of Love* might well have reminded his friend of a similar moment in the *Legend*.[73] The slyly exclusionary cross-lingual reference to Jason's 'craft and art of love' works, like the Thomas Daverse's letter, to insinuate readers capable of recognising the literary reference into an exclusive group implicitly differentiated from the unaware woman on whom their attention focuses. As a homosocial bonding exercise (whether between Paston intimates or Jason and the male readers of the *Legend*), it excludes even those women who seek to model their intimacies with men on such male–male exercises of affection, depending on a Latinity that cannot be acquired by imitation.

This ominous beginning prepares for a second departure from Ovid, this time more subtle. When Medea laments her attraction to Jason, she does so in words Chaucer borrows almost exactly from Ovid's *Heroides*. Ovid's Medea berates herself, asking herself 'why did I take more pleasure than I should in your golden hair, and your comeliness, and the lying favours of your tongue?' (*Heroides* XII, lines 13–14).[74] Chaucer's Medea, unlike Ovid's, omits to categorise Jason's speech as lies, and where Ovid's Medea regrets her

---

[72] Quoted by Rachel E. Moss, *Fatherhood and its Representations in Middle English Texts* (Cambridge: D. S. Brewer, 2013), p. 35.

[73] London, British Library, MS Additional 43391, f. 26r.

[74] cur mihi plus aequo flavi placuere capilli
et decor et linguae gratia ficta tuae?

delight in 'the lying favours of your tongue', Chaucer omits the 'lying' from his translation, instead adding a superlative to render the phrase: 'of thy tonge, the infynyt graciousnesse' (line 1675). The change has two effects. Firstly, it signals Medea's desire as aberrant through a crudely genital innuendo. As Jane Burns observes at length in *Bodytalk* and as we saw in Chapter One, the tongue and the clitoris are frequently represented as analogues of each other. In this context, Medea's omission of 'ficta' leaves the categorisation of the activity of the tongue more open to interpretation. The pleasures of Jason and Medea's relationship are coded as lingual, not phallic, and whereas in Ovid the pleasing action of Jason's tongue is unquestionably employed in producing fictions, in Chaucer there is a risqué ambiguity as to *which* of the many activities in which tongues can be used so pleased Medea. Secondly, however, the excision of 'ficta' from Chaucer's version hammers home the point made in the previous Latinate pun: Medea is deceived not so much by pleasing fictions as by her own gender-bounded lack of language. Ultimately, for all her attempts to construct 'poynt[s]' through her strategic words, it is her lack of Latin 'tongue' that enables Jason to trick her by flaunting Ovid's warning of his deceit in her uncomprehending face.

CONCLUSION

The 'Legend of Hipsiphyle and Medea' lingers over an embodied desire always implicitly present within the *relicta* narrative: the desire of a female protagonist to play a quasi-masculine or lesbian-like role in relation to a male protagonist displaying what Classical and medieval *auctores* castigate as effeminacy, and what we might call male femininity. Hipsiphyle and Medea in effect 'revisit' the narrative of Dido, both in that Chaucer positions their narrative directly after hers, and in that her story (though chronologically later in Classical history) takes a prior and paradigmatic place in relation to other *relicta* narratives. Yet whereas masculine readers of Dido from Augustine to Chaucer represent themselves as successful emulators of Aeneas, able to break free from desire and follow a masculine trajectory, Hipsiphyle and Medea become trapped in language, deceived by Jason's capacity simultaneously to play masculine or feminine roles. A degraded inversion of Constance of the *Canterbury Tales*, swept by sea from shore to shore and sliding fluently across registers of language, Jason epitomises the linguistic and libidinal dangers of translation, as he persistently reinvents himself through slippery rhetoric. Constantly reorienting his course and transforming his gender identity in the process, he leaves in his wake a debris of women, whose abbreviated narratives are overtly marked by absences of source material. As Chaucer excises Hipsiphyle's Amazonian past and Medea's maternity, constantly directing readers to fill in the gaps in his text, he invites readers to participate in the same process of looking back to a prior narrative in order to extend and supplement a current one. Yet as Medea signally fails to graft herself into the prior story of Jason's intimate relations, she reveals herself to be less successful in this practice than Chaucer imagines his readers might be. The rhetorical prosthesis she seeks only emphasises her innate lack. The pleasures of a 'lesbian-like' mode of reading, a mode of reading that returns to gaps and absences in the text, is appropriated by the Jasons of the story, by the Latinate reader Chaucer interpellates. By contrast, Hipsiphyle and Medea are pejoratively coded, not as women desirous of male femininity, but as 'capouns': bodies defined by their phallic lack. As the 'Legend of Hipsiphyle and Medea' ends by looking forward to Jason's third courtship and betrayal of 'the doughter of the kyng Creon' (lines 1661), it resists any form of *telos*, whether the ending claimed by Dido for herself or the masculine trajectory of Aeneas towards Rome. It offers up a 'castrated' narrative whose form is, like that of the 'Legend of Philomela', unpleasantly mimetic of the 'caponised' and vulnerable bodies of its heroines.

4

STONY FEMININITY AND THE LIMITS OF DESIRE IN *THE SOWDONE OF BABYLON*

The early fifteenth-century *Sowdone of Babylon* has its roots in a twelfth-century *chanson de geste*.¹ This *chanson* blends romance with chivalric violence and nationalistic piety, describing how Charlemagne's knights reclaimed the stolen relics of Christ's crucifixion for the nascent empire of France. Its heroine is the Muslim princess Floripas.² Flooded with fiery passion and weeping emotion, she exemplifies the *belle sarrasin* trope so beloved of French *chanson de geste* and English romance: the beautiful Muslim woman whose aberrant femininity delimits the boundaries of ideal Christian womanhood, and who is ultimately contained within the structure of Christian marriage.³ Yet in *The Sowdone of Babylon*, all certainties are called into question. To anyone familiar with the *chanson* or the subsequent Anglo-Norman and Middle English versions of the text, the *Sowdone*

---

1   The *Sowdone of Babylon* survives in a single manuscript, Princeton, MS Garrett 140, dating to around 1440. The text has been edited by Alan Lupack, in *Three Middle English Charlemagne Romances* (Kalamazoo, MI: Medieval Institute Publications, 1990). All quotations are from this edition.
2   In this chapter, I draw on Shokoofeh Rajabzadeh's persuasive argument that the term 'Saracen', as part of a medieval Islamophobic rhetoric of misrepresenting Muslims, should be kept for direct quotations from medieval texts, rather than being used as a general label for a people. See Rajabzadeh, 'The Depoliticised Saracen and Muslim Erasure', *Literature Compass Special Issue: Critical Race and the Middle Ages* 16.9–10 (2019): e12548. I discuss this argument in more detail later in this chapter.
3   Much has been written about unions between Christians and Muslims in medieval English and French romance. See, for example, Geraldine Heng, *The Invention of Race in the European Middle Ages* (Cambridge: Cambridge University Press, 2018), pp. 127–62; Amy Burge, *Representing Difference in the Medieval and Modern Orientalist Romance* (New York: Palgrave Macmillan, 2016); Akbari, *Idols in the East*, pp. 176–99; Sharon Kinoshita, *Medieval Boundaries: Rethinking Difference in Old French Literature* (Philadelphia, PA: University of Pennsylvania Press, 2006), pp. 46–73, 176–99; Siobhain Bly, *Saracens and the Making of English Identity* (New York: Routledge, 2005), pp. 61–96; Heng, *Empire of Magic*, pp. 181–238; Heffernan, *The Orient in Chaucer and Romance*; Dorothee Metlitzki, *The Matter of Araby in Medieval Romance* (New Haven, CT: Yale University Press, 1977).

of Babylon's most striking quality is what it does *not* contain. The profuse language of sensuality, which washes through the counterpart texts to infuse both the female protagonist and the religious relics with an almost interchangeable desirability, is nowhere to be found.[4] Desire in the *Sowdone* is puzzlingly difficult to locate. In this respect, the text stages one of the central questions of this book. Women who do not desire men baffle both medieval and modern categories. How can female desires and emotions defined by resistance to erotic or emotional contact with men be understood, not merely as negative or lacking states, but also as autonomous expressions of sexuality? Related to this enquiry, and often pressed into service in the attempt to pin down these elusive, negatively defined sexualities, is the question of how femininity relates to female sexuality, and how aberrations in gender reflect, predict, coexist with or qualify alternative sexualities. The conversation is not confined to the medieval period, and can be found submerged in some very recent ecofeminist and queer theory. This chapter probes the implications of that seldom-acknowledged relationship between medieval and contemporary, yoking together medieval medical and philosophical theories of female fertility with late medieval anxieties about the pregnant body and the pregnant potential of the relic, to shed light on more recent theories of female, queer and posthuman embodiment. In this chapter, I explore the cultural discourses that inform the *Sowdone of Babylon* and its tradition, and I argue that the *Sowdone*'s rejection and reconfiguration of those discourses might offer a model for transforming contemporary theorisations of gender and desire.

POROUS BODIES, SEALED VESSELS: FLUID CONSTRUCTIONS OF FEMININITY

Since Carolyn Dinshaw's ground-breaking analysis of the association between covert desires and religious deviancies, the two topics have often been brought into conversation. Earlier in this book I argued that the enclosed, mutilated and prosthetically supplemented body of Philomela evokes the censorious suspicions some writers express concerning the inappropriate sexual or erotic activities of enclosed women religious. However, the narratives I discuss in this chapter allow that topic to take centre stage. In their focus on a woman defined by her divergence from Christian ideals of femininity, the Floripas narratives reflect a particular nexus of medieval ideas about gendered bodies

---

[4] In this, the *Sowdone* runs counter to the general trend, identified by Akbari, for later medieval versions of the narrative to increase the emphasis on Floripas' sensual and exoticised beauty. See Suzanne Conklin Akbari, 'Woman as Mediator in Medieval Depictions of Muslims: The Case of Floripas', in *Medieval Constructions in Gender and Identity: Essays in Honour of Joan M. Ferrante*, ed. Teodolinda Barolini (Tempe, AZ: Arizona Centre for Medieval and Renaissance Studies, 2005), pp. 151–67 (p. 154).

and desires. As relic narratives, they focus questions concerning these religious objects and their place in affective practices. Increasingly, in a late medieval English context, relics condense a particularly gendered set of anxieties relating to the display and direction of emotion, the boundaries between animate and inanimate, and the turning of women's desires away from reproductive sexuality.[5] These narratives thus carry the potential to accommodate anxieties about these topics. Equally, however, these texts explore the ways in which a pejorative construction of racial and religious alterity manifests as aberrant performance of gender. As Suzanne Conklin Akbari has shown, medieval English and French narratives depicting marriages of Muslims and Christians are rooted in centuries-old medico-philosophical discourses of femininity, which construct the ideal female body as a fertile, fluid and penetrable 'matter'.[6] The tradition to which the *Sowdone of Babylon* belongs thus has potential both for arousing and for resolving anxieties. However, to understand how it achieves this position, we must look to the discourses that circulate around it.

Medieval discourses contesting the definition of femininity orbit around the idea of the gestational body. We can identify an affective model of femininity that conflates fluidity, emotional openness and fertility; this is countered by a monitory discourse, which idealises feminine containment, enclosure and chastity. At its heterodox fringes, the latter discourse gives way to an animosity towards the female body and its messy fluidity, and suspicion of pregnant bodies, including even that of the Virgin Mary. This animosity is inflected by the closely related discourses surrounding relics. In their potential to attract misdirected or excessive emotion (the wrong kind of adoration), relics function as a dangerously emotive focus of feminine desire and aberrant sexuality. The discourse is also specifically imbricated with ideas about the gestational body, for the fears generated by relics open out from the 'ordinary' anxiety and even distrust occasioned by the everyday pregnant body, with which relics share the basic capacity to contain an excess of themselves.[7] The interpenetration of relic discourse with religious anxieties about female fertility and sexuality and both with much older ideas about the gestational body gives us the highly charged culture of the early fifteenth century, into which the *Sowdone* was translated.

To understand these debates, we must look backwards from the late medieval period. The alignment of the feminine with the fluid and emotional is perhaps the most enduring model of femininity in Western culture. Its

---

[5] These ideas underlie Dinshaw's *Getting Medieval*; they also feature in Lochrie's examinations of heresy in *Covert Operations*, pp. 177–228 and *Heterosyncrasies*, pp. 47–60.
[6] Akbari, *Idols in the East*, pp. 155–99.
[7] Chaganti, *Poetics of the Reliquary*, p. 75. For discussion of the everyday pregnant body as a source of fear, see Julia Kristeva, *Powers of Horror: An Essay on Abjection*, trans. Leon S. Roudiez (New York: Columbia University Press, 1982), p. 77.

implications underpin this book from the introduction onwards, and I here revisit the medical theories (notably the writings of Isidore) discussed elsewhere, with a particular view to what they imply about the generative functions of the female body. Women, we saw in the introduction, were held to be naturally more imperfect, and in medical terms this was understood in terms of their humoral state. Galenic traditions of medicine posited that four humours (cold and hot, wet and dry) governed the body and also the temperament of each person, with women predisposed to a colder and moister state than the more perfect balance of men.[8] Accordingly, in the now familiar formulation of the seventh-century bishop Isidore of Seville, woman (*mulier*) takes her name from the fact that she is *mollior* (softer; gentler) than a man. Femininity is to be associated with softness and penetrability, with nurturing fertile potential and fluid emotional expression.[9] Dominated by moist humours, the female body is softened into liquidity, like melted wax. Just as wax is receptive to the imprint of the seal thrust into it, so too the female body is receptive to impregnation, and a watery body promises fertility. These same watery elements work upon the female body's affective processes, expressing their presence in effusions of emotion, which reciprocally bear witness to the fluid fertility they enable. This model of femininity may best be understood in relation to its quintessential example, the Virgin Mary. Mary's body overflows with liquid expressions of emotion intimately related to her role as mother of Christ. The liquids that spill forth from her body – milk, tears, amniotic fluid, blood – may be understood as manifestations of the same substance, the moist humour of the medical theory, and they exist in a reciprocal relation to her emotions.[10] As *virgo lactans*, she feeds her infant breastmilk that symbolises her outpouring of compassion for humanity; as the weeping mother of the *pietà*, her tears express the depths of her sorrow.

Modern reinterpretations of the same ideas help show how such a model of femininity might be both powerful and transformative. Astrida Neimanis' 2016 monograph proposes an ecofeminist exploration of fluid embodiment, mobilising the concept of 'bodies of water' as a weapon against 'masculinist

---

[8] See Robert M. Stelmack and Anastasios Stalikas, 'Galen and the Humour Theory of Temperament', *Personality and Individual Differences* 12.3 (1991): 255–64; Rebecca Flemming, *Medicine and the Making of Roman Women: Gender, Nature, and Authority from Celsus to Galen* (Oxford: Oxford University Press, 2000), pp. 228–358; for specifically medieval perspectives, see Sauer, *Gender in Medieval Culture*, pp. 24–31.

[9] For detailed discussion of French and English descriptions of Muslims more generally, see Akbari's *Idols in the East*, pp. 155–99 and 'From Due East to True North: Orientalism and Orientation', in *The Postcolonial Middle Ages*, ed. Jeffrey Jerome Cohen (New York: Palgrave, 2001), pp. 19–34.

[10] Karine van 't Land, 'Sperm and Blood, Form and Food: Late Medieval Medical Notions of Male and Female in the Embryology of Membra', in *Blood, Sweat and Tears: The Changing Concepts of Physiology from Antiquity into Early Modern Europe*, eds Manfred Horstmanshoff, Helen King and Claus Zittel (Leiden: Brill, 2012), pp. 363–92.

logic'.[11] Neimanis observes that the same water that circulates through the cells of the human body permeates natural and artificial ecosystems. This shared wateriness offers a model through which to challenge the idea of the human as discrete, autonomous and sovereign, 'those discrete, zipped up skins of Enlightenment individualism'.[12] Made up mostly of water, bodies are permeable and porous; these same qualities are, in medieval thought, associated with the fluidity of the female body.[13] Neimanis' feminist exploration of this bodily fluidity charts the transmission of drugs into and through breast milk, as she concludes that the watery operations of bodies implicate us all in ethical interactions reaching beyond our individual human bodies and beyond the human species.[14] She accords 'gestational' liquids such as amniotic fluid an important role in her description of this watery anatomy, and does so primarily to topple the male-as-default model that has given us the assumption that human beings are discrete, autonomous, bounded beings. Further, she uses the idea of water to break down the binaries between human and non-human, animate and inanimate. Water constitutes the human body, yet the same water that washes through the cells of the human bodies may also flow through rivers, seas and lakes and even water-treatment plants, drains and sewers, for 'the bodies from which we siphon and into which we pour ourselves are certainly other human bodies ... but they are just as likely a sea, a cistern, an underground reservoir of once-was-rain'.[15] From this commonality, she draws up a political manifesto for recognising our ethical implication in these watery systems. Neimanis' central argument is that this conceptual model of the body as watery will take us beyond an Anthropocene, human-centred view of the planet; it will induce us to recognise our commonalities with the bodies of water into which and from which we are constantly being transformed. She reads this process in terms of queer theory, insofar as it effects a blurring of the binary distinctions between the animate and inanimate, the human and non-human, and also insofar as she places the human 'reprosexual' anatomy, the gestational waters of the womb in particular, only on a continuum with other generative bodies of water not constrained by a binary of masculine/feminine. However, she explicitly identifies her feminine-coded language of amniotic and lactational fluids as a rhetorical means of combatting the phallogocentrism of the discourse with which she takes issue. For her, the

---

[11] Neimanis, *Bodies of Water*, p. 3.
[12] Ibid., p. 33.
[13] *The Diseases of Women*, attributed to Hippocrates, claimed that women's flesh was 'spongier' than men's and therefore more porous and absorbent. See discussion of this by Helen King, 'The Mathematics of Sex: One to Two, or Two to One?', in *Sexuality and Culture in Medieval and Renaissance Europe*, eds Philip M. Soergel and Andrew Barnes (New York: AMS Press, 2005), pp. 47–58 (p. 51).
[14] Neimanis, *Bodies of Water*, pp. 33–34.
[15] Ibid., p. 2.

feminine connotations of somatic fluidity and effusive emotion are not to be excluded from the expansion from human to posthuman, but rather, they are the rhetorical means whereby such an expansion can be strategised. Arguing that we are implicated in the endless porous circulations between bodies and their surroundings, between organic and inorganic waters and waterways, Neimanis valorises fluidity to expose the limitations of the masculinist ideal of the sovereign and discrete individual.

Neimanis' model makes it possible for us to see how an Isidorean model of female emotionality and fluidity might underpin an imagery of radical transformation, and obtain real conceptual power. The expressive reciprocality of emotion and liquid is not limited in its operations to the fertile female body, but also works in a more broadly generative way to produce from seemingly inanimate materials the substances that testify to emotional and biological processes. This is best illustrated by the genre of miracle stories in which stone statues of saints melt into real tears in response to imploring prayers, or wooden images bleed to signify divine passion.[16] Such effusions of liquid may be understood as humoral proof of the reality of the emotion through which they were brought into being, an emotion coded as feminine. Thus, Mary's own tears are human tears, but they gesture towards a complete and coherent affective system reaching beyond the human. The Isidorean model of the porous feminine body, manifesting affect beyond its corporeal limits, is not so dissimilar from Neimanis' watery body, implicated in networks of fluid contact beyond its own permeable boundaries. This model of the fluid female body is therefore generative, not merely in terms of being descriptive of what makes female fertility, conception and gestation possible, but also in ontological terms, as it produces new understandings of matter (water, stone, blood, tears), and of the ways in which matter may be transformed from the inanimate to the animate.

The radically transformative power inherent in this model of the feminine as fluid and affective generates predictable anxieties. If the female body is fluid, it is also porous, leaking liquids uneasily associated with affect or sexuality, taking in foreign matter and confusing ideological and conceptual categories. If feminine affect offers a model for transforming our sense of the animate and the inanimate, the human and the non-human, the transformation may also be imagined in reverse, as objects involved in human relations become lifeless or too lively, even monstrous. Robert Mills and Gary Waller discuss the paradoxes through which medieval religious dissenters approach the crying

---

[16] The weeping or bleeding of statues generates considerable anxiety: Knighton records a story of Lollards who cut the head off a statue of St Katharine, to see whether it would bleed. See Sarah Stanbury, *The Visual Object of Desire in Late Medieval England* (Philadelphia, PA: University of Pennsylvania Press, 2008), p. 107; see also Gary Waller, *The Virgin Mary in Late Medieval and Early Modern Literature and Popular Culture* (Cambridge: Cambridge University Press, 2011), pp. 14–15.

statues and other miracles discussed above, and Mills notes that their rhetoric simultaneously exposes the mechanical operations of such statues (such as the Boxley Rood of Grace, operated using strings and sticks to move the parts) and is filled with images of organic decay and collapse mobilised in opposition to this mechanical operation.[17] These statues, these mechanical structures, are *machina* in the medieval sense as well as machines (or identity-machines) in the terminology used by contemporary queer theorists.[18] They are therefore not merely 'queer' in the sense of troubling the boundaries between animate and inanimate, human and cyborg, but also in the sense of being conceptually aligned with the deviant sexual practices the writers of penitentials associate with the *machina*: the sexual practices of women that rely on some non-human, inanimate substitute for a male penis.[19] As Dinshaw and Lochrie both note, the *Twelve Conclusions* sets up disconcerting parallels between the sexual deviances of women, especially nuns, who have intercourse 'with hemself or with creature that beris no lyf', and the religious deviancies of those who venerate relics and mistake the 'lifeless' objects for the human saints they memorialise.[20] This reading of feminine deviancy is grounded in a negative reading of the imbrication of liquid and emotion, and a particular suspicion of its capacity to blur or collapse boundaries between animate and inanimate bodies. It is far from unique to heterodox texts, appearing also in such vivid narratives as the Middle English romance *The King of Tars*, which produces a nightmarish image of formless flesh in place of a living baby, as the result of a Christian woman's intimacy with a Muslim man.[21] Inanimate objects thus become touchstones for women's excessive or misdirected desires, which spill over limits and flow between categories.

Predictably, much medieval writing on the subject of feminine embodiment and affect seeks to idealise that which is contained, not overflowing; enclosed, not open; controlled, not emotionally effusive; and chaste or virginal, not fertile. Lochrie locates the task of rhetorical containment of unsettled, 'fissured' femininity primarily in the hagiographic and mystical

---

[17] Robert Mills, 'Queering the Un/Godly: Christ's Humanities and Medieval Sexuality', in *Queering the Non/Human*, eds Noreen Giffney and Myra J. Hird (Aldershot: Ashgate, 2008), pp. 111-36 (pp. 126-27); Waller, *The Virgin Mary*, pp. 14-15.

[18] Mills, 'Queering the Un/Godly', p. 127.

[19] I discuss this more fully in my introduction.

[20] The text of the *Twelve Conclusions* is edited by Anne Hudson, *Selections from English Wycliffite Writings* (Toronto: University of Toronto Press, 1997), pp. 24-29 (p. 28). Quoted and discussed in Lochrie, *Heterosyncrasies*, pp. 47-60, and Dinshaw, *Getting Medieval*, pp. 88-90.

[21] Siobhain Bly Calkin, 'Marking Religion on the Body: Saracens, Categorization, and *The King of Tars*', *Journal of English and Germanic Philology* 104 (2005): 219-38; Jane Gilbert, 'Unnatural Mothers and Monstrous Children in *The King of Tars* and *Sir Gowther*', in *Medieval Women: Texts and Contexts in Late Medieval Britain: Essays for Felicity Riddy* (Turnhout: Brepols, 2000), pp. 329-44.

discourses, which valorise instead the 'sealed' woman – silent, cloistered, virginal – who keeps to her boundaries.[22] It is something of an irony that these discourses seek to analogise the female body, as far as is possible, to an inanimate object. Devotional and mystical texts urge their female readers to imagine their bodies as stone structures, monasteries or cells whose chambers are locked against ingress; romances represent their heroines' bodies as coterminous with the towers and castles they inhabit. Tellingly, the thirteenth-century *Hali Meidhad* even describes virginity as a balm that prevents the body from rotting, implicitly constructing the virginal female body as a form of living relic, a 'treasure' preserved from physical or spiritual decay.[23] Thus the 'sealed' female body is imagined as a body preserved from the corruptions of the flesh, much like a relic. In an endless transfer of anxieties, there develops a rhetoric wherein the fluid and porous potential of the Virgin's generative womb is limited by reference to the stony, inanimate qualities of reliquaries or statues – the very objects whose lack of animate fluidity arouses suspicion. The Virgin's pregnant body is imagined in terms that downplay its messy and fluid femininity, its capacity to gush amniotic fluid or blood, and its in- or supra-organic nature is emphasised. For example, as Jacqueline Tasioulas observes, artists picturing the Virginal womb visualised a 'smoothly sculpted' space rather than a realistic uterus.[24] Mystics such as Gertrude of Helfta and Bridget of Sweden described this space in great detail, in terms of gold, silk and crystals that evoke the reliquary. Thus, the Virgin's womb was 'immaculate ... as transparent as the purest crystal, through which her internal organs, penetrated and filled with divinity, shone brightly, just as gold, wrapped in silk of various colours, shines' and with 'the caul, that the child was born with, lined all in white'.[25] In visual culture, the moving statues known as *vierges ouvrantes* represent the Virginal womb as a gilded, painted space, a cavity that may contain a tiny, fully formed Trinity, but no fluid or suggestion of fluid. Within the *vierge ouvrante* we find the smooth, hard surfaces that reify the architectural metaphors of Mary as *turris David* or

---

[22] Lochrie, *Margery Kempe and Translations of the Flesh*, p. 6.
[23] *Hali Meidhad*, ed. Bella Millett (London: Oxford University Press, 1982), line 6. For the rhetoric of virginal bodies as treasures or sealed vessels, see Jane Tibbetts Schulenburg, *Forgetful of Their Sex: Female Sanctity and Society ca. 500–1100* (Chicago, IL: University of Chicago Press, 2001), p. 128; for images of virginity and balm, see Clarissa Atkinson, '"Precious Balsam in a Fragile Glass": The Ideology of Virginity in the Later Middle Ages', *Journal of Family History* 8 (1983): 131–43.
[24] Tasioulas, 'The Foetal Existence of Christ', p. 28.
[25] Gertrude of Helfta, *Œvres spirituelles, Le Héraut*, ed. P. Doyère et al. (Paris: Editions du Cerf, 1968–78), IV, 50–52, 4.3.3–4. Quoted in Tasioulas, 'The Foetal Existence of Christ', p. 30 and Jeffrey Hamburger, *The Visual and the Visionary: Art and Female Spirituality in Late Medieval Germany* (New York: Zone Books, 1998), p. 118. See also Sarah Elliott Novavich, 'Transparent Mary: Visible Interiors and the Maternal Body in the Middle Ages', *Journal of English and Germanic Philology* 166.4 (2018): 464–90 (p. 467).

turris eburnea in the Song of Songs. These are not images of a sealed organic body, but of a body made inorganic, transformed into mineral, from within. The qualities attributed to the Virgin's body – its refusal to be acted upon as ordinary maternal bodies are acted upon by pregnancy; its aloofness from sin; its rejection of feminine fluidity and leakiness – are disconcertingly close to inertness. The Virgin's hard, white, bloodless womb is grotesquely evocative of a body drained of blood in miscarriage, or of a statue of marble and paint. These strenuous attempts to represent the Virgin's body as stony, bloodless, contained and inorganic, succeed in negating those somatic qualities of fluidity and softness typically associated with female fertility and capacity to conceive. Seeking to define the perfected feminine body as lacking the messy fluidity and fleshliness of woman in her natural state, these writers and artists succeed in transforming the Virgin into something disturbingly akin to the inanimate objects that, elsewhere, disclose deviant female desires and deviant female capacities to trouble the boundary between human and inhuman.

In heterodox discourses, the imagery of the pregnant Virgin provokes predictable animosity. Elina Gertsman notes that the *vierges ouvrantes* aroused (and continue to arouse) violently coercive responses, often disfigured by being (tellingly) 'glued shut or gutted'.[26] A similar form of rhetorical violence likewise targets the Virgin's womb in post-Wycliffite English writings, where the emphasis is on the emptiness of that space: a 'sack', a 'saffron bag' or a 'pudding when the meat was taken out'.[27] Motivated in part by the desire to distinguish the substance of Christ's body from that of his mother – to deny her maternal contributions and represent her simply as a vessel – these epithets rhetorically seal off her body from his by insisting on its inanimacy, its emptiness, its separateness. The imagery of bags, sacks or statues glued shut suggests a paranoia about the too-open body that expresses itself by denying the organic and reproductive functions of that body. This literal and rhetorical violence is also part of a larger tradition of violence and censure directed at relics and reliquaries, exposing the conceptual exchangeability of the idea of the relic and the idea of the pregnant body.

In the final twist of this double helix of discourses constructing femininity and its embodied aberrations, relics are also analogised to the female body in pregnancy. Reliquaries in the shape of the pregnant Virgin Mary bear witness to a shared logic of materiality. As Sarah Stanbury cogently argues, the relic is a part whose inner meaning always exceeds its material substance, an object enclosed within structures definitively lesser than itself.[28] The paradox of 'heaven and earth in little space', of the containment of Christ

---

[26] Elina Gertsman, *Worlds Within: Opening the Medieval Shrine Madonna* (University Park, PA: Pennsylvania State University Press, 2015), p. 2.

[27] Mary E. Fissell, *Vernacular Bodies: The Politics of Reproduction in Early Modern England* (Oxford: Oxford University Press, 2004), p. 25.

[28] Stanbury, *The Visual Object of Desire*, p. 17.

within a human, female body, is analogous to the paradox of the relic. It is conceptually aligned with the body of the Virgin Mary – the quintessential reliquary – which, carrying the Word within itself, 'contains the modes of its own representation and is contained by them'.[29] As Robyn Malo points out, relics operate in terms of *translatio*, which is both the term for their movement from shrine to shrine, and the grammatical name for metaphor, the rhetorical expression of a gap.[30] Relics never achieve fixed meaning, never communicate stably, but remain semiotically fluid, and their fluidity and quasi-gestational enclosure in reliquaries condense anxieties relating to female fertility and result, predictably, in monitory emphases on their stony inanimacy.[31]

This conversation is tensely, even claustrophobically, drawn in on itself, even as it spreads out across the centuries. Women are associated with excess, with transformation, with pregnant potential, with affect reaching beyond the body, and with the collapsing of boundaries between animate and inanimate. Attempts to control, diffuse or police these qualities are advanced from both orthodox and heterodox religious perspectives, and the nature of these attempts bears witness not only to anxiety but also to disgust and fear of female desires orientated towards taboo objects. In the medieval context, relic discourse is drawn by an almost centripetal force into the ambit of constructions of femininity, offering a parallel discourse of the valorising and the policing of desires. Consequently, the pre-existing structures for thinking about female desire are imbricated with religious writings, and a circular transfer of anxieties recurs over and over through medieval writing. In early fifteenth-century England, these circulating anxieties are highly visible in Wycliffite and anti-Wycliffite contexts, and spill over into much popular writing. The narrative of Floripas, with its juxtaposition of desire for relics and desire for a woman, offers a tantalising context for exploring deviant female sexuality and female gender noncomformity.

FEMININE FLUIDITY AND THE COLONISING ROMANCE

The tradition of narratives of which the *Sowdone* is part stretches from the twelfth-century *chanson* to an early fourteenth-century Anglo-Norman text that is the *Sowdone*'s direct source, to the two independent late medieval English poems, both dating from within a few years of the *Sowdone*, that were translated more directly from the *chanson*.[32] These two Middle English

---

[29] Chaganti, *Poetics of the Reliquary*, p. 75.
[30] Malo, *Relics and Writing*, p. 8. Malo draws on Carolyn Dinshaw's comments on translation in *Chaucer's Sexual Poetics*, pp. 133–34.
[31] See Malo, *Relics and Writing*, p. 134.
[32] For discussion of the evolution of the Floripas narrative across medieval Europe, see Hans-Erich Keller, 'La Belle Sarrasin dans *Fierabras* et ses dérivés', in *Charlemagne in the North: Proceedings of the Twelfth International Conference of the Société Rencesvals,*

analogues of the *Sowdone* exist in unique witnesses, as does the *Sowdone* itself, and are to be found in London, British Library MS Additional 37492 (the Fillingham *Firumbras*, which I abbreviate to F), and in Oxford, Bodleian Library MS Ashmole 33 (the Ashmole *Ferumbras*, which I abbreviate to A). The *Sowdone* itself survives in Princeton, MS Garrett 140.[33] These narratives are all deeply concerned with the ways in which bodies labelled as 'Saracen' – and especially the bodies of women – might fit into the evolving discourses of feminine fluidity and relic-like containment discussed in the previous section. Thus they participate in the construction of a caricatured and fictionalised version of Muslim embodiment, which functions as point of contrast to Christianity. As Shokoofeh Rajabzadeh has observed, the construction of 'the Saracen' in medieval Western literature is 'not a real identity' nor yet a name for a character existing only in fiction, but rather the label under which pejorative misrepresentation of Muslims is inscribed.[34] Yet despite their near-contemporaneity, the *Sowdone* is very different from its Middle English analogues, and from the older versions. Its constructions of gendered Muslim bodies are very unlike those of the main tradition, and thus it carries potential for a radical reconfiguration of the Christian nexus of ideas about femininity, fluidity and the fertile body, which the existing rhetoric of race seeks to cement. In this section, I will explore these differences in detail.

The *Sowdone*'s earliest source text, the twelfth-century French *chanson*, sets up a rich network of images of feminine sensuality, concentrated on the figure of Floripas. This sensual imagery intermingles with the almost eroticised devotion with which the relics are treated, and Floripas and the relics are frequently portrayed as almost interchangeable objects within a Christian male orbit of desirous acquisition. In this, the *chanson* is inflected by the discourses I have discussed in the previous section, drawing on a wealth of ideas about femininity, emotion, relics and the body, but the text neatly resolves and contains implicit tensions. Instead of circulating anxieties endlessly, worrying about the excessive fluidity of a fertile woman's body or expressing horror at its polar opposite, the image of stony containment, the *chanson* cleverly uses the relics and the desirable female body as safety valves for the anxieties that attach to each polarised idea: thus the relics function as sanctioned and licit objects of desire in place of Floripas' disturbingly sensual Muslim body, and

---

Edinburgh 4th to 11th August 1991, eds Philip E. Bennett, Anne Elizabeth Cobby and Graham A. Runnalls (London: Grant and Cutler, 1993), pp. 299–307; for more on the versions written in England, see Phillipa Hardman and Marianne Ailes, *The Legend of Charlemagne in Medieval England: The Matter of France in Middle English and Anglo-Norman Literature* (Cambridge: D. S. Brewer, 2017), pp. 264–345.

33 A version of the Anglo-Norman survives in London, British Library MS Egerton 3028, and has been edited by Louis Brandin, '*La Destruction de Rome* et *Fierabras*, MS Egerton 3028 de Musée Britannique', *Romania* 64 (1938): 18–100. Quotations and line references are from this edition.

34 Rajabzadeh, 'The Depoliticised Saracen', p. 5.

then in turn, she acts as an appropriately sexual target of desire that displaces any concerns about excessive or misdirected emotion orientated towards the relics. This remarkably successful dynamic persists into the translations of the *chanson*. The two Middle English translations of the *chanson* that are contemporary with the *Sowdone* seem keen to deepen the emphasis on the relics as proxies for Floripas' body, in a manner suggestive of pointed defensive response to Lollard critiques of relics and devotion. Yet the *Sowdone* is quite different. It works to move beyond the endlessly polarising binaries I identify above, to break through those constant oppositions of boundless fertility and generative, fluid emotion countered by contained sterility and stony inanimacy. In so doing, it transforms the figure of Floripas into a gender-nonconforming heroine, a warrior woman who transforms her narrative.

In the *chanson*, Floripas' story of conversion and romance begins when the princess falls into sympathy with her father's enemies. Flooded with compassion for her father's Christian prisoners, she saves them, revealing that it is she who has guardianship of the holy relics of Christ's crucifixion, stolen from Rome. Her father is defeated and she is baptised before a dazzled and grateful French court and married to Guy of Burgundy, bringing Iberia into Christian control. Her sexualised femininity marks her amenability to conversion and her potential to perform the *sine qua non* of the romance genre by conceiving children for her French husband. Akbari refers to the Floripas of the *chanson* as 'the fertile ground that gives rise to a Christian Self that incorporates the Muslim Other'; for Vance the text offers 'male fantasies of the woman's body ... as a pliable, waxlike entity whose boundaries are vulnerable and changing, but whose penetration can also nurture new fulfilments'.[35] A *belle sarrasin* conforming to that trope's expectations of fertility and amenability to conversion, she is also, in Akbari's view, unlike other *belles sarrasins* in that her long-standing presence in the narrative and her keeping of her name post-baptism result in an unusually 'extended period during which Floripas is neither wholly Saracen nor wholly Christian', which 'constitutes a liminal phase during which not only Floripas's identity, but also the feminine ideal itself, is in flux'.[36] The basic plot proves an appealing vehicle for late medieval English translators, easily accommodating topical anxieties, notably those concerning relics and the imbricated deviations of religious and sexual desires. However, the *Sowdone* is unique in its reframing of the source tradition's treatment of gender. In it, Floripas embodies a stony and impenetrable femininity, a resolute refusal to yield or soften with emotion. The radical rewriting of her character here constitutes a searching involvement with the wider controversies

---

[35] Akbari, *Idols in the East*, p. 189; Eugene Vance, 'Style and Value: From Soldier to Pilgrim in the Song of Roland', *Yale French Studies* (special issue), *Contexts: Style and Values in Medieval Art and Literature* (1991): 75–96 (p. 95).

[36] Akbari, 'Woman as Mediator', p. 153.

surrounding the construction of femininity itself, which will become apparent as we compare the Middle English text with its sources and analogues.

The twelfth-century *chanson* represents Floripas as a heroine before the fact, a beauty whose disposition and appearance predict her swift defection from her father's faith. Despite her geographic origins, her physical appearance conforms to French ideals of femininity, 'white like flowers in summer … crimson like a meadow rose'.[37] This whiteness is, Akbari observes, a clichéd and racist mechanism for indicating inner virtue, hinting at an unseen temperateness of disposition.[38] Although Floripas displays unfeminine anger, her emotions also spill out of her in a more correctly feminine way, in weeping compassion. She sheds tears for the French (line 2074), and as she approaches more closely to the French and Christian ideal of femininity, she becomes more somatically open, more permeable. In the Anglo-Norman translation of the *chanson* on which the *Sowdone* is based, this transformation is cleverly mapped onto both romantic and geographic structures, as Floripas is translated into a temperate climate (suggestive of the humoral moisture that would presage feminine fertility) at the very moment her emotions dissolve into sympathy for the French knights. The text describes her walking in an orchard filled with roses and the distinctively Northern European 'violet' (Anglo-Norman *Fierabras* II, line 543), and listening to the song of 'the nightingale' (line 542, 'le russinole'), the bird that symbolises both romance and rape. Rhetorically translated, she is also geographically translated, and the same processes open up her body to the predatory sexual gaze that operates upon the literary space.

This imagery reinforces the characterisation of Floripas' spatial and somatic openness, both of which are sexualised. Floripas' chamber is described as a place of sensory luxury and excess, part of the stereotype of the sexualised Muslim woman. Central to it is Floripas' magic girdle, an object that maintains Floripas' tower as a place of bodily comfort where appetites are sated, for it has the power to make its wearer feel neither hunger nor thirst. The girdle itself is part of a much wider arsenal of magical paraphernalia Floripas uses, including magical clothes from the land where Jason went, 'où Jason ala' (*chanson*, line 2032), a reference that aligns her with the enchantress Medea. These gendered images of exotic sensory indulgence and magic bring with them connotations of sexual openness and sensuality. Architectural parallels deepen this imagery of bodily openness, as Floripas' body is conflated with the tower she inhabits. As Floripas arouses the suspicions of her former peers, her tower comes under threat of siege, while her body comes under parallel threat of sexual aggression. When the Muslim warrior Lucafere storms into Floripas' chamber to investigate her treatment of Christian prisoners, his ingress reads as a sexual

---

[37] 'blance comme flours en este … vermellette come rose de pré' (lines 2008–9). *Chanson de Fierabras*, eds A. Kroeber and G. Servois (Paris: Vieweg, 1860). All quotations are taken from this edition.

[38] Akbari, *Idols in the East*, p. 48.

threat. An even more overt violation of architectural and bodily space follows. The Sultan sends a thief to steal a magic girdle owned by Floripas, and on seeing Floripas lying asleep in her chamber, the thief decides to rape her, and is only prevented when Floripas summons help with her desperate cries. These episodes of sexual threat, though prevented, function as part of the familiar, misogynistic machinery of romance, in publicising Floripas' body as a target of sexual desire and a locus of vulnerability.[39] In its penetrability, the stone tower functions as a somatic entity, a proxy for penetrable female orifices.

This imagery of blended architectural and somatic vulnerability takes on heightened significance as it is layered with another analogy, that of the tower *and* the body to the reliquary or the relic. The tower itself is a literal reliquary, because it contains the relics of Christ's crucifixion, which Floripas reveals that she has been entrusted with following the sack of Rome.[40] Enclosed within and conflated with the tower, Floripas herself is both figurative relic and a container of relics, an organic reliquary and a living tower, and thus her guardianship of the relics takes on a somatically enclosing connotation, a form of spiritual pregnancy. This connotation is strengthened by an imagery of liquid suggestive of amniotic fluid. Floripas' tower is washed by seawater, which penetrates the dungeon in which the French lie in chains. As Floripas herself weeps salt tears of compassion for the imprisoned knights, water equally saline swirls around their confined bodies. When Floripas transforms emotion into action, delivering the French from prison, the act resembles childbirth, not only because of the conflation of the tower with the body, but also because of the pre-existing medieval imagery of the womb as an imprisoning, watery space whose waters are often saline or brackish.[41] The overlapping images render any attack on Floripas' tower simultaneously a

---

[39] For discussion of this dynamic elsewhere, See, for example, Nicole Nolan Sidhu, *Indecent Exposure: Gender, Politics, and Obscene Comedy in Middle English Literature* (Philadelphia, PA: University of Pennsylvania Press, 2016), pp. 94–100; Karras, *Sexuality in Medieval Europe*, p. 164; Saunders, *Rape and Ravishment*, p. 187.

[40] For further analysis of the conflation of the tower and the reliquary in the Middle English analogues to the *Sowdone*, see Elizabeth Jane Watkins, 'French Romance and English Piety: Genre and Codex in Insular Romance', unpublished PhD thesis, University of Toronto, 2014, pp. 224–25.

[41] The *Prick of Conscience*, for example, describes how, in the 'modur wombe':

There dwelled mon in a dongyon
In stede of foule fylth and corrupcyoun,
Where he had noon othur foode
Bot foule glet and lipered bloode
And stynke and fylthe as I seyde ore
Therwith was he norysshed thore.

Prik of Conscience, ed. James H. Morey (Kalamazoo, MI: Medieval Insitute Publications, 2012), Part I, lines 84–91.

rape and a desecration, an act of violence against a pregnant woman and a composite horror greater than the sum of its parts.

Both of the late medieval English versions share an emphasis on the animate power of relics, and they intensify the elements of sensuality and sexual violence found in the *chanson*.[42] This deepened emphasis works to mobilise the pre-existing logic of the narrative in such a way as to combat or pre-empt Lollard attacks on relics. The romances take on some of the functions of prayer or religious observance, 'translat[ing] the boundary between secular romance and religious artifact'.[43] Thus, in the A text, Floripas laments that her father's warrior Lucafere 'haf … my dore y-broke' (A, line 2192) as he attempts to enter and find out what she has done with her father's prisoners. The words evoke the popular trope of Mary as an inviolate door closed against sexual penetration. Later, the would-be rapist thief Maupyn begins to feel Floripas with 'hondes … doun benyþe hure breste' (A, line 2428) and falls on her, kissing and clutching, as he begins 'hure legges oundo' (A, line 2439), as if she were a locked box to be forcibly opened. The F text gives the thief direct speech, dramatically declaring his intention to 'byreue the thy maydenhede'. (F, line 145). Floripas' sexual vulnerability is thus coded as a Marian or relic-like quality and her body as a reliquary, while the sensual emphases of the text perform the inverse function, as the relics become almost sexually charged. The Christian knights venerate the relics with kisses, and their licit devotion becomes startlingly suggestive in the A text's observation that Floripas has produced these relics from a 'pryue plas' (A, line 2115) in her chamber, a location euphemistically indicative of her own 'pryuetee' or genitalia. In the F text, the narrative concludes with the marriage between Floripas and Guy and, interpolated where a typical romance would detail the results of that sexual union, there is a prayer invoking the relics. These English texts pointedly heighten the sense of sympathy due to Floripas in her sexual vulnerability and mobilise that sympathy in the service of religious objects under threat from Lollard attacks.

This treatment of desire and devotion is very much rooted in the religious discourses I discussed earlier in this chapter. Like relics, like the Marian body, the Floripas narrative disrupts multiple boundaries, collapsing temporal as well as emotional categories. Illicit Christian desire for Floripas' nubile body is anticipated in the venerating kisses that take relics as a substitute for her not-yet-baptised body, while her somatically charged enclosure of the relics prefigures the pregnancy that might result from her future marriage.[44]

---

[42] For F, see Watkins, 'French Romance and English Piety', pp. 248–49. For A, see Siobhain Bly Calkin, 'Devotional Objects, Saracen Spaces and Miracles in Two Matter of France Romances', in *Medieval Romance and Material Culture*, ed. Nicholas Perkins (Cambridge: D. S. Brewer, 2015), pp. 59–74 (p. 69).

[43] Watkins, 'French Romance and English Piety', pp. 248–49.

[44] Akbari makes the point about the relics as substitute for Floripas' not-yet-baptised body

Floripas' body is positioned as a nexus of fluidly unstable emotion, always threatening to dissolve into something else, or to spill across boundaries; always sliding into the past or melting into the future. Consequently, the desires organised around Floripas elude categorisation, collapsing into other forms of desire orientated towards other objects. However, like much interaction that might be labelled 'queer', such boundary-collapsing touches and desires are deeply implicated in the hegemonic regulation of female sexuality and of the fertile female body.[45] Floripas and the relics exist in a state of reciprocal substitution, each repeatedly accommodating the desires or touches that cannot or should not be applied to the other. They are safety valves for potentially deviant masculine desires, conveniently pliable objects, whose potential is neatly brought under control by the end of the narrative.

At that point, the imagery that advertises the potential vulnerability of Floripas' permeable, emotional, fluid body is transformed to mark the elevation of that body into a new order of meaning. After the defeat of Floripas' father the Sultan, she is welcomed into the French court. There the relics' sanctity is tested in a ceremony where they are unwrapped, displayed to onlookers hanging miraculously unsupported in the air, and then laid upon a cloth of 'silk, worked with gold' (*chanson*, line 6098, 'paile, qui fu à or ouvrés'). The image echoes the descriptions of Floripas' sexualised body, 'with its wrap of silk' (*chanson*, line 2826, 'drap de soie'). As the text collapses distinctions between the living female body and the relics, it maintains the teleological pressure towards redemption and reproduction, sanctioning the sexualisation of Floripas' body by its analogy to the ritual display of the relics. As Floripas disrobes, her emergence from her silky wrappings has an electrifying effect on onlookers, a blend of erotic and spiritual awe. Aptly, given the role of silk in the economy of transfer of female bodies through the medieval Mediterranean, the silk performs a function not dissimilar to that of the water that marks the mobility of Floripas' body, implicating her in a fluid network of cultural translations which enable connotations of 'Saracen' excess and exoticism to be transformed into a Christian idiom of religious containment.[46] The silk is rewritten, not as erotic luxury, but as sacred wrapping. Like the relics, displayed in order that, their veracity confirmed, they may be distributed about the churches of France and safely returned to enclosing shrines, Floripas' body is revealed in order that she may be subsumed into the social order of marriage, her fluid fertility likewise safely contained. Meanwhile, the conflation of Floripas' body with the relics works

---

in relation to another version of the narrative, the text of Jean Bagnyon, dating from later in the fifteenth century. Akbari, 'Woman as Mediator', p. 161.

[45] For the (contested) capacity of the queer to reinforce the hegemony, see Tison Pugh, *Sexuality and its Queer Discontents in Middle English Literature* (New York: Palgrave Macmillan, 2008), p. 1.

[46] Burns, *Sea of Silk*, p. 2.

to naturalise relic discourse into the reproductive teleology of the romance, coding the French knights' desire to reclaim them as a fertile and generative desire, which is fulfilled in Floripas' spiritual rebirth, in her marriage and in the genesis of a sanctified French empire under Charlemagne.[47] The baptism is analogous to insemination: the liquid waters of the font carry a seminal potential to form and shape that which they touch, a directed fluidity distinct from the watery porousness of the fertile female body, and which imbues Floripas with Christian grace. The early fourteenth-century *King of Tars* elucidates this association, culminating in a scene of miraculous (and profoundly racist) baptism that makes good the formal defects caused to a newborn infant as a result of its Muslim father's lack of seminal power to form a Christian baby. The narrative concludes with a juxtaposition that is, in this context, unpleasantly loaded with latent violence. Floripas is disrobed, baptised and married to Guy and the relics are distributed piecemeal to the churches of France. The separation of the relics seems good, practical sense, a lessening of the risk of their repeated theft, but it also suggests a reciprocal sundering or disempowering of their human counterpart, through an incorporation of her body into the religious and marital structures that might also be seen as a dismemberment or curtailment of her agency.

The *Sowdone* differs radically from this established narrative. In the *Sowdone*, the familiar combination of romantic imagery with a 'Westernised' Muslim love interest recurs, yet oddly displaced; likewise, the imagery of liquid signifying a feminine amenability to conversion and a fertile potential for marriage is strangely distorted. Much as the 'Legend of Hipsiphyle and Medea' constructs itself around a patchwork of inverted misogynistic commonplaces, so too the *Sowdone* takes the imagery of its source tradition, dismantles it and reassembles the pieces in a distorted new form that radically undermines the older model. The *Sowdone* casts the masculine as the defective gender, in sharp contrast to the Isidorean positioning of the female as an excessively fluid, porous inferior to the male. It locates generative failure in masculine lack of fluidity, taking as its targets both Floripas' father, the patriarch and Sultan of Babylon, and the epitome of literary *paternitas*, Chaucer himself. It is this *paternitas*, and not the feminine body or the relic, that is circumscribed and broken down into its constituent parts.

The Sultan features in the established *chanson* tradition as a figure of hypermasculine aggression and authority. Yet in the *Sowdone* he is swiftly and vividly incorporated into a fertile, sexualised and temperate Northern European romance idiom. This new Sultan appears as peaceable victim of Christian aggression and 'vilané' (line 82), not in an exoticised 'Babylon', but in a landscape of 'grene woode[s]' (line 50) and 'grene tre[es] (line 46) whose verdant foliage and singing 'nightingalis' evoke the *locus amoenus* of countless

---

[47] Calkin, 'Devotional Objects, Saracen Spaces', p. 69.

romantic encounters. The rhetorical strategy is borrowed directly from the *Sowdone*'s Anglo-Norman source, as it places Floripas in just such a temperate, European-vernacular location. Moreover, the scene conveys similar connotations of sexualised violence, forming a backdrop to a hunt for 'the bore or the veneson, / The wolfe, the bere and the bawson' (lines 51–52).[48] This common metaphor for sexual pursuit is, in other versions of the narrative, depicted as so quintessentially Christian a pastime that it is unfamiliar to Muslim men; here it is represented as a natural 'kynde' response to the springtime season, that time when 'every wight desirith his like, / Whan lovers slepen with opyn yye' (lines 44–45). However, this familiar rhetorical strategy of translating a Muslim character into a sexualised and geographically temperate, Northern European *locus amoenus* is spiked with startling difference because its subject is not the beautiful maid Floripas, but her father, the Sultan of Babylon. The *Sowdone*'s opening depiction of the Sultan in this idiom has no precedent; elsewhere he is invariably a caricature of brutality and aggression. The transformation catapults him disconcertingly into the narrative space we might expect his daughter to occupy: the space of the unmarried, would-be lover, already implicated in the tropes of desirable Christian youth. The image of the courteous hunter is a masculine ideal, yet this image mobilises rhetorical strategies typically used to characterise a female character, giving it a strangely emasculatory undertone. Exposing an unmarked lack within the Muslim familial structure, the scene dislocates narrative chronology, placing the Sultan (who, we now notice, never seems to have a wife or mother for his children) in the position of a romance suitor, seeking a sexual partner, rather than in the position of the father of adult children. These incongruities expose the latent strangeness of the tropes that furnish the scene, much as Chaucer's inversions of gender in the 'Legend of Hipsiphyle and Medea' expose the strangeness of tropes of femininity by organising them around Jason. The Sultan's unexpected presence discloses the fact that the tropes of the hunt, the springtime wood and the singing nightingales are the machinery through which medieval English literature typically renders violence against women palatable, decorative and acceptable.

The text de-naturalises its own rhetoric, and with good reason. Primed to see something out of keeping with the fabric of the romance, we notice that this material is lifted from Chaucer, in patchwork with an older lyric. The *Sowdone* lines run:

> Hit bifelle bytwyxte March and Maye,
> Whan kynde corage begynneth to pryke,
> Whan frith and felde wexen gaye,

[48] Ryan Judkins, 'The Game of the Courtly Hunt: Chasing and Breaking Deer in Late Medieval English Literature', *Journal of English and Germanic Philology* 112.1 (2013): 70–92.

> And every wight desirith his like,
> Whan lovers slepen withe opyn yye
> As nightyngalis on grene tre,
> And sore desire that thai cowde flye,
> That thay myghte withe here lovere be.
> (lines 41–48)

The first two lines adapt the Harley love lyric addressed to 'Alysoun', which begins:

> Bytuene mersh & aueril
> When spray biginneþ to springe
> þe lutel foul haþ hire wyl
> on hyre lud to synge.[49]

This quintessentially English lyrical voice provides a springtime setting for the *Sowdone* author to borrow, and the *Sowdone* then picks up the *Canterbury Tales* prologue a few lines from the beginning, where Chaucer describes how 'smale foweles maken melodye, / That slepen al the nyght with open ye / (So priketh hem Nature in hir corages)' (*CT* I, lines 9–11). Grafted into a romance whose lineage goes back to a French *chanson*, the Chaucerian and English material stands as metonym for the idea of Chaucerian *paternitas*, just beginning to coalesce in contemporary fifteenth-century writings. In this vein, Hoccleve eulogises his 'maistir deere and fadir reverent'; Lydgate writes of drawing inspiration distilled from the 'golde dewe drops' of Chaucerian eloquence; the anonymous *Book of Curtasye* recalls the 'lusty lyquour / of that fulsome fontayne' whose source is 'fader Chaucer'.[50] These formulations have in common an imagery of fluid that is seminal, looking back to the *General Prologue*'s references to 'shoures soote' and to procreative 'licour'.[51] However, Roberta Magnani identifies a subversive tendency in this nascent tradition, noting that the above writers seek as much to displace Chaucer as literary patriarch, as to celebrate him.[52] The *Sowdone*'s particular brand of destabilisation results in a pointedly emasculatory omission. Its patchwork quotation includes everything in the opening lines of the *General Prologue*, either in paraphrase (the lyric) or in close imitation – everything, *except* the imagery of spurting showers and sap-filled veins.

Dryly insufficient, this grafted Chaucerian material signally fails to strike root in the text. Rapidly, the picture of the temperate, romantic Sultan would-be

---

[49] *The Harley Lyrics: The Middle English Lyrics of MS Harley 2253*, ed. G. L. Brook (Manchester: Manchester University Press, 1948), no. 33, lines 1–4.
[50] John M. Bowers, 'Thomas Hoccleve and the Politics of Tradition', *Chaucer Review* 36.4 (2002): 352–69.
[51] Dinshaw, *Getting Medieval*, p. 119.
[52] Magnani, 'Constructing the Father', pp. 4–6.

lover is blotted out in favour of a hypermasculine and aggressive warrior king. Feasting on 'beestes bloode' (line 684) and 'serpents in oyle … fryed', (line 687), he ingests the excesses of hot liquid that medical texts associate with hypermasculine rage, casting him as polar opposite to the idealised Christian woman whose watery nature produces effusions of compassionate tears.[53] No longer emasculated – indeed, the reverse – the Sultan bears witness to the failure of an impotent Chaucerian *paternitas* in a romance narrative, and this metatextual insufficiency is soon paralleled with an equally ignominious failure of the French Christians of the text, who adopt the orphaned infants of two giants allied to the forces of the Sultan of Babylon, only to see them die for lack of the maternal fluid they cannot provide.[54] Though the adopted infants appear elsewhere in the tradition, the *Sowdone* is unique in stressing that the babies' failure to thrive results from a specifically *liquid* maternal absence: 'Here dammes mylke they lakked there; / Thay deyden for defaute of here dam' (lines 3035–36). Whereas in the sources and analogues fluidity is a feminine characteristic charged with almost too much affective potential, in the *Sowdone*, the lack of fluidity is that which renders paternity sterile and ineffective.

The *Sowdone*'s rewriting of its titular character inverts the anxieties of the wider tradition. Its arid, impotent and sterile imagery marks failures of rhetorical translation and of generative function, disrupting the operations of gender by marking primarily the masculine, not the feminine, as defective and insufficient. The fluid sensuality that identifies Floripas as an amenable subject for Christian baptism exposes, when 'written' onto an unexpectedly masculine Muslim body, the violence and the strangeness of the tropes of romance. In response, the romance itself – textual 'matter' and thus coded feminine – functions as a recalcitrant female body, rejecting the insertion of Chaucerian *paternitas* briefly thrust into its narrative. This early section of the *Sowdone* thus prepares us for a heroine whose embodiment of desire is configured quite differently from the other female protagonists of the tradition.

STONE (BUTCH) BODIES AND THE TRANSFORMATION OF DESIRE

The *Sowdone* makes substantial changes to its material, and amongst the most significant is its treatment of the relics, so central to the *chanson* and its later translations. The emotional pivot of the original plot, the organisation of desires around the twin foci of Floripas' body and the relics of Christ's crucifixion, is broken apart, as the relics lose their central significance, disappearing

---

[53] Jeffrey Jerome Cohen, 'On Saracen Enjoyment: Some Fantasies of Race in Late Medieval England', *Journal of Medieval and Early Modern Studies* 31 (2001): 113–46.
[54] For comparison, the Anglo-Norman observes that the infants died 'car lour mer lour failli, qi lour voit alaitant' (lines 1600-1, 'for they lacked their mother, who had been nursing them'); there is less emphasis on the fluid itself, and more on the mother.

from the narrative for most of its length, until Floripas casually offers them to Charlemagne: 'Here I presente to you, as I can, / Relikes of grete honoure / That were at Rome iwonnen' (lines 3137–39). No longer implicated in rituals of enclosure and display, Floripas' body also loses its more-than-erotic resonance, and indeed it is also stripped of its sensuality, as the *Sowdone* removes the flirtatious exchanges, the descriptions of physical beauty and the imagery of romantic expectation that cross-hatch the source texts. In this version of the narrative, Floripas emerges as a cold, even chilling, warrior-like figure, rarely showing uncontrolled emotion, let alone the tearful compassion and yielding desire of the source tradition. For example, when she overpowers her father's jailor – a scene other versions of the plot represent as one of rash fury – she acts with a cool efficiency only exceeded by her calm recounting of the event. We are told that she grabbed a 'keye cloge' to give the jailor 'harde grace' (lines 1602–3); in report, Floripas depicts this attack in the language of approved battle, elevating her key block into a real weapon: 'I slough him with a mace' (line 1613). Her actions code her as masculine: as Ruth Karras puts it, 'the need to prove oneself in competition with other men and to dominate others' was 'one core feature of medieval masculinity'.[55] This martial and strategic language prepares for Floripas' betrothal to (or rather, negotiation for) Guy of Burgundy. With a mixture of bargaining and threat uniquely devoid of romance, Floripas asserts:

> For his love wille I cristenede be
> And lefe Mahoundes laye ...
> And but he wole graunte me his love,
> Of you askape shalle none here.
> (lines 1895–900)[56]

As with Medea, 'love' and strategies for battle overlap, with Floripas taking the roles of suitor to Guy and ruthless tactical advisor simultaneously. No sooner has the betrothal been solemnised with kisses and vows than Floripas unfolds a plan for the invasion of her father's 'castel' (line 1950), using strategies and weapons she provides (lines 1940–50). The penetration of the fortress by the French thus takes the place of a wedding night for Guy and Floripas, in an audacious twisting of tropes that rewrites the familiar analogy of the feminine

---

[55] Karras, *From Boys to Men*, p. 10.
[56] By comparison, the Anglo-Norman reads: 'I love a knight of France: Guy is his name. ... For his love I will be baptised and washed, and I will return the relics, which are so precious, and deliver you all without any harm coming to you.'

Jeo aime un chivaler de France: Gy l'en fait nomer. ...
Par s'amour me feroi baptiser et laver
Et rendrai les reliques, qi tant funt a preiser,
Et vous delivererai touz sanz nol mal aver.'
(lines 827–31)

chamber and the female body while simultaneously undermining patriarchal authority with daughterly disobedience. Insofar as Floripas' tower is never precisely conquered, but rather is the site *from which* Christian penetration into Islamic territory occurs, this tower/body has a penetrative function with its own sexual suggestiveness and its own generative power to drive forward the narrative.

In this firmly de-eroticised, relic-free context, Floripas' tower functions as a fortress against ingress, a bulwark battered by the sea, and the ultimate means of Christian penetration into Islamic territories. It is not imagined as a reliquary: though the relics are presumably there, no mention is made of them. The space is instead defined by its 'harde stone' (line 1550), with Floripas' own chamber furnished with 'iren and stele' (line 1849). The entire tower (not only the lower part) is characterised as a 'dungeon' (line 2296) or 'prisone' (line 1559). The tower remains firmly conflated with Floripas' body, and its boundaries with her boundaries. This is evocatively communicated by the aural echoes between the Sultan's bitter reference to Floripas as a 'stronge hore' (lines 2065, 2125, 2223, 2580, 3131) and her 'stronge tour' (lines 2079 and 2128). The irony of the term 'hore' is brought home by Floripas' reversal of the classic romance trope of sexual ingress, the trope of masculine penetration of the feminised tower, epitomised by the *Roman de la Rose*, as 'Floripe and here maydyns kept the toure/ And woonde up the brigges on hye' (lines 2547–48). This emphasis on architectural impenetrability extends to the threat of sexual violence, for when Floripas' Muslim fiancé Lucafere enters, he comes seeking not sexual intimacy but 'debate' (line 1966), and although he knocks hard on the door, he does not smash through it. These implications are strengthened in the would-be rape scene, which so graphically establishes Floripas' sexual vulnerability in the pre-*Sowdone* tradition. Here it is Floripas' own cry that stops the violence. Paralysing the would-be rapist, her words leave him 'Stondinge amased for drede' (line 2364), seemingly unable to move. The reaction recalls a pivotal moment in medieval drama, where the sceptical midwife Salome attempts to penetrate the Virgin's vagina to test the truth of her claims of chastity.[57] The midwife's hand is struck still, withered, as it attempts to penetrate the inviolate body. Likewise, Floripas' body appears to exert an almost magnetic repulsion, preventing the thief's touch.[58] The *Sowdone* thus casts Floripas as a Marian figure in a firmly non-affective

---

[57] The N-Town Salome declares:

'Alas, alas, and weleawaye,
For my grett dowth and fals beleve!
Myne hand is ded and drye as claye!'

('Play 15: Nativity', in *The N-Town Plays*, ed. Douglas Sugano [Kalamazoo, MI: Medieval Institute Publications, 2007], lines 254–56). See Novavich, 'Transparent Mary', p. 471.

[58] The analogy between affective response and magnetic repulsion (or attraction) exists in

tradition, a body inviolate against penetration, the boundaries of her body fortified to withstand siege.

Deepening these Marian connotations is the image of the *turris eburnea* of the Song of Songs, the ivory tower hung about like a fortress with 'shields of mighty men', which is echoed in Floripas' assurance that her tower contains 'armure i-nowe'. Since the *Sowdone*, unlike its analogues, never displaces Floripas' racial origins with protestations of her whiteness or Northern European appearance, she might evoke the Song of Songs woman's colour, 'fusca ... quia decoloravit me sol' ('darkened by the sun'). Since the Song of Songs woman is both the Church and the Virgin, both an architecture and a female structure, the parallel works to construct Floripas' body as an inorganic, fortified and impenetrable space, and this conferred stoniness inverts the miracles wherein stone statues cast off their inanimacy to weep, bleed or lactate. Bernard of Clairvaux constructs the Song of Songs woman as a 'virile bride' (in Shawn Krahmer's wording), offering a model of Marian female masculinity for Floripas.[59] The transformation radically reorients the characterisation of Floripas' body, from a yielding openness to a contained substance that resists sexual and erotic contact and displays a masculine self-control and self-fortification.

An imagery of somatic regulation and discipline complements this transformation, centred on an object laden with symbolism from the *chanson* onwards: the magic girdle that enables Floripas and her companions to stave off hunger or thirst as they withstand the siege. In the *Sowdone*, the girdle is stripped of its context of non-Christian magic and indulgence, allowing a Marian parallel to emerge, rooted in the imagery not of magic but of its closely related discipline of medicine.[60] Floripas tells the peers:

> I knowe a medycyne in my thoughte
> To comforte you with-alle.
> I have a girdil in my forcere,
> Whoso girde hem therwith aboute,
> Hunger ner thirste shal him never dere
> (lines 2301–5)

The framing of the girdle as 'medycyne' evokes the metaphor of spiritual 'medycyne', a prescription that is conceptual ('in my thoughte') rather than literal, like the spiritual 'balm' of virginity discussed in *Hali Meidhad*. In

---

medieval texts, notably those characterising devotion to Christ. See Walter, 'Fragments for a Medieval Theory of Prosthesis', pp. 1358–59.

[59] Krahmer, 'The Virile Bride of Bernard of Clairvaux', p. 304.
[60] See Diane Watt, 'Mary the Physician: Women, Medicine and Gender in the Middle Ages', in *Medicine, Religion and Gender in Medieval Culture*, ed. Naoë Kukita Yoshikawa (Cambridge: D. S. Brewer, 2015), pp. 27–44.

its form, the girdle recalls the rolls of prayers known as birth girdles and associated with the Virgin Mary in her role as healer, thought to aid women in labour.[61] Written rolls of parchment, these 'girdles' could be worn on the body in an attempt to preserve its integrity through the rigours of childbirth. Margaret Healy argues that they might be read as a form of prosthetic and 'ideal' skin, 'to counter the deficiency of the all too permeable and vulnerable human skin envelope ... a material-fantasy armoury of medical, spiritual and social defence'.[62] Floripas' girdle works to render her body impermeable, but also to transform that body into something more-than-feminine, for the defensive function Healy identifies with her term 'armoury' indeed suggests a body protected against violent attack. There are other hints to support this reading of Floripas' medicalised means of preservation. As we have seen, the Anglo-Norman text introduces a suggestive image of Floripas, about to rescue the Christian knights, walking for pleasure in a *locus amoenus* of flowers and ominous nightingale song, which at once translates her into romance idiom and publicises her body as a potential site of sexual desire or sexual violence. The *Sowdone* changes the scene deftly, representing Floripas in the garden as a woman with a task in hand, 'To geder floures in morne colde' (line 1553). The chilly temperature and the purposive verb 'geder' suggest a task in hand, calling to mind the medicinal uses of flowers, which dictate their preservation before the heat of the day. In combination, the imagery conflates Floripas with the Virgin-as-medic, an authoritative figure in control of her body. As an object disciplining the body's natural need for the entry of water and food, Floripas' girdle recalls the practices Caroline Walker Bynum identifies amongst religious women, of using a restrictive diet to subdue the female body and bring about a cessation of one of its 'leaky' properties, that of menstruation.[63] It therefore renders Floripas legible within the established medieval paradigm of the virago, whose aggression or agency are sometimes represented as the organic results of a disrupted or absent menstrual cycle. In negating the need for food or water, the girdle renders Floripas' body inorganic, doubly impenetrable, and identifies her with the Virgin not in her affective, maternal role, but in her sealed, contained presentation. This stony, impenetrable and sexually resistant figure condenses anxieties relating to feminine fluidity and its containment, revealing the disturbing potential of

---

[61] See Mary Morse, '"Thys moche more ys oure Lady Mary longe": Takamiya MS 56 and the English Birth Girdle Tradition', in *Middle English Texts in Transition: A Festschrift Dedicated to Toshiyuki Takamiya on his 70th birthday*, eds Simon Horobin and Linne Mooney (York: York Medieval Press, 2014), pp. 199–219.

[62] Margaret Healy, 'Wearing Powerful Words and Objects: Healing Prosthetics', *Textual Practice* 30.7 (2016): 1233–51 (p. 1236).

[63] Caroline Walker Bynum, *Holy Feast and Holy Fast: The Religious Significance of Food to Medieval Women* (Berkeley, CA and Los Angeles, CA: University of California Press, 1987), pp. 202–74.

the female body to sublimate the boundary between human and non-human, animate and inanimate.

The concluding moments of the *Sowdone*, which reveal that the relics stolen from Rome were always safely hidden in Floripas' tower, continue the now predictable pattern of differences from the source tradition. There is no scene of lingering disrobing here, and the event itself is distanced from the return of the relics, which Charles accepts with a venerating kiss. Tucked away at the end of the text, three lines summarise: 'Dame Florip was baptysed than / And here maydyns alle / And to Sir Gye i-maryed' (lines 3191–93). In the *Sowdone*, Floripas' baptism is not an individual event, but a ceremony she shares with her maidens. Likewise, Charlemagne does not distribute the relics to be displayed, but instructs his treasurer:

> To kepe the relikes of grete pris
> And his other tresoure
> And bringe hem safe to Parys,
> There to abide in store.
> (lines 3207–10)

Like Floripas' own body, the relics are to be preserved out of sight. Their value is not dismissed, nor their appropriateness for tactile and affective veneration, but they are not made objects for display, consumption or disunification.

In some respects, Floripas is legible within paradigms of female deviant behaviour we have encountered before. Like Medea, she embodies a paradoxical conjunction of excess and lack. She is insufficiently fluid and yielding to conform to the feminine ideal, lacking the emotional warmth of her analogues; yet her body is also excessive in its prosthetic extension, in the girdle she wears and the stone tower she inhabits. The tower, in particular, with its phallic shape and its stony hardness harnessed by Floripas as a means to organise the penetration of the Islamic stronghold, codes Floripas' body as more-than-feminine, quasi-lesbian, much as Philomela's body was so coded. The *Sowdone*'s characterisation of Floripas as hard, cold and impenetrable accords her a metaphorical sterility, in terms of the medical theories that define fluidity and softness as preconditions for female fertility. Such sterility might diffuse tensions concerning Muslim fertility. A metaphorically sterile Floripas mitigates the threat a fertile, non-Western female body poses to an anxiously xenophobic Christian community, which would answer to topical concerns. As with Dido, the archetypal 'Eastern' woman who threatens the destiny of Western Christendom by seducing one of its founding fathers, Floripas' fertility is a potential concern as much as it is a means of manifesting her amenability to conversion: for what are the limits of Christendom, and whom can it accommodate? David Abulafia identifies a 'hardening of external boundaries' between Christianity, Islam and Judaism in the later Middle Ages, and we could see the *Sowdone* Floripas as a somatic literalisation of this process.[64] However, the depiction of Floripas also extends beyond these reasonably familiar constructions (and containments) of femininity, offering something that is not simply sterile, insufficient, excessive or absent.

A present-day model of nonconforming female desire shares with the medieval romance a reliance upon the affective imagery of stone. This enduring association between stone and (female) desire to resist touch is most famously expressed in Leslie Feinberg's semi-autobiographical novel *Stone Butch Blues*. Feinberg's novel memorialises the 'stone butch' as a lesbian who resists sexual contact, and imaginatively plays with ideas of typical femininity and emotional openness as forms of fluidity that the stone butch resists. In a generative analysis of female masculinity, Halberstam argues that 'the stone butch defines an enigmatic core of lesbian sexual and social practice', making visible 'female masculinity' as something distinct from, rather than subordinate to, masculinity in general, complicated 'the idea that butches are bad copies of men'.[65] The *Sowdone*, of course, far predates not only the categories of 'butch' and 'femme', but even the taxonomies of gender and sexuality in reaction to which they operate. However, Halberstam cautiously identifies resonances between the 1950s novel and the diaries of the famously Sapphic Anne Lister, written well over a century before, and I replicate her extension of the tenure of the term backwards to the medieval.[66] Halberstam suggests that this stony identity represents an epistemic barrier, a site of incomprehension and puzzlement, amongst those who struggle to recognise that, for a stone butch, 'being untouchable did not and does not signify an absence of desire or pleasure'.[67] This imagery of 'stone' (contrasted to a 'normative' feminine desire constructed in terms of fluidity), and its imaginative use to capture a feminine desire that is impenetrable and resistant to touch, evokes the Floripas of the *Sowdone*.

The parallel between Floripas and the twentieth-century 'stone butch' helps us to consider how female desires may be separated out from and made visible within the category of negation to which they are typically assigned. In her almost inorganic embodiment, the *Sowdone* Floripas resembles a nightmare version of the relics she displaces from the narrative, as they are constructed in the insinuating subtext of Lollard polemic: a body 'without lyf', like the stony statues whose calcified wombs stir up such unease. Despite the relics' erasure from the larger narrative of the *Sowdone*, relic discourse provides a crucial framework for understanding the workings of Floripas' own embodied desires, as much of the logic applied to the relics elsewhere is applied to her in this rewritten version. For example, the tower – which in earlier versions

---

[64] David Abulafia, 'Seven Types of Ambiguity, *c*. 1100–*c*. 1500', in *Medieval Frontiers: Concepts and Practices*, eds David Abulafia and Nora Berend (Aldershot: Ashgate, 2002), p. 33.
[65] Halberstam, *Female Masculinity*, p. 124.
[66] Ibid., pp. 111–12.
[67] Ibid., p. 124.

is overtly coded as a reliquary – here retains its properties of protecting and yet publicising the precious nature of what it contains. It 'enshrines' Floripas' body, in the sense Malo establishes in her work on relic discourse, where she argues that 'practices of enshrinement' work to withhold the contained relic from outside contact. Floripas' untouchability manifests itself on the bodies of those who seek to violate it as a quasi-religious awe, much like the response engineered by a shrine. In the same way, the logic of the relic and the reliquary underpins the *Sowdone*'s presentation of Floripas as a (desiring) subject. It is a crucial tenet of orthodox theology that relics are neither empty (absences), nor does their material substance comprehend the thing they signify, the spiritual presence they mediate. Relics signify, as Bynum puts it, 'the presence and absence of the divine'.[68] They point to a reality, even if that reality is beyond touch or sensation of their own material bodies, their own physical substance. In the same way, we might see the *Sowdone* Floripas' body not as a locus of absent desire, but as a locus of desires not comprehended by the structures of thought typically applied to feminine bodies in romances – or medieval women in general.

As we have seen, writers as different and distant from each other as Isidore of Seville and Astrida Neimanis bear witness to the fact that the operations of watery female bodies are implicated in a patriarchal reproductive economy (though for the former the implication is a matter of natural order, whereas for the latter it is an acute problem). As Floripas' body is rendered stone-like and impenetrable, she mobilises those anxieties that circulate endlessly between monitory discourses of femininity and its enclosure: the fear of porousness or of unfeminine, inhuman hardness; the spectre of excessively fluid and yielding sensuality or the suspicion of desires prosthetically satisfied or fixing on inanimate objects. Because of her subaltern position, emerging out of the tropes of idealised femininity and relic devotion and yet monstrously different from their products, she offers a site through which to think not only about the local medieval context, but also about the submerged assumptions about femininity, embodiment and desire that radiate out into post-medieval discourses. Even in Neimanis' post-humanist philosophy, which insistently targets the phallogocentric valorisation of the discrete, autonomous, presumptively male individual, the valorisation of fluidity often seems to invert, rather than deconstruct, the binary. Water remains presumptively feminine, opposed to a presumptively masculine discreteness and autonomy; it is insistently valorised through Neimanis' rhetoric, which is laden with metaphors of fluidity and infusion, only inverting the pejorative connotations of seepage and overflow implicit in medieval condemnations of 'leaky' female bodies.[69]

---

[68] Caroline Walker Bynum, *Wonderful Blood: Theology and Practice in Late Medieval Northern Germany and Beyond* (Philadelphia, PA: University of Pennsylvania Press, 2006), p. 16.

[69] Neimanis does acknowledge – though without a solution – the potential tension

By contrast, the *Sowdone* constructs a model of nonconforming femininity that is truly newly generated, not merely inverted or recirculated. Floripas resists being subsumed into the watery rhetorics that construct her analogues, but her resistance does not take the form of the 'sealing' that Lochrie identifies in hagiographic and mystical writing. She remains generative, albeit through mechanisms of impregnating power that suggest weaponised *paternitas* rather than female fertility, as her tower enables penetration of Muslim space and her impregnable form is echoed in the impregnable generic operations of the romance. Her reconfigured character involves a rethinking of the implications of stony (as opposed to watery) embodiment. As Jeffrey Jerome Cohen reminds us, medieval philosophers understood stones to be admixtures of water and earth.[70] They considered that, as the proportions of water to earth varied, so too did the properties of stones themselves, from lumpen rocks resembling mud solidified, to translucent, crystalline structures of water held in fixity. Jewels – precious stones – were understood to be water transmuted, hardened, organised into its most impenetrable form. Middle English romances are in touch with this philosophy of watery stoniness, as *Pearl*, written by the author of the romance *Sir Gawain and the Green Knight*, bears witness. In her strangely unyielding rectitude, the *Pearl* maiden – that 'myry juele' – appears in feminine form, but a feminine form whose watery nature has been elevated, transmuted, into the impenetrable, hard surfaces of a pearl.[71] The *Pearl* maiden might therefore offer an analogy for a femininity that resembles a crystalline, not a fluid, materiality: a hardness that retains some of the properties of water.[72] Like Feinberg's 'stone butch', she is not merely a 'bad copy' of a masculine hardness, nor merely an 'invert' form of femininity. In this imagery of jewel-like stony fluidity, we can identify a rhetorical means to go beyond the binaries that reproduce themselves so endlessly in ongoing constructions of femininity, even to the present day.

CONCLUSION

The *Sowdone*'s radical rewriting of femininity through the figure of Floripas necessarily carries equally radical implications for thinking about female desire and literary hegemony. The text rejects (indeed, exposes the sterility of) a Chaucerian imagery of romantic desire. Like Chaucer's 'Legend of

---

between her strategy and the feminist emphasis on 'difference and disaggregation', citing in particular the feminisms of women of colour such as Lorde. *Bodies of Water*, pp. 27–28.

[70] Cohen, *Stone: An Ecology of the Inhuman*, p. 15.

[71] *Pearl*, ed. Sarah Stanbury (Kalamazoo, MI: Medieval Institute Publications, 2001), line 23.

[72] I would like to thank my students, Finley Kidd and Beatrice Obe, for essays and discussions relating *Pearl* to discourses of racial alterity and to Neimanis' work.

Hipsyphile and Medea', the text takes on the form accorded to its female protagonist(s). That narrative becomes a sterile, cyclic structure, a castrated form cruelly mimetic of the 'capoun[s]' to which its heroines are compared. The *Sowdone* meanwhile acts as an impenetrable feminine body, rejecting the insertion of Chaucerian *paternitas* much as its heroine refuses masculine penetration of her tower and her body. Unlike Jason, whose betrayals spiral on beyond the confines of the *Legend*, Floripas' consort Guy of Burgundy remains in the *Sowdone* (as, indeed, in most of its analogues) a blank page, an entirely un-particularised cipher, on whom Floripas writes her own desires. In this logic, however, Chaucerian *paternitas* is reassigned to the role of the aggressor, analogised to the would-be rapist Muslims who seek to break down Floripas' door and must be beaten back, rejected and exposed as threats. The romance thus finds a space for a nonconforming female desire that is neither an absence nor a negation of affect, and as it does so, it calls into question the colonising logic of masculine writing on the feminine body.

5

VEILED INTERPRETATIONS AND ARCHITECTURES OF DESIRE IN THE 'LEGEND OF THISBE' AND THE 'LEGEND OF ARIADNE'[1]

Of the 'goode women' Chaucer includes in his *Legend*, two of the most obviously blameless and innocent are Thisbe, heroine of the second tale, and Ariadne, protagonist (or co-protagonist, as she shares all but the title of her tale with her more savvy and ultimately luckier-in-love sister, Phaedra) of the sixth. Neither woman is particularly notorious prior to the *Legend*. In neither case might Chaucer claim the need to excise a gory narrative of revenge or infanticide (as in the cases of Philomela and Medea), or of conspicuous aggression towards men (as in the case of Hipsyphyle). Yet these legends offer rich sites for Chaucer's ongoing project of interrogating the implications of considering female desire as an active, or even authorial, impulse. The 'Legend of Thisbe' shatters convention, featuring a disconcertingly feminised Pyramus, a decidedly dissident Thisbe, and a supporting cast of oddly gendered objects and animals. The retelling undermines the Latin hermeneutic tradition of correlating grammatical structures with sexual and gendered hierarchies of behaviour, taking as its target no less an authority than St Jerome himself. It ends in a moment of remarkably transgressive feminine authority, as Thisbe constructs a text, a 'compleynte', from raw material she takes from her lover's supine body. Yet this seeming autonomy is all too soon curtailed, both by Chaucer's bitingly ironic reconfiguring of images from Thisbe's tale in his later 'Wife of Bath's Prologue' and, closer to home, in the 'Legend of Ariadne', which offers a crudely inverted reworking of the same tropes, now deployed only to demonstrate the sexual and semantic incapability of female desire to shape or structure its chosen subjects. The 'Legend of Ariadne' participates in the *Legend*'s persistent imagery of prosthesis, but whereas for Philomela the prosthesis is a marker of female sexual deviancy and for Medea, the indication of an aberrantly

---

[1] An early version of this chapter appeared as an article. See Lucy Allen-Goss, 'Transgressive Desire in Chaucer's "Legend of Thisbe"', *Chaucer Review* 53.2 (2018): 194–212.

feminine body, for Ariadne (whose legend offers the closing word on the matter she shares with Thisbe), prosthesis is a marker of lack, an indication of definitive feminine inability to make meaning.[2] Together, these texts expose the hopelessness of the project that began with Philomela's textile communication and Medea's attempts to construct a linguistic phallus: the impossibility of female subjects taking control of a masculinised language.

WALLED DESIRE IN THE 'LEGEND OF THISBE'

The tale of Pyramus and Thisbe is best known to modern readers from the play put on by Shakespeare's 'rude mechanicals' in *A Midsummer Night's Dream*. Two unfortunate young lovers are forbidden by their parents to meet. They whisper to each other through a tiny crack in a wall and plot a clandestine meeting, which is doomed to end prematurely in misunderstanding and double suicide. First, however, an unwise casting decision makes the anthropomorphised Wall between the lovers the literal butt of a crude joke. As the actor playing Thisbe puckers up to the nether regions of the actor playing Wall, s/he laments to the unseen Pyramus on the other side: 'I kiss the wall's hole, not your lips at all!'[3] The slapstick humour has overshadowed Chaucer's version of the tale for 400 years. However, this subversive representation of gender and sexuality has its true roots in the *Legend*, whence its radical potential to destabilise expectations derives. Despite this, the presence of the 'Legend of Thisbe' within the *Legend of Good Women* has puzzled scholars, who search in vain for any spice of transgression in the text. Unlike Medea, Dido or Cleopatra, Thisbe is no obvious virago; unlike Philomela or Lucrece, she is not the victim of notorious wrongs at the hands of a man. The commonplace criticism of the *Legend*, that it reduces women to 'weak martyrs of love', diluting distinctive characters to an anodyne suffering meekness by cutting out the salacious or violent details of their own actions, does not apply here.[4] The masculine and feminine protagonists are blamelessly united from the start; the changes Chaucer makes to Ovid's version are small. Thisbe is well known for being virtuous and innocent; her lover Pyramus is hapless, but entirely faithful. As James W. Spisak (delightfully) puts it: 'Praising [Thisbe] is hardly a penance …

---

[2] My analysis of prosthesis draws upon recent work in the fields of disability theory and queer theory, notably Shildrick, 'Border Crossings', pp. 137-69 and 'Prosthetic Performativity: Deleuzian Connections and Queer Corporalities', in *Deleuze and Queer Theory*, eds Chrysanthi Nigianni and Merl Storr (Edinburgh: Edinburgh University Press, 2009), pp. 115-33; Richard H. Godden, 'Prosthetic Ecologies: Vulnerable Bodies and the Dismodern Subject in *Sir Gawain and the Green Knight*', *Textual Practice* 30.7 (2016): 1273-90.

[3] *A Midsummer Night's Dream*, Act V, sc. i, line 202.

[4] Dinshaw, *Chaucer's Sexual Poetics*, p. 75.

it's like giving up leeks for Lent'.[5] Accordingly, Nancy Bradley Warren dismisses Thisbe, in passing, as 'one of the most passive of the heroines of the *Legend*', while McDonald claims that the story is 'the least ambiguous. ... totally devoid of sexuality', and Kara Doyle suggests there is nothing in Chaucer's treatment of his sources to invite more than 'a fairly straightforward reading'.[6] The retelling is accorded little credit for innovation: Lisa Kiser, Priscilla Martin and Florence Percival all repeat the claim that the 'Legend of Thisbe' is a boringly close translation of Ovid and give the narrative scant attention.[7] Hansen argues that all the men of the *Legend* are emasculated in one way or another, but she singles out Pyramus as a character barely worth Chaucer's effort to emasculate, being already youthful and timid.[8] She and Doyle briefly consider Thisbe's potentially 'manly' boldness in pursuit of love, but neither contributes more than a passing aside.[9] Their analyses predate (and substantiate) Michelle Sauer's criticism of the scholarly tendency to look within a narrow ambit for female deviant desire, and to privilege interactions that replicate modern heterosexual stereotypes, with an active 'manly' woman and a passive 'womanly' woman.[10] Thisbe, whose behaviour deviates little if at all from medieval ideals of femininity, passes under the radar. Even Delany, who devotes much time to Chaucer's use of the *Moralisé* as well as Ovid and uncovers the beginnings of a promising network of innuendos drawn from both sources, minimises the significance of the narrative.[11] She brings her analysis to an abrupt close, claiming with tired Chaucerian *occupatio*: '[e]xamples of sexual wordplay could be further multiplied, but these will suffice'.[12] It would seem there is nothing in Thisbe's story to provoke the slightest whisper of controversy.

5   James W. Spisak, 'Chaucer's Pyramus and Thisbe', *Chaucer Review* 204.3 (1984): 204–10 (p. 204).
6   Warren, '"Olde Stories" and Amazons', p. 86; McDonald, 'Chaucer's *Legend*, Ladies at Court', p. 27; Kara A. Doyle, 'Thisbe out of Context: Female Readers and the Findern Manuscript', *Chaucer Review* 40.3 (2006): 231–61 (p. 254).
7   Kiser, *Telling Classical Tales*, pp. 120–21; Priscilla Martin, *Chaucer's Women: Nuns, Wives and Amazons* (Iowa City: University of Iowa Press, 1990), pp. 203, 207. In *Chaucer's Legendary Good Women*, Percival devotes sections to Ariadne, Medea, Cleopatra, Dido, Lucrece and Phyllis, but not to Thisbe (pp. 173–296).
8   Hansen, *Chaucer and the Fictions of Gender*, p. 5.
9   Ibid., p. 6, and Doyle, 'Thisbe out of Context', p. 253.
10 Sauer, '"Where are the Lesbians in Chaucer?"', p. 334. See also Watt, 'Why Men Still Aren't Enough', pp. 451–64.
11 The 'Legend of Thisbe' shows familiarity with both the Latin and French sources. See Delany, *The Naked Text*, pp. 123–36, and Kathryn L. McKinley, 'Gower and Chaucer: Readings of Ovid in Late Medieval England', in *Ovid in the Middle Ages*, eds James G. Clark, Frank T. Coulson and Kathryn L. McKinley (Cambridge: Cambridge University Press, 2011), pp. 197–230 (pp. 210–14).
12 Delany, *The Naked Text*, p. 130.

Yet while it is true that the basic plot details of Chaucer's narrative do remain – to the frustration of scholars seeking a daring new twist – faithful to the established version originating with Ovid, the Latin tale Chaucer chooses is quite promising in terms of potential innuendos. Ovid's lovers whisper to each other through a chink in a wall, which permits only oral intercourse, and arrange a secret tryst. Leaving the shelter of her home, Thisbe arrives at the meeting place first, but is startled by a wild beast that threatens to maul her body. As Chaucer describes it, 'as she ran hire wympel let she falle / And tok non hed, so sore she was awhaped' (lines 813–14). This fallen veil is seized upon by the animal, bloodied in its jaws and left lying at the meeting place, where a horrified Pyramus sees it and jumps to the worst possible conclusion, assuming Thisbe to be dead and stabbing himself in despair. The animal takes the place of the lover whom Thisbe expects to meet, and its lust for her flesh offers a dark parody of the sexual urge. The loss of the wimple is a quasi-sexual despoiling, the bloody veil recalling the blood-spotted bedsheets indicative of lost virginity. The scene tips over into an absurd parody of sex: in extravagant grief and death throes Pyramus quivers, gushing from his *membra* (limbs), while Thisbe, who has returned to find him dying, shakes and trembles.[13] Like the mutually un-penetrative intercourse whispered through the wall, this quasi-orgasmic writhing is doomed to end not in reproduction but in death: the story as a whole would seem to illustrate the failures of faithful love, rather than to censure faithless men.

I argue, however, that the 'Legend of Thisbe' deserves far more careful attention than it has received. Chaucer's choice of narrative is carefully judged, and he exploits its potential through a series of carefully twisted innuendos, which put him in touch with a much wider hermeneutic debate. In telling contrast to her unobtrusive presence in modern scholarly responses to the *Legend*, in pre-Chaucerian writings Thisbe is a remarkably prominent figure. Writers from Juvenal onwards present her story as a byword for overwhelming sexual desire and excitingly taboo lust, reducing the character of Thisbe to little more than a penetrable vagina, consistently conflated with the orifice through which her would-be lover Pyramus whispers to her.[14] Innuendos concerning this crack in the wall proliferate, giving the narrative something of the cultural significance of a smutty *Romeo and Juliet*. This is certainly how Alan of Lille treats the tale in the *De planctu Naturae*, as he sets out his famous attack on the deforming powers of deviant sexual desire and gender nonconformity to enact reciprocal disruptions in the structure of

---

[13] Returning to Pyramus, Thisbe 'sees his pulsing limbs quivering on the bloody earth' (*Mets* IV, lines 133–34, 'tremebunda videt pulsare cruentum / membra solum'), while she is compared to the sea, which 'tosses' (*Mets* IV, line 136, 'tremit') when the wind shakes it.

[14] Delany, *The Naked Text*, p. 128.

grammatical gender and of language itself.[15] Casting about for a rhetorically transgressive image to illustrate his point, he can come up with no more shockingly disruptive possibility than that of Pyramus renouncing Thisbe's feminine charms, euphemistically described as her 'Veneris rimula' or 'little chink of Venus' (*De planctu*, line 53), and thus patently identified with her genitalia.[16] This essentialised femininity also lies beneath the treatment of the character in the *Ovide Moralisé*, for the fourteenth-century poem emphasises the respective femininity and masculinity of Thisbe and Pyramus through a series of risqué genital puns.[17] The *Moralisé* identifies the two characters respectively with the gendered archetypes of *anima*, the feminine soul, and Christ, the masculine lover of the soul. This interpretation maps the divine relationship between the deity and the soul brought into being by his Word onto a love described in terms of genital complementarity, in another version of the gendered paradigm of textual authorship. 'Thisbe' is, therefore, steeped in associations with the old established hermeneutic paradigm, in which the operations of language and of human desire are inextricably linked, moving parts of the same universal mechanism, wherein grammar and genitalia testify to the same rigid binary. For Chaucer, inheriting these rich source materials, the tale of Thisbe is ripe for subversive rewriting.

Chaucer's 'Legend of Thisbe' constructs images of deviant desire and gender nonconformity in its very opening lines. The narrator locates himself within the city of Babylon:

> The whyche toun the queen Semyramus
> Let dychen al aboute and walles make
> Ful hye, of hard tiles wel ybake.
> (lines 707–9)

The queen Semiramis is the notorious 'virago' of the 'Man of Law's Tale' (*CT* II, line 359). In much medieval literature, she was known for her unnatural sexual desires, and for gender deviancies including the wearing of trousers.[18] Chaucer's setting for his tale is, then, literally constructed under the hand of a gender-transgressing queen, and its very 'walles' partake of her questionable sexuality and gender. Semiramis is, and indeed Thisbe herself is, Babylonian. Like Medea, whose homeland of Colchis is pointedly located by the narrator as being 'Beyonde Troye, estward in the se' (line 1426), Thisbe participates in the ideological geographies that locate 'Eastern' women at the margins of the category of the feminine. Chaucer makes a point of this geographic identity,

---

[15] I discuss this text both in my introduction and in Chapter 3.
[16] See Guynn, *Allegory and Sexual Ethics*, p. 110.
[17] For discussion of these puns, see Delany, *The Naked Text*, pp. 128–29.
[18] See Kruger, 'Passion and Order in Chaucer's "Legend"', pp. 230–31; Delany, 'Geographies of Desire', p. 235; Johnstone Parr, 'Chaucer's Semiramis', *Chaucer Review* 5.1 (1970): 57–61.

introducing Thisbe herself as 'the fayreste / That estward in the world was tho dwellynge' (lines 717–18). As with the Muslim women of Middle English romance, her passionate character might be reduced to a racial stereotype, an innate marker of her Babylonian femininity. The narrative anticipates this charge, offering a description of the Babylonian custom that results in Thisbe's immured relationship, as visibly foreign to readers of the *Legend*:

> ... in *that* contre yit, withouten doute,
> Maydenes been ykept, for jelosye,
> Ful streyte, lest they diden som folye.
> (emphasis mine; lines 721–23)

This image of exotically enclosed femininity, of Babylonian womanhood protected against its own lust, sets up tantalising expectations of what form this 'folye' might take. Conjuring up the familiar imagery of the 'Eastern' woman as excessively lustful or viragolike, Chaucer invites his readers to participate in a racist fantasy of imagining how such female desire might react to this attempted containment.[19]

Expanding on this image of a racialised heroine, whose race implicates her in sexual deviancy, Chaucer translates Thisbe's enclosure from the Babylonian to the English. This translation performs the rhetorical manoeuvre Heng describes, when she acknowledges that 'race can ... function as sexuality', as Chaucer implicates his enclosed lovers within an English discourse of sexual deviancy.[20] Unlike his sources, Chaucer constructs the enclosure in which Babylonian 'maydens' are 'ykept' as something akin to an English religious architecture, describing Pyramus and Thisbe whispering together in a muttering reminiscent of confession, 'softe as any shryfte' (line 745). By locating his lovers in quasi-religious seclusion, Chaucer introduces a new set of suggestive associations. Medieval English literature addressed to immured women is monitory, and it anticipates not only chastity, but also sexual deviancy. As we saw in chapter 1, the *Ancrene Wisse* warns its audience that some enclosed women 'of hire ahne suster haveth ... i-beon i-temptet' ('have been tempted by their own sisters'), while Aelred's *De institutione inclusarum* cautions female recluses against the belief that men are the only threat to chastity.[21] Diane Watt reads the convent of Marie de France's *Eliduc* as a 'lesbian-like' space; Sauer writes of the way in which the walls of the anchoress's cell could create a space, a '"lesbian void" in which the anchoress could explore woman-woman

---

[19] Chaucer's racial rhetoric here evokes what we saw in Chapters 3 and 4 with regard to Medea, Floripas and the idea of the virago.
[20] Heng, *Inventions of Race*, p. 20.
[21] *Ancrene Wisse*, ed. Hasenfratz, II, lines 180–81; *De institutione inclusarum*, eds Ayto and Barratt, p. 287. For a summary of this tradition of writing, see Lochrie, 'Between Women', pp. 77–81.

possibilities', and Lochrie discusses the historical abbess Heloise's seemingly pragmatic awareness of female same-sex desire within the monastic enclosure.[22] The monastic space whispers, not with 'shrifte', but with insinuations of lesbian-like desire that both translate into English, and reinforce, the connotations of deviant femininity already pejoratively associated with the lovers' Babylonian origins.

Aptly for a structure raised up by a trouser-wearing virago of a queen, the wall of Chaucer's 'Legend of Thisbe' continues this pattern, as Chaucer departs from convention in his presentation of its gendered construction. Where earlier writers made the wall a feminine extension of Thisbe's sexualised body, Chaucer explains that the wall that separates the lovers '[w]as clove a-two, ryght from the cop adoun, / Of olde tyme of *his* fundacioun' (emphasis mine; lines 738–39). The wall is, as Delany notes, made of 'lym and ek ... ston' (line 765): lime and stones, but also, in slang, the 'limb' of the penis and the 'stones' of testicles.[23] The hole through which Pyramus and Thisbe communicate is described as a 'clyfte', and Chaucer gleefully uses the words three times in quick succession. The term can mean 'crotch' (in a non-gendered sense), but it primarily means 'the cleft in the buttocks'.[24] Chaucer uses the word in an anatomically precise sense ('bynethe my buttok') in the scatological portion of the 'Summoner's Tale' (line 2142), and recycles the joke of a posterior unexpectedly kissed through an opening in the wall in his 'Miller's Tale', indicating that the term to him meant 'anus' and not 'vagina'. No longer the feminine aperture of the earlier texts, Chaucer's wall is an inanimate version of nether regions which (since they are equipped with testicles and penis as well as buttocks) we may identify as masculine.

Both Pyramus and Thisbe use the wall as proxy for their bodily intimacies, much as the relics of the *Sowdone* tradition serve as proxies for the intimacies that the French knights are tempted to visit upon the desirable and taboo body of Floripas. We are told that 'The colde wal they wolden kysse of ston' (line 768). The phrasing is slightly odd; the adjective 'colde' picks up on an earlier cliché wherein Pyramus and Thisbe's love is compared to a burning 'glede' and hot 'fyr' (line 735). Since the terminology of temperature is used throughout the *Legend* to evoke emotional states, the term 'colde' does not so much emphasise the wall's inanimacy (its literal coldness) as suggest a chilly unwillingness to respond, blurring the boundaries between inanimate and unwilling states. In its association with feminine humours (generally understood to be cooler than those of male bodies), the word re-complicates

[22] Watt, 'Why Men Still Aren't Enough', pp. 451–64; Sauer, 'Representing the Negative', p. 70; Lochrie, *Heterosyncrasies*, pp. 26–46.
[23] See Delany, *The Naked Text*, pp. 130–31, and *MED*, headwords 'lim', n. (1 and 2) and 'ston', n. (1 and 14).
[24] *MED*, headword 'clift', n. (2a).

the gendered construction of the wall, suggesting something akin to female masculinity or male femininity, a cold yet testicular structure.[25] This blurring of boundaries is suggestive of the same confusion, associated with female deviant desires, which I discussed in Chapter Four, in the context of late medieval religious anxieties, while the deferred syntax that places 'of ston' obtrusively and unexpectedly at the end of the line draws attention to the obvious testicular pun and, by extension, to the conflation of such testicular 'stones' and relics (*coilles* and *reliques*) that animates both the *Roman de la Rose* and Chaucer's 'Pardoner's Tale'. The description of Pyramus and Thisbe mutually kissing the cold stones of the wall might, then, suggest not so much a frustrated desire for sexual intimacy as the achievement of an alternative and deviant form of that intimacy.

These implications are kept to the fore by Chaucer's description of the place at which Pyramus and Thisbe seek to meet, to elope together and consummate their love. We are told:

> They sette mark here metynge sholde be
> There kyng Nynus was grave under a tre –
> For olde payens that idoles heryed
> Useden tho in feldes to ben beryed.
> (lines 784–87)

The tomb of Ninus, unfortunate husband of the virago Semiramis, provides another architectural reminder of Babylonian depravities. As Chaucer hints with his reference to pagans who 'idoles heryed', Ninus' medieval reputation was as the inventor of idolatry as a practice. The meeting place is therefore multiply ominous, a reminder both of the decidedly unromantic outcome of Ninus and Semiramis' marriage (which, in some traditions, ended in the murder of the former by the latter) and of a misdirected and heretical religious devotion, an excessive attraction to an inanimate object.[26]

This possibility of atypical sexual activity is retrospectively strengthened by Chaucer's later revisiting of the tale of Pyramus and Thisbe, which occurs in the initially somewhat surprising context of the 'Merchant's Tale'. There, the Merchant refers his listeners to Ovid, as proof that love will always discover some stratagem whereby it may achieve its ends, and cites in particular the example of Pyramus and Thisbe, who 'Thogh they were kept ful longe streite overal, / They been accorded, rownynge thurgh a wal' (*CT* IV, lines 2129–30). The example is an odd one, as Emerson Brown notes, both because the Merchant appears to believe that the 'rowynynge thurgh a wal' forms the successful conclusion to Pyramus and Thisbe's frustrated

---

[25] For discussion of the role of temperature in medieval theories of the gendered body, see Cadden, *Nothing Natural is Shameful*, p. 123. I am grateful to an anonymous reader of this book for this suggestion.
[26] Kruger, 'Passion and Order in Chaucer's "Legend"', p. 231.

love, and because the example is cited in the context of Damian and May's distinctly earthy and pragmatic sexual lust, wherein, as he puts it, 'the victory of love is conceived of in completely physical terms'.[27] One might assume 'rowynynge' here is intended to imply something rather sexually charged ('moaning', perhaps), or to refer euphemistically to some kind of more-than-verbal contact. Otherwise, the reference in the 'Merchant's Tale' makes little sense in context (nothing has ever prevented Damian and May from talking). Reading back into the 'Legend of Thisbe', we might affirm that Chaucer's emphasis is not so much on prevention of sexual activity as on widening the definition of what 'sexual' activity is, in this context of inanimate phallic substitutes and of erotic touches that arise from the nexus of suggestive images conflated in the relic-like, testicular stone of the wall's construction. In this context, the inanimate nature of the wall is as important as its genital configuration. We need not again rehearse the long-standing associations between inanimate versions of male genitalia and connotations of female sexual deviancy, especially in this already suggestive context of female enclosure and Semiramic gender nonconformity. As Chaucer renders the wall's topography reminiscent of disembodied and inanimate male members, he locates both Pyramus and Thisbe amongst disturbingly indeterminate categories of sexual deviancy, which might be legible as anything from male–male genital activity (the kissing of stones) to lesbian-like appropriation of an inanimate male member (Thisbe's use of the phallic wall). The wall is both a prosthetic extension to a desiring body, and a component part of that body; it is a 'machine' that radically interrogates the construction of the body as a stable site of desire for the opposite sex that is satisfied, only and always, through essentialised genital contact.[28] As Chaucer makes the expression of Pyramus' and Thisbe's desire dependant upon an autonomous or separable structure, a 'clyfte' or chink in a wall, he pushes back against the idea of genital penetration as the definitive act of sexual satisfaction. As he structures his description of this desirous intercourse around a rhetoric of ambiguity and innuendo that stops short of explicit definition, he locates Pyramus and Thisbe within the discourse of *lacunae* which, as we have seen, so frequently expresses a female same-sex desire.[29]

---

[27] Emerson Brown, Jr, 'Hortus Inconclusus: The Significance of Priapus and Pyramus and Thisbe in the "Merchant's Tale"', *Chaucer Review* 4.1 (1969): 31–40 (p. 40).
[28] On the essentialisation of sex as genital contact, and the role of prosthesis in challenging this formulation, see Shildrick, 'Prosthetic Performativity', pp. 118–24.
[29] I discuss this, in particular, in Chapter 1; see also Freeman, *Time Binds*, pp. 95–125; Farina, 'Lesbian History and Erotic Reading', pp. 69–116; Kłosowska, *Queer Love in the Middle Ages*, pp. 69–116.

INVERTING GENDER, DISTURBING ST JEROME

The suggestive location of Thisbe and Pyramus on either side of the architectural structure that codes them as sexually deviant is only the beginning of Chaucer's narrative. Yet Thisbe's example carries suggestive connotations that far predate the *Legend*. The story of the Babylonian lovers has a special place within the hermeneutic tradition of Latin writings that proceed from Jerome's writings comparing interpretation to sexual penetration.[30] In one sense this is generally true of the category of narratives from which Chaucer takes material for the *Legend*: Thisbe is the heroine of a Classical *fabula*, and *fabulae* must be 'stripped' of their rhetorical integuments. Yet Thisbe herself, more specifically, functions as personification of Jerome's veiled woman, as her own clothing – and the sexualised yet hermeneutically disorderly manner of its removal – form the middle section of Chaucer's narrative.

After Thisbe leaves the walls and the city of Babylon, she encounters another ambiguously gendered sexual proxy: this time, a lion/ess who frightens Thisbe away from her meeting place at the crucial moment, convincing Pyramus that his lover is dead. When Thisbe first sees the animal that startles her to panic, the narrator explains: 'Allas! Than cometh a wilde lyonesse / Out of the wode, withoute more arrest' (lines 805–6). The clumsy rhyme with 'arrest' draws attention to the use of the feminine form, 'leonesse', and its aural awkwardness suggests something slightly out of joint about the suffix. Soon afterwards Pyramus, thinking Thisbe has been killed, exclaims:

> How shulde I axe mercy of Tisbe,
> Whan I am he that have yow slayn, allas!
> …
> Now what *lyoun* that be in this forest,
> My body mote *he* renten, or what best
> That wilde is, gnawe mote *he* now myn herte!
> (emphasis mine; lines 835–44)

Pyramus' repeated use of the gendered pronoun draws attention to his use of the masculine. In this shifting from feminine to masculine, Chaucer follows Ovid, whose narrator refers to a 'leaena' and 'lea', both words meaning 'lioness' (*Mets* IV, lines 97 and 102), and whose Pyramus later speaks of 'leones' (lions in masculine plural, *Mets* IV, line 114). However, Chaucer's manipulation of the lion's gender is more pointed than that of Ovid, and he stresses Thisbe's correct identification of it as feminine, in consensus with the narrator.[31] To emphasise the point, Thisbe refers a final time to the gender of the animal,

---

[30] For discussion of Jerome's writings, see the introduction to this book.
[31] Spisak suggests that Ovid used the feminine form simply to fill out the line, whereas Chaucer's focus on sex invites us to notice it. Spisak, 'Chaucer's Pyramus and Thisbe', p. 205.

as she decides to return to tell her lover 'of the lyonesse and al my drede' (line 861). That both characters perceive the animal as a creature of their own gender may be indicative of the narrative's homonormative gaze, but Pyramus' mistaken identification of the lion as male based on a footprint and a bloody veil establishes him as a poor judge of masculinity and an incompetent reader of gender. By contrast, Thisbe's encounter naturalises female lust after female flesh.

A careful reassignment of the innuendos established in Chaucer's French and Latin sources provides the final twist to this suggestive picture. The French *Ovide Moralisé* participates in a long tradition of emphasising Thisbe's genital femininity, by peppering its retelling of the story with genital innuendos relating to both main characters. Delany, the only scholar to date to offer a detailed discussion of the innuendo of the tale and of Chaucer's departures from his sources, believes that much of the smutty punning of the *Moralisé* simply disappears.[32] However, it is in fact reassigned in a systematic way. In the French text, Pyramus cries seminal masculine tears, while Thisbe displays a gaping, genitally suggestive feminine wound. The innuendos are easily understood in terms of visual similarities, but there is also a linguistic component to the imagery. As Delany observes, when the *Moralisé* author describes Thisbe's metaphorical wound of love, he puns obscenely on an innocent conjunction ('con', *Moralisé* IV, line 765) and a vulgarity ('con', meaning 'cunt'), and this punning calls to mind the commonplace *Latin* pun on the words *vulnus* ('wound') and *vulva* (genitalia).[33] By contrast, Chaucer neatly inverts the attribution of imagery, and displaces the mention of tears and wounds to the passage describing the lovers' final, single, face-to-face meeting. When Thisbe returns, too late, to find her lover's dying body, she 'wep of teres ful *his* wounde' (line 873). Her lacrimal fluid, analogous to semen in medieval medical theory, penetrates and fills Pyramus' body. In Ovid's Latin, that body was already depicted as being open to phallic penetration, albeit self-inflicted, for Pyramus picks up his sword and stabs himself 'in the groin' ('in ilia', *Mets* IV, line 129), pulling the suggestively warm ('ferventi', *Mets* IV, line 120) weapon from his body. In Chaucer, no mention is made of the object with which Pyramus 'smot' himself, and the classic phallic image is appropriated by Thisbe, as, like Dido, she swiftly snatches up Pyramus' discarded sword and stabs herself.[34] As she declares:

---

[32] Delany, *The Naked Text*, p. 130.
[33] Ibid., pp. 129–30.
[34] I discuss Dido's suicide in Chapter 3. With phallic implication, Chaucer's Aeneas leaves his 'swerd stondying' (line 1332) in Dido's bed, and she, like Thisbe, appropriates this symbol of masculinity in order to kill herself. Ovid – on whom Chaucer may be drawing in his depiction of Thisbe's suicide – stresses that the 'Trojan sword' Dido uses to kill herself will be stained with mingled tears and blood. See *Heroides* VII, lines 186–88.

> My woful hand ...
> Is strong ynogh in swich a werk to me
> For love shal yeve me strengthe and hardynesse
> To make my wounde large ynogh, I gesse.
> (lines 890–93)

This act stands in pointed opposition to the paradigm of female behaviour set out by Chaucer's Hypermnestra later in the *Legend*, where that character declares that her female body will not permit her to wield a weapon. Insofar as it is an 'unfeminine' act, it is also one that resonates with the established innuendos of same-sex desire that place phallic objects in female hands, and Delany sees the image of hands working in wounds as a risqué evocation of female masturbation.[35] Chaucer's death scene thus equips both characters with matching feminine 'wounds', and places at Thisbe's disposal multiple means of erotic, phallic or quasi-seminal penetration of those wounds.

On the linguistic level, the 'Legend of Thisbe' pointedly draws attention to its source tradition, and to Chaucer's careful redeployment and reconfiguration of the Latin and French puns borrowed from the *Moralisé*. Chaucer prepares the ground by stressing the Latin origins of his narrative just when he wishes to call that language to mind. He employs Ovid's signature anaphora drawn out to absurdity (lines 871–79), retains Ovid's striking and unusual comparison of Pyramus' gushing wound to a broken water pipe (lines 851–52) and interpolates a characteristically Latinate simile (nowhere else used by Chaucer) to describe Thisbe's face as 'pale as box' (line 866).[36] As Thisbe approaches the bleeding body of her lover, she sees 'hire wympel and his empty shethe, / And ek his swerd that hym hath don to dethe' (lines 887–89). Primed by the profusion of Ovidian and Latinate language, the Middle English words evoke their Latin counterparts, just as the 'con' of the French recalls the familiar Latin pun on *vulnus* and *vulva*. Confronting the Middle English word 'shethe', Latin-literate readers might suddenly remember the double meanings of its Latin counterpart *vagina*. Such a cross-linguistic pun would rest on perfectly standard Middle English: 'shethe' is a natural translation for the Latin word *vagina* (scabbard). Chaucer uses the word, with clear sexual innuendo, in the *Envoy to Scogan*, where the aged speaker renounces both poetic and sexual activity and allows his 'swerd' to rest in its 'shethe' (line 39). However, it is a rare part of his vocabulary, cropping up only two more times: once in the parodic tale of Sir Thopas in the *Canterbury Tales* (*CT* VII, line 876), and once more in *Troilus* (*T&C* IV, line 1185). The wider context of that part of *Troilus* foreshadows Thisbe's lament here, for Troilus considers

---

[35] See Doyle, 'Thisbe out of Context', p. 253, and Delany, *The Naked Text*, p. 131.
[36] The first simile is 'oraque buxo pallidiora' ('her face paler than boxwood'); the second 'non aliter quam cum vitiato fistula plumbo scinditur' ('not unlike the way that a pipe, at a weak point in the lead, splits', *Mets* IV, lines 134–35).

suicide when he believes Criseyde to be dead and weeps, like Thisbe, over the prone body of his lover.[37] These instances build up a suggestive connotative range for the term in Chaucer's lexicon, casting the wounded Pyramus as a feminised figure, with Thisbe in the role of Troilus, confronted with an orifice whose gendered connotations have come bewilderingly adrift.

When we look back to the *Metamorphoses*, however, for precedent for this cross-linguistic pun, we discover it is a translational red herring. Ovid mentions only that Thisbe sees her own abandoned veil and 'ense / vidit ebur vacuum': 'she saw the ivory [sheath] empty of the sword' (*Mets* IV, lines 147–48). The Latin word for sheath is omitted. Like Pyramus, glancing at the bloody veil and leaping to an unsupported conclusion, readers seeking a Latin body part are bound to be disappointed.[38] The 'vagina' readers might glimpse behind Thisbe's 'shethe' sees exists only as a cross-linguistic innuendo, a suggestively feminised body part visible only to those with the linguistic capacity – the tongue, perhaps – to penetrate the obscure joke. The innuendo forcibly reminds a particular subset of readers that they are reading a narrative already multiply retold in different versions and different languages, influentially pressed into service by Alan of Lille to illustrate the putative congruence of genital and grammatical gender: in such a narrative, the teasing suggestion of a Latin *vagina* on a seemingly masculine body belongs to a venerable tradition in which deviancies of gender and desire may always be glimpsed on the margins of the 'authoritative' tradition.

These glimpses of deviancy culminate in the final lines of the text, in which Thisbe mourns her lover through gestures and actions that code her as transgressively authoritative. Bending over Pyramus' supine body, weeping seminal tears into the suggestively feminised opening in his body, she echoes – through her posture and through the vocabulary that surrounds her – Chaucer's own repudiated hero Troilus, as he weeps over Criseyde. The moment is not only one of lamentation, but also one of textual production. The narrator describes how Thisbe 'medeleth she his blod with hire compleynte; / How with his blod hireselve gan she peynte' (lines 874–75). Thisbe's mingling of Pyramus' blood with her 'compleynte' is plainly a generative image, a form of artistic creativity, as the word 'peynte' indicates.[39] The substance Thisbe uses as raw material –

---

[37] Troilus' choice of word is polyptoton, echoing Criseyde's earlier resolution that, since she dares not stab herself to death, she will starve '[t]il I my soule out of my breste unshethe' (*T&C* IV, line 776).

[38] Chaucer certainly could have drawn on Ovid's *Metamorphoses* for such a sexualised pun. The very same innuendo on vagina/sheath is used to unpleasant effect in Ovid's description of Tereus drawing his sword as he prepares to rape Philomela (*Mets* VI, line 551). In his legend of Philomela, Chaucer does not replicate Ovid's wording, but the text occurs shortly after that of Thisbe, and it is possible that the 'shethe' here is transferred from the other Ovidian narrative.

[39] We might compare this to the scene in which Gower's Canace writes to her brother. As Martha Driver observes, a miniature illustrating the scene shows her 'plunging a dagger

the very blood of her lover – is also the substance medieval medics understood to be the raw material through which foetuses were nourished in the womb.[40] Like tears, blood could be seen as analogous to generative material, whether the masculine semen or the menses thought to nourish a foetus in the womb, and thus the image answers equally well to either interpretation of Pyramus as feminine or masculine.[41] Meanwhile, the term 'compleynte' dignifies Thisbe's weeping with a title used formally for several Chaucerian poems and sections of poems. The episode not only inverts the gendered paradigm of sexualised masculine textual creation, but it also complicates that binary and complementary paradigm, for Thisbe achieves what no male figure in the hermeneutic tradition manages, and makes 'hireselve' both author and blank canvas on which to 'peynte', as she becomes the author of her own matter and the creator of her own text.

As a pagan woman stepping out of her own *fabula* to offer a moment of textual creation, Thisbe flies in the face of Jerome's rigidly gendered depiction of textual agency. However, Chaucer's treatment of her constitutes an even more striking corrective to the positions expressed by Alan of Lille and Jean de Meun. Their texts, as we have seen, posit that misdirected masculine desire is cause and consequence of disruptions to grammatical gender and to the communicative functioning of language in general. The 'Legend of Thisbe' explores the unexamined parallel process: the hermeneutic disruptions resulting from *female* same-sex desire. We might conclude that, since Thisbe's lover Pyramus ends the 'Legend of Thisbe' a thoroughly feminised figure who engages errant masculine pronouns to describe a lioness, Chaucer only replicates the dire warnings of Alan and Jean, that same-sex desire results in emasculated men and grammatical incoherence. However, the culminating of Thisbe's story with the depiction of her textual creation marks a subversive shift away from the established theories concerning male same-sex desire. What results from Thisbe's dissident desire is not the sterility of language that accompanies male same-sex desire in Alan and Jean, but a subversively generative image of feminine linguistic production.

---

into her heart and writing on a scroll with her own blood'. Driver, 'Women Readers and Pierpont Morgan MS M. 126', in *John Gower: Manuscripts, Readers, Contexts*, ed. Malte Urban (Turnhout: Brepols, 2009), pp. 71–107 (p. 82).)

[40] Karine van 't Land discusses medieval theories of the relationships between sperm and blood, acknowledging the degree to which these substances were often conflated. See van 't Land, 'Sperm and Blood, Form and Food: Late Medieval Medical Notions of Male and Female in the Embryology of Membra', in *Blood, Sweat and Tears: The Changing Concepts of Physiology from Antiquity into Early Modern Europe*, eds Manfred Horstmanshoff, Helen King and Claus Zittel (Leiden: Brill, 2012), p. 379.

[41] Collette argues that this identification of blood and semen underlies the very gory imagery of Boccaccio's version of the story of Thisbe, though there it carries no implications of gender nonconformity. See *Rethinking Chaucer's* Legend, p. 38.

If Thisbe's 'compleynt' functions as a tongue-in-cheek riposte to the hermeneutic traditions Chaucer engages with in his prologues, the 'Legend of Thisbe' offers even more startlingly irreverent possibilities for thinking about those traditions. The narrative quite literally inverts the grammatical slippage Alan of Lille condemns in his treatise, when he refers to same-sex desire that turns 'hes' into 'shes' or 'illos facit illas' (*De planctu*, line 5), as Pyramus' error of gender turns the lion into a 'he'. When reading the narrative from the perspective of a diligent interpreter of *fabulae* and other allegorical materials, it is hard not to notice that the 'lion' acquired a symbolic referent during the years between Ovid's composition and Chaucer's rewriting: it became the avatar of none other than St Jerome. Worse still, its unintentional gender fluidity – so offensive to the saint's own perception of natural order – recalls a shameful but well-known incident in the venerable patristic author's biography, found in the *Legenda Aurea*. There, de Voragine recounts a dastardly plot through which Jerome was tricked into dressing in women's clothes, by enemies who sought to impugn his reputation for chastity.[42] The unfortunate parallel is strengthened by a second marked resemblance. Thisbe herself, with her precarious veil, recalls Jerome's personified pagan text, which likewise appears clothed in a removable veil, a rhetorical *integument*. Chaucer capitalises on the comedy, and gives the veil much greater prominence than either his Latin or his French source. Pyramus launches into a lengthy, new passage of apostrophe, beginning 'Wympel, allas!' and addressed to the discarded garment (lines 847–50). The speech bears witness to Pyramus' catastrophic succession of misinterpretations, from his mistaken certainty of Thisbe's death to his grammatical misgendering of the lioness who attacked her. Laura Getty suggests that Pyramus misreads the veil on a grammatical level, taking it as a metonym for Thisbe's body, but the failure is more deeply implicated in the hermeneutic system than this.[43] Like a textual interpreter who fails miserably to understand Jerome's analogy of *fabula* and integument, maiden and veil, Pyramus fixes on the wimple rather than the woman, and misreads the situation as he fixes on the element he should strip away.

It might seem that the joke of the 'Legend of Thisbe' is not on 'goode' women, but rather on the male authorities whose writings seek to keep women in their proper position within the textual and sexual hierarchy. The 'Legend of Thisbe' explores the subversive potential of deviant female desire to disrupt the gendered hermeneutic paradigm originating with Jerome, and to do so in a way that is not sterile, but generative. Chaucer's Thisbe emasculates – or feminises – her lover Pyramus, but her *fabula* goes one step further, and implicates St Jerome himself in dissident imagery, by disturbing

---

[42] *The Golden Legend: Readings on the Saints*, trans. William Granger Ryan (Princeton, NJ and Oxford: Princeton University Press, 1993), Legend 146, p. 598. See Mills, *Seeing Sodomy*, pp. 5–7.
[43] Getty, "'Other Smale Ymaad Before'", p. 59.

the gendered stability of his hermeneutic and of his symbol. The problem is that this presumes a considerable – even implausible – familiarity with highly erudite hermeneutic theory, much of it written in Latin. The *Legenda Aurea* story of Jerome's inadvertent wearing of women's clothing and the association of the saint with the symbol of a lion might not present much difficulty, but the complex grammatical arguments, the cross-linguistic puns and the detailed allusions to multiple sources are another matter. The obscure Latinate and patristic innuendos of the 'Legend of Thisbe' carry more than a hint of gendered coterie exclusivity, of *pas devant les femmes*.

Chaucer's Wife of Bath looms large over his later works, exceeding the boundaries of her own text to appear in the 'Envoy to Buxton' as well as the *Canterbury Tales*. The Wife grapples her way through an argument with Jerome, and Jerome's model of textual interpretation, famously and pithily exposing the interaction between gender and interpretative authority. Listening to her husband's censures of women who – like Thisbe – roam free from the house, and bare their heads, Alisoun responds robustly with the rhetorical question 'who peyntede the leon?' (*CT* III, line 692).[44] The beast to which she refers is ultimately from Aesop's fable, but it also evokes both Jerome's avatar and the ambiguously gendered lion(ess) of the 'Legend of Thisbe', the animal whose actions Pyramus badly misconstrues and whose gender, seemingly incidentally, he also mistakes. In Alisoun, perhaps created while Chaucer was still writing the *Legend*, we see the learned and Latinate subtext of the 'Legend of Thisbe' brought combatively to the surface of the text. We also see the fictional creation of a female readership for the hermeneutic tradition. Over the fifteenth century, the text plainly reached audiences distant from both courtly and aristocratic circles, finding itself in manuscripts read by both men and women, and sometimes divorced from its contextualising and puzzling prologues. The 'Legend of Thisbe' appears as a stand-alone narrative in the unusual and interesting Findern Manuscript, Cambridge, University Library MS Ff. 1. 6, which contains many woman-oriented texts and, perhaps even more interestingly, a host of gentry women readers' names.[45] It remains

---

[44] For discussion of this passage, see Mary Carruthers, 'The Wife of Bath and the Painting of Lions', *PMLA* 94.2 (1979): 209–22; Cox, *Gender and Language in Chaucer*, pp. 18–38; Hansen, *Chaucer and the Fictions of Gender*, pp. 26–57.

[45] Julia Boffey, '"Twenty Thousand More": Some Fifteenth- and Sixteenth-Century Responses to The Legend of Good Women', in *Middle English Poetry: Texts and Traditions*, ed. A. J. Minnis (York: York Medieval Press, 2001), pp. 279–97 (pp. 280–81); McDonald, 'Chaucer's *Legend*, Ladies at Court', pp. 22–42; Coleman, 'The Flower, the Leaf, and Philippa of Lancaster', pp. 33–58; Doyle, 'Thisbe out of Context', pp. 231–61; Carol Meale, 'The Tale and the Book: Readings of Chaucer's Legend of Good Women in the Fifteenth Century', in *Chaucer in Perspective: Middle English Essays in Honour of Norman Blake*, ed. Geoffrey Lester (Sheffield: Sheffield Academic Press, 1999), pp. 118–38 (pp. 123–24). For details of the manuscripts, see *The Legend of Good Women*, eds Cowen and Kane, pp. 1–19. The manuscripts not containing the story of Thisbe

disputed whether or not such women – living in a rural community distant from the court and probably exposed to little of the cultural and textual material that would give the innuendos of the 'Legend of Thisbe' context – took the text as ludic banter or as a straightforward exemplary narrative of faithful love. The Wife of Bath is imagined as a woman of similar social, educational and geographic position to the historical women who would, across the fifteenth century, read the 'Legend of Thisbe' in manuscripts such as Cambridge, University MS Ff. 1. 6. Her conveniently imperfect awareness of Jerome is always enough to facilitate Chaucer's own barbs; never so much as to suggest true female hermeneutic authority. Chaucer's Alisoun functions as a textual means of containing the dangerously subversive, outspokenly authorial voice of Thisbe. Her rhetorical question 'who peyntede the leon' is simultaneously an outspoken challenge to masculine interpretative authority, and the undoing of that challenge. The answer to the question, in the case of both Alisoun and Thisbe, is of course Chaucer himself. Chaucer's voice, ultimately, stands behind both women, and the 'Wife of Bath's Prologue' flags up this authorial ventriloquism more pointedly than the 'Legend of Thisbe'. Like Bottom the Weaver, Chaucer seeks to voice all the parts at once.

Indeed, this same manuscript offers an ending to the narrative that works to undermine the conclusion Chaucer puts into the mouth of his narrator. Seemingly forced to concede the masculine rectitude of Pyramus, the narrator observes:

> Of trewe men I fynde but fewe mo
> In alle my bokes, save this Piramus,
> And therfore have I spoken of hym thus.
> For it is deynte to us men to fynde
> A man that can in love been trewe and kynde.
> Here may ye se, what lovere so he be,
> A woman dar and can as wel as ~~sche~~ he.[46]

The text in MS Ff. 1. 6 originally ended with an aberrant feminine pronoun. The scribe mistakenly refers to Pyramus, Chaucer's young male hero, as 'sche'. In its context here, it functions as a teasing proof of the success of Chaucer's reassignment of gendered innuendos, which briefly equip Pyramus as a 'sche'. However, the error is also cancelled with a single stroke and a superscript reinscription of masculinity, as good a metaphor as any for female same-sex desire in Middle English literature, which – despite the best efforts of scholars – tends to remain 'twice marginal and twice invisible'.

To draw together these allusions, puns and inversions of grammar into an *exemplum* of masculine misreading and deviant female textual agency

---

are Oxford, Bodleian Library, MS Rawlinson C. 86, which contains the legend of Dido alone, and London, British Library, Additional MS 12524, whose text is acephalous.
[46] Cambridge, University Library, MS Ff. 1. 6, f. 67v.

is, then, a very male-oriented in-joke, one that places Chaucer as *auctor* alongside Jerome, Alan of Lille and Jean de Meun. Thisbe's story is the canvas on which Chaucer projects erudite innuendos for educated masculine readers to penetrate, while he preserves her famous innocence with a veil of linguistic modesty for less erudite female audiences. Her subversiveness is therefore only ever a linguistic possibility, contained with a discourse that constantly returns its female voices to their places within the dynamics of masculine control and feminine enclosure.

INVERTING THISBE AND REINSTATING JEROME

The 'Legend of Ariadne' takes this dynamic of staging feminine desire as a force of agency and expressiveness, only to circumscribe it. This legend interrogates the running theme of prosthesis as the means of coding female desire as deviant, reusing the key elements of the 'Legend of Thisbe'. The architectural euphemisms, with their genital and anal connotations; the imagery of whispered intercourse through a hole in a wall; the hurried attempt of a young woman to meet her lover; the threat of wild beasts; and the mistaken significance attached to a veil – all recur. However, the legend features not one female character, but two, for Ariadne's sister Phaedra is almost as significant in the narrative as the eponymous heroine. It is Phaedra who is accorded a prosthetic competency, while Ariadne is a still more brutally silenced echo of the veiled woman of Jerome. The 'Legend of Ariadne' is thus a doubled extension of Thisbe's story, an 'addition that threatens to become an excess', a prosthetic response that struggles to impose coherency on its fragmented matter.[47] Through it, Chaucer hammers home the message that neither feminine materiality, nor its prosthetic supplementation, accords women true and lasting power to make meaning and shape narrative.

The 'Legend of Ariadne' begins in such a way as to call Thisbe clearly to mind. Another young, virginal female protagonist defies her father to pursue a love affair with a forbidden partner; another relationship is established through an innuendo-laden architecture that allows conversation but does not permit direct contact or sight. The legend begins, as Thisbe's does, with the covert reminder of past sexual deviancies living on into present realities. Instead of Semiramis, famed for her incestuous and gender-nonconforming practices, we have Minos, king of Crete, who has a captive 'monstre' (line 1928), the bestial offspring of intercourse between the queen Pasiphae and a bull. Instead of Pyramus, there is Theseus, chosen by lot to feed the Minotaur. The smutty punning that transforms Thisbe's wall's 'limb and stone' into genitalia reappears in refracted form. As is the case with Thisbe and her lover, Ariadne and her sister Phaedra communicate by means of architectural gaps,

---

[47] Godden, 'Prosthetic Ecologies', p. 1275.

fissures and openings, while he is invisible to them, and they to him. We are told that Theseus is confined in a 'tour', the location so often conflated with the beautiful and penetrable bodies of women likewise confined.[48] However, unlike the clichéd lady in the tower, Theseus is imprisoned somewhere with rather ignominious connotations:

> Doun in the botom derk and wonder lowe,
> Was joynynge in the wal to a foreyne;
> And it was longynge to the doughtren tweyne
> Of Mynos, that in hire chaumbers grete
> Dwellten above.
> (lines 1960–64)

Many scholars, from Lowes onwards, have noted that the rather scatological location of Theseus in a 'foreyne' (a privy) is not only an insinuation of the lack of romantic atmosphere in the emerging love affair, but also betrays the influence of Boccaccio's *Teseida* on the narrative.[49] In the *Teseida*, Palamon and Arcite make contact with Emily because their prison adjourns her garden; here, the same situation is twisted into a cruder conversation, whose reliance on the pragmatic details of plumbing remind us that words are not the primary matter that travels from chamber to 'foreyne'. As the 'foreyne' carries the anal connotations of the 'clyfte' that facilitated Pyramus and Thisbe's intercourse, so too the phallic and testicular punning of the earlier legend soon reappear, gleefully expanded but also displaced, in the passages that immediately follow.

Hearing Theseus' laments, Ariadne and her sister take pity on him, and Ariadne suggests to her sister 'if ye wol assenten, by my trouthe, / He shal ben holpen, how so that we do' (lines 1983–84). Eagerly, Phaedra proposes 'we shul make hym balles', (line 2003) and she organises the provision of 'His wepne, his clewe, his thyng' (line 2140). Thus begins a passage of such densely packed innuendos as have delighted scholars struggling with the *Legend*. Delany explains, carefully, how the objects with which the sisters equip Theseus in his

---

[48] In the romance Sir Degrevant, whose approximate date is not very far from that of Chaucer's *Legend*, the hero likewise makes rather unromantic use of the castle plumbing in order to reach his beloved. See *Sir Degrevant*, in *Sentimental and Humorous Romances*, ed. Erik Kooper (Kalamazoo, MI: Medieval Institute Publications, 2005), lines 921–25.

[49] Unsurprisingly, interpretations of these lines have often been advanced in relation to the putative chronological order of the *Legend* and the 'Knight's Tale'. See J. L. Lowes, 'The Prologue to the *Legend of Good Women* Considered in Its Chronological Relations', PMLA 20 (1905): 794–864 (pp. 809–10); Frank, *Chaucer and* the Legend, p. 187; Percival, *Chaucer's Legendary Good Women*, pp. 187–88; David Wallace, *Chaucerian Polity: Absolutist Lineages and Associational Forms in England and Italy* (Stanford, CA: Stanford University Press, 1997), p. 114. Nicole Nolan Sidhu notes that Chaucer's 'strange slip' in locating Ariadne and Phaedra's Cretan bedchamber next to the 'maysterstrete / Of Athenes', (lines 1965–66) further indicates this influence. See Sidhu, *Indecent Exposure*, pp. 105–6.

task to penetrate the Minotaur's lair pun unmistakably on phallic and testicular aids. Dinshaw dedicates no less time to describing how the 'krynkled ... queynte weyes' (lines 2012–13) of the labyrinth itself evoke female genitalia. The puns betray their speaker's suspicious familiarity with the construction of inanimate substitutes for masculine genitalia and the navigation of vaginal depths. However, it is Phaedra, not Ariadne, who maintains control over the phallic mechanisms of Theseus' equipment; Phaedra, not Ariadne, who shows herself to be conversant with their production and use. In this, Chaucer departs tellingly from his source, which here is the *Ovide Moralisé* (VIII, line 1201). The French text details Ariadne's strategic bargaining over marriage plans, but where it goes on to specify her invention of the 'engin' that would enable Theseus to succeed, Chaucer transfers the material from Ariadne to her sister.[50] Florence Percival observes that Chaucer's treatment of the story thus has 'quite peculiar emphases', not only because it draws on Classical and medieval sources that offer very different versions of the narrative (including the presence or absence of Phaedra), but also because, in presenting Phaedra as the beautiful originator of the rescue plan, Chaucer makes it somewhat difficult to see why Theseus owes loyalty primarily to Ariadne.[51] The details code Phaedra as lesbian-like in her capacity to produce a substitute phallus, and no less so in her seemingly intimate knowledge of the 'krynkled' and 'queynte' passages Theseus must navigate. Rather like Medea, who schools Jason in the 'poynt[s]' of his oncoming battle for that which teasingly evokes a female pudendum, Phaedra takes on a position of quasi-masculine authority, initiating Theseus into a new mode of penetrative activity.

This whispered intercourse through the unromantic orifice of the 'foreyne', and this plan to conquer the Minotaur, both succeed. Theseus sails away home with both Ariadne and Phaedra, making a short pit stop en route. Yet the similarities to the 'Legend of Thisbe' persist, as Ariadne awakens the morning after her wedding night with Theseus. With comedic double meaning that recalls the punning allocation of a *vagina* to Pyramus, Ariadne 'gropeth in the bed and fond ryght nought' (line 2186). The verb implies a sexual 'groping', and thus the lines momentarily suggest a specifically genital disappointment for Ariadne, before it becomes clear that the man himself (and not merely that which a wife might grope for in the dark on her wedding night) is gone. Nor do the similarities to the 'Legend of Thisbe' end here. Dashing to the seashore in search of her absent lover, Ariadne calls aloud:

> 'Where be ye, that I may nat with yow mete,
> And myghte thus with bestes ben yslayn?'
> ...

[50] Sanford Brown Meech, 'Chaucer and the *Ovide Moralisé*: A Further Study', *PMLA* 46.1 (1931): 182–204 (p. 196).
[51] Percival, *Chaucer's Legendary Good Women*, pp. 177–79.

Hire coverchef on a pole up steked she,
Ascaunce that he shulde it wel yse.
(lines 2191–203)

Ariadne's 'coverchef' or veil serves as a mute message, as it did for Thisbe's lover Pyramus. Yet the whole dynamic is inverted. Whereas Pyramus sees and misinterprets the 'veil' that has been unintentionally dropped, and Thisbe has fled for fear of the 'bestes wilde' and cannot correct him, Theseus presumably does not care whether or not he sees Ariadne's quite deliberate message, and would be entirely content if the beasts whose violence she risks were to devour her. The parallel between this legend and Jerome's analogy therefore becomes a cruel joke on Ariadne. As she attempts to use her 'coverchef' as a message to her lover, he – so we are told – has already penetrated her naked body and found it wanting. It transpires that Theseus' reason for this abandonment of Ariadne is the discovery that her sister Phaedra 'fayrer was than she' (line 2172). In the context of Jerome's analogy, the greater physical beauty of Phaedra implies not the shallowness or fickleness of Theseus, but rather his excellent hermeneutic judgement; preference for feminine naked 'beauty' is implicitly sanctioned, indeed valorised, in Jerome's model of interpretation. With this in mind, it is no surprise that, unlike Thisbe, Ariadne is unable to transform her minimal prosthetic agency into a textual creation. Chaucer cuts short her 'complenynge' (line 2218) with characteristic, quasi-surgical *occupatio*, declaring 'It is so long, it were an hevy thyng' (line 2219).[52] The clunky and predictable pun on 'thyng' (meaning genitalia) looks back to Phaedra's construction of Theseus' 'wepne ... clewe ...thyng' (line 2140), ironically reinforcing the emphasis on Ariadne's genital and linguistic lack.

This failure of language looks back once again to the earlier episode in the 'Legend of Ariadne'. Delany observes that the thread that winds through the labyrinth may be read as a narrative 'thread', especially in proximity to the next legend's much stronger and more familiar imagery of Philomela's conflated textile and narrative production. This, then, codes Ariadne as 'unwinder of thread' and, Delany proposes, as 'generator of narrative'.[53] However, this seems to me exactly the wrong conclusion to draw, especially if we think (as Delany suggests we should) of women's professional expertise in the textile trade. No professional textile worker would imagine unwound thread to be productive in the way that weaving is productive. An unwound spool cannot be used, and anyone who knows anything about thread, yarn or wool knows that something re-wound hastily after snagging over several hundred feet of dank passage is unlikely to have emerged in a fit state to be

---

[52] The line suggests either castration or that clitoral excision of an enlarged member, sometimes considered to indicate female masculinity, which I discuss in Chapter 1. See Lochrie, *Heterosyncrasies*, p. 87.
[53] Delany, *The Naked Text*, p. 210.

recovered. The thread allows Theseus to come and go through the labyrinth without harm, and it is functional in this respect, but its function in aiding this masculine penetrator of uncharted depths is precisely what undoes, and unwinds, its useful potential in the context of the feminine domain of textile production. Deprived of this feminine means of making meaning, Ariadne is subsumed into a structure not of her own making, a structure whose implication in acts of masculine sexual violence aligns it hegemonically with Jerome's paradigm of the captive woman. At the end of the narrative, Chaucer cuts out a substantial portion of the Classical story, skipping to the end. He refers his readers to Ovid for the missing material, and says only that, like Alceste before her, Ariadne is at last transformed:

> In hire Epistel Naso telleth al;
> But shortly to the ende I telle shal.
> The goddes han hire holpen for pite,
> And in the signe of Taurus men may se
> The stones of hire corone shyne clere
> (lines 2220–24)

This stellification makes manifest the structures of sexual violence within which Ariadne is contained: not only the *Legend* itself, but also constellation of Taurus. This constellation memorialises another narrative of violence against women, referring as it does to the story of Europa, the mother of the same king who imprisoned Theseus and controlled the Minotaur. This Europa was, in her youth, raped by Jupiter, who took on the form of a bull, as Ovid reports in *Metamorphoses* II.[54] As Irina Dumitrescu points out, Chaucer has alluded to this violent narrative before.[55] In the F Prologue, the narrator makes an astronomical reference to the season, explaining that when he woke to worship his beloved daisy, the sun was 'in the brest ... of the beste, that day / That Agenores doghtre ladde awey' (F, lines 113–14). The *Riverside Chaucer* is complicit in the erasure of rape from these lines, glossing them as a reference to 'Europa, *loved* by Jupiter in the form of a bull'.[56] The location of Ariadne in the constellation of Taurus is a reminder of this rape, and it reinforces the underlying point of the narrative, that, unlike Theseus, Ariadne does not finally escape the bull-shaped aggressor. She is the collateral damage to his exploits.

---

[54] Ovid uses the term 'deceptive' (*Mets* II, line 871) in relation to the bull's intent; he specifies Europa's fear (*Mets* II, line 873 'pavet', 'she is afraid') and her dishevelled clothing falling from her as the bull carries her away: 'her clothes wound in the wind, fluttering', (*Mets* II, line 875, 'tremulae sinuantur flamine vestes').

[55] Irina Dumitrescu, 'Beautiful Suffering and the Culpable Narrator in Chaucer's Legend of Good Women', *Chaucer Review* 52.1 (2017): 106–23 (p. 112).

[56] F, line 114. See James Simpson, *Reform and Cultural Revolution* (Oxford: Oxford University Press, 2002), pp. 172–73.

What Chaucer omits of what Ovid relates is scarcely more detailed in the original. The *Metamorphoses* offer a few rather cryptic lines noting that it was Bacchus who took pity on Ariadne, and he who took her crown from her head and set it amongst the stars, with the intention 'perenni / sidere clara foret' ('that she should shine forever amongst the stars', *Mets* VIII, lines 177–78). The *Heroides* of course provides Ariadne's lament on her own behalf, but no word about this final episode of her stellification. As often, Chaucer does have sources for his material, but they are not quite what he claims. Percival suggests that the passage 'conceals and reveals' the omitted story of Ariadne's relationship with Bacchus, who set her diadem amongst the stars, and notes that Machaut also draws attention to the suspicious speed with which Ariadne finds a new lover.[57] However, it seems to me that the most overt absence here is not textual but physical: not a matter of Chaucer's missing sources, but of his suddenly missing heroine. Without the intervening narrative that would make the vague reference intelligible, the mention of Ariadne's 'stones' and 'corone' might cause one to be bewildered as to where the heroine's actual body has gone. Does she die? What of her, aside from her crown, is subsumed into that other structure of the starry sky? The questions point to a hermeneutic invasion of Ariadne's bodily and epistemic integrity. The legend stages the collapse of Ariadne's capacity firstly to shape her own narrative, then to understand it and finally to keep her body and her name from being silently subsumed into other representational structures whose meanings differ drastically from those she might choose. Aridne's inability to prevent the mobile, unceasing reinterpretation of her body's meaning raises questions as to the ethics of representation, and their gendered asymmetry: for reading a woman as a 'constellation' is to impose a unity of meaning upon her from outside, while acknowledging that this unity is at best illusory, at worst a radically inaccurate perception of matter.[58] Indeed, this representation of Ariadne as a constellation denies that she *has* matter, reducing her body to a fiction.

This violence has its roots in Jerome's hermeneutics of rape, which treats the female body simultaneously and paradoxically both as unreal (having no desires or agency of its own) and as entirely material, being a surface to inscribe and inseminate. Like the captive woman of Jerome's narrative, Ariadne is made to memorialise sexual violence (as part of the constellation of Taurus), while her own capacity to make meaning is violently disturbed and bewildered, as that final line 'I can myselven in this cas nat rede' (line 2217) indicates, with its reflexive pronoun ambiguously suggesting Ariadne's inability to interpret both the 'cas' and her own role in it. Ariadne appears again, in Sherman's striking

---

[57] Percival, *Chaucer's Legendary Good Women*, p. 181.

[58] I have in mind Deleuze and Guattari's formulation of the 'constellation', and the ethical implications of their valorisation of ever-shifting embodiment. See *Anti-Oedipus*, pp. 238–43; Thomas Nail, 'What is an Assemblage', *SubStance* 46.1 (2017): 21–37 (pp. 24–25).

phrase, 'under erasure', in the 'Knight's Tale', as Chaucer borrows the imagery of the lovers speaking through the tower, which I discussed at the beginning of this section. Thus, like Thisbe whose lion 'reappears' in the 'Wife of Bath's Prologue', Ariadne is finally reassumed into later Chauceriana, overwritten by a new narrative. Both Thisbe and Ariadne are circumscribed by these subsequent reconfigurations of their constitutive material; their feminine 'matter' is endlessly formed and reformed, fluidly rearranged to suit a new narrative.

Yet if Ariadne's story illustrates the failure of that heroine's rather partial attempt to wrestle her way out of the gendered paradigms of desire and interpretation that constrain her, that story is only half of the narrative. Phaedra fares no better than her sister. Despite her prosthetic competency and her intimate understanding of 'krynkled' passages, her textual and sexual generativity are abruptly circumscribed. Initially, it seems that her lesbian-like intimacy with Theseus demonstrates the success of her instruction in prosthetic penetration beyond the maze of the Minotaur, as their relationship becomes both sexually and textually productive. Alone of all the female protagonists of the *Legend*, Phaedra gives birth to a child who features as a central character in a subsequent tale. The next-but-one legend features this son, Demophon. His tale illustrates the truism that 'wiked fruit cometh of a wiked tre' (line 2395). Demophon replicates his father's offence, seducing Phyllis who is (ironically) taken in by his good 'lynage' (line 2526). The narrator comments 'ye ben lyk youre fader as in this, / For he begiled Adriane, ywis' (lines 2544–45). Phaedra herself is virtually written out of her own narrative, her sister reclaiming her pairing with Theseus in the final evaluation. She contributes no formative influence on Demophon's character; her role (like her prosthetic constructions) seems to have been handed over entirely to Theseus, reducing her once more to mere forgettable 'mateere'.

CONCLUSION

Through Thisbe and Ariadne, Chaucer presents twisted and manipulated echoes of the famous pagan woman of Jerome's analogy of correct masculine interpretative activity: the veiled woman, whose veil must be stripped away and ignored in order that the beauty of her naked body may be penetrated and evaluated. Both women leave their veils to be interpreted, as Thisbe's 'wympel' flutters from her head and into the bloody jaws of a lion, and as Ariadne desperately wrenches off her own 'coverchef' to raise it up as a message, destined to be ignored, for her betraying lover Theseus. Yet both women are also placed in suggestive proximity to the trappings of masculine writerly and reproductive agency, to phallic and genital proxies that undercut their seeming innocence with seamy and crude innuendo. In these two legends, feminine attempts to take on *auctoritas* – whether of a 'compleynte' or a strategic plan – end in the reabsorption of female bodies into larger textual structures imbued with implications of sexual violence.

6

OPENING MECHANISMS, ENCLOSING DESIRE: THE EROTIC AESTHETICS OF *UNDO YOUR DOOR*

Few Middle English authors save Chaucer can claim so widespread a presence in the works of sixteenth-century authors as the anonymous creator of the late fifteenth-century romance *Undo Your Door*.[1] The text was printed at least twice in the sixteenth century, survives in two different versions and is listed in the Day Book of John Dorne alongside other well-known romances.[2] Spenser retells the tale in the *Faerie Queene*; Thomas Nashe knows it; Beaumont and Fletcher use its alternative title 'Squire of Low Degree' as an insulting epithet in their plays, and Shakespeare borrows its striking image of anagram-solving for Malvolio.[3] Yet scholars have struggled with its chaotically amalgamated representations of romantic desire, taking refuge in the ascription of its popularity to its parodic undermining of an 'outmoded' genre steadily going out of fashion.[4] Recent reconsiderations of romance as a genre and periodisation as a practice urge us to reconsider that reading, and to ask again what earlier readers found so compelling, so suggestively

---

[1] The earliest complete witness to the text is Copland's printed edition of *c.* 1560, which ends with a colophon identifying the text as 'undo your doore, otherwise called the squyer of lowe degré'. Nicola McDonald makes a convincing case for using the former phrase, and not the latter, as a title. I follow her practice. See McDonald, 'Desire Out of Order and *Undo Your Door*', *Studies in the Age of Chaucer* 34 (2012): 247–75. All quotations are from *The Squire of Low Degree*, in *Sentimental and Humorous Romances*, ed. Kooper. All line references, unless otherwise stated, are to this edition.

[2] John Dorne, 'The Day-book of John Dorne, Bookseller in Oxford, AD 1520', ed. Falconer Madan, *Collectanea* 1 (1885): 453–78.

[3] For the first three instances, see: Stephen Guy-Bray, *Loving in Verse: Poetic Influence as Erotic* (Toronto: University of Toronto Press, 2006), pp. 50–58; Thomas Nashe, *The Works of Thomas Nashe*, ed. Ronald B. McKerrow, 3 vols (Oxford: Basil Blackwell, 1904–5), vol. 1, p. ii, quoted by Sid Ray, 'Tragical-Comical-Historical-Pastoral', *Shakespeare and the Middle Ages: Essays on the Performance and Adaptation of Plays with Medieval Settings*, eds Martha W. Driver and Sid Ray (Jefferson, NC: McFarland, 2009), pp. 195–200 (p. 196); Helen Cooper, *Shakespeare and the Medieval World* (London: Bloomsbury, 2010), p. 177. I discuss Shakespeare's Malvolio later in this chapter.

[4] McDonald critiques the application of this term to *Undo Your Door*. McDonald, 'Desire Out of Order', p. 247.

evocative, in *Undo Your Door*. I argue that the romance pointedly locates itself within a Chaucerian tradition of subversive writing, and that it layers together tropes and images associated with female desire, which we have seen operating in various texts and contexts earlier in this book. We see female sexuality represented as a transgressive yet creative force, which disrupts expectations of male–female sexual and erotic relations and assembles its own objects of desire from inanimate materials and from mechanisms disturbingly reminiscent of the objects medieval writers associated with same-sex desire and female autoerotic satisfaction. In this, the romance upends and dissects the paradigm of masculine authority and female passivity in both textual and sexual operations.

CRACKED COPIES: THE REPRODUCTIVE AESTHETICS OF *UNDO YOUR DOOR*

Undo Your Door has been widely interpreted as the last gasp of the medieval romance tradition, a retrospective parody of the genre that undermines the long-established tropes of chivalric masculinity and reproductive desire. Certainly, the characters are recognisable from earlier romances. There is the low-born hero who proves his worth as a knight; the jealous steward who arranges ham-fisted sabotage; the capricious father, who ultimately capitulates to his son-in-law; and, above all, the desired lady. Yet the plot that draws these familiar elements together is oddly out of joint. Knightly adventures are treated with casual unconcern, as the author flings his hero from Hungary to Spain to Christ's tomb without more than the most cursory detail, concentrating instead on the heroine's experiences during his absence.[5] Generically mandated paternal hostility is complicated by a subplot of desire which, McDonald astutely notes, 'functions queerly' between father and would-be son-in-law.[6] But it is the reproductive arc of the traditional romance, with its progress from desire to marriage to children, that is most severely disrupted. The heroine persistently deviates from invoked models of passively reproductive femininity, displaying a forthright sexuality that reduces potential love interests to all-but-inanimate objects. Unforgettably, the text centres on an episode in which the princess misidentifies her steward's dead body as that of her lover. She promptly eviscerates and embalms it, keeping it in a box and engaging in protracted acts of necrophiliac intimacy. Both the remainder of the text, and most of the scholarship to date, are taken up with increasingly awkward attempts to understand or explain away this strange manifestation of female desire, and to return it to some form of social, generic, or physical containment. Yet the princess's desire is not merely a startling digression or

---

[5] These adventures are largely described in just twelve lines, 884–96.
[6] See McDonald, 'Desire Out of Order', p. 258.

an unexpected caprice. In its bold disruptions of the expected time, space, and narrative structure of romance, the text recalls Freeman and Ahmed's theorisations of those 'queer' temporalities and orientations that make room for female same-sex desires. Reframing female deviant desire as the main plot, *Undo Your Door* makes visible a gendered textual aesthetic that permeates the whole narrative, eroticising processes of dissection and recombination in ways that evoke both medieval and modern discourses of female same-sex desire.

The romance is a promiscuous consumer of its own textual antecedents, crowded with knowing allusions to such stalwart heroes and heroines as Guy of Warwick, Sir Gawain, Lybeus Desconus and the Lady of Synadowne. The text is bursting at its seams with borrowed material, espousing an aesthetic of dissection and recombination, realised both in the author's magpie-like assembly of citations, quotations, allusions and stereotypes, and in its heroine's construction of a macabre object of desire from a dead body. This aesthetic speaks to preoccupations extending beyond medieval romance, into sixteenth-century culture and technology. The romance participates in representational innovations paralleled in print culture and in architecture, concentrating on the capacity of structuring mechanisms to shape perceptions of familiar material. It evokes various mechanisms used to manipulate boundaries between inside and outside, including the hinges of a window and the boards of a codex. These structures serve as metaphors for the princess's control over her own sexuality and over her penetrable body. In a text consumed by inaction and located almost entirely in the princess's chamber as she waits for her lover, the moving parts of inanimate mechanisms constitute a substitute focus for human activity, and form part of a wider eroticised aesthetic that moves female desire into an entirely new context.

The first surviving material witness to *Undo Your Door* aptly reflects the romance's self-conscious preoccupation with reused material, right down to the detail of its cracked and broken surface. This witness is the fragmentary print copy by Wynkyn de Worde, dated to about 1520.[7] A quarto edition, it opens with factotum woodcut featuring a man and woman, richly dressed in contemporary fashions and standing in a garden, in the act of exchanging a ring.[8] The woodblock was one de Worde had used several times before. A title page offered the frame through which a speculative buyer might be introduced to a new text (or an old text reissued), and de Worde's output

---

[7] Wynkyn de Worde, 'Here begynneth vndo your Dore', San Marino, CA, Huntington Library, Rare Books 62181 (STC 23111.5). The date of these fragments is attained through analysis of the title page in comparison to de Worde's earlier work, and by reference to the Day Book of the bookseller John Dorne, who lists *Undo Your Door* in his entry for 1520. See W. E. Mead, *The Squyr of Lowe Degre* (Boston, MA: Ginn, 1904) and 'The Day Book of John Dorne', ed. Madan, p. 116.

[8] See Edward Hodnett, *English Woodcuts, 1480–1535*, 2nd edn (Oxford: Oxford University Press, 1973), no. 1009.

shows his astute awareness of the value of such reuse as a marketing tool.[9] Firstly, he used the image in his editions of the courtly love poems of Stephen Hawes in 1509.[10] When he printed *Troilus and Criseyde* in 1517, the same woodcut served to suggest Chaucer's famous scene of the exchange of rings.[11] Later still, buyers of de Worde's edition of *The Four Leaves of True Love* were enticed towards the religious treatise with the woodcut's not-entirely-accurate promise of racy reading matter.[12] By the time de Worde pressed the woodblock into service for the title page of *Undo Your Door*, it was a familiar sight, and had acquired several small cracks across its surface.[13] Some forty years later, William Copland reprinted the text.[14] This enduring title page frames the text of *Undo* with an image whose reuse was visibly evident, and whose content was fragmented through the mechanical processes of its reproduction, offering a neat parallel for the romance's own treatment of objects of desire. The reproductive logic of *Undo* resembles a reused woodcut, a cracked copy of sources that range from the annunciation to the works of Chaucer. Like the *Sowdone of Babylon*, which invokes Chaucerian literary *paternitas* to expose its sterile limitations, *Undo Your Door* stages flawed reproductions of earlier texts, revealing their degraded states and exposing their limitations.

The Chaucerian connotations of de Worde's woodcut are realised in the opening scene of *Undo*, which a casual reader might associate with the woodcut's image of lovers in a garden. The squire stands, lamenting his putatively unrequited love for the princess, in a tree-lined courtyard. This 'arber' (line 28) recalls the *locus amoenus* ubiquitous in Chaucer's dream visions and drawn from the continental courtly love tradition. Specifically, it echoes the *Parliament of Fowls* in featuring a lengthy list of trees catalogued by name, from the 'cypresse' to the 'pyany, the poplar, and the plane' (lines

---

[9] See, for example, Martha Driver, 'Illustration in Early English Books: Methods and Problems', *Books at Brown* 33 (1986): 1–49; A. S. G. Edwards, 'From Manuscript to Print: Wynkyn de Worde and the Printing of Contemporary Poetry', *Gutenberg Jahrbuch* (1991): 143–48; Carol Meale, 'Caxton, de Worde, and the Publication of Romance in Late Medieval England', *The Library* 14 (1992): 283–98. I am indebted to Alex da Costa for thought-provoking discussions of speculative buyers and the marketing of early print.

[10] Seth Lerer, 'The Wiles of a Woodcut: Wynkyn de Worde and the Early Tudor Reader', *Huntington Library Quarterly* 59 (1996): 381–403 (p. 382).

[11] See Lerer, 'Wiles of a Woodcut', pp. 385–86. Lerer builds on Schibanoff's argument about sixteenth-century 'gender-selective recollection' of Chaucer's works. See Susan Schibanoff, 'Taking Jane's Cue: Phyllyp Sparowe as a Primer for Women Readers', *PMLA* 101 (1986): 832–47. Her reading of the implications of de Worde's print stress Pandarus' surveillance and spying, elements of the plot that would bring Chaucer's text considerably closer in theme to *Undo Your Door*.

[12] Lerer, 'Wiles of a Woodcut', pp. 381–403.

[13] Ibid., p. 383.

[14] London, British Library, C. 21.c.58 (STC 23112).

31–40).¹⁵ Like the garden of that archetypal courtly dream vision, the *Roman de la Rose*, this 'arber' is 'enclosed … and walled well' (line 139), and crowded with a catalogue of birds who inhabit the garden, including the 'lavorocke and the nightyngale, / The ruddocke, the woodwale, / The pee and the popinjaye' (lines 45–47).¹⁶ The names recall the birds that recur through Chaucer's works, from the *Parliament of Fowls* (*Parl*, lines 323–64) to the prologues of the *Legend* (F, line 37), to *locus amoenus* of the *Book of the Duchess* (*BoD*, line 295), and above all to the list in the Middle English translation of the *Roman de la Rose*, with its 'nyghtyngales, / Alpes, fynches, and wodewales … turtles and laverokkes. Chalaundres … thrustles, terins, and mavys' (*Romaunce*, lines 657–65). The Middle English *Romaunce* places its catalogue of birds in 'ordre' and depicts a carefully orchestrated harmony of 'summe high and summe eke lowe' (*Romaunce*, lines 712 and 717), but in *Undo Your Door* we find restless movement of '[t]he swalowe whippynge to and fro' (line 50) and discordant noise as 'the jay jangled' (line 51). The sheer length of the list of birds – a full fifteen lines – disrupts the narrative memorably. Yet, the list is not merely the result of a taste for conspicuous detail. In a self-consuming process, which we will see is typical of the text, the author of *Undo* produces a second catalogue of birds, appearing some lines later plucked and dressed for the king's banquet table:

> … partryche, pecoke, and plovere,
> With byrdes in bread ybake,
> The tele, the ducke, and the drake,
> The cocke, the curlewe, and the crane,
> With fesauntes fayre, theyr were no wane;
> Both storkes and snytes ther were also.
> (lines 318–23)

In a matter of 400 lines, the author of *Undo* invokes a *locus amoenus* and overwhelms it with excess of detail, transforming its component parts into the furnishings of a gluttonous feast. It is a process of material and textual reuse that transforms familiar objects of desire – the *locus amoenus* and its inhabitants – into material that serves a different and more mundane appetite.

The same aesthetic of fragmentation and reconstruction characterises the erotic relations of the princess and her squire. Both characters seek in vain

---

¹⁵ The list *Undo Your Door* echoes is *Parl*, lines 176–82.

¹⁶ The similarities between this list and instances of such lists elsewhere in Chaucer's works were noted well over a century ago; Laura Hibbard Loomis discusses them as she dismisses the theory that Chaucer's Sir Thopas derived its lists from *Undo Your Door*. See Laura A. Hibbard (Loomis), *Mediæval Romance in England: A Study of the Sources and Analogues of the Non-cyclic Metrical Romances* (New York: Oxford University Press, 1924; rev. 1963), p. 263.

to construct the squire as a knightly hero and chivalric lover, patchworking together disparate tropes and images in the process. Lamenting his low birth as he stands beneath the princess's window, the squire offers a notoriously dissonant combination of romance prototypes for his desired identity, bringing together the romance heroes Lybeus, Gawain and Guy with the giant Colbrand. He wishes:

> Wolde God that I were a kynges sonne,
> That ladyes love that I myght wonne!
> Or els so bolde in eche fyght
> As was Syr Lybius that gentell knyght,
> Or els so bolde in chyvalry
> As Syr Gawayne, or Syr Guy;
> Or els so doughty of my hande
> As was the gyaunte Syr Colbrande.
> (lines 75–82)

The combination is ominous, for the squire's desire to be 'doughty of my hande' takes on connotations of rapacious violence in the context of the notorious villain Colbrand, legendary enemy of English knights.[17] As with the catalogue of birds, swiftly transposed from the garden to the banquet table, the listing of romance antecedents exposes the disjunctivity of the sources from which the romance and its characters are constructed.

The princess responds swiftly with a new combination of elements, suggestive of a blazon in its itemised detail.[18] The princess specifies each item of the clothing she desires for the squire, as if his body were a blank page on which she might inscribe her image of chivalry and her heraldic signs of choice. This itemised list of clothing newly constitutes the squire's body as a knightly figure, and a target of her desiring eyes, unfixing associations between gender and gaze.[19] The squire is told he should wear: 'armes …Of gold and goules sete with sable … a shelde of blewe' (lines 203–5) with a complicated motto and design, armour featuring 'starres of gold' (line 223) and 'covered with good velvet' (line 224) and such exotic and regal decoration as 'oystryche fethers' (line 226) and 'armyne' [ermine] (line 230). The shield is to feature a 'ladyes head' (line 212) – a disembodied part of a body – and a motto, strangely expressed by the princess as:

---

[17] See Myra Seaman, 'The Waning of Middle English Chivalric Romance in "The Squyr of Lowe Degre"', *Fifteenth Century Studies* 29 (2004): 174–99 (p. 191).

[18] On the adaptation of the 'blazon' to figure women's sexual agency, see Michelle M. Sauer, 'Divine Orgasm and Self-Blazoning: The Fragmented Body of the Female Medieval Visionary', in *Sexuality, Sociality and Cosmology in Medieval Literary Texts*, eds Jennifer N. Brown and Marla Segol (New York: Palgrave, 2013), pp. 123–43.

[19] E. Jane Burns, *Courtly Love Undressed: Reading through Clothes in Medieval French Culture* (Philadelphia, PA: University of Pennsylvania Press, 2002), pp. 4–5.

> A reason for the love of me:
> Both O and R shall be therin,
> With A and M it shall begynne.
> (lines 214–16)

The letters spell out *amor* in a comically contorted form that anticipates Shakespeare's Malvolio, delightedly spelling out 'M O A I ... every one of these letters is in my name!'[20] They offer desire constructed by means of reconfiguration, love literally constructed from jumbled fragments put together. Recalling Freeman's image of a 'lesbian' form of erotic textual practice that takes pleasure in the suturing together of such fragmented material and the contingency of such a mixture of sources, the construction of the princess's desire hints at its underlying dissidence.[21] Collected and recombined, the 'archaic ... debris' of romance fragments and heraldic fantasies function as 'signs that [desire] has been and could be otherwise'.[22] Despite their comedic excess, the lines look forward to the more gruesome acts of dissection and reassembly the princess will later perform on the body she believes to be her lover's, an instance of foreshadowing grimly emphasised by the princess's passing fear that, were their love discovered, the squire might risk being 'hanged and drawe' (line 168).[23] The passage casts the princess as active agent in the construction of her own desires, a role tellingly unshared by her lover, whose attempt at self-fashioning in the mould of a romance hero is swiftly brushed aside for her lengthier revision of his image.

'QUEER' DESIRE AND THE INTERRUPTED GAZE

The princess herself is constructed from more promising materials than old-fashioned romances, appearing at first in a setting that evokes nothing less than the iconography of the annunciation to the Virgin Mary, updated with strikingly modern technological details. The frame through which she converses with her lover is a simpler innovation than that of the woodcut that opens the early print copy, but it is an innovation all the same: an oriel window, whose stained-glass casements open and close. This window, both enclosing and bisecting the imagined scene of the lovers, parallels the simultaneous dissection of the Chaucerian dream vision in the ongoing narrative, which locates the relationship insistently amongst the *disiecta membra* of

---

[20] *Twelfth Night*, Act II, sc. v (1160–62).
[21] See Freeman, *Time Binds*, pp. 95–135.
[22] Ibid., p. xvi.
[23] In this, the romance anticipates the parallels between literary trope and corporeal dissection, which Jonathan Sawday explores in his *The Body Emblazoned: Dissection and the Human Body in Renaissance Culture* (London and New York: Routledge, 1995).

Chaucerian courtly love poetry. We are told that the princess looks out onto a courtyard garden:

> In her oryall there she was,
> Closed well with royall glas.
> Fulfylled it was with ymagery
> ...
> And wyd the windowes she open set,
> The sunne shone in at her closet.
> (lines 93–102)

The passage exploits long-established and ubiquitously displayed iconography. The image of the woman sitting behind a sunlit window and surrounded by a garden is instantly legible as the Virgin Mary in the garden that represents the *hortus conclusus* of the Old Testament, as she awaits the message of the Angel Gabriel. The *hortus conclusus* is the world in microcosm, the inversion of Eden and of Eden's cataclysmic effects on language, the symbol of rediscovered unity and completeness.[24] The garden typically features lilies and a tree, representing the tree of the Cross and the tree of the Garden of Eden, which *Undo* replicates in its depiction of the courtyard garden's 'lyly-floure' (line 34) and 'tre that Jesu chose' (line 32). Within this garden is an enclosed chamber (or 'closet'), representing Mary's chaste body, while her miraculously intact virginity is represented by the window. These architectural features carry symbolic meaning. As the sun shines, its beams penetrate the glass without breaking it, a metaphor for Christ's capacity to enter the womb of a Virgin.[25] A fourteenth-century lyric sums up the familiar argument:

> Ase the sonne taketh hyre pas
> Wythoute breche thorghout that glas,
> Thy maydenhod onwemmed hyt was
> For bere of thyne chylde.[26]

Undo's configuration of these components of garden and enclosed chamber, listening woman and speaking visitor, and sunbeams shining through glass cast the princess as a secularised Virgin Mary to the squire's extremely unpromising Christ, who is destined to undergo a gruesome parody of death and resurrection later in the narrative.[27]

---

[24] See Sauer, *Gender in Medieval Culture*, pp. 50–51; Liz Herbert McAvoy, 'The Medieval *hortus conclusus*: Revisiting the Pleasure Garden', *Medieval Feminist Forum: A Journal of Gender and Sexuality* 50.1 (2014): 5–10.

[25] See Nicola F. McDonald, 'Gender', in *A Handbook of Middle English Studies*, ed. Marion Turner (Chichester: Wiley-Blackwell, 2013), pp. 63–76 (p. 72).

[26] 'Marye, mayde mylde and fre', in *Middle English Marian Lyrics*, ed. Karen Saupe (Kalamazoo, MI: Medieval Institute Publications, 1997), lines 73–76.

[27] McDonald, 'Desire Out of Order', pp. 265–66.

However, the romance does not merely offer this annunciatory image for shock value, or for the pleasures of subverting its associations with unity and intactness. Its modifications represent an exploration of the ways in which a new image of female sexuality might be configured out of the disrupted and disturbed fragments of the annunciation tradition. The metaphorical medium that stands in for the princess's sexualised body (or, to be less euphemistic, her broken or unbroken hymen) is not innocently blank, like the plain glass of the Virgin's window, but stained with images, historiated with prior narratives. As Spearing observes, the fact that the glass is stained accords the princess scopic agency in her interchange with the squire. She is able to see (and hear) him, but the coloured glass prevents her from being seen or heard until she chooses to open her window.[28] The window that enables the princess to control her desiring gaze also implicates her within a wider iconography of gazes and desires, subject, at the time of the text's composition, to recent and radical new interpretations. As Anne Harris notes, stained glass is 'an indiscrete medium', allowing coloured light to move beyond the constraints of its frame or pane, 'imping[ing] upon the … space that surrounds it'.[29] As such, this stained glass feeds into the princess's authoritative re-emblazoning of the squire's patchwork chivalric identity. As she looks through the panes 'fulfylled with ymagerie' (line 95), she transfers the image from her glass to his body like a pool of light falling from a window, envisaging him likewise dressed in clothing 'fulfylled with ymagerie' (line 209). This mobile glazed imagery recalls Chaucer's famous scene in the *Book of the Duchess* in which the dreamer falls asleep in a chamber whose windows are glazed with 'ymagery' in the form of the story of Troy. Light from those windows shines unbroken onto the body of the dreamer, 'al naked', as he prepares to conceive his poetic text, and symbolises the continuity of masculine authorial inspiration.[30] Reused here, the image, like de Worde's recycled woodcut, recalls an earlier Chaucerian iteration in degraded form, pressed into service to construct the princess as the author of her own *female* desires, practised on the unpromising material of her boorish squire.

The subversive implications of the princess's window are augmented by a further 'twist' on the traditional annunciation narrative.[31] The medium that symbolises the accessibility of the Virgin's body to the penetrating sun is transformed into one that facilitates the princess's active choice to allow or

---

[28] A. C. Spearing, *The Medieval Poet as Voyeur: Looking and Listening in Medieval Love-Narratives* (Cambridge: Cambridge University Press, 1993), p. 179.

[29] Anne Harris, 'Glazing and Glossing: Stained Glass as Literary Interpretation', *Journal of Glass Studies* 56 (2014): 303–16 (pp. 303, 306).

[30] For this reading of Chaucer's text as an annunciatory image, see Helen Barr, *Transporting Chaucer* (Manchester: Manchester University Press, 2014), pp. 10–11. The quotation is from *The Book of the Duchess*, line 293.

[31] McDonald, 'Gender', p. 72.

disallow access.³² The princess's oriel window features a casement that is both glazed and made to open.³³ Its glass need not break, for it can be moved aside. Its intactness is achieved by sleight of hand, by manipulation of a mechanism, and not because it is penetrated only by the intangible beams of the sun. Metaphorically, it represents the possibility of sexual contact that does not necessitate the tell-tale penetrative rupture of the hymen. The fact is revealed in a description of unprecedented detail. We are told that:

> Every wyndowe by and by
> On eche syde had there a gynne,
> Sperde with many a dyvers pynne.
> Anone that lady, fayre and fre,
> Undyd a pynne of yveré.
> (lines 96–100)

As the most recent editor of the text observes, windows with glass were still a rarity, worth remarking upon; windows with stained glass made to open, even more so.³⁴ Yet the detailed explanation is not merely a necessity of plot or unfamiliar content. The paraphernalia of locks, bolts and windows are often featured in bawdy *fabliaux*, with their sexual entanglements and (apparent) willingness to accord women sexual agency.³⁵ By placing the princess in control of her own locked window, the romance metaphorically characterises her as a woman in charge of her own sexuality, and the description of her manipulation of the specific technology is enriched with erotic suggestion. This extends to the details of the casement. The word 'gynne' used here means 'device' and refers to a closing mechanism that may be opened by manipulating the pointed object slotted into it. The 'pynne' is part of the standard construction for a casement window: a protruding bar with a corresponding slot or ring, which enabled a glazed wooden panel to be closed onto or unlatched from its surrounding frame. Pins used to fasten a window 'gynne' would typically be made of metal, and yet *Undo* provides us with a pin of 'yveré', a detail that remains tellingly consistent even in the

---

³² This representation of the princess's 'active choice' to control her sexuality raises issues of consent around the image of the female body as a closed structure; for more on this imagery of consent see Carissa M. Harris, "'A drunken cunt hath no porter": Medieval Histories of Intoxication and Consent', *Medieval Feminist Forum: A Journal of Gender and Sexuality* 54.2 (2019): 109–34.

³³ See Kooper, ed., *The Squire of Low Degree*, n. 93 and n. 94.

³⁴ Kooper, ed. *The Squire of Low Degree*, n. 94.

³⁵ See, for example, Chaucer's two *fabliaux* in the *Canterbury Tales*, the 'Miller's Tale' and the 'Merchant's Tale'. For discussion, see Nicole Sidhu, '"Famulier foo": Wives, Male Subordinates, and Political Theory in the *Merchant's Tale*', *Chaucer Review* 54.3 (2019): 292–314; Glenn Burger, *Chaucer's Queer Nation*, pp. 26–37, 107–11; Holly A. Crocker, 'Performative Passivity and Fantasies of Masculinity in the Merchant's Tale', *Chaucer Review* 38.2 (2003): 178–98.

considerably abbreviated later version of the narrative in the Percy Folio.[36] The unexpectedly luxurious material, and the strangely detailed focus on the mechanism for opening and closing the window, construct this component of the casement as an oddly eroticised zone, like a desired body part imagined in heightened aesthetic terms. The device the author refers to with the nonspecific term 'pynne' is, technically, a form of 'pintel' (a pin designed to be used as a fastening in conjunction with a slot), and both words are terms that also mean 'penis', the former euphemistic and the latter more blunt.[37] The penis/bolt innuendo is picked up by the verb 'sperde', with its suggestion of thrusting motion. The 'gynne' itself, the slot or hinge, is glossed into Latin as *machina*, the term repeatedly used as a euphemism for a dildo.[38] The modern technology of the casement window frames the princess not only as a woman in charge of her own sexuality, but even hints that she is a woman capable of meeting her sexual desires without the direct participation of a man, as it provides her with a *machina* or inanimate phallic substitute before she even speaks to the squire.

This intense focus on an opening mechanism located within an annunciatory scene has precedent, not in literary antecedents of the romance, but in innovations in visual culture that had been emerging through the fifteenth century. The annunciation is innately concerned with issues of access and mediation, representing as it does Mary's mediatory role as *porta coelis*, the way to heaven, and Christ's intercessory role as God Incarnate. It was a popular site for images of donors and patrons, depicted kneeling beside or below the main scene in manuscript illuminations and panel paintings. The miraculous mechanics of Mary's virginal womb gave rise to statues of the Virgin, known as *vierges ouvrantes*, which I discuss at length in Chapter Four. These statues were, like the 'pynne', often made of ivory, and featured hinged compartments that could be opened to display an image of the Trinity tucked inside the womb of the statue.[39] As I have observed, these statues aroused equal measures of devotional fascination and horror, and may be associated with the deep anxieties surrounding autonomous female desires and uncontrolled female bodies that manipulate their own boundaries. In wider culture, this fascination with the epistemological implications of the space of the annunciation drew to its height in the fifteenth-century triptychs depicting

---

[36] The word is not necessitated by an important rhyme, for it rhymes with a stock filler phrase 'faire and fre' (line 99). The Percy Folio text paraphrases the scene, but retains the detail of the princess moving the ivory pin: 'Shee pulled forth a pin of ivorye, / Like the sun itt shone by and by' (lines 37–38). The Percy Folio text (from London, British Library MS Additional 27879) is also edited by Kooper, as *The Squire of Low Degree; Percy Folio*, in *Sentimental and Humorous Romances*.

[37] See *MED* headwords pin (n.) and pintel (n.).

[38] See Lochrie, *Heterosyncrasies*, p. 52 and *MED* headword gin(ne), n. 3a: 'Get or gyn: Machina'.

[39] See Tasioulas, 'The Foetal Existence of Christ', pp. 24–48.

the partially shared space between human viewer and sacred icon. As Lynn Jacobs points out, fifteenth-century artists of the Northern Renaissance such as Campin, van der Weyden and van Eyck began to exploit the hinged form of the triptych, a popular medium for annunciation images, to introduce subtle visual discontinuities between the spaces depicted on the panels. Jacobs discusses instances of hinged triptychs that employ subtly inconsistent perspective as the scenes of donors kneeling in the left and right panels give way to the sacred space of the centre panel, images that feature discontinuities of space across the hinged pivot that separates the panels of the triptych.[40] The visual discontinuities that result from this trouble the eyes, while the mechanism that holds the triptych together, the hinged joint between the panels, tempts viewers to move and touch, as well as look at, the image. Would the image 'line up' if we adjusted the angle of the panels by manipulating the hinge? In her analysis of these triptychs, Jacobs interprets the treatment of the 'doors' (the contemporary term for the side panels) as a means of constructing 'miraculous thresholds' that tantalise viewers with the daring possibility of human incorporation into sacred space.[41] As with the annunciation iconography incompletely incorporated into the romance narrative, these images call attention to their internal disunity and incongruity, and, as with the princess's window, their hinges offer the suggestive possibility of human hands meddling with pre-ordained structures of thinking about devotion.

In the subversively secularised annunciation scene of the romance, the window between the princess and her lover offers the possibility of sexual, not sacred, penetration. The scene arrests the viewer's gaze as it falls on the 'gynne' that manipulates the boundary between viewer and viewed, according a simple inanimate mechanism a profound significance. It participates in the wider late medieval interest in the dissection and recombination of past materials, and in the synthesis, hinging or joining together of these materials by means of new mechanisms. However, this pivotal first exchange of sentiments between the lovers in effect constructs a defaced copy of the moment of sacred conception of Christ. Its reproduction of the annunciation is a faulty reinscription, which casts doubt on the validity of textual and sexual reproductions alike. In its reliance upon imagery uncomfortably laden with connotations of female same-sex activity (the dildo) and lesbian erotics (the *lacunae* and the patchworked identities), it suggests a strong antipathy towards the traditional, (hetero)sexually reproductive conclusions of romance. Accordingly, this subverted iconography directs the princess's sexual desire away from either the chaste obedience of the Virgin or the reproductive receptivity of traditionally desirable romance heroines, destined for motherhood. In literary terms, the punning imagery equips the princess, like Philomela, like

---

[40] See Lynn F. Jacobs, *Opening Doors: The Early Netherlandish Triptych Reinterpreted* (University Park, PA: University of Pennsylvania Press, 2012), p. 42.
[41] Ibid., pp. 304–5.

Thisbe, like Floripas, with a form of prosthetic penis and a mode of authorial agency, subverting the popular hermeneutic model of writing as analogous to sex and requiring an active, penetrating masculine body and a passive, receptive female surface. Locating the princess within the dissected fragments of a courtly love trope, and describing her eager accumulation of disparate chivalric images around her lover, the author of *Undo* poises us to expect a heroine who rewrites the textual traditions in which she is situated.

THE BODY IN THE BOX: DESIRING MECHANISMS

The second phase of the romance concentrates upon the responses to this pivotal conversation between the princess and the squire. Generic expectations lead us to expect that the princess's display of sexual autonomy will be swiftly curtailed, or at least challenged, by masculine containment, probably paternal. Instead, however, the romance abruptly confounds these expectations with a display of intimacy and desire coloured with remarkably overt same-sex innuendo, between the squire and the princess's father. After the princess and the squire have taken their leave of one another in the garden, we are told that the princess's steward has overheard their entire conversation and seeks to betray their love to the king. The expected scene of paternal fury fizzles out, as the squire returns to his duties about the court. In the king's hall, the squire:

> ... toke a white yeard in his hande,
> Before the kynge than gane he stande,
> And sone he sat hym on his knee,
> And served the kynge ryght royally.
> (lines 213–16)

The staff of office, the 'white yeard', offers a crude pun, for a 'yeard' is a euphemism for a penis.[42] Its whiteness visually evokes the penile punning on the 'pynne of yveré' the princess manipulated with *her* hands. Meanwhile, the ambiguous pronouns in the third line allow for a momentarily shocking visual image of the king sitting on the knee of the steward while the latter 'serve[s]' the former, the verb suggesting service of a sexual as well as a menial nature.[43] In return, the king conceives of a sudden and consuming passion

---

[42] The same pun appears in the late fifteenth-century N-Town play of the marriage of Mary and Joseph, where suitors to Mary come with 'whyte yardys in ther honde' (Play 10, 'The Marriage of Mary and Joseph', in *The N-Town Plays*, ed. Sugano, line 691). This is one of several intersections between *Undo Your Door* and the N-Town Plays, amongst them the shared interest in the traditional religious image of the suitor imploring his beloved to 'undo your door' (see Play 12, 'Joseph's Doubt', in *The N Town Plays*, ed. Sugano, line 1 and note 1).

[43] Here, 'hym' is a reflexive pronoun referring back to the squire, but is easily misread as

for the squire, deciding that 'he was the semylyest man / That ever in the worlde he sawe or than' (lines 335–36). Fulfilling all the stereotypes of lovesick longing, the king 'sate ... and eate ryght nought, / But on his squyer was all his thought' (lines 337–38). This display functions as a 'queer decoy' of sorts, in Schibanoff's sense, an obtrusive distraction from the suggestive imagery of the princess's desire that is beginning to unfold.[44] Like the crude penile punning of the *Morte*, with its images of violent male-on-male penetration, the king's exaggerated passion for the squire grabs attention away from the subtler suggestiveness of the earlier scene. Yet like so much of this narrative, the scene of decoy desire is constructed from images borrowed from earlier passages of the text itself, for the whiteness of the 'yeard' visually evokes the 'yveré' pin and semantically echoes the penile punning of the princess's window bars. As a result, it distracts conscious attention away from the princess's transgressive sexuality while simultaneously keeping the inanimate objects that characterise that sexuality firmly present in the subtext.

The king's unexpectedly affectionate attitude towards the squire facilitates further interaction between squire and princess, as the king gives his servant permission to prove his bravery in daring exploits abroad. Dashing away, the squire realises (or pretends to realise) that he 'had forgete' (line 498) to bid farewell to his beloved, and returns, attempting for many lines to gain access to her chamber and repeating over and over the refrain of the title: 'undo your dore' (lines 534–46). The princess, who has slept through the entire episode, awakens, and displays a distinctly lukewarm interest in her would-be lover, insisting he undertake lengthy quests to distant lands before seeking her hand in marriage, modelling his exploits on those of numerous heroes of well-known romances (lines 605–25). Meanwhile, the princess's jealous steward plots to kill the squire, and sets upon him with his men in the corridor outside the princess's chamber. In the ensuing scuffle the steward is killed and the squire captured, and the steward's men decide, inexplicably, to imprison the squire and to leave the steward's corpse, disfigured about the face so that it is unrecognisable and dressed in the squire's clothes, outside the princess's door. When the princess at last opens her door, enticingly 'naked as she was bore' (line 673), she is greeted with the sight of the 'styffe' corpse (line 658). Receiving what she believes to be the body of her dead lover, the princess loses no time:

> His bowels soone she dyd out drawe,
> And buryed them in Goddes lawe.
> She sered that body with specery,
> With vyrgin waxe and commendry.
> (lines 685–88)

---

referring to the king.
[44] Schibanoff, *Chaucer's Queer Poetics*, p. 28.

The scene looks back to Cleopatra's treatment of Antony's corpse in the *Legend*, as she takes 'spicerye' and 'let the cors embaume', (lines 675–76) before leaping, 'naked' (line 696), into a burial pit next to his sepulchre. Here, however, the physical cutting and reassembling of the dead man to form an object of devotion is grotesquely separate from the final burial, especially because the princess's speedy and decisive actions in reassembling the body suggest the fulfilment of a premeditated desire to keep the corpse rather than to subject it to the usual rituals. This skilled mortician's art preserves the eviscerated corpse for no fewer than seven years, during which time the princess keeps the corpse in her bedroom.

In its dissected, embalmed state, this body powerfully recalls the relics so central to devotional and affective practice and, as Dinshaw and Lochrie observe, so insistently imbricated in ideas about deviant female sexuality.[45] In *Undo*, the embalmed body (treated, like a relic, in such a way as to preserve its human tissues) replaces the desired-but-absent person in the affections of its owner. The princess's devotion to this unnaturally preserved body part risks spilling over from fond thoughts of the departed lover into something attached more directly to the object itself, much as orthodox devotion to a departed saint as conduit to the divine might risk spilling over into idolatry focused on the saint's relics as objects.[46] The ideas are much the same as those evoked by the earlier *Sowdone* and other relic romances of the fifteenth century. Once again, a relevant text is the *Twelve Conclusions of the Lollards*, which describes sexually unnatural acts carried out by women in terms that suggest the eroticisation of a relic-like object. The passage castigates women for 'knowing with hemself or irresonable beste or creature þat beris no lyf', a practice whose possible meanings include autoerotic or same-sex sexual knowledge.[47] Dinshaw glosses the phrase 'creature þat beris no lyf' as referring to dildos, which she takes to be the ubiquitous signifier of same-sex female desire.[48] Lochrie, commenting on the unusual phrasing of 'creature þat beris no lyf' as a euphemism for a dildo, questions why the Latin author did not use a more familiar term such as *machina* or *instrumentum*, but notes (pertinently for our discussion here) that it might be 'because dildos were often made of leather or wood, hence formerly of creatures bearing life'.[49] In answer to her

---

[45] The parallel to relics is acknowledge by Piero Boitani, *English Medieval Narrative in the Thirteenth and Fourteenth Centuries* (Cambridge: Cambridge University Press, 1982), p. 57, and discussed in more detail by Kenneth Rooney, *Mortality and Imagination: The Life of the Dead in Medieval English Literature* (Turnhout: Brepols, 2012), pp. 72–80.

[46] For the theology, see Margaret Aston, *Lollards and Reformers: Images and Literacy in Late Medieval Religion* (London: Hambledon Press, 1984), p. 141.

[47] *Twelve Conclusions*, ed. Hudson, p. 28. Quoted and discussed in Lochrie, *Heterosyncrasies*, p. 48, and Dinshaw, *Getting Medieval*, pp. 88–90.

[48] Dinshaw, *Getting Medieval*, p. 88

[49] Lochrie, *Heterosyncrasies*, p. 52.

own question, she relates the sin to the more widespread Lollard horror of excessive attachment to images and relics, to 'inanimate' objects 'of tre and ston'.[50] The formulation in the *Twelve Conclusions* suggests that the inanimate objects in question, 'creatures þat beris no lyf', are troubling because they disrupt the animate/inanimate binary, inviting users to manipulate them for uses proper to the animate human body, and because their sterility, their inability to 'bear life', carries sodomitic undertones.[51] The focus of the princess's desire condenses in these anxieties into one grotesque object, troubling the animate/inanimate boundary, and arousing suspicions of desires disturbed from their natural targets and fixed in an embalmed and dissected corpse.

Yet even within the orthodox devotion that provides the princess with her annunciatory iconography, the preserved corpse evokes powerful parallels. It calls to mind the popular trope wherein the features of Christ's crucified body are itemised, one by one, and mapped onto the features of a manuscript book, in a rhetorical process that stresses the shared life – the shared skin and blood and wounding – that marks both body and parchment book.[52] The trope involves a blazon-like dissection of the components of a parchment codex, including skins of animals, the red ink and nails used to fasten the wooden boards in which codices are bound.[53] One author explains how, seeing the nailed boards and red letters of the book, '[m]y lorde I likne to þat signe', for '[þ]e body was bored *and* on borde bete'.[54] The word 'bored' puns not only on 'borde' – the tree of the cross or the wood of the book's binding – but also on the words meaning 'speared' or 'hollowed out', suggesting the spear-thrust wound in Christ's side but also the evisceration of the animal whose hide is used for parchment. Like these books, the body in *Undo* is transformed through a process of evisceration and preservation. The skin is embalmed, and in the later Percy Folio version, the 'flax' – hair – is also removed, as

---

[50] Ibid., p. 54. She quotes from the *Twelve Conclusions*, ed. Hudson, p. 27.

[51] I am grateful to an anonymous reader for Boydell and Brewer for this latter interpretation.

[52] For discussion of the *arma Christi* tradition more widely, see Lisa H. Cooper and Andrea Denny-Brown, eds, *The Arma Christi Tradition in Medieval and Early Modern Material Culture* (Farnham: Ashgate, 2013).

[53] See H. Leith Spencer, *English Preaching in the Late Middle Ages* (Oxford: Clarendon Press, 1993), pp. 139–42; Mary Caroline Spalding, ed., 'The Middle English Charters of Christ' (Bryn Mawr, PA: Bryn Mawr College, 1914), pp. xlii–li; Kathryn Rudy, 'An Illustrated Mid-Fifteenth Century Primer for a Flemish Girl: British Library, Harley MS 3828', *Journal of the Warburg and Courtauld Institutes* 69 (2006): 51–94 (p. 56); and Sarah Noonan, 'Bodies of Parchment: Representing the Passion and Reading Manuscripts in Late Medieval England', unpublished PhD thesis, Washington University in St Louis, 2010, pp. 33–100.

[54] 'The Disputation Between Mary and the Cross', lines 191–93. Quoted by Noonan, 'Bodies of Parchment', p. 9 n. 14.

animal hair is removed from skin prepared for parchment.[55] The eviscerated and dried body is 'closed ... in a maser tre' which is, in turn, bound with 'lockes thre' (lines 689–90). The verb 'closen' may be used to refer specifically to the binding of parchment, while the 'maser tre' (maple wood) suggests the wooden boards to which parchment manuscripts were bound, and the 'lockes' the clasps used for fastening codices shut.[56] The macabre mortuary practices thus continue the narrative's representation of the princess as the author of her own desires, and an author who makes startlingly subversive use of repurposed images from religious iconography.

The containment of the body also recalls the construction of the original window that enclosed the princess within her chamber. Outside its container of 'maser tre', the princess further encloses the body in 'a marble stone, / With quaynt gynnes many one' (lines 691–92). The wooden frame with its stone surround suggests the architecture of an oriel window with its moveable wooden casement set in a stone frame, while the 'quaynt gynnes' echo the earlier description of each window fastened with 'a gynne / Sperde with many a dyvers pynne' (lines 97–98). The body is secured in its wooden case, which can be opened in much the same way as the annunciatory window. The window, the body and the book are evoked in such a way that their properties map onto one another, architectural, visual, somatic and textual, frames of reference overlapping. Intended to conceal and contain, the chest of wood and stone is, instead, revealing. Insistently, it draws the details of the earlier scene – the 'gynne' and 'pynne' of the window frame, which attract attention seemingly unmerited for such innocuous mechanisms – back into focus. Like a relic, it troubles the boundary between animate and inanimate object, arousing anxieties through its propensity to attract excessive and misdirected devotion. A *point de caption*, it forges connections between different representations of intimacy, touch and affection due to the very different objects (the window, the book, the relic and the body itself). The profusion of undifferentiated intimate emotion the object generates resembles the excessive, unbounded desire which, as we saw in Chapters Three and Four, medical authorities associated with women exhibiting pathological symptoms of sexual and gender transgression. Powerfully gruesome and yet desired, the body in the box makes the dissidence of the princess's desire unmistakably visible, evoking the objects, the practices and the characteristic excesses and boundary transgressions that are the targets of innuendos and hints of female same-sex desire.

These objects play prosthetic functions within *Undo*, both in the sense that they represent the prosthetic devices that define female same-sex desire to medieval audiences, and in the sense that they offer extended possibilities

---

[55] *Percy Folio*, ed. Kooper, line 93.
[56] See *MED* headword closen (v. 8).

of action to an individual constructed, within a male discourse, as suffering 'impairment'.[57] These objects offer the princess the means to overcome containment and stasis, to overcome the 'impairment' of her gender and of the expectations imposed by her genre. Like a relic, the embalmed body is swiftly involved in rituals of intimate touch and affection, which exceed the bounds of propriety. The 'lockes' of the casket are designed to be opened, and the princess sets the entire object 'at hir beddes head, / And every day she kyst that dead' (lines 693–94). By the end of seven years the princess's touch – which we might, following Dinshaw, theorise as a 'queer touch', a touch that is transgressive in its emotional impetus – is fast wearing the body into powder.[58] The activity might recall the worn devotional images we find as testimony to the same intensity of desire for physical contact in Books of Hours. Readers were encouraged to touch or stroke their books *because* they evoked the dead body, as the vividly red painted blood drops of manuscripts such as British Library MS Egerton 1821, with its much-rubbed surface, bear witness.[59] This activity takes on particular pertinence when we think of the touching and kissing with which other enclosed women – nuns – venerated images of the Wound of Christ depicted on the stretched-skin manuscript page, an activity whose attraction, Lochrie provocatively argues, may have had its origins in the similarity of the image to female genitalia rather than to Christ's body.[60] When the princess kisses and touches the relic-like, book-like body as a substitute for her presumed wounded lover, she evokes these parallel forms of intimacy with a vicarious object that may not represent quite what it seems to represent.

After the embalmed body has been so over-used that it threatens to fall into dust, the princess determines to bury the remains. Referring to them as 'treasure' at risk of 'theves' (lines 936–38), she uses imagery commonly associated with female genitalia, rather than a male body, and laments:

> I have thee kept this seven yere,
> And now ye be in powder small,
> I may no lenger holde you with all.
> (lines 930–32)

In response to the princess's apparent despair, the king attempts to entice her back to worldly pleasures with descriptions of luxuries. The king's suggested 'remedies' are, effectively, attempts to warm the princess's chilly sexual desire,

---

[57] Mitchell and Snyder, *Narrative Prosthesis*, p. 8.
[58] Dinshaw, *Getting Medieval*, p. 143.
[59] London, British Library MS Egerton 1821, ff. 1v–2r. See Nancy Thebaut, 'Bleeding Pages, Bleeding Bodies: A Gendered Reading of British Library MS Egerton 1821', *Medieval Feminist Forum*, 45.2 (2009): 175–200 (p. 178).
[60] See Karma Lochrie, 'Mystical Acts, Queer Tendencies', in *Constructing Medieval Sexualities*, eds Karma Lochrie, Peggy McCracken and James Schultz (Minneapolis, MN: University of Minnesota Press, 1997), pp. 180–200 (pp. 189–92).

beginning with a prescription of heating wines ('rumney and malmesyne ... Mountrose and wyne of Greke' including spiced 'ypocrasse' (lines 753–55), and with sexualised pastimes such as hunting.[61] Finally, he proposes that

> An hundreth knightes truly tolde
> Shall play with bowles in alayes colde,
> Your disease to drive awaie.
> (lines 803–5)

The 'aleyes' suggest the intimate passages of the female body, 'colde' in their sexual frigidity, while the 'bowles' pun on masculine genitalia. In short, the king's cure for his daughter's seeming lack of sexual interest is a dose of good old-fashioned heterosex. The prescription is, however, doomed to fail: as a collection of medical remedies intended to promote sexual desire, it can have little effect on the princess whose passion seems, if anything, too heated. Slyly, the text punningly reminds us that the 'bowles' the princess has been playing with most recently are neither masculine genitalia nor games, but the viscera she so professionally removed from her putative lover's body during the embalming process.[62] Predictably, her response to the lengthy catalogue of sensory pleasures is strikingly laconic: 'Gramercy, father, so mote I the, / For all these thinges lyketh not me' (lines 853–54).[63] Bidding farewell to a lengthy catalogue of worldly pleasures, the princess vows:

> Nowe wyll I take the mantell and the rynge,
> And become an ancresse in my lyvynge.
> And yet I am a mayden for thee.
> (lines 955–57)

The princess's vow echoes the famous withdrawal of romance heroines such as Guinevere to a nunnery at the end of her paradigmatic doomed love affair with Lancelot, but we also find it given a more unsavoury gloss. The anchorhold and the women's monastery are both spaces frequently invoked in medieval innuendos and warnings about female same-sex desire.[64] This resolution to pursue an anchoritic life – especially one understood from the outset to result from earthly passions rather than devotion to Christ – may

---

[61] See Jennifer Evans, *Aphrodisiacs, Fertility and Medicine in Early Modern England* (Woodbridge: Royal Historical Society/Boydell Press, 2014), p. 91; C. M. Woolgar, *The Senses in Late Medieval England* (New Haven, CT and London: Yale University Press, 2007), p. 126.

[62] I am grateful to Hope Docherty for identifying this pun on bowles/bowels.

[63] The formulation recalls Kłosowska's discussion of the much earlier romance *Yde and Olive*, in which Olive tacitly expresses her same-sex desire by using similar terms. See *Queer Love in the Middle Ages*, p. 105.

[64] Ancrene Wisse, II: 71; Watt, 'Why Men Still Aren't Enough', pp. 451–64; Sauer, 'Representing the Negative', p. 70.

be seen as a natural progression of dissident desire. The *Twelve Conclusions* juxtapose the discussion of intemperate desire for relics and transgressive female desire that seeks sexual gratification in 'creature[s] þat beris no lyf' with particular slurs on religious women, and with anxieties about abortive interference into reproduction. The passage in full, from the eleventh conclusion, describes women's lack of 'continence' leading to the

> most horrible synne possible to mankynde. For þou sleyng of children or þei ben cristenid, aborcife and stroying of kynde be medicine ben ful sinful, 3et knowing with hemself or irresonable beste or creature þat beris no lyf passith in worthinesse to be punischid in peynis of helle. Þe correlary is þat widuis, and qwiche as han takin þe mantil and þe ryng deliciousliche fed, we wolde þei were weddid, for we can nout excusin hem fro priue synnis.[65]

The passage associates women who engage in procuring abortion or infanticide with women whose sexual satisfaction involves carnal knowledge with each other or with the above-mentioned 'creature þat beris no lyf', and with women who 'han takin þe mantil and þe ryng'. *Undo* draws together the two latter images, and indeed uses the same commonplace phrase, 'the mantell and the rynge' (line 955), to describe the princess's desire for religious enclosure. The first image, the image of destruction of children, begins to make sense of the princess's similarly reproduction-resistant desires.

The eroticised aesthetic of deconstruction and reassembly in *Undo Your Door* has its parallels in earlier medieval women's textual, visual and material practices, often associated with the expression of female sexual agency and even same-sex desire.[66] Michelle Sauer argues medieval devotional and mystical works conveyed an 'emphasis on female body parts that suggests an eroticisation, perhaps self-inflicted'. She sees this emphasis as a means of reclaiming female agency from the discourses of the patriarchy, likening depictions of eroticised body parts to a blazon that expresses female sexual agency through the repurposing of a masculine literary practice.[67] This anticipates the process described by Horne and Lewis, whereby 'lesbians and gays have ... to form identities out of appropriations and adaptations of existing codes', or the 'lesbian' mode of reading that proceeds through patchworking together of materials, through *lacunae* and omissions.[68] We might associate this dynamic with Chaucer's Medea, who imaginatively cut-and-pastes herself into the masculine role of lover in a homoerotic dynamic, or with Kłosowska's description of the role of 'cut-and-recombined' materials in the fashioning of a

---

[65] *Twelve Conclusions*, ed. Hudson, p. 28.
[66] Caroline Walker Bynum, *Fragmentation and Redemption: Essays on Gender and the Human Body in Medieval Religion* (Cambridge, MA and New York: MIT Press and Zone Books, 1992).
[67] Sauer, 'Divine Orgasm and Self-Blazoning', p. 125.
[68] Horne and Lewis, 'Introduction, Reframed', p. 4.

'lesbian-like identity' amongst the manuscript makers in women's convents.[69] In just this manner, the princess of *Undo* constructs a patchwork object of desire from the (sometimes violently) dismembered remnants not only of her putative lover, but also of the iconographies and anxieties, the canonical texts and the generic predecessors, that haunt her romance. The *machina* that satisfies her desire is both the mechanism of hinge, and the prosthesis she constructs from her putative lover's body; it is the 'desiring machine' Deleuze and Guattari describe, which reframes our sense of the boundaries of the body and frees that body from the sedimented expectation of feminine orientation towards masculinity.[70]

CONCLUSION

This reading of the princess's desire allows us to draw some final conclusions that look back from *Undo Your Door* to the wider fifteenth-century romance tradition, to the influence of Chaucer over the fifteenth century and, ultimately, to broader late medieval attempts to harness the subversive potential of female deviant desire. Scholars have recognised *Undo Your Door* as a parody of the mechanisms through which romances typically engineer reproduction: the formulaic plots ending in procreative marriage, and the predictable tropes that perpetuate themselves from one tale to the next. Yet the text's interrogation of reproductive mechanisms has, I submit, a distinctly contemporary focus on technological means of framing, reframing and re-presenting material. Its lengthy descriptions of new devices are not merely overblown conspicuous consumption, and its insistent reuse of old material is not merely the sign of a genre decayed past the point of innovation. Its aesthetic, which recombines a new object from piecemeal fragments of the old material, evokes those *lacunae* and tactile, erotic gaps that have featured in medieval representations of female dissident desire throughout this book. As hybrids of mechanism and body, the objects on which *Undo* places such intense and disconcerting focus – the genital 'pynne' in the princess's hand; the body in the box – anticipate Haraway's thought experiments about the way in which the gendered, hierarchised structures of representation and reproduction are threatened by the disruption of the perceptual boundary between human and machine, animate and inanimate.[71] These objects participate in the religious unease surrounding relic culture, but transmit the anxieties they generate from the narrow context of objects to the wider representational context of other artistic forms, such as the triptychs representing the annunciation, the board books figuring the

---

[69] Kłosowska, *Queer Love in the Middle Ages*, pp. 91–94. Kłosowska quotes from Bennett, '"Lesbian-Like" and the Social History of Lesbianisms', p. 11 n. 17.
[70] See Deleuze and Guattari, *Anti-Oedipus*, pp. 28–29; I draw also on Ahmed, *Queer Phenomenology*, p. 56.
[71] Haraway, 'A Cyborg Manifesto', pp. 149–81.

crucifixion, and the romance narrative itself. As *Undo Your Door* explores the functions of objects that are mechanical, inanimate or gruesomely suspended between the two, to represent or express sexual desire, it implicitly constructs a framework in which sexuality that relies upon the manipulation of an inanimate object is linked, by analogy, to somatic, visual, textual, architectural modes of desiring, whose most sacred form is that of the annunciation. That which initially appears bizarre, gruesome and entirely transgressive is given a surrounding frame of context that allows us to see it as part of a wider set of concerns about desire and perception, and the mechanics of representation.

CONCLUSION: THE ENDS OF DESIRE

This book seeks to contextualise the hermeneutic construction of women's bodies as dangerous and unstable conduits to the expression of deviant desire. I argue that Chaucer's *Legend* and the Middle English romances explore the possibility of a feminine hermeneutic that considers how differently language might work if we contemplated the possibility of women speaking their desires. In the *Legend*, this feminine hermeneutic is a nightmarish possibility, in which woman's expressions of desire function as monstrous prostheses, failing to articulate or signify, and simultaneously rendering the bodies they supplement grotesque and deviant. By contrast, the feminine hermeneutic of the romances functions as a technological prosthesis, equipping female characters with new, innovative mechanisms through which they may express and structure their desires. These two representations of feminine hermeneutics are not purely and simply polar opposites, the one negative and pejorative, the other positive and affirming. The *Legend*, even as it constructs female desires as irrevocably deviant in their articulation, also necessarily constructs a space in which those desires *are* articulated. It affords them visibility and substance, however circumscribed by censure. The romances, meanwhile, rely upon a surrogacy of embodied desire, constantly using male bodies to ventriloquise female emotions, and thus they insinuate that female emotion is only truly visible, truly palpable, when articulated by and through men. The tensions within these differing attempts to construct a feminine hermeneutic shed light on interpretative practices in a wide sense. In this conclusion, I use the *Legend* and the romances read both backwards and forwards across hermeneutic traditions. I re-situate the Latin hermeneutics of Jerome and the work of Jean de Meun in relation to an English fourteenth- and fifteenth-century intervention that makes visible the female desires so often left out of consideration. I also seek to reinterpret our own practices as medievalists working on medieval texts, and on medieval women, their embodied desires and emotions.

THE FAILED ENDS OF THE *LEGEND*'S WOMEN

My reading of Chaucer's *Legend* locates that text within a complex hermeneutic tradition stretching from Jerome's patristic Latin to Jean de Meun's influential vernacular poetics. There the feminine is coded as a blank space, a tablet to be inscribed or a body to be impregnated. This works to displace or occlude female desires and emotions, to render them rhetorically null. She who has no agency has no desires worth considering. Chaucer's response is not to deny female desire, but to represent it, and in representing it, to make it monstrous. The *Legend* exposes the latent anxieties of the hermeneutic tradition, but simultaneously uses those anxieties to shore up its own masculine *auctoritas*. As I argued in my introduction, Chaucer justifies the construction of a feminine hermeneutic and a feminine rhetoric with an inverted trope borrowed from Jerome via Guillaume de Lorris. He transforms the image of the text as a desirably feminine body veiled in rhetoric and transforms it into a shockingly exposed naked man. By placing a naked male body where Jerome leads us to expect desirably penetrable femininity, Chaucer exposes the sexual violence of the analogy between naked text and penetrable body, and the anxiety that is latent in that violence. The trope extends the 'ordinary' hermeneutic fear of masculine sexual deviancy (which we see repeatedly, notably in Alan of Lille's *De planctu Naturae*) with the possibility of further inversions. A female subject, no longer violently subjugated, might respond to the invitation to penetrate the naked body of the text. The means of her penetration must be prosthetic, since within this logic of gendered embodiment she is not naturally (genitally) equipped. Consequently, a feminine hermeneutic codes its female agents as sexually and somatically deviant in their prosthetic activity.

The main portion of the *Legend* confirms and extends this initial proposition. When equipped with an extension of a lingual or phallic variety, women's bodies variously become over-equipped, lesbian-like, surgically reduced, mutilated or erased. We see Chaucer's heroines repeatedly seeking language as a prosthetic and finding themselves prosthetically equipped in a manner that codes them as sexually deviant. Philomela's tongueless mouth is grotesquely replaced by the phallic loom and the coarse tapestry it produces; her eerily unbleeding body implicates her in discourses of unnatural feminine embodiment. Dido uses Aeneas' sword to perform the 'sterile transgression' of a murder that would destroy her unborn foetus. Medea and Hipsiphyle are identified with castrated male birds, 'capoun[s]', constructed as masculine bodies *manqué*, surgically reduced to satisfy a carnal appetite. Lucrece is raped and stabs herself; Phyllis drowns herself; Thisbe kills herself. Her blood-dabbled 'compleynte' sees her bending over a feminised body, inseminating its gaping wound with her tears. Ariadne becomes the raw material from which the stellified image of Taurus is constructed, memorialising a violent rape and erasing her human body from the narrative. Hypermnestra's truncated narrative is suffused with images of extreme fears of bleeding, of sexual activity and of violence which so overwhelm the title character that they cause her to 'dissociat[e]' her knife-wielding hands from her virginal body.[1] Trauma –

---

[1] She says 'I am a mayde … Myne handes ben nat shapen for a knyf' (lines 2690–92). It

physical, emotional, psychic and epistemic injury that leaves a wound, a gap – is represented as an inevitable accompaniment to the expression of female emotion; the prostheses that seek to cover these gaps fail.

These failures of prosthesis might be understood, like the inversion of the 'naked erthe', in relation to the established hermeneutic tradition. To Alan of Lille, metaplasm is the fault men commit when they fall into sexual and grammatical deviancy: the meaningless distortion of the form of a word or the orientation of a body, carried out for the sake of metrical ornament. The term appears in that classic medieval school text, Donatus' Latin grammar, where one of its varieties is the trope of prosthesis: the change to the form of a word in which syllables are added to the beginning of a word without changing its meaning (for example, 'arise' for 'rise').[2] The *Legend* is prosthetic in this sense, a series of narratives that differ at the beginning but which all end in the same sterile *occupatio*, the same absence of a meaningful conclusion, and which all express the same 'meaning': the perfidies of men and the sufferings of women. Mimetically, the poem reflects the feminine body's sexual and somatic lack of 'ends' and 'poynts', which leave their bodies perpetually inconclusive and unclosed. The attempt to construct a feminine hermeneutic only exposes the prosthetic workings of that hermeneutic, which always draws attention to its own lack, and which invariably becomes deviant as it seeks (and fails) to signify. The teleological evasions of the narrative are thus the natural result of representing female desires that refuse to 'end' where they should. Chaucer pointedly shears away the impassioned speeches, eloquent laments and fiery denigrations that Ovid gives to his heroines in the *Heroides*. After eight tattered fragments of Classical tales, punctuated with self-important declarations of narratorial *occupatio*, the *Legend* ends – or does it? – almost but not quite at the close of the final legend of Hypermnestra. 'This tale is seyd for this conclusioun – ' (line 2723) declares the narrator, tantalisingly leaving us hanging.

The *Legend* attributes this failure of ending to the endless play of tropes and figures, through which feminine rhetoric attempts to construct its prostheses. Thus the tales of Philomela and Lucrece hinge upon the violence inherent in metonymic substitution of part for whole. The female body is conflated with the architectural edifice around it, and the pen, tongue, penis and loom substitute metonymically for each other. When Philomela cannot speak literally of her rape, she is forced to make recourse to a substitute, a textile euphemism as it were. Her prosthetic language works to propel her

---

is Dinshaw who argues that this expression of perceived bodily incongruity expresses Hypermnestra's 'dissociation from her own body'. Dinshaw, *Chaucer's Sexual Poetics*, p. 76.

2   See James Jerome Murphy, *Rhetoric in the Middle Ages: A History of Rhetorical Theory from Saint Augustine to the Renaissance* (Berkeley, CA, Los Angeles, CA and London: University of California Press, 1974), p. 34.

into a pejorative imagery of deviant female desire, rather than enabling her to speak literally of her mutilation. In the *relicta* narratives of Dido, Hipsiphyle and Medea, the governing rhetorical (and geographic) trope is *translatio*. In displacing masculinity as a *telos* for female desire, these legends reciprocally disrupt the referential operations of metaphor, producing the chaos of language in which a feminised Jason collides endlessly with feminine *formae*. The circular narrative with its lack of phallic point cruelly resembles the pejorative 'caponisation' of Medea, demonstrating the incapacity of her rhetorical prosthesis to grant her masculine agency. Finally, in the legends of Thisbe and Ariadne, Chaucer returns to the old trope of the veiled feminine text, demonstrating the failure of each woman's attempts to authorise her own embodied desires, and cynically recycling both stories as raw material for later narratives in which female desire is subordinated to masculine sexual violence. Feminine language fails to signify, because its figurative extensions cannot be brought back to a substantive core.

The *Legend* explores these anxieties relating specifically to a feminine hermeneutic and its prosthetic rhetoric, but we can see these same anxieties submerged within the wider hermeneutic tradition, and implicated in its gendered construction. The sexual violence Chaucer exposes in Jerome's analogy of the text and the body bears witness to a fear of what an unsubjugated female body might do; it visits pain upon the female body to deny that body the possibility of pleasure. The prosthetic construction of feminine rhetoric in the *Legend* might be understood as an indication of the possible nature of this denied pleasure: an unsubjugated female body might satisfy itself with prostheses, rendering a male body unnecessary, or even penetrably passive, like the 'naked erthe' of the *Legend* prologue. This latent fear of female rhetoric as a self-satisfying pleasure may be detected elsewhere in medieval hermeneutic writings. The grammarian Walter of Wimborne refers to rhetoric as the *lingue machina*, the 'machine of the tongue' that flatters but does not signify, as opposed to the machine of prayer that speaks through the spirit.[3] Echoing an aspect of his terminology, Fradenburg argues that postlapsarian language, as an extension of knowledge or perception into the world outside the speaker, always threatens to escape its boundaries and elude control. In this propensity to become separated from its origin in a human body experiencing human emotion, rhetoric is 'a contraption of language that operates with no reference to the truth as perceived by a feeling individual'. Both the medieval 'machina' and modern 'contraption' bear witness to the underlying imbrication of these anxieties concerning language with anxieties concerning

---

[3] Jenifer Sutherland, 'Repuerascere: Christianizing Classical Rhetoric through Play in Walter of Wimborne's *De Palpone*', *Exemplaria* 17.2 (2005): 381–412 (p. 391). She acknowledges her debt to Fradenburg, *Sacrifice Your Love*, pp. 12–20, and to Elaine Scarry, *The Body in Pain: The Making and Unmaking of the World* (Oxford: Oxford University Press, 1985), pp. 253–85.

female deviant sexuality and its modes of satisfaction. Thus the feminine hermeneutic of the *Legend* that expresses female desire through deviant prostheses is only the explicit and visible version of this anxiety, the version of this anxiety given full expression.

By representing his feminine hermeneutic, then, Chaucer deploys the image of the deviant woman with her prosthetic *lingue machina* as a warning, a monitory *exemplum* that justifies the return to masculine *auctoritas*. The narratives of the *Legend* end by cutting off women's words and reinstating the narrator's own voice as he imposes his interpretations upon his tales. With cynical insincerity, he repeatedly urges women to recognise the treachery of men (or, in one case, the treachery of all men but himself); he insistently laments their trauma and their mutilation, while cropping their stories. The masculine hermeneutic reinstates itself to mansplain the failures of a feminine hermeneutic. This, too, we may trace back to that first and programmatic inversion of the hermeneutic paradigm, in the prologue. As Chaucer inverts the gender of the 'naked text', he grafts onto Jerome's image another set of connotations. A textual body that is impenetrably masculine may be understood as a Latin body, the body of the Latin textual tradition, as read by women. The idea is grounded in the commonplace association of Latin with masculinity, as opposed to the English 'mother tongue'. The 'naked erthe' is then an ambivalent trope, seeming to sanction (or even necessitate) a feminine hermeneutic, while also providing the means of its frustration. Across the legends, Chaucer deploys Latinity as a form of gender-policing, using Latinate puns to expose his female protagonists' lack of comprehension and inability to transcend their female bodies. At the end of each legend is an anxious authorial gesture of control, a clutching grasp that seeks to pull the whole unwieldy and expressive textual matter back into the safe control of the Latinate voice and the paternal tradition of *auctoritas* circumscribing feminine material. The poem represents itself as a body in need of prosthetic supplementation to supply its missing endings. As its female protagonists fail to construct their own linguistic prostheses, the poem draws attention to the lack that permeates it. It repeatedly directs readers to seek and adduce sources and analogues, adding a silent *coda* of further reading. As Chaucer's narrator constantly points beyond the limits of his text to other sources, he signposts other versions, other details. Seek out Ovid; read Guido of Colonne. Find the details in the *Heroides*; look to Virgil. The *Legend* is thus akin to the body of Eve: constantly making reference to the masculine bodies out of which it is taken (Ovid, Virgil, Guido). The *Legend* is thus also the misogynistic fantasy of the lesbian body: a textual corpus that constantly seeks to extend itself prosthetically, yet in so doing, calls attention to its lack, to the men whose contents it refuses to take in.

DESIROUS TECHNOLOGIES IN ROMANCE

At first glance, the romances appear to enact the same literal and epistemic violence upon their characters that we find in the *Legend*, and to implicate those characters in fragmented and mutilated narrative structures that are, likewise, cruelly mimetic of broken bodies. The *Morte* is filled with images of violently penetrated and consumed female bodies. Women are split open, like the spitted meat the giant consumes; they are imprisoned, and are always threatened by rape as a consequence of bloody warfare. These women, from the duchess to the giant's textile-worker slaves to the foster mother, are nameless and almost voiceless, spoken for only in that single lament by the foster mother, which is so paradoxically filled with horrific detail and with unsettling *lacunae*. Jarringly strange penile puns grotesquely parody the feminine-voiced *lacunae* of the text, and the poem as a whole constructs a Philomela narrative splintered into three sets of female bodies suffering, speaking and weaving. The possibility of physical, sexual and poetic violence also permeates the *Sowdone of Babylon*, as its female protagonist resists her would-be rapist and evades the patriarchal demands of her father and the fiancé approved by that father. The *Sowdone of Babylon* mobilises a rapacious imagery of trespass and a corresponding stony resistance to ingress in such a way as to enact the metaphorical sterilisation of Floripas, bringing to the fore a strand of anxiety concerning gestational bodies and relics that reduces the narrative of triumphant *translatio* to one of uneasy conquest. Finally, *Undo Your Door* fractures the image of the annunciation into a mechanism for deploying desirous agency. The romance offers up a mutilated, disembowelled and reconstituted corpse to the touches and kisses that wear its substance to powder, and in the absence of this bizarre object of erotic gratification, the narrative crumbles into a weirdly self-consuming romance patchworked together from fragments of earlier texts. In all three romances, and as in the *Legend*, disintegrative violence on both corporeal and textual levels is imbricated with innuendos of sexual deviancy, with hints of same-sex desires and misplaced erotic charges that threaten to break down the distinctions between animate and inanimate, licit and illicit bodies and touches.

However, there is an obvious and crucial difference between the *Legend* and the romances. The *Legend* translates into English the idea of a masculinised textual body that disrupts the hermeneutic paradigm wherein presumptively male interpreters are invited to analogise reading and writing with eroticised acts of sexual violence. This idea foreshadows the equally subversive rewriting of the Arthurian knights in the *Morte*, the Sultan in the *Sowdone of Babylon* and the squire and steward in *Undo Your Door*. In those texts, too, male bodies are repackaged as targets of violent desire. Yet whereas Chaucer deploys the spectre of the naked male body as a shock tactic that bursts in on the sterile and stale poetics of the dream vision with an unwelcome form of indecent exposure, the romances dwell on its possibilities. They treat male bodies, rather than female bodies, as the canvases on which to explore emotional questions. Male bodies, not female ones, are the blank surfaces ever ready for penetration, dissection and reassembly, in both the *Morte* and, most grotesquely, in *Undo Your Door*. In the *Sowdone*, it is the textual body of Chaucer that is objectified, while the Sultan – the eponymous anti-hero – is briefly but vividly feminised. In the romances, it is the literary canon that becomes fragmented, quoted or cited piecemeal, like the nightingale that figures Philomela in the *Morte* or the sections of Chaucer that appear, cut up and repurposed for consumption, in the *Sowdone* and in *Undo Your Door*. Masculine bodily integrity is exposed as faulty when men's bodies are put in the positions (of sexual victim, of mother, of sexualised beloved) habitually associated with women. The men of the *Morte* are penetrated and mutilated. The knights of the *Sowdone* are revealed as lacking the fluidity that would nurture their adopted children. The squire of *Undo Your Door* is rhetorically dismembered via blazon, and his alter ego the steward literally eviscerated, embalmed and pulverised. *Undo Your Door* transfers its erotic anxieties onto its male characters, involving the king of Hungary and the squire in a more overt homoerotic relationship that deflects attention from the princess's own lesbian-like desires, while enabling their (temporary) fulfilment. As with the penile puns of the alliterative *Morte*, the romance uses the image of male same-sex activity in order to demarcate a space of transgressive sexuality in which women's experiences and emotions are visible.

As Lochrie points out, much medieval literature finds enjoyment, rather than a source of anxiously self-flagellating shame, in confessional discourses, including those concerning seemingly hidden or taboo sexualities.[4] The romances bear witness to this. The *Morte* translates a horrific and unspeakable trauma into an inescapably comedic series of penile puns. Gleefully constructing bathetic images of overblown grief, the text produces a personified penis so appealing that he appears not only in the original poem (as Sir Ienitall) but also in Malory, as the rubricated knight *Genytrottys*. The *Sowdone of Babylon* audaciously fragments the seminal imagery of the *General Prologue* in such a way as to equip its masculine antagonist and patriarch in the unexpected garb of a youthful romance heroine. In *Undo Your Door*, jaunty rhymed couplets emphasise the sensationalist speed with which the princess, apparently still 'naked as she was bore' (line 673), whips out her embalming tools and sets to work, creating an unavoidably tantalising picture. The sheer audacity with which the author marries the clichés of courtly romance with annunciatory innuendos is as delightful as it is eyebrow-raising. These taboo images, these puns and innuendos, admit a Foucauldian pleasure in the disclosure of what is hidden or unspeakable. The difference between the *Legend* and the romances

---

[4] Lochrie's target is Foucault, whose views on shame and sexual secrecy in the Middle Ages she interrogates. See *Covert Operations*, p. 14.

may be related to their differing constructions of *auctoritas*. The romances do not constantly attempt to construct *auctoritas* (indeed, all three are pointedly anonymous), and they therefore exhibit none of the anxieties of ownership that we find in the established hermeneutic tradition, those anxieties that are so threatened by the possibility of a feminine prosthetic intruding upon the hermeneutic process. In romance prostheses are marvellous technologies, extensions whose power to extend agency is fascinating and amazing, rather than evidence of power slipping out of a narrowly defined human grasp. A sense of wonder at technology suffuses these texts. As Katherine Little and Nicola McDonald remark, 'romance … [is] one of medieval culture's most important staging grounds for especially cutting-edge technological innovation'; it is, McDonald continues, a site of 'wonder'.[5] The romances work hard to conflate feminine desire with the technological, the artificial and the prosthetic, and in this they offer a valuable corrective to our contemporary tendency to associate the feminine with the natural, the bodily and the organic (and the masculine with the technological). The kinds of pleasure that arise from making sense of these innuendos and subtexts, *lacunae* and omissions, are pleasures that belong to a lesbian erotic.

Romance imagines supplemented female bodies, not as monsters (the lesbians, 'capouns' and tongueless women of the *Legend*), but as new possibilities for somatic expression of desire. Images of female embodiment and emotion are at once technological and architectural, grotesque and sanctifying, disintegrative and comprehensive. The distinction between natural and artificial, human and not human, is often squeamishly or grotesquely blurred. We encounter body parts that are indistinguishable from metal weapons and bodies that metaphorically cleave to stones, or are separated into multiple component parts speaking in ventriloquised, fractured voices. We find metaphors for female genitalia that range from the masculine anus to the opening mechanism of a casement window, and wombs that evoke the architectural space surrounding a foetus and the *porta clausa* of the Virgin, the brackish dungeon and the sacred reliquary. Above all, the romances display a fascination with technologies and innovations, with objects that stand in for human efforts or extend human potential, from siege engines to navigational technology to miraculous girdles to architectural novelties. These objects overlap suggestively with the categories of the prosthetic and the relic/*coille*, those prominent symbols of deviant desire from the hermeneutic tradition. Like the 'desiring machines' of Deleuze and Guattari, the prosthetically equipped bodies of romance women are not fragmented by their incompleteness and their unstable incorporation of supplementary material; rather,

[5] Little and McDonald, 'Introduction', p. 3.

these 'interruption[s]' and break[s]' to their bodily and textual corpora are innate, just as the interruption is necessary and functional to the machine.⁶

In this, romance's *modus operandi* recalls what Eileen Joy says about the rhetorical and epistemic ways in which activists might combat dehumanising histories and definitions:

> to take the marker of 'less than human' as an opportunity to finally bid the human adieu and start inventing those 'improbable' virtualities and 'diagonal lines' that Foucault talked about'.⁷

Romance acknowledges the reality of bodily prosthesis. In the *Morte*, horrific ambiguity renders the giant's penis indistinguishable from his sword, and the giant himself straddles the division between human and monster, while the violated woman, or women, fragment amongst their several bodies the individual experience of the archetypal rape survivor Philomela. In the *Sowdone*, Floripas is both woman and fortress, both a carapace and a female body, in a tradition of narratives that liken a fertile female body to the eroticised, gilded hollows of the reliquary. In *Undo Your Door*, the princess's body is conflated with her chamber and her genitalia with its window. These imagined hybrid bodies might be understood in terms of the biological metaphor of metaplasm as Haraway considers it, as relating to changes in cell structures. Haraway claims metaplasm as that which can 'signify a mistake, a stumbling, a troping that makes a fleshly difference', and cites as an example how 'a substitution in a string of bases in a nucleic acid can be a metaplasm, changing the meaning of a gene and altering the course of a life'.⁸ Romance's prostheses might be understood as a kind of creative metaplasm, the metaplasm that constructs fleshly difference, and makes possible new and differently embodied desires.

BEGINNING AGAIN

This book began with the conviction that Chaucer's *Legend* had something to say about hermeneutic practice, about representations of desire and about the deviant desires that remain unspoken in much medieval literature and much modern scholarship. 'Where are the lesbians in Chaucer?' asks Michelle Sauer. They – and the host of women who embody dissident desires and desire nonconforming bodies – are everywhere in the *Legend*. More than that: they are fundamental to the hermeneutic and poetic project Chaucer attempts with the *Legend*, a project that is not so much about women's emotions as it is about

---

6   Deleuze and Guattari, *Anti-Oedipus*, p. 38.
7   Eileen Joy, 'Improbable Manners of Being', *GLQ: A Journal of Lesbian and Gay Studies* 21.2–3 (2015): 221–24 (p. 223).
8   Donna Haraway, *Manifestly Haraway* (Minneapolis, MN and London: University of Minnesota Press, 2016).

the very origins of the gendering of poetic generativity, the very basis of the epistemic structure that denies women a capacity to speak without becoming deviant, monstrous and misunderstood. This project is characteristically cynical and self-servingly ambivalent, misogynistic in its insincere promise to work on behalf of women while simultaneously exploiting that posture in order to shore up Chaucerian *auctoritas*. But it does make visible the desires and the embodiments of women who otherwise slip out of visibility, in both medieval and post-medieval contexts. The romances I discuss expand and extend this representational possibility with vigour and innovative imagination. They seek to make visible a host of graphic, extreme, grotesque and audacious and shocking female emotions, from the deep horror of trauma, to the profound desire to withstand erotic touch, to the irrepressible yearning for sexual agency and feminine-authored modes of sexual satisfaction. Both the *Legend* and the romances have long been criticised for their unsatisfying discontinuities and jarring imperfections, their *lacunae* and poetic stumblings. Yet we might associate all these texts with a medieval 'lesbian erotic' organised around *lacunae*, the gaps and seams and interstices.[9] The discontinuities of these narratives – defects and mistakes; innuendos and jarring euphemisms – are only 'faults' if we accept that the purpose of a text is to rise towards a conclusion, to organise itself into completeness and to shut out co-participants who might respond to its gaps and silences.

---

[9] See Farina, 'Lesbian History and Erotic Reading'; Kłosowska, *Queer Love in the Middle Ages*, pp. 69–116.

BIBLIOGRAPHY

MANUSCRIPTS AND PRINTS

Cambridge, Trinity College, MS. R. 3. 19.
Cambridge, University Library, MS Ff. 1. 6.
London, British Library, C. 21.c. 58 (STC 23112).
London, British Library, MS Additional 12524.
London, British Library, MS Additional 27879.
London, British Library, MS Additional 37492.
London, British Library, MS Additional 43391.
London, British Library, MS Additional 59678.
London, British Library, MS Egerton 1821.
London, British Library, MS Egerton 3028.
London, British Library, MS Royal 20 C VII.
Lincoln, Cathedral Library, MS 91.
Oxford, Bodleian Library, MS Ashmole 33.
Oxford, Bodleian Library, MS Rawlinson C. 86.
Paris, Bibliothèque nationale de France, MS Fr. 25526.
Princeton, University Library, MS Garrett 140.
San Marino, CA, Huntington Library, Rare Books 62181 (STC 23111.5).

PRIMARY TEXTS

Alan of Lille, *De planctu Naturae*, ed. Nikolaus M. Häring (Spoleto: Fondazione CISAM, 1978).
The Plaint of Nature, trans. James J. Sheridan (Toronto: Pontifical Institute of Mediaeval Studies, 1980).
Arnold, I. D. O., and M. M. Pelan, *La Partie arthurienne du Roman de Brut* (Paris: Klincksiek, 1962).
Augustine, *Confessions*, ed. and trans. Carolyn J. B. Hammond, 2 vols (Cambridge, MA: Harvard University Press, 2014–15).
Ayto, John, and Alexandra Barratt, eds, *Aelred of Rievaulx's De institutione inclusarum: Two English Versions*, EETS o.s. 2 (London: Oxford University Press, 1984).
Benson, Larry D., ed, rev. by Edward E. Forster, *The Alliterative Morte Arthure*, in *King Arthur's Death: The Middle English Stanzaic Morte Arthur and*

Bibliography

Alliterative Morte Arthure (Kalamazoo, MI: Medieval Institute Publications, 1994).
Bracton, Henry, *Bracton de legibus et consuetudinibus Angliae: Bracton on the Laws and Customs of England*, ed. George E. Woodbine, trans. Samuel E. Thorne, 4 vols (Cambridge, MA: The Belknap Press of Harvard University, 1968–77).
Brandin, Louis, ed., '*La Destruction de Rome* et *Fierabras*, MS Egerton 3028 de Musée Britannique', *Romania* 64 (1938): 18–100.
Brook, G. L., ed, *The Harley Lyrics: The Middle English Lyrics of MS Harley 2253* (Manchester: Manchester University Press, 1948).
Caxton, William, *The Booke of Ovyde Named Methamorphose*, ed. Richard J. Moll (Toronto and Oxford: Pontifical Institute of Mediaeval Studies/Bodleian Library, 2013).
Chaucer, Geoffrey, *The Riverside Chaucer*, gen. ed. Larry D. Benson, 3rd edn (Oxford: Oxford University Press, 2008).
Chrétien de Troyes, *Cligès*, in *The Romances of Chrétien de Troyes*, ed Joseph J. Duggan (New Haven, CT and London: Yale University Press, 2001.
Cowen, Janet, and George Kane, eds, *Geoffrey Chaucer: The Legend of Good Women* (East Lansing, MI: Colleagues Press, 1995).
de Boer, Cornelius, ed., *Ovide Moralisé: Poème du commencement du quatorzième siècle*, 4 vols (Amsterdam: Johannes Müller, 1915–38).
Dorne, John, 'The Day-book of John Dorne, Bookseller in Oxford, AD 1520', ed. Falconer Madan, *Collectanea* 1 (1885), 453–78.
Gertrude of Helfta, *Œvres spirituelles, Le Héraut*, ed. P. Doyère et al. (Paris: Editions du Cerf, 1968–78).
Gower, John, *Confessio Amantis*, ed. Russell A. Peck with Latin translations by Andrew Galloway, 3 vols (Kalamazoo, MI: Medieval Institute Publications, 2004).
Guillaume de Lorris and Jean de Meun, *Le Roman de la Rose*, ed. Felix Lécoy, 3 vols (Paris: Fermin-Didot, Champion, 1914–24).
The Romance of the Rose, trans. Charles Dahlberg, 3rd edn (Princeton, NJ: Princeton University Press, 1995).
Hasenfratz, Robert, ed., *Ancrene Wisse* (Kalamazoo, MI: Medieval Institute Publications, 2000).
Hudson, Anne, ed. *Selections from English Wycliffite Writings* (Toronto: University of Toronto Press, 1997).
Isidore of Seville, *The Etymologies of Isidore of Seville*, eds Stephen A. Barney, W. J. Lewis, J. A. Beach and Oliver Berghof (Cambridge: Cambridge University Press, 2006).
Jerome, *Jerome: Letters and Select Works*, trans W.H. Fremantle, in *A Select Library of Nicene and Post-Nicene Fathers of the Christian Church*, ed. Philip Schaff and rev. Henry Wace, 2nd series, vol. 6 (New York: Christian Literature Company, 1893).

Bibliography

Kooper, Erik, ed., *Sentimental and Humorous Romances* (Kalamazoo, MI: Medieval Institute Publications, 2005).

Kroeber, A., and G. Servois, eds, *Chanson de Fierabras* (Paris: Vieweg, 1860).

Lupack, Alan, ed., *Three Middle English Charlemagne Romances* (Kalamazoo, MI: Medieval Institute Publications, 1990).

Millett, Bella, ed., *Hali Meidhad*, EETS o.s. 284 (London: Oxford University Press, 1982).

Ovid, *Heroides, Amores*, trans. Grant Showerman, rev. G. P. Goold (Cambridge, MA: Harvard University Press, 1914).

Ovid, *Metamorphoses Books I–VIII*, trans. Frank Justus Miller (London: William Heineman, 1916).

Ovid: The Art of Love and Other Poems, ed. G. P. Goold and trans. H. J. Mozley, 2nd edn (Cambridge, MA: Harvard University Press, 1985).

Mead, William Edward, ed., *The Squyr of Lowe Degre: Edited in all the Extant Forms with Introduction, Notes and Glossary* (Boston, MA: Ginn, 1904).

Morey, James H., ed., *Prik of Conscience* (Kalamazoo, MI: Medieval Insitute Publications, 2012).

Nashe, Thomas, *The Works of Thomas Nashe*, ed. Ronald B. McKerrow, 3 vols (Oxford: Basil Blackwell, 1904–5).

Ryan, William Granger, trans., *The Golden Legend: Readings on the Saints* (Princeton, NJ and Oxford: Princeton University Press, 1993).

Saupe, Karen, ed., *Middle English Marian Lyrics* (Kalamazoo, MI: Medieval Institute Publications, 1997).

Spalding, Mary Caroline, ed., *The Middle English Charters of Christ* (Bryn Mawr, PA: Bryn Mawr College, 1914).

Stanbury, Sarah, ed., *Pearl* (Kalamazoo, MI: Medieval Institute Publications, 2001).

Statius, *Thebaid, Books 1–7*, ed. and trans. D. R. Shackleton Bailey, 2 vols (Cambridge, MA: Harvard University Press, 2003).

Sugano, Douglas, ed., *The N-Town Plays* (Kalamazoo, MI: Medieval Institute Publications, 2007).

Thomas of Chobham, *Summa confessorum*, ed. F. Broomfield (Louvain: Nauwelaerts, 1968).

Trevisa, John, *On the Properties of Things: John Trevisa's Translation of Bartholomaeus Anglicus De proprietatibus rerum*, ed. M. C. Seymour, 3 vols (Oxford: Clarendon Press, 1975–88).

Virgil, *Eclogues, Georgics, Aeneid, Minor Poems*, trans. H. Rushton Fairclough, rev. by G. P. Goold, 2 vols (Cambridge, MA: Harvard University Press, 1999).

Yunck, John A., ed. and trans., *Eneas: A Twelfth-Century French Romance* (New York: Columbia University Press, 1974).

Bibliography

SECONDARY TEXTS

Abulafia, David, 'Seven Types of Ambiguity, c. 1100–c. 1500', in *Medieval Frontiers: Concepts and Practices*, eds David Abulafia and Nora Berend (Aldershot: Ashgate, 2002), pp. 1–34.

Adler, Gillian, '"ȝit þat traytour alls tite teris lete he fall": Arthur, Mordred, and Tragedy in the Alliterative *Morte Arthure*', *Arthuriana* 25.3 (2015): 3–21.

Ahmed, Sara, *Queer Phenomenology: Orientations, Objects, Others* (Durham, NC and London: Duke University Press, 2006).

Akbari, Suzanne Conklin, 'From Due East to True North: Orientalism and Orientation', in *The Postcolonial Middle Ages*, ed. Jeffrey Jerome Cohen (New York: Palgrave, 2001), pp. 19–34.

—— 'Woman as Mediator in Medieval Depictions of Muslims: The Case of Floripas', in *Medieval Constructions in Gender and Identity. Essays in Honour of Joan M. Ferrante*, ed. Teodolinda Barolini (Tempe, AZ: Arizona Centre for Medieval and Renaissance Studies, 2005), pp. 151–67.

—— *Idols in the East: European Representations of Islam and the Orient, 1100–1450* (Ithaca, NY: Cornell University Press, 2009).

Alcoff, Linda, and Laura Grey, 'Survivor Discourse: Transgression or Recuperation?', *Signs* 18.2 (1993): 260–90.

Allen-Goss, Lucy, 'Queerly Productive: Women and Collaboration in Cambridge, University Library, MS Ff. 1. 6', *Postmedieval* 9.3 (2018): 334–48.

—— 'Transgressive Desire in Chaucer's "Legend of Thisbe"', *Chaucer Review* 53.2 (2018): 194–212.

Armstrong, Dorsey, 'The Alliterative *Morte Arthure* and Arthur's Sword of Peace', *Parergon* 25.1 (2008): 81–101.

Aston, Margaret. *Lollards and Reformers: Images and Literacy in Late Medieval Religion* (London: Hambledon Press, 1984).

Atkinson, Clarissa, '"Precious Balsam in a Fragile Glass": The Ideology of Virginity in the Later Middle Ages', *Journal of Family History* 8 (1983): 131–43.

Baden-Daintree, Anne, 'Kingship and the Intimacy of Grief in the Alliterative *Morte Arthure*', in *Emotions in Medieval Arthurian Literature: Body, Mind, Voice*, eds Frank Brandsma, Carolyne Larrington and Corinne J. Saunders (Cambridge: D. S. Brewer, 2015), pp. 87–104.

Bahr, Arthur, *Fragments and Assemblages: Forming Compilations in Medieval London* (Chicago, IL: University of Chicago Press, 2013).

Baker, Joan, and Susan Signe Morrison, 'The Luxury of Gender: *Piers Plowman* B. 9 and *The Merchant's Tale*', in *William Langland's Piers Plowman: A Book of Essays*, ed. Kathleen M. Hewett-Smith (New York: Routledge, 2001), pp. 41–68.

Barr, Helen, *Transporting Chaucer* (Manchester: Manchester University Press, 2014).

Bartlett, Anne Clark, 'Cracking the Penile Code: Reading Gender and Conquest in the Alliterative "Morte Arthure"', *Arthuriana* 8.2 (1998): 56–76.

Bibliography

Baswell, Christopher, *Virgil in Medieval England: Figuring the Aeneid from the Twelfth Century to Chaucer* (Cambridge: Cambridge University Press, 1995).

Batt, Catherine, *Malory's* Morte D'Arthur: *Remaking Arthurian Tradition* (New York and Basingstoke: Palgrave, 2002).

Battles, Dominique, *The Medieval Tradition of Thebes: History and Narrative in the OF Roman de Thèbes, Boccaccio, Chaucer and Lydgate* (New York and London: Routledge, 2004), pp. 1–18.

Berlant, Lauren, 'Trauma and Ineloquence', *Cultural Values* 5 (2001): 41–58.

Benkov, Edith, 'The Erased Lesbian: Sodomy and the Legal Tradition in Medieval Europe', in *Same Sex Love and Desire among Women*, eds Sautman and Sheingorn, pp. 101–22.

Bennett, Judith M., and Amy M. Froide, 'A Singular Past', in *Singlewomen in the European Past, 1250–1800*, eds Judith M. Bennett and Amy M. Froide (Philadelphia, PA: University of Pennsylvania Press, 1999).

Bennett, Judith M., 'Remembering Elizabeth Etchingham and Agnes Oxenbridge', in *The Lesbian Premodern*, eds Giffney, Sauer and Watt, pp. 131–43.

Benson, Larry D., 'The Date of the Alliterative *Morte Arthure*', in *Medieval Studies in Honour of Lillian Herlands Hornstein*, eds Jess Bessinger and Robert K. Raymo (New York: New York University Press, 1976), pp. 19–40.

Bildhauer, Bettina, *Medieval Blood* (Cardiff: University of Wales Press, 2006).

Bleeth, Kenneth, 'The Image of Paradise in the Merchant's Tale', in *The Learned and the Lewed: Studies in Chaucer and Medieval Literature*, eds Larry Benson and David Strains (Cambridge, MA: Harvard University Press, 1974), pp. 45–60.

Bloch, Howard R., *The Scandal of the Fabliaux* (Chicago, IL: University of Chicago Press, 1986).

Blud, Victoria *The Unspeakable, Gender and Sexuality in Medieval Literature 1000–1400* (Cambridge: D. S. Brewer, 2017).

Boffey, Julia, '"Twenty Thousand More": Some Fifteenth- and Sixteenth-Century Responses to *The Legend of Good Women*', in *Middle English Poetry: Texts and Traditions*, ed. A. J. Minnis (York: York Medieval Press, 2001), pp. 279–97.

Boitani, Piero, *English Medieval Narrative in the Thirteenth and Fourteenth Centuries* (Cambridge: Cambridge University Press, 1982).

Bowers, John M., 'Thomas Hoccleve and the Politics of Tradition', *Chaucer Review* 36.4 (2002): 352–69.

Brown, Emerson, Jr, 'Hortus Inconclusus: The Significance of Priapus and Pyramus and Thisbe in the "Merchant's Tale"', *Chaucer Review* 4.1 (1969): 31–40.

Brownlee, Kevin, and Sylvia Huot, eds, *Rethinking the Romance of the Rose: Text, Image, Reception* (Philadelphia, PA: University of Pennsylvania Press, 1992).

Bullough, Vern L., 'On Being a Male in the Middle Ages', in *Medieval Masculinities*, ed. Lees, pp. 31–45.

—— with Gwen Whitehead Brewer, 'Medieval Masculinities and Modern Interpretations: The Problem of the Pardoner', in *Conflicted Identities and*

Multiple Masculinities: Men in the Medieval West, ed. Jacqueline Murray (New York and London: Garland, 1999), pp. 93–110.

Burge, Amy, *Representing Difference in the Medieval and Modern Orientalist Romance* (New York: Palgrave Macmillan, 2016).

Burger, Glenn, 'Kissing the Pardoner', *PMLA* 107 (1992): 1143–56.

—— '"Pite renneth soone in gentil herte": Ugly Feelings and Gendered Conduct in Chaucer's *Legend of Good Women*', *Chaucer Review* 52.1 (2017): 66–84.

Burgwinkle, William, *Sodomy, Masculinity and Law in Medieval Literature: France and England, 1050–1230* (Cambridge: Cambridge University Press, 2004).

Burns, E. Jane, *Bodytalk: When Women Speak in Old French Literature* (Philadelphia, PA: University of Pennsylvania Press, 1993).

—— 'Raping Men: What's Motherhood Got to Do With It?' in *Representing Rape* eds Robertson and Rose, pp. 127–60.

—— *Courtly Love Undressed: Reading Through Clothes in Medieval French Culture* (Philadelphia, PA: University of Pennsylvania Press, 2002).

—— *Sea of Silk: A Textile Geography of Women's Work in Medieval French Literature* (Philadelphia, PA: University of Pennsylvania Press, 2009).

Butler, Judith, *Bodies that Matter: On the Discursive Limits of 'Sex'*, 2nd edn (New York: Routledge, 2011).

Butterfield, Ardis, *The Familiar Enemy: Chaucer, Language and Nation in the Hundred Years War* (Oxford: Oxford University Press, 2009).

Bychowski, M. W., Howard Chiang, Jack Halberstam, Jacob Lau, Kathleen P. Long, Marcia Ochoa and C. Riley Snorton, '"Trans Historicities": A Roundtable Discussion', *Transgender Studies Quarterly* 5.4 (2018): 658–85.

Bynum, Caroline Walker, *Holy Feast and Holy Fast: The Religious Significance of Food to Medieval Women* (Berkeley, CA and Los Angeles, CA: University of California Press, 1987).

—— *Fragmentation and Redemption: Essays on Gender and the Human Body in Medieval Religion* (Cambridge, MA and New York: MIT Press and Zone Books, 1992).

—— *Wonderful Blood: Theology and Practice in Late Medieval Northern Germany and Beyond* (Philadelphia, PA: University of Pennsylvania Press, 2006).

Cadden, Joan, *Nothing Natural is Shameful: Sodomy and Science in Late Medieval Europe* (Philadelphia, PA: University of Pennsylvania Press, 2013).

Calkin, Siobhain Bly, *Saracens and the Making of English Identity* (New York: Routledge, 2005).

—— 'Marking Religion on the Body: Saracens, Categorization, and *The King of Tars*', *Journal of English and Germanic Philology* 104 (2005): 219–38.

—— 'Devotional Objects, Saracen Spaces and Miracles in Two Matter of France Romances', in *Medieval Romance and Material Culture*, ed. Nicholas Perkins (Cambridge: D. S. Brewer, 2015), pp. 59–74.

Campbell, Thomas P., *Tapestry in the Renaissance: Art and Magnificence* (New Haven, CT and London: Yale University Press, 2002).

Bibliography

Carruthers, Mary, 'The Wife of Bath and the Painting of Lions', *PMLA* 94.2 (1979): 209–222.

—— *The Book of Memory: A Study of Memory in Medieval Culture*, 2nd edn (Cambridge: Cambridge University Press, 2008).

Caruth, Cathy, *Unclaimed Experience: Trauma, Narrative and History* (Baltimore, MD: Johns Hopkins University Press, 1996).

Chaganti, Seeta, *The Medieval Poetics of the Reliquary: Enshrinement, Inscription, Performance* (New York: Palgrave Macmillan, 2008).

Chin, Catherine M., *Grammar and Christianity in the Late Roman World* (Philadelphia, PA: University of Pennsylvania Press, 2008).

Chism, Christine, 'Friendly Fire: The Disastrous Politics of Friendship in the Alliterative "Morte Arthure"', *Arthuriana* 20.2 (2010): 66–88.

Cixous, Hélène, 'Castration or Decapitation?', trans. Annette Kuhn, *Signs* 7.1 (1981): 41–55.

Clark, Robert L. A., 'Jousting without a Lance: The Condemnation of Female Homoeroticism in the *Livre Des Manières*', in *Same Sex Love and Desire Among Women*, eds Sautman and Sheingorn, pp. 143–77.

Cohen, Jeffrey Jerome, *Of Giants: Sex, Monsters and the Middle Ages* (Minneapolis, MN: University of Minnesota Press, 1999).

—— 'On Saracen Enjoyment: Some Fantasies of Race in Late Medieval England', *Journal of Medieval and Early Modern Studies* 31 (2001): 113–46.

—— *Medieval Identity Machines* (Minneapolis, MN: University of Minnesota Press, 2003).

—— *Hybridity, Identity and Monstrosity in Medieval Britain: On Difficult Middles* (New York: Palgrave, 2007).

—— *Stone: An Ecology of the Inhuman* (Minneapolis, MN and London: University of Minnesota Press, 2015).

Coleman, Joyce, 'The Flower, the Leaf, and Philippa of Lancaster', in *The Legend of Good Women: Context and Reception*, ed. Carolyn P. Collette (Cambridge: Cambridge University Press, 2006), pp. 33–58.

Collette, Carolyn, ed., *Rethinking Chaucer's* Legend of Good Women (York: York Medieval Press, 2014).

—— 'Chaucer's Poetics and Purposes in the *Legend of Good Women*', *Chaucer Review* 52.1 (2017): 12–28.

Cooper, Helen, *Shakespeare and the Medieval World* (London: Bloomsbury, 2010).

Cooper, Lisa H., and Andrea Denny-Brown, eds, *The Arma Christi Tradition in Medieval and Early Modern Material Culture* (Farnham: Ashgate, 2013).

Conway, Martin A., and C. W. Pleydell Pearce, 'The Construction of Autobiographical Memories in the Self Memory System', *Psychological Review* 107 (2000): 261–88.

Copeland, Rita, *Rhetoric, Hermeneutics, and Translation in the Middle Ages* (Cambridge: Cambridge University Press, 1995).

Cormier, Raymond, 'Taming the Warrior: Responding to the Charge of Sexual Deviance in Twelfth-Century Vernacular Romance', in *Literary Aspects of*

Courtly Culture: Selected Papers from the Seventh Triennial Congress of the International Courtly Literature Society, eds Donald Maddox and Sara Sturm-Maddox (Woodbridge: D. S. Brewer, 1994), pp. 153–60.

Cox, Catherine S., *Gender and Language in Chaucer* (Gainesville, FL: University Press of Florida, 1997).

Crofts, Thomas H., 'Perverse and Contrary Deeds: The Giant of Mont Saint Michel and the Alliterative *Morte Arthure*', in *The Erotic in the Literature of Medieval Britain*, eds Andrea Hopkins and Cory Rushton (Cambridge: D. S. Brewer, 2007), pp. 116–31.

Crocker, Holly A., 'Performative Passivity and Fantasies of Masculinity in the Merchant's Tale', *Chaucer Review* 38.2 (2003): 178–98.

Davis, Isabel, *Writing Masculinity in the Later Middle Ages* (Cambridge: Cambridge University Press, 2007).

—— 'Introduction', in *Chaucer and Fame: Reputation and Reception*, eds Isabel Davis and Catherine Nall (Cambridge: D. S. Brewer, 2015), pp. 1–20.

Delany, Sheila, *The Naked Text: Chaucer's Legend of Good Women* (Berkeley, CA, Los Angeles, CA and Oxford: University of California Press, 1994).

—— 'Geographies of Desire: Orientalism in Chaucer's *Legend of Good Women*', in *Chaucer's Cultural Geography*, ed. Kathryn L. Lynch (New York and London: Routledge, 2002), pp. 225–47.

Deleuze, Gilles, and Félix Guattari, *Anti-Oedipus: Capitalism and Schizophrenia*, trans. Robert Hurley, Mark Seem and Helen R. Lane (London and New York: Continuum, 2004).

—— *A Thousand Plateaus: Capitalism and Schizophrenia*, trans. Brian Massumi (Minneapolis, MN: University of Minnesota Press, 1987).

DeMarco, Patricia, 'An Arthur for the Ricardian Age: Crown, Nobility, and the Alliterative Morte Arthure', *Speculum* 80 (2005): 464–93.

Derrida, Jacques, *Of Grammatology*, trans. Gayatri Chakravorty Spivak, 2nd edn (Baltimore, MD: Johns Hopkins University Press, 1998).

Desmond, Marilynn, *Reading Dido: Gender, Textuality and the Medieval Aeneid* (Minneapolis, MN and London: University of Minnesota Press, 1994).

—— 'The Translatio of Memory and Desire in The Legend of Good Women: Chaucer's Vernacular *Heroides*', *Studies in the Age of Chaucer* 35 (2013): 179–207.

—— *Weeping for Dido: The Classics in the Medieval Classroom* (Princeton, NJ: Princeton University Press, 2019).

Diamond, Arlyn, '*Sir Degrevant*: What Lovers Want', in *Pulp Fictions of Medieval England*, ed. Nicola McDonald (Manchester: Manchester University Press, 2004), pp. 82–101.

Dinshaw, Carolyn, 'Eunuch Hermeneutics', *English Literary History* 55.1 (1988): 27–51.

—— *Chaucer's Sexual Poetics* (Madison, WI: University of Wisconsin Press, 1989).

—— 'Rivalry, Rape and Manhood: Gower and Chaucer', in *Chaucer and Gower:*

Difference, Mutuality, Exchange, ed. Robert F. Yeager (Victoria, BC: English Literary Studies, 1991), pp. 130–52.

—— 'A Kiss is Just a Kiss: Heterosexuality and its Consolations in *Sir Gawain and the Green Knight*', *Diacritics* 24 (1994): 205–26.

—— 'Chaucer's Queer Touches/A Queer Touches Chaucer', *Exemplaria* 7.1 (1995): 75–92.

—— *Getting Medieval: Sexualities and Communities, Pre- and Postmodern* (Durham, NC and London: Duke University Press, 1999).

—— *How Soon is Now? Medieval Texts, Amateur Readers, and the Queerness of Time* (Durham, NC: Duke University Press, 2012).

Driver, Martha, 'Illustration in Early English Books: Methods and Problems', *Books at Brown* 33 (1986): 1–49.

—— 'Women Readers and Pierpont Morgan MS M. 126', in *John Gower: Manuscripts, Readers, Contexts*, ed. Malte Urban (Turnhout: Brepols, 2009), pp. 71–107.

Doyle, Kara A., 'Thisbe out of Context: Female Readers and the Findern Manuscript', *Chaucer Review* 40.3 (2006): 231–61.

Dumitrescu, Irina, 'Beautiful Suffering and the Culpable Narrator in Chaucer's *Legend of Good Women*', *Chaucer Review* 52.1 (2017): 106–23.

Edwards, A. S. G., 'From Manuscript to Print: Wynkyn de Worde and the Printing of Contemporary Poetry', *Gutenberg Jahrbuch* (1991): 143–48.

Edwards, Robert R., 'Medieval Statius: Belatedness and Authority', in *Brill's Companion to Statius*, eds W. J. Dominik, C. E. Newlands and K. Gervais (Leiden and Boston: Brill, 2015), pp. 497–511.

Edwards, Suzanne M., *The Afterlives of Rape in Medieval English Literature* (New York: Palgrave Macmillan, 2016).

Evans, Jennifer, *Aphrodisiacs, Fertility and Medicine in Early Modern England* (Woodbridge: Royal Historical Society/Boydell Press, 2014).

Farina, Lara, 'Lesbian History and Erotic Reading', in *The Lesbian Premodern*, eds Giffney, Sauer and Watt, pp. 49–60.

Farmer, Sharon, ed., *Gender and Difference in the Middle Ages* (Minneapolis, MN: University of Minnesota Press, 2003).

Federico, Sylvia, 'Queer Times: Richard II in the Poems and Chronicles of Late Fourteenth-Century England', *Medium Ævum* 79.1 (2010): 25–46.

Fein, Susanna, and David Raybin, 'About This Issue', *Chaucer Review* 52.1 (2017): 1–2.

Fein, Susanna, and Michael Johnston, eds, *Robert Thornton and His Books: Essays on the Lincoln and London Thornton Manuscripts* (York: York Medieval Press, 2014).

Field, P. J. C., '*Morte Arthure*, the Montagus and Milan', *Medium Ævum* 78.1 (2009): 98–117.

Finlayson, John, 'Two Minor Sources for the Alliterative *Morte Arthure*', *Notes & Queries* 9.4 (1962): 132–33.

—— '*Morte Arthure*: The Date and a Source for the Contemporary References', *Speculum* 42.4 (1967): 624–38.

Fissell, Mary E., *Vernacular Bodies: The Politics of Reproduction in Early Modern England* (Oxford: Oxford University Press, 2004).

Flannery, Mary, 'A Bloody Shame: Chaucer's Honourable Women', *Review of English Studies* NS 62.255 (2011): 337–57.

—— 'Gower's Blushing Bird, Philomela's Transforming Face', *Postmedieval* 8.1 (2017): 35–50.

Flemming, Rebecca, *Medicine and the Making of Roman Women: Gender, Nature, and Authority from Celsus to Galen* (Oxford: Oxford University Press, 2000), pp. 228–358.

Fradenburg, L. O. Aranye, *Sacrifice Your Love: Psychoanalysis, Historicism, Chaucer* (Minneapolis, MN: University of Minnesota Press, 2002).

—— 'Beauty and Boredom in the *Legend of Good Women*', *Exemplaria* 22.1 (2013): 65–83.

Frank, Robert Worth, 'The Legend of the *Legend of Good Women*', *Chaucer Review* 1.1 (1966): 110–33.

—— *Chaucer and the 'Legend of Good Women'* (Cambridge, MA: Harvard University Press, 1972).

Freeman, Elizabeth, *Time Binds: Queer Temporalities, Queer Histories* (Durham, NC: Duke University Press, 2010).

Freud, Sigmund, *Beyond the Pleasure Principle*, trans. James Strachey (London and New York: Norton, 1961).

Fricker, Miranda, *Epistemic Injustice: Power and the Ethics of Knowing* (Oxford: Oxford University Press, 2007).

Fries, Maureen, 'The Poem in the Tradition of Arthurian Literature', in *A Reassessment of the Poem*, ed. Göller, pp. 30–43.

Furrow, Melissa, *Expectations of Romance: The Reception of a Genre in Medieval England* (Cambridge: D. S. Brewer, 2009).

Fyler, John M., *Chaucer and Ovid* (New Haven, CT and London: Yale University Press, 1979).

Gaunt, Simon, 'Straight Minds/"Queer" Wishes in Old French Hagiography', in *Premodern Sexualities*, eds Louise Fradenburg and Carla Freccero, with the assistance of Kathy Lavezzo (New York and London: Routledge, 1996).

—— 'From Epic to Romance: Gender and Sexuality in the *Roman d'Eneas*', *Romanic Review* 83.1 (1992): 1–27.

Gertsman, Elina, *Worlds Within: Opening the Medieval Shrine Madonna* (University Park, PA: Pennsylvania State University Press, 2015).

Getty, Laura J., '"Other Smale Ymaad Before": Chaucer as Historiographer in the "Legend of Good Women"', *Chaucer Review* 42.1 (2007): 48–75.

Gibson, Gail McMurray, *The Theatre of Devotion: East Anglian Drama and Society in the Late Middle Ages* (London and Chicago, IL: University of Chicago Press, 1989).

Bibliography

Giffney, Noreen, Michelle M. Sauer and Diane Watt, eds, *The Lesbian Premodern* (New York: Palgrave Macmillan, 2011).

Gilbert, Jane, 'Gender, Oaths and Ambiguity in *Sir Tristrem* and Béroul's *Roman de Tristan*', in *The Spirit of Medieval Popular Romance: A Historical Introduction*, eds Ad Putter and Jane Gilbert (Harlow: Pearson Education, 2000), pp. 237–57.

—— 'Unnatural Mothers and Monstrous Children in *The King of Tars* and *Sir Gowther*', in *Medieval Women: Texts and Contexts in Late Medieval Britain: Essays for Felicity Riddy* (Turnhout: Brepols, 2000), pp. 329–44.

Godden, Richard H., 'Prosthetic Ecologies: Vulnerable Bodies and the Dismodern Subject in *Sir Gawain and the Green Knight*', *Textual Practice* 30.7 (2016): 1273–90.

Goldberg, Jeremy, *Women, Work and Life Cycle in a Medieval Economy: Women in York and Yorkshire, c. 1300–1520* (Oxford: Clarendon Press, 1992).

—— 'John Rykener, Richard II, and the Governance of London', *Leeds Studies in English* NS 45 (2014): 49–70.

Göller, Karl Heinz, 'Reality versus Romance: A Reassessment of the Alliterative *Morte Arthure*', in *A Reassessment of the Poem*, ed. Göller, pp. 15–29.

Göller, Karl Heinz, ed., *The Alliterative Morte Arthure: A Reassessment of the Poem* (Cambridge: D. S. Brewer, 1981).

Gravdal, Kathryn, *Ravishing Maidens: Writing Rape in Medieval French Literature and Law* (Philadelphia, PA: University of Pennsylvania Press, 1991).

Green, David, *The Hundred Years War: A People's History* (New Haven, CT: Yale University Press, 2014).

Griffiths, Jeremy, and Derek Pearsall, eds, *Book Production and Publishing in Britain, 1375–1475* (Cambridge: Cambridge University Press, 2007).

Griffin, Miranda *Transforming Tales: Rewriting Metamorphosis in Medieval French Literature* (Oxford: Oxford University Press, 2015).

Gutmann, Sara, 'Chaucer's Chicks: Feminism and Falconry in the "Knights' Tale", "The Squire's Tale", and *The Parliament of Fowls*', in *Rethinking Chaucerian Beasts*, ed. Carolynn Van Dyke (New York: Palgrave, 2012), pp. 69–83.

Guy-Bray, Stephen, *Loving in Verse: Poetic Influence as Erotic* (Toronto: University of Toronto Press, 2006).

Guynn, Noah D., *Allegory and Sexual Ethics in the High Middle Ages* (New York: Palgrave Macmillan, 2007).

Hagedorn, Suzanne, *Abandoned Women: Rewriting the Classics in Dante, Boccaccio, and Chaucer* (Ann Arbor, MI: University of Michigan Press, 2004).

Halberstam, Jack (Judith), *Female Masculinity* (Durham, NC: Duke University Press, 1998).

—— *In A Queer Time and Place: Transgender Bodies, Subcultural Lives* (New York: New York University Press, 2005).

Hamburger, Jeffrey, *The Visual and the Visionary: Art and Female Spirituality in Late Medieval Germany* (New York: Zone Books, 1998).

Hamel, Mary, ed., *Morte Arthure: A Critical Edition* (New York and London: Garland, 1984).

───── 'Adventure as Structure in the Alliterative "Morte Arthure"', *Arthurian Intentions* 3.1 (1988): 37–48.

Hanna, Ralph, *Pursuing History: Middle English Manuscripts and their Texts* (Stanford, CA: Stanford University Press, 1996).

Hanna, Ralph, and Thorlac Turville-Petre, 'The Text of the Alliterative *Morte Arthure*: A Prolegomenon for a Future Edition', in *Robert Thornton and His Books*, eds Fein and Johnston, pp. 131–56.

Hansen, Elaine Tuttle, 'The Feminization of Men in Chaucer's *Legend of Good Women*', in *Seeking the Woman in Late Medieval and Renaissance Writings: Essays in Feminist Contextual Criticism*, eds Janet Halley and Sheila Fisher (Knoxville, TN: University of Tennessee Press, 1989), pp. 51–70.

───── *Chaucer and the Fictions of Gender* (Berkeley, CA, Los Angeles, CA and Oxford: University of California Press, 1992).

Haraway, Donna, 'A Cyborg Manifesto: Science, Technology, and Socialist-Feminism in the Late Twentieth Century', in *Simians, Cyborgs and Women: The Reinvention of Nature* (New York: Routledge, 1991), pp. 149–81.

───── *Manifestly Haraway* (Minneapolis, MN and London: University of Minnesota Press, 2016).

Hardman, Philippa, and Marianne Ailes, *The Legend of Charlemagne in Medieval England: The Matter of France in Middle English and Anglo-Norman Literature* (Cambridge: D. S. Brewer, 2017).

Harlan-Haughy, Sarah, 'The Circle, the Maze and the Echo: Sublunary Recurrence and Performance in Chaucer's *Legend of Ariadne*', *Chaucer Review* 52.3 (2017): 341–60.

Harris, Anne, 'Glazing and Glossing: Stained Glass as Literary Interpretation', *Journal of Glass Studies* 56 (2014): 303–16.

Harris, Carissa M., '"A drunken cunt hath no porter": Medieval Histories of Intoxication and Consent', *Medieval Feminist Forum: A Journal of Gender and Sexuality* 54.2 (2019): 109–34.

───── '"For Rage": Rape Survival, Women's Anger, and Sisterhood in Chaucer's *Legend of Philomela*', *Chaucer Review* 54.3 (2019): 253–69.

Hartman, Geoffrey, 'The Voice of the Shuttle: Language from the Point of View of Literature', *Review of Metaphysics* 23 (1969): 240–58.

Healy, Margaret, 'Wearing Powerful Words and Objects: Healing Prosthetics', *Textual Practice* 30.7 (2016): 1233–51.

Heffernan, Carol F., *The Orient in Chaucer and Romance* (Cambridge: D. S. Brewer, 2003).

Heng, Geraldine, *The Invention of Race in the European Middle Ages* (Cambridge: Cambridge University Press, 2018).

───── *Empire of Magic: Medieval Romance and the Politics of Cultural Fantasy* (New York: Columbia University Press, 2003).

Henry, Nicola, *War and Rape: Law, Memory and Justice* (London and New York: Routledge, 2011).

Hexter, Ralph, *Ovid and Medieval Schooling: Studies in the Medieval School*

Commentaries on Ovid's Ars Amatoria, Epistulae Ex Ponto, *and* Epistulae Heroidum (Munich: Arbeo-Gesellschaft, 1986).

Hibbard (Loomis), Laura A., *Mediæval Romance in England: A Study of the Sources and Analogues of the Non-cyclic Metrical Romances* (New York: Oxford University Press, 1924; rev. 1963).

Hodnett, Edward, *English Woodcuts, 1480–1535*, 2nd edn (Oxford: Oxford University Press, 1973).

Hohl, Katrin, and Martin A. Conway, 'Memory as Evidence: How Normal Features of Victim Memory Lead to the Attrition of Rape Complaints', *Criminology and Criminal Justice* 17.3 (2016): 248–65.

Holton, Amanda, *The Sources of Chaucer's Poetics* (Aldershot: Ashgate, 2008).

Horne, Peter, and Reina Lewis, 'Introduction, Reframed – Inscribing Lesbian, Gay and Queer Presences in Visual Culture', in *Outlooks: Lesbian and Gay Sexualities and Visual Culture*, eds Peter Horne and Reina Lewis (London: Routledge, 1996).

Hume, Cathy, *Chaucer and the Cultures of Love and Marriage* (Cambridge: D. S. Brewer, 2012).

Huot, Sylvia, *The Romance of the Rose and its Medieval Readers: Interpretation, Reception, Manuscript Transmission* (Cambridge: Cambridge University Press, 1993), pp. 273–322.

Hsy, Jonathan, *Trading Tongues: Merchants, Multilingualism, and Medieval Literature* (Columbus, OH: Columbus University Press, 2013).

Inal, Tuba, *Looting and Rape in Wartime: Law and Change in International Relations* (Philadelphia, PA: University of Pennsylvania Press, 2013).

Ingham, Patricia Clare, *The Medieval New: Ambivalence in the Age of Innovation* (Philadelphia, PA: University of Pennsylvania Press, 2015).

Ireland, Richard, 'Lucrece, Philomela (and Cecily): Chaucer and the Law of Rape', in *Crime and Punishment in the Middle Ages*, ed. T. S. Haskett (Victoria, BC: University of Victoria, 1998), pp. 37–61.

Jacobs, Lynn F., *Opening Doors: The Early Netherlandish Triptych Reinterpreted* (University Park, PA: University of Pennsylvania Press, 2012).

Jantzen, Grace, *Becoming Divine: Towards a Feminist Philosophy of Religion* (Bloomington, IN: University of Indiana Press, 1999).

Jones, E. A., 'Ceremonies of Enclosure: Rite, Rhetoric and Reality', in *Rhetoric of the Anchorhold: Space, Place and Body within the Discourses of Enclosure*, ed. Liz Herbert McAvoy (Cardiff: University of Wales Press, 2008), pp. 34–49.

Jones, Nancy A., 'The Daughter's Text and the Thread of Lineage in the Old French Philomena', in *Representing Rape*, eds Robertson and Rose, pp. 161–88.

Joplin, Patricia Klindienst, 'The Voice of the Shuttle is Ours', in *Rape and Representation*, eds Lynn A. Higgins and Brenda R. Silver (New York: Columbia University Press, 1991, pp. 35–64.

Jordan, Mark D., *The Invention of Sodomy in Christian Theology* (Chicago, IL: University of Chicago Press, 1997).

Joy, Eileen, 'Improbable Manners of Being', *GLQ: A Journal of Lesbian and Gay Studies* 21.2–3 (2015): 221–24.

Judkins, Ryan, 'The Game of the Courtly Hunt: Chasing and Breaking Deer in Late Medieval English Literature', *Journal of English and Germanic Philology* 112.1 (2013): 70–92.

Karras, Ruth Mazo, *Common Women: Prostitution and Sexuality in Medieval England* (New York: Oxford University Press, 1996).

—— *From Boys to Men: Formations of Masculinity in Late Medieval Europe* (Philadelphia, PA: University of Pennsylvania Press, 2002).

—— *Sexuality in Medieval Europe: Doing Unto Others*, 2nd edn (New York: Routledge, 2005).

Keiser, George R., 'Edward III and the Alliterative Morte Arthure', *Speculum* 48 (1973): 37–51.

Keller, Hans-Erich, 'La Belle Sarrasin dans *Fierabras* et ses dérivés', in *Charlemagne in the North: Proceedings of the Twelfth International Conference of the Société Rencesvals, Edinburgh 4th to 11th August 1991*, eds Philip E. Bennett, Anne Elizabeth Cobby and Graham A. Runnalls (London: Grant and Cutler, 1993), pp. 299–307.

Kennedy, Edward D., 'Malory and his English Sources', in *Aspects of Malory*, eds Toshiyuki Takamiya and Derek Brewer (Cambridge: D. S. Brewer, 1981), pp. 27–56.

King, Helen, 'The Mathematics of Sex: One to Two, or Two to One?', in *Sexuality and Culture in Medieval and Renaissance Europe*, eds Philip M. Soergel and Andrew Barnes (New York: AMS Press, 2005), pp. 47–58.

Kinoshita, Sharon, *Medieval Boundaries: Rethinking Difference in Old French Literature* (Philadelphia, PA: University of Pennsylvania Press, 2006).

Kiser, Lisa J., *Telling Classical Tales: Chaucer and the Legend of Good Women* (Ithaca, NY: Cornell University Press, 1993).

Kolve, V. A., 'From Cleopatra to Alceste: An Iconographic Study of *The Legend of Good Women*', in *Signs and Symbols in Chaucer's Poetry*, eds John P. Hermann and John J. Burke (Tuscaloosa, AL: University of Alabama Press, 1981), pp. 130–78.

Kozák, Dániel, 'Traces of the Argo: Statius' *Achilleid* 1 and Valarius' *Argonutica* 1–2', in *Flavian Epic Interactions*, eds Gesine Manuwald and Astrid Voigt (Berlin and Boston, MA: De Gruyter, 2013), pp. 247–66.

Krahmer, Shawn M., 'The Virile Bride of Bernard of Clairvaux', *Church History* 69.2 (2000): 304–27.

Kristeva, Julia, *Powers of Horror: An Essay on Abjection*, trans. Leon S. Roudiez (New York: Columbia University Press, 1982).

Kruger, Steven, 'Passion and Order in Chaucer's *Legend of Good Women*', *Chaucer Review* 23.3 (1989): 219–35.

Lacan, Jacques, *The Ego in Freud's Theory and in the Technique of Psychoanalysis (The Seminar of Jacques Lacan, Book II: 1954–1955)*, ed. Jacques-Alain Miller, trans. Sylvana Tomaselli (New York: Norton, 1991).

―――― *The Psychoses (The Seminar of Jacques Lacan, Book III: 1955–1956)*, ed. Jacques Alain-Miller, trans. R. Grigg (New York: Norton, 1993).

Lankewish, Vincent A., 'Assault from Behind: Sodomy, Foreign Invasion, and Masculine Identity in the *Roman d'Eneas*', in *Text and Territory: Geographical Imagination in the European Middle Ages*, eds Sylvia Tomasch and Sealy Gilles (Philadelphia, PA: University of Pennsylvania Press, 1998), pp. 207–46.

Lees, Clare A., ed., *Medieval Masculinities: Regarding Men in the Middle Ages* (Minneapolis, MN: University of Minnesota Press, 1994).

Leupin, Alexandre, *Barbarolexis: Medieval Writing and Sexuality*, trans. Kate M. Cooper (Cambridge, MA and London: Harvard University Press, 1989).

Little, Katherine C., and Nicola McDonald, eds, *Thinking Medieval Romance* (Oxford: Oxford University Press, 2018).

―――― 'Introduction', in *Thinking Medieval Romance*, eds Little and McDonald, pp. 1–14.

Lochrie, Karma, *Margery Kempe and Translations of the Flesh* (Philadelphia, PA: University of Pennsylvania Press, 1994).

―――― 'Mystical Acts, Queer Tendencies', in *Constructing Medieval Sexualities*, eds Karma Lochrie, Peggy McCracken and James Schultz (Minneapolis, MN: University of Minnesota Press, 1997), pp. 180–200.

―――― *Covert Operations: The Medieval Uses of Secrecy* (Philadelphia, PA: University of Pennsylvania Press, 1999).

―――― 'Between Women', in *The Cambridge Companion to Medieval Women's Writing*, eds Carolyn Dinshaw and David Wallace (Cambridge: Cambridge University Press, 2003), pp. 70–90.

―――― *Heterosyncrasies: Female Sexuality When Normal Wasn't* (Minneapolis, MN: University of Minnesota Press, 2005).

Lerer, Seth, 'The Wiles of a Woodcut: Wynkyn de Worde and the Early Tudor Reader', *Huntington Library Quarterly* 59 (1996): 381–403.

Lowes, J. L., 'The Prologue to the Legend of Good Women Considered in Its Chronological Relations', *PMLA* 20 (1905): 794–864.

―――― 'Chaucer and the *Ovide Moralisé*', *PMLA* 33 (1918): 302–25.

Magnani, Roberta, 'Constructing the Father: Fifteenth-Century Manuscripts of Chaucer's Works', unpublished PhD thesis, Cardiff University, 2010.

Mallory, Sarah W., 'Designing and Defining Tapestries: The Three Stages of Tapestry Production', in *Grand Design: Pieter Coecke van Aelst and Renaissance Tapestry*, ed. Elizabeth Cleland (New York: Metropolitan Museum of Art and Yale University Press, 2014), pp. 110–11.

Malo, Robyn, *Relics and Writing in Late Medieval England* (Toronto: University of Toronto Press, 2013).

Mann, Jill, *Feminizing Chaucer*, 2nd edn (Cambridge: D. S. Brewer, 2002).

Martin, Priscilla, *Chaucer's Women: Nuns, Wives and Amazons* (Iowa City: University of Iowa Press, 1990).

Matthews, William, *The Tragedy of Arthur: A Study of the Alliterative 'Morte Arthure'* (Berkeley and Los Angeles, CA: University of California Press, 1960).

Bibliography

McCarthy, Terence, 'Malory and His Sources', in *A Companion to Malory*, eds Elizabeth Archibald and A. S. G. Edwards (Cambridge: D. S. Brewer, 1996), pp. 75–95.

McCormick, Betsy, Leah Schwebel and Lynne Shutters, 'Introduction: Looking Forward, Looking Back on the *Legend of Good Women*', *Chaucer Review* 52 (2017): 3–11.

McDonald, Nicola F., 'Chaucer's *Legend of Good Women*, Ladies at Court and the Female Reader', *Chaucer Review* 35.1 (2000): 22–42.

—— 'Desire Out of Order and Undo Your Door', *Studies in the Age of Chaucer* 34 (2012): 247–75.

—— 'Gender', in *A Handbook of Middle English Studies*, ed. Marion Turner (Chichester: Wiley-Blackwell, 2013), pp. 63–76.

—— 'The Wonder of Middle English Romance', in *Thinking Medieval Romance*, eds Little and McDonald, pp. 13–36.

McKinley, Kathryn L., 'Gower and Chaucer: Readings of Ovid in Late Medieval England', in *Ovid in the Middle Ages*, eds James G. Clark, Frank T. Coulson and Kathryn L. McKinley (Cambridge: Cambridge University Press, 2011), pp. 197–230.

Meale, Carol, 'Caxton, de Worde, and the Publication of Romance in Late Medieval England', *The Library* 14 (1992): 283–98.

—— 'The Tale and the Book: Readings of Chaucer's *Legend of Good Women* in the Fifteenth Century', in *Chaucer in Perspective: Middle English Essays in Honour of Norman Blake*, ed. Geoffrey Lester (Sheffield: Sheffield Academic Press, 1999), pp. 118–38.

Meech, Sanford Brown, 'Chaucer and the *Ovide Moralisé*: A Further Study', *PMLA* 46. 1 (1931): 182–204.

Meron, Theodor, *War Crimes Law Comes of Age: Essays* (Oxford: Oxford University Press, 1998).

Metlitzki, Dorothee, *The Matter of Araby in Medieval Romance* (New Haven, CT: Yale University Press, 1977).

Mills, Robert, 'Queering the Un/Godly: Christ's Humanities and Medieval Sexuality', in *Queering the Non/Human*, eds Noreen Giffney and Myra J. Hird (Aldershot: Ashgate, 2008), pp. 111–36.

—— 'Homosexuality: Specters of Sodom', in *A Cultural History of Sexuality in the Middle Ages*, ed. Ruth Evans (Oxford: Blackwell, 2011), pp. 57–80.

—— *Seeing Sodomy in the Middle Ages* (Chicago, IL and London: University of Chicago Press, 2014).

Minnis, Alastair J., 'A Note on Chaucer and the *Ovide Moralisé*', *Medium Ævum* 48 (1979): 254–57.

—— *Magister Amoris: The Roman de la Rose and Vernacular Hermeneutics* (Oxford: Oxford University Press, 2001).

—— *Fallible Authors: Chaucer's Pardoner and the Wife of Bath* (Philadelphia, PA: University of Pennsylvania Press, 2008).

Mitchell, David T., and Sharon L. Snyder, *Narrative Prosthesis: Disability and the Dependencies of Discourse* (Ann Arbor, MI: University of Michigan Press, 2000).

Moll, Richard J., *Before Malory: Reading Arthur in Later Medieval England* (Toronto, Buffalo, NY and London: University of Toronto Press, 1996).

Morse, Mary, '"Thys moche more ys oure Lady Mary longe": Takamiya MS 56 and the English Birth Girdle Tradition', in *Middle English Texts in Transition: A Festschrift Dedicated to Toshiyuki Takamiya on his 70th Birthday*, eds Simon Horobin and Linne Mooney (York: York Medieval Press, 2014).

Morse, Ruth, *The Medieval Medea* (Cambridge: D. S. Brewer, 1996).

Moss, Rachel E., *Fatherhood and its Representations in Middle English Texts* (Cambridge: D. S. Brewer, 2013).

Murphy, James Jerome, *Rhetoric in the Middle Ages: A History of Rhetorical Theory from Saint Augustine to the Renaissance* (Berkeley, CA, Los Angeles, CA and London: University of California Press, 1974).

Murray, Jacqueline, '"Twice Marginal and Twice Invisible": Lesbians in the Middle Ages', in *The Handbook of Medieval Sexuality*, eds Vern L. Bullough and James A. Brundage (New York: Garland, 1996), pp. 191–222.

Nail, Thomas, 'What is an Assemblage', *SubStance* 46.1 (2017): 21–37.

Neimanis, Astrida, *Bodies of Water: Posthuman Feminist Phenomenology* (London: Bloomsbury, 2016).

Ngai, Sianne, *Ugly Feelings* (Cambridge, MA: Harvard University Press, 2005).

Nievergelt, Marco, 'Introduction: The Alliterative *Morte Arthure* in Context', *Arthuriana* 20.2 (2010): 3–4.

—— 'Conquest, Crusade and Pilgrimage: The Alliterative *Morte Arthure* in its Late Ricardian Crusading Context', *Arthuriana* 20.2 (2010): 89–116.

—— 'From *disputatio* to *predicatio* – and Back Again: Dialectic, Authority and Epistemology between the *Roman de la Rose* and the *Pèlerinage de Vie Humaine*', *New Medieval Literatures* 16 (2015): 135–71.

Noonan, Sarah, 'Bodies of Parchment: Representing the Passion and Reading Manuscripts in Late Medieval England', unpublished PhD thesis, Washington University in St Louis, 2010.

Norris, Ralph, *Malory's Library: The Sources of the* Morte Darthur (Cambridge: D. S. Brewer, 2008).

Novavich, Sarah Elliott, 'Transparent Mary: Visible Interiors and the Maternal Body in the Middle Ages', *Journal of English and Germanic Philology* 166.4 (2018): 464–90.

Osborn, Marijane, 'Transgressive Word and Image in Chaucer's Enshrined "Coillons" Passage', *Chaucer Review* 37 (2003): 365–84.

Oswald, Dana M., *Monsters, Gender and Sexuality in Medieval English Literature* (Cambridge: D. S. Brewer, 2010).

Parr, Johnstone, 'Chaucer's Semiramis', *Chaucer Review* 5.1 (1970): 57–61.

Pearman, Tory Vendeventer, *Women and Disability in Medieval Literature* (New York: Palgrave Macmillan, 2010).

Peck, Russell A., 'Willfulness and Wonders: Boethian Tragedy in the Alliterative

Morte Arthure', in *The Alliterative Tradition in the Fourteenth Century*, eds Bernard S. Levy and Paul E. Szarmach (Kent, OH: Kent State University Press, 1981), pp. 153–82.

Percival, Florence, *Chaucer's Legendary Good Women* (Cambridge: Cambridge University Press, 1998).

Poellinger, Mary Michele, '"The rosselde spere to his herte rynnes": Religious Violence in the Alliterative *Morte Arthure* and the Lincoln Thornton Manuscript', in *Robert Thornton and His Books*, eds Fein and Johnston, pp. 157–76.

Porter, Chloe, Katie L. Walter and Margaret Healy, eds, *Prosthesis in Medieval and Early Modern Culture* (Special Issue), *Textual Practice* 30.7 (2016).

Porter, Elizabeth, 'Chaucer's Knight, the Alliterative *Morte Arthure*, and Medieval Laws of War: A Reconsideration', *Nottingham Medieval Studies* 27 (1983): 56–78.

Puff, Helmut, 'Female Sodomy: The Trial of Katherina Hetzeldofer (1477)', *Journal of Medieval and Early Modern Studies* 30.1 (2000): 41–61.

Pugh, Tison, *Sexuality and its Queer Discontents in Middle English Literature* (New York: Palgrave Macmillan, 2008).

Rajabzadeh, Shokoofeh, 'The Depoliticised Saracen and Muslim Erasure', Critical Race and the Middle Ages (Special Issue), *Literature Compass* 16.9–10 (2019): e12548.

Ray, Sid, 'Tragical-Comical-Historical-Pastoral', *Shakespeare and the Middle Ages: Essays on the Performance and Adaptation of Plays with Medieval Settings*, eds Martha W. Driver and Sid Ray (Jefferson, NC: McFarland, 2009), pp. 195–200.

Roberts, Anna Kłosowska, *Queer Love in the Middle Ages* (New York: Palgrave Macmillan, 2005).

Robertson, Elizabeth, and Christine M. Rose, 'Introduction', in *Representing Rape*, eds Robertson and Rose, pp. 1–20.

Robertson, Elizabeth, and Christine M. Rose, eds, *Representing Rape in Medieval and Early Modern Literature* (New York: Palgrave, 2001).

Rollo, David, *Kiss My Relics: Hermaphroditic Fictions of the Middle Ages* (Chicago, IL and London: University of Chicago Press, 2011).

Rooney, Kenneth, *Mortality and Imagination: The Life of the Dead in Medieval English Literature* (Turnhout: Brepols, 2012).

Rowe, Donald W., *Through Nature to Eternity* (Lincoln, NE: University of Nebraska Press, 1988).

Rudy, Kathryn, 'An Illustrated Mid-Fifteenth Century Primer for a Flemish Girl: British Library, Harley MS 3828', *Journal of the Warburg and Courtauld Institutes* 69 (2006): 51–94.

Sauer, Michelle M., 'Representing the Negative: Positing the Lesbian Void in Medieval English Anchoritism', *Thirdspace* 3.2 (2004): 70–88.

—— '"Where are the Lesbians in Chaucer?": Lack, Opportunity and Female Homoeroticism in Medieval Studies Today', *Journal of Lesbian Studies* 11.3/4 (2007): 331–45.

—— 'Divine Orgasm and Self-Blazoning: The Fragmented Body of the Female Medieval Visionary', in *Sexuality, Sociality and Cosmology in Medieval Literary Texts*, eds Jennifer N. Brown and Marla Segol (New York: Palgrave, 2013), pp. 123–43.

—— *Gender in Medieval Culture* (London: Bloomsbury, 2015).

Saunders, Corinne J., 'Classical Paradigms of Rape in the Middle Ages: Lucretia and Philomela', in *Rape in Antiquity*, eds Susan Deacy and Karen F. Pierce (London: Classical Press of Wales, 1997), pp. 243–66.

—— *Rape and Ravishment in the Literature of Medieval England* (Cambridge: D. S. Brewer, 2001).

—— 'Affective Reading: Chaucer, Women and Romance', *Chaucer Review* 51:1 (2016): 11–30.

Sautman, Francesca Canadé, and Pamela Sheingorn, *Same Sex Love and Desire Among Women in the Middle Ages* (New York: Palgrave, 2001).

Sawday, Jonathan, *The Body Emblazoned: Dissection and the Human Body in Renaissance Culture* (London and New York: Routledge, 1995).

Scarry, Elaine, *The Body in Pain: The Making and Unmaking of the World* (Oxford: Oxford University Press, 1985).

Schibanoff, Susan, 'Taking Jane's Cue: Phyllyp Sparowe as a Primer for Women Readers', *PMLA* 101 (1986): 832–47.

—— 'Sodomy's Mark: Alan of Lille, Jean de Meun, and the Medieval Theory of Authorship', in *Queering the Middle Ages*, eds Glenn Burger and Steven F. Kruger (Minneapolis, MN: University of Minnesota Press, 2001), pp. 28–56.

—— *Chaucer's Queer Poetics: Rereading the Dream Trio* (Toronto, Buffalo, NY and London: University of Toronto Press, 2006).

Schulenburg, Jane Tibbetts, *Forgetful of Their Sex: Female Sanctity and Society ca. 500–1100* (Chicago, IL: University of Chicago Press, 2001).

Schultz, James A., 'Heterosexuality as a Threat to Medieval Studies', *Journal of the History of Sexuality* 15.1 (2006): 14–29.

Seal, Samantha Katz, *Father Chaucer: Generating Authority in* The Canterbury Tales (Oxford: Oxford University Press, 2019).

Seaman, Myra, 'The Waning of Middle English Chivalric Romance in "The Squyr of Lowe Degre"', *Fifteenth Century Studies* 29 (2004): 174–99.

Sedgwick, Eve Kosofsky, *Tendencies* (Durham, NC: Duke University Press, 1993).

Shildrick, Margrit, 'Prosthetic Performativity: Deleuzian Connections and Queer Corporalities', in *Deleuze and Queer Theory*, eds Chrysanthi Nigianni and Merl Storr (Edinburgh: Edinburgh University Press, 2009), pp. 115–33.

—— 'Reimagining Embodiment: Prostheses, Supplements and Boundaries', *Somatechnics* 3.2 (2013): 270–86.

—— 'Border Crossings: The Technologies of Disability and Desire', in *Culture-Theory-Disability: Encounters Between Disability Studies and Cultural Studies*, eds Anne Waldschmidt, Hanjo Berressem and Moritz Ingwersen (Bielefeld: Transcript, 2017), pp. 137–69.

Sidhu, Nicole Nolan, *Indecent Exposure: Gender, Politics and Obscene Comedy in Middle English* (Philadelphia, PA: University of Pennsylvania Press, 2016).

—— '"Famulier foo": Wives, Male Subordinates, and Political Theory in the Merchant's Tale', *Chaucer Review* 54.3 (2019): 292–314.

Simpson, James, *Reform and Cultural Revolution* (Oxford: Oxford University Press, 2002).

—— 'Derek Brewer's Romance', in *Traditions and Innovations in the Study of Medieval English Literature: The Influence of Derek Brewer*, eds Charlotte Brewer and Barry Windeatt (Cambridge: D. S. Brewer, 2013), pp. 154–72.

Smith, D. Vance, 'Destroyer of Forms: Chaucer's Philomela', in *Readings in Medieval Textuality: Essays in Honour of A. C. Spearing*, eds Christina Maria Cervone and D. Vance Smith (Cambridge: D. S. Brewer, 2016), pp. 135–56.

Spearing, A. C., *The Medieval Poet as Voyeur: Looking and Listening in Medieval Love-Narratives* (Cambridge: Cambridge University Press, 1993).

Spencer, H. Leith, *English Preaching in the Late Middle Ages* (Oxford: Clarendon Press, 1993).

Spisak, James W., 'Chaucer's Pyramus and Thisbe', *Chaucer Review* 204.3 (1984): 204–10.

Spivak, Gayatri Chakrvorty, 'Can the Subaltern Speak?' in *Marxism and the Interpretation of Culture*, eds Cary Nelson and Lawrence Grossberg (Urbana, IL: University of Illinois Press, 1988), pp. 271–313.

Stanbury, Sarah, *The Visual Object of Desire in Late Medieval England* (Philadelphia, PA: University of Pennsylvania Press, 2008).

Stelmack, Robert M., and Anastasios Stalikas, 'Galen and the Humour Theory of Temperament', *Personality and Individual Differences* 12.3 (1991): 255–64.

Sutherland, Jenifer, 'Repuerascere: Christianizing Classical Rhetoric Through Play in Walter of Wimborne's De Palpone', *Exemplaria* 17.2 (2005): 381–412.

Sutton, John William, 'Mordred's End: A Reevaluation of Mordred's Death Scene in the Alliterative *Morte Arthure*', *Chaucer Review* 37.3 (2003): 280–85.

Tasioulas, Jacqueline, '"Heaven and Earth in Little Space": The Foetal Existence of Christ in Medieval Literature and Thought', *Medium Ævum* 76 (2007): 24–48.

Thebaut, Nancy, 'Bleeding Pages, Bleeding Bodies: A Gendered Reading of British Library MS Egerton 1821', *Medieval Feminist Forum*, 45.2 (2009): 175–200.

Tolhurst, Fiona, *Geoffrey of Monmouth and the Feminist Origins of the Arthurian Legend* (New York: Palgrave Macmillan, 2012).

Tolhurst, Fiona, and K. S. Whetter, 'Memories of War: Retracting the Interpretative Tradition of the Alliterative *Morte Arthure*', *Arthuriana* 29.1 (2019): 88–108.

Trembinski, Donna, 'Comparing Premodern Melancholy/Mania and Modern Trauma: An Argument in Favour of Historical Experiences of Trauma', *History of Psychology* 14.1 (2011): 80–99.

—— 'Trauma as a Category of Analysis', in *Trauma in Medieval Society*, eds Turner and Lee, pp. 13–24.

Trigg, Stephanie, 'Weeping Like a Beaten Child: Figurative Language and the Emotions in Chaucer and Malory', in *Medieval Affect, Feeling and Emotion*, eds Glenn D. Burger and Holly A. Crocker (Cambridge: Cambridge University Press, 2019), pp. 25–46.

Turner, Wendy J., and Christina Lee, 'Conceptualising Trauma for the Middle Ages', in *Trauma in Medieval Society*, eds Wendy J. Turner and Christina Lee (Leiden and Boston, MA: Brill, 2018), pp. 3–12.

Tuten, Belle S., 'Power and Trauma in the "Maid of Arras", *Cantigas de Santa María*', in *Trauma in Medieval Society*, eds Turner and Lee, pp. 105–21.

Vale, Juliet, 'Law and Diplomacy in the Alliterative Morte Arthure', *Nottingham Medieval Studies* 23 (1979): 31–46.

Vance, Eugene, 'Style and Value: From Soldier to Pilgrim in the Song of Roland', *Yale French Studies* (special issue), *Contexts: Style and Values in Medieval Art and Literature* (1991): 75–96.

van 't Land, Karine, 'Sperm and Blood, Form and Food: Late Medieval Medical Notions of Male and Female in the Embryology of Membra', in *Blood, Sweat and Tears: The Changing Concepts of Physiology from Antiquity into Early Modern Europe*, eds Manfred Horstmanshoff, Helen King and Claus Zittel (Leiden: Brill, 2012).

Wallace, David, *Chaucer and the Early Writings of Boccaccio* (Cambridge: D. S. Brewer, 1985).

—— *Chaucerian Polity: Absolutist Lineages and Associational Forms in England and Italy* (Stanford, CA: Stanford University Press, 1997).

Waller, Gary, *The Virgin Mary in Late Medieval and Early Modern Literature and Popular Culture* (Cambridge: Cambridge University Press, 2011).

Walter, Katie L., 'Fragments for a Medieval Theory of Prosthesis', *Textual Practice* 30.7 (2016): 1345–63.

Warren, Nancy Bradley, '"Olde Stories" and Amazons: The *Legend of Good Women*, the Knight's Tale, and Fourteenth-Century Political Culture', in *Re-thinking Chaucer's Legend*, ed. Collette, pp. 83–104.

Watkins, Elizabeth Jane, 'French Romance and English Piety: Genre and Codex in Insular Romance', unpublished PhD thesis, University of Toronto, 2014.

Wakelin, Daniel, and Alexandra Gillespie, eds, *The Production of Books in England 1350–1500* (Cambridge: Cambridge University Press, 2011).

Watt, Diane, *Amoral Gower: Language, Sex, and Politics* (Minneapolis, MN: University of Minnesota Press, 2003).

—— 'Why Men Still Aren't Enough', *GLQ: A Journal of Lesbian and Gay Studies* 16.3 (2010): 451–64.

—— 'Mary the Physician: Women, Medicine and Gender in the Middle Ages', in *Medicine, Religion and Gender in Medieval Culture*, ed. Naoë Kukita Yoshikawa (Cambridge: D. S. Brewer, 2015).

Weiss, Judith, 'Modern and Medieval Views on Swooning: The Literary and Medical Contexts of Fainting in Romance', in *Medieval Romance, Medieval Contexts*, eds Rhiannon Purdie and Michael Cichon (Woodbridge: D. S. Brewer, 2011), pp. 121–34.

Westover, Jeff, 'Arthur's End: The King's Emasculation in the Alliterative "Morte Arthure"', *Chaucer Review* 32.3 (1998): 310–24.

Whetter, K. S., 'Genre as Context in the Alliterative *Morte Arthure*', *Arthuriana* 22.2 (2010): 45–65.

White, Allon, 'Prosthetic Gods in Atrocious Places: Gilles Deleuze/Francis Bacon', in *Carnival, Hysteria, and Writing: Collected Essays and Autobiography* (Oxford: Oxford University Press, 1993), pp. 160–77.

Wills, David, *Prosthesis* (Stanford, CA: Stanford University Press, 1995).

Woods, Marjorie Curry, 'Performing Dido', in *Public Declamations: Essays on Medieval Rhetoric, Education, and Letters in Honour of Martin Camargo*, eds Georgiana Donavin and Denise Stodols (Turnhout: Brepols, 2015), pp. 253–65.

Woolgar, C. M., *The Senses in Late Medieval England* (New Haven, CT and London: Yale University Press, 2007).

Ziolkowski, Jan, *Alan of Lille's Grammar of Sex: The Meaning of Grammar to a Twelfth-Century Intellectual* (Cambridge: Medieval Academy, 1985).

INDEX

Abulafia, David   136
Achilles   11, 85, 88–89, 99
Adam   1–2, 22, 97
Adler, Gillian   73
Aelred of Rievaulx, *De Institutione Inclusarum*   42, 146
Ahmed, Sara   4, 9, 44, 50, 58, 82, 83 n. 2, 167, 185
Akbari, Suzanne Conklin   113
Alan of Lille   7, 17, 33, 158
  De Planctu Naturae
    and corruption of language   11–14, 39, 51, 98, 153–55, 188–89
    and drag or disguise   88–89, 99
    and grammar as morality   85
    and Pyramus and Thisbe   11, 144–45
Alceste   22–24, 162
Alcoff, Linda   70, 81
anchoritism   41–43, 44, 46, 55, 146–47, 183–84
Ancrene Wisse   41 n. 19, 42, 146, 183 n. 63
Anglo-Norman *Fierabras*   123, 128, 134
  (*see also Chanson de Fierabras, Ferumbras, Firumbras, Sowdone of Babylon*)
annunciation   168, 171, 173–76, 185–86, 192
Augustine
  City of God   39–40
  Confessions   85–87, 89–90, 102, 108

Baden-Daintree, Anne   76
Bahr, Arthur   57
Bartlett, Anne Clark   64, 74, 77–80
Baswell, Christopher   89, 94
Bennett, Judith M.   4 n. 14, 15, 50
  (*see also* lesbian-like)

Bernard of Clairvaux   133
Bildhauer, Bettina   46
birds   21, 38, 43, 64–65, 67, 97, 123, 129, 169
blood   45–52, 54, 144, 151–54, 180–82, 153 n. 39
  of beasts   130
  and the humours   114–19
  and reproductive fluids   39, 46, 94, 124 n. 41, 154, 188
  shed in battle   27, 63, 66, 72, 192
  and tears   94, 151 n. 34, 153–54
  (*see also* castration, mutilation, rape, trauma, wounds)
Blud, Victoria   46
Brown, Emerson Jr.   148
Burger, Glenn   18, 92–93
Burns, E. Jane   54, 65 n. 62, 108
Butler, Judith   4–5
Bynum, Caroline Walker   134, 137

Caruth, Cathy   80–81
castration   2, 32, 48, 72–73, 104–05, 161 n. 52
  (*see also* blood, mutilation, wounds)
Caxton, William   14, 17 n. 53
Chaganti, Seeta   32
Chanson de Fierabras   32, 111, 120–27, 129, 130, 133
  (*see also* Anglo-Norman *Fierabras, Ferumbras, Firumbras, Sowdone of Babylon*)
Chaucer, Geoffrey   7–8, 21, 26
  Book of the Duchess   102 n. 62, 169
  Canterbury Tales   17 n. 53, 19, 26,
    General Prologue   22, 46–47, 129, 193
    Man of Law's Prologue   17 n. 54, 24, 102 n. 62

219

Index

Man of Law's Tale   108
Merchant's Tale   148–49, 174 n. 34
Miller's Tale   174 n. 34
and the Pardoner   19, 20–21, 23–25, 105, 148
Second Nun's Prologue   104
'Sir Thopas'   152
and the Wife of Bath   25–26, 141, 156–57, 164
Legend of Good Women   17–18, 195
Prologues   18–25, 155–56, 162, 169, 190–91
echoes of the Philomela myth   38
list of legendary women   102 n. 62
'Legend of Ariadne'   49, 53 n. 52, 143 n. 7, 158–164
and circumscription of women's language   32, 188, 141–42, 161–64, 190
and sterile repetition   96 n. 45
'Legend of Cleopatra'   25 n. 75, 53 n. 52, 85, 142, 143 n. 7, 179
'Legend of Dido'   31, 53 n. 52, 83–95, 142, 151, 188, 190
and influence on 'The Legend of Hipsiphyle and Medea'   99, 108–09
as manuscript extract from the *Legend*   156 n. 45
'Legend of Hipsiphyle and Medea'   31–32, 83–109, 127–28, 188, 190
'Legend of Hypermnestra'   152, 188, 189
'Legend of Lucrece'   30, 39–43, 49–50, 101, 143 n. 7, 188–89
and shame   92
'Legend of Philomela'   30–31, 35–60, 101, 153 n. 38, 161, 189
and lesbian-like prosthesis   112, 135, 141–42, 176–77, 188
and truncated narrative   102, 109, 141
'Legend of Phyllis'   101, 143 n. 7, 164, 188
'Legend of Thisbe'   32, 49, 141–64, 177, 188, 190

as manuscript extract from the *Legend*   57, 156–57
Parliament of Fowls   38, 169
Romaunce of the Rose   169, 30 n. 9, 21 n. 69
Troilus and Criseyde   38, 64 n. 12, 92, 152–53
Chism, Christine   75
Chrétien de Troyes   35 n. 1, 68
(*see also Ovide Moralisé*)
Cixous, Hélène   4
Cloth   51–59, 67–68, 80–81
Clothing   56, 123, 126, 144, 161, 170, 173
as disguise   178
as integument   10, 19–23, 150, 155–58, 161, 162 n. 54, 164, 188–90
men wearing women's clothing   88, 99
as raw material   56, 94
women wearing men's clothing   145
(*see also* weaving, thread)
Cohen, Jeffrey Jerome   7, 12 n. 86, 30 n. 84, 63 n. 8, 73, 138
Coleman, Joyce   18
Collette, Carolyn   18, 56 n. 60, 154 n. 41
Conway, Martin A.   70
cross-dressing, *see* drag

Davis, Isabel   6, 105
Delany, Sheila
on the 'Legend of Ariadne'   49, 159–60, 161
assessment of the *Legend*   18, 46, 101, 104
on the 'Legend of Dido'   87, 92–93
on the 'Legend of Hipsiphyle and Medea'   101, 104
on the 'Legend of Lucrece'   40
on the 'Legend of Philomela'   46
on the 'Legend of Thisbe'   143, 147, 151–52
Deleuze, Gilles   7, 30 n. 84, 163 n. 58, 185, 194
Derrida, Jacques   1, 7, 49
Desmond, Marilynn   86

Index

de Voragine, Jacobus, *Legenda Aurea*   155–56
Driver, Martha   153 n. 39
Dinshaw, Carolyn   6, 9, 14, 17–18, 49, 50, 83, 160,
   on eunuch hermeneutics   19, 21, 105
   on queer touch   86 n. 13, 182
   relations between religious and sexual deviancy   32, 112, 117, 179
Dorne, John   165
Doyle, Kara A.   143
drag   1–2, 88–89, 145
   and language   20–23, 102–05
   and time   76, 84–87
Dumitrescu, Irina   162

écriture feminine   51–52
Edwards, Suzanne   41–42
effeminacy, *see* male femininity
eunuch hermeneutics, *see* Dinshaw, Carolyn
Eve   1–2, 9, 22, 103, 191

Farina, Lara   16, 82
Farmer, Sharon   5 n. 16
Feinberg, Leslie   136, 138
female masculinity   3, 6, 46–47, 93, 131, 133
   and the clitoris   161 n. 52
   and phallic supplementation   1 n. 2, 3–4, 13–14, 83–84, 101–06, 148, 151–52
   and the stone butch   136–38
   and the virago   31, 93, 98–106, 134–36, 142–43, 145–47
   (*see also* drag, male femininity, gender)
Ferumbras (Ashmole)   120–21, 125–26
   (*see also* Anglo-Norman *Fierabras*, *Chanson de Fierabras*, *Firumbras*, *Sowdone of Babylon*)
Firumbras (Fillingham)   120–21, 125–26
   (*see also* Anglo-Norman *Fierabras*, *Chanson de Fierabras*, *Ferumbras*, *Sowdone of Babylon*)

Flannery, Mary   92
flesh   47–48, 76, 100, 115 n. 13, 117, 195
   consumption of   23, 37, 67–69, 97, 114
   and deviant desire   14, 23, 67–69, 78, 114, 151
   and gender   4–5, 46, 86, 119
   and human creation   1–2
   incorruptibility of   118
   as opposed to the spirit   10, 24, 95
   as prosthesis   3, 24
Fradenburg, L. O. Aranye   190
Frank, Robert Worth   17 n. 53, 18 n. 61
Freeman, Elizabeth   56, 82
   and lesbian erotohistoriography   16, 24, 36, 44, 58–59, 171, 196
   and metre and rhythm   50, 52 n. 47
   and temporality   76, 83–87, 167
Froide, Amy   4 n. 14

Gaunt, Simon, 9 n. 29
gender
   in grammar   10–12, 22, 145, 155–58, 189
   construction of   1–7, 9–13, 15–16, 46–47, 74–75, 113–20
Gertrude of Helfta   118
Gertsman, Elina   119
Getty, Laura   155
Giffney, Noreen   8
Gilbert, Jane   26
Göller, Karl Heinz   71, 76, 77–78, 80
Gower, John   29
   Confessio Amantis   38 n. 8, 45–46, 47 n. 34, 46 n. 36, 153 n. 39
Grey, Laura   70, 81
Guattari, Félix   7, 30 n. 84, 163 n. 58, 185, 194
Guillaume de Lorris   12
   and poetic inspiration for the *Roman de la Rose*   19–20, 21, 22, 188
   as depicted by Jean de Meun   20–21, 23
   (*see also* Jean de Meun, *Roman de la Rose*)

Index

Halberstam, Jack (Judith)   1 n. 2, 6, 105, 136
Hali Meidhad   118, 133
Hamel, Mary   78
Hanna, Ralph   29 n. 82
Hansen, Elaine   18, 98, 100 n. 56, 143
Haraway, Donna   7, 185, 195
Harris, Anne   173
Harris, Carissa M.   174 n. 31
Healy, Margaret   134
Helen of Troy   11, 13, 87
Heng, Geraldine   63 n. 8, 66, 74, 80, 98, 146
Henry V   72
heterosex   52 n. 47, 143, 183
 and constructions of medieval sexuality   12 n. 40, 143
 and modern lesbian readers   16
 aversion towards   13, 112, 134
Hohl, Katrin   70
Horne, Peter   16, 184
Hume, Cathy   18
Hsy, Jonathan   83, 84 n. 3, 87

Isidore of Seville   3, 88, 114–16, 127

Jacobs, Lynn F.   176
Jantzen, Grace   23 n. 72
Jean de Meun, *Roman de la Rose*   7, 12–13, 27, 29, 33, 148, 154, 158
 and the *Legend* Prologues   18–23, 187–88
 and Paris, Bibliothèque nationale de France, MS Fr. 25526   2–3
 and the enclosed *locus amoenus*   132, 169
Jerome   7, 18, 104, 141, 155–58
 and hermeneutic allegory of the captive woman   9–10, 35–36, 59, 86, 150, 154–55, 158, 187
 and Chaucer's adaptations of hermeneutic allegory   19–22, 32–33, 39, 160–64, 188–91
Jones, Nancy   56
Joy, Eileen   195

Karras, Ruth Mazo   6, 66
King of Tars   117, 127

Kiser, Lisa J   143
Kłosowska, Anna   5–6, 8, 183 n. 62
 and lesbian erotics of recombination   16, 32, 57, 82, 184–85
Krahmer, Shawn   133

Lacan, Jacques   4, 21, 47, 105
Lees, Clare   6
Leupin, Alexandre   13
Lewis, Reina   16, 184
Little, Katherine C.   26, 194
Lochrie, Karma   8, 9, 12 n. 40, 38, 147, 193
 on theories of the flesh   3, 117–18, 138
 relations between religious and sexual deviancy   32, 117, 179, 182
Lowes, J. L.   159

Magnani, Roberta   129
male bodies
 as surrogates for female emotion and experience   5–6, 19–24, 74–77
 as sexually penetrable   6, 22, 153–54
 (*see also* castration)
male femininity   20, 31–32, 71, 83–101, 128
 and grammatical pronouns   11–13, 155–57
 (*see also* drag, female masculinity, gender)
Malo, Robyn   32, 120, 137
Malory, Thomas, *Morte Darthur*   28, 63, 78–79, 193
Mann, Jill   92
manuscripts
 Cambridge, Trinity College, MS R. 3. 19   53
 Cambridge, University Library, MS Ff. 1. 6   57, 156–57
 London, British Library, MS Additional 12524   39 n. 12, 156 n. 45
 London, British Library, MS Additional 27879   175 n. 35, 180–81

Index

London, British Library, MS Additional 37492   53
London, British Library, MS Additional 43391   107
London, British Library, MS Additional 59678   79
London, British Library, MS Egerton 1821   182
London, British Library, MS Egerton 3028   121 n. 33
London, British Library, MS Royal 20 C VII   75 n. 41
Lincoln, Cathedral Library, MS 91   62–63, 72, 79
Oxford, Bodleian Library, MS Ashmole 33   121
Oxford, Bodleian Library, MS Rawlinson C. 86   156 n. 35
Paris, Bibliothèque nationale de France, MS Fr. 25526   2–3
Princeton, University Library, MS Garrett 140   111 n. 1
Martin, Priscilla   143
Matthews, William   71, 80
McDonald, Nicola F.   18, 26, 29, 96, 143, 165 n. 1, 166, 194
metaphor, theories of   13–14, 98, 189–90, 194–95
metaplasm, *see* prosthesis (grammar)
Mills, Robert   12 n. 40, 50, 116–17
Morte Arthure (alliterative poem)   28, 31, 61–82, 178, 192–93, 195
    and Philomela   61–69, 82
Moss, Rachel   107
Murray, Jacqueline   8, 157
mutilation   30, 35–36, 41–43, 44–48, 65–67, 102–05, 119, 178–79
    (*see also* blood, castration, rape, trauma, wounds)

nakedness   76
    of the female body   25 n. 75, 178–79, 193
    of the male body   21–23, 66, 188, 190–93
    and mortification of the flesh   55
    and textual creation   19, 173
    and textual interpretation   10, 22–23, 32, 161, 164, 188–93
Nashe, Thomas   165
Nature (personification of)   11, 13–14, 19–22, 129
Neimanis, Astrida   7, 114–16, 137–38
N-Town Plays   132 n. 57, 177 n. 41

Ovid   90, 94–95, 99, 148, 152, 191
    Ars Amatoria   87, 106–07
    And Caxton's glosses   14
    Heroides   17 n. 54, 189, 191
        Ariadne   162–63
        Dido   85, 89, 93–95, 151 n. 34
        Medea   107–08
        Thisbe   162–63
    Metamorphoses
        Arachne and Athena   68
        Ariadne   163
        Europa   162
        Medea and Jason   104
        Philomela, Procne and Tereus   35, 45–48, 52, 53, 55–56, 153 n. 38
        Thisbe and Pyramus   142–44, 148, 150–53, 155
Ovide Moralisé   25 n. 1
    Medea and Jason   106
    Philomela, Procne and Tereus   48–49, 52, 54, 56, 68
    Thisbe and Pyramus   143, 145, 151–52, 160

Paston, John II   107
Paston, John III   107
Pearl   138
Pearce, C. W. Pleydell   70
Percival, Florence   143, 160, 163
Poellinger, Mary Michele   75
pregnancy   3, 13, 93–94, 104, 113–20, 124–25, 134
    (*see also* procreation)
Prick of Conscience   124 n. 41
printed books
    San Marino, CA, Huntington Library, Rare Books 62181 (STC 23111.5)   167 n. 7
    London, British Library, C.21.c.58 (STC 23112)   168 n. 14

223

Index

procreation   104, 122, 126–27, 151, 77, 172–73
  as metaphor for textual creation   19–20, 59, 153–55, 164, 166–71
  failures of   13, 93–94, 101–02, 128–30, 135–37, 164, 188
prosthesis   134
  and construction of woman   1–4, 10, 22, 44, 135, 188–95
  as symbol of deviant sexuality   13–15, 30, 48–50, 60, 112, 137, 177, 188–95
  as sexual supplement   2, 14, 149, 158, 164, 181–82, 185
  in grammar   11–12, 189, 195
  as marker of lack   16, 17, 24, 44, 48, 101–09, 142, 187–190
  as masculinising supplement   3, 15, 101–09, 190
  in modern theory   1–2, 7, 49, 142 n. 2, 149 n. 28, 185, 195
  and poetic structure   19–21, 25, 29–30, 82, 187–88, 191–92
  (*see also* drag)
Putter, Ad   26

Rajabzadeh, Shokoofeh   121
rape   64, 70–71
  and Europa   162–63
  and the Duchess of Brittany (*Alliterative Morte*)   31, 61–73, 77–82, 192
  and Floripas (*Sowdone of Babylon*)   123, 124–25, 132, 192
  and Philomela   30–31, 35–54, 58–60, 67–68, 153 n. 38, 190
  and the *Wife of Bath's Tale*   25
  as hermeneutic allegory   9–11, 188–89, 190–91
  (*see also* mutilation, trauma, wounds)
Richard II   72, 75–77
relics   111, 127, 130–32
  and the pregnant body   112–22, 124–27, 136–37, 192
  and sexual desire   28, 32, 113, 120–22, 125–26, 136–37, 147, 179–85
  and the testicles   20–25, 105, 148–49, 194
Roberts, Anna Kłosowska, *see* Kłosowska, Anna
Rollo, David   13
romance
  generic expectations of   25–26, 29–30, 61 n. 2, 107, 122, 182
  scholarly assessments of   7–8, 26–29, 165–66, 185
Roman d'Eneas   68, 88
Rowe, Donald W   104–05

same-sex desire
  intimacies between men   5–6, 31–32, 64, 74–82, 99–109, 166, 177–78, 184, 193
  intimacies between women   6, 8, 14–16, 42–43, 95, 97, 101–02
  the 'lesbian-like'
    Judith Bennett's coinage   15, 30–32, 95, 108–09, 146–49
    Lesbian-like erotic   8, 15–16, 30–32, 149, 160–64, 185, 188–93
    prosthesis as symbol of   13–15, 48–51, 60, 101–09, 135–36, 149, 185, 188
  (*see also* female masculinity, gender, male femininity, sodomy)
Sauer, Michelle M.   8, 39, 143, 146, 184, 195
Saunders, Corinne   66
Schibanoff, Susan   13, 80, 178
Schultz, James A.   12 n. 40
Sedgwick, Eve Kosofsky   87 n. 19
Shakespeare, William
  A Midsummer Night's Dream   142
  Henry V   28
  Titus Andronicus   45, 48–49
  Twelfth Night   165, 171
Shildrick, Margrit   7
sodomy
  sex between men   11–12, 33, 80, 88
  sexual penetration of a male

body 22–24, 78–79, 151, 188, 193
  and the medieval categorisations of sexual sin 12 n. 40, 14 n. 47, 51
Spearing, A. C. 173
Spisak, James W. 142, 150 n. 31
Squire of Low Degree, see *Undo Your Door*
Stanbury, Sarah 119
Statius
  Achilleid 88, 99
  Thebaid 99
Sutton, John William 78, 80

Tasioulas, Jacqueline 118
Thomas of Chobham, *Summa confessorum* 8 n. 25
thread 47, 48, 51–52, 55–59, 68, 81, 159, 161–62
  (see also cloth, weaving)
Tolhurst, Fiona 63 n. 8, 65 n. 14, 71–72, 78 n. 53
tongues 35, 41, 44–50, 92, 107–08, 153, 189, 190–91
trauma 72, 188–89, 191, 193, 196
  and memory 31, 43, 51, 58–59, 61–70, 77–82
  (*see also* blood, castration, mutilation, rape, wounds)
Trevisa, John, *On the Properties of Things* 3
Trigg, Stephanie 75
Twelve Conclusions of the Lollards 29, 117, 179–80

Undo Your Door (*Squire of Low Degree*) 28, 32–33, 165–86, 192–93, 195

Vance, Eugene 122
Venus 11–12, 90–91, 145
Virgil 38, 85–96, 191
Virgin Mary 172
  annunciation 171–72
  and the body as closed structure 40, 118–19, 125, 132–33, 172, 194
  and female masculinity 133
  as healer 133–34
  as intercessor 175
  pregnancy and maternity 46, 113–114, 118–20, 132, 172, 175
  and relics 119–20, 125
  and tears 116

Waller, Gary 116
Walter of Wimbourne 190–91
Warren, Nancy Bradley 99, 143
Watt, Diane, 8, 48 n. 36, 146
weaving 30, 35, 45, 48, 52–59, 68, 80–82
  (*see also* cloth; thread)
Weiss, Judith 74–75
Westover, Jeff 74, 77–78, 79–80
Whetter, K. S. 71–72
Wills, David 7
wounds 78–79, 150–53, 178, 182
  (*see also* blood, castration, mutilation, rape, trauma)

GENDER IN THE MIDDLE AGES

I *Gender and Medieval Drama*, Katie Normington, 2004
II *Gender and Petty Crime in Late Medieval England: The Local Courts in Kent, 1460–1560*, Karen Jones, 2006
III *The Pastoral Care of Women in Late Medieval England*, Beth Allison Barr, 2008
IV *Gender, Nation and Conquest in the Works of William of Malmesbury*, Kirsten A. Fenton, 2008
V *Monsters, Gender and Sexuality in Medieval English Literature*, Dana M. Oswald, 2010
VI *Medieval Anchoritisms: Gender, Space and the Solitary Life*, Liz Herbert McAvoy, 2011
VII *Middle-Aged Women in the Middle Ages*, edited by Sue Niebrzydowski, 2011
VIII *Married Women and the Law in Premodern Northwest Europe*, edited by Cordelia Beattie and Matthew Frank Stevens, 2013
IX *Religious Men and Masculine Identity in the Middle Ages*, edited by P. H. Cullum and Katherine J. Lewis, 2013
X *Reconsidering Gender, Time and Memory in Medieval Culture*, edited by Elizabeth Cox, Liz Herbert McAvoy and Roberta Magnani, 2015
XI *Medicine, Religion and Gender in Medieval Culture*, edited by Naoë Kukita Yoshikawa, 2015
XII *The Unspeakable, Gender and Sexuality in Medieval Literature, 1000–1400*, Victoria Blud, 2017
XIII *Popular Memory and Gender in Medieval England: Men, Women, and Testimony in the Church Courts, c.1200–1500*, Bronach C. Kane, 2019
XIV *Authority, Gender and Space in the Anglo-Norman World, 900–1200*, Katherine Weikert, 2020
XV *Female Desire in Chaucer's* Legend of Good Women *and Middle English Romance*, Lucy M. Allen-Goss, 2020
XVI *Treason and Masculinity in Medieval England: Gender, Law and Political Culture*, E. Amanda McVitty, 2020
XVII *Holy Harlots in Medieval English Religious Literature: Authority, Exemplarity and Femininity*, Juliette Vuille, 2021
XVIII *Addressing Women in Early Medieval Religious Texts*, Kathryn Maude, 2021
XIX *Women, Dance and Parish Religion in England, 1300–1640: Negotiating the Steps of Faith*, Lynneth Miller Renberg, 2022
XX *Women's Literary Cultures in the Global Middle Ages: Speaking Internationally*, edited by Kathryn Loveridge, Liz Herbert McAvoy, Sue Niebrzydowski and Vicki Kay Price, 2023

www.ingramcontent.com/pod-product-compliance
Lightning Source LLC
Chambersburg PA
CBHW070802230426
43665CB00017B/2456